CHINA'S EXTERNAL ECONOMIC RELATIONS

CHINA'S EXTERNAL ECONOMIC RELATIONS

Edited by Liu Saili and Zhou Lin

Enrich Professional Publishing

Published by

Enrich Professional Publishing (S) Private Limited
16L, Enterprise Road,
Singapore 627660
Website: www.enrichprofessional.com
A Member of Enrich Culture Group Limited

Hong Kong Head Office:
2/F, Rays Industrial Building, 71 Hung To Road, Kwun Tong, Kowloon, Hong Kong, China

China Office:
Rm 1800, Building C, Central Valley, 16 Hai Dian Zhong Jie, Haidian District, Beijing

United States Office:
PO Box 30812, Honolulu, HI 96820, USA

Translated by Freda Wan
Edited by Glenn Griffith and Vivien Lee

ISBN (Hardback)	978-981-4332-13-2
ISBN (ebook)	978-981-4332-11-8 (pdf)
	978-981-4332-09-5 (epub)

Enrich Professional Publishing is an independent globally-minded publisher focusing on the economic and financial developments that have revolutionized New China. We aim to serve the needs of advanced degree students, researchers, and business professionals who are looking for authoritative, accurate, and engaging information on China.

Printed in Hong Kong with woodfree paper from Japan

Contents

Foreword

In order to understand China's unprecedented economic growth, it is essential to understand its economic relations with the rest of the world. As China enjoys the success of its open-door policy and economic reforms since 1978, and continues to fully liberalize its economy since its WTO accession in 2001, its economic relations with major trading partners and world powers have evolved and progressed. Trade used to dominate China's economic interaction with other countries. Yet today, economic relations are multi-faceted. They encompass foreign trade, economic aid, as well as utilizing foreign investment, importing technology, developing international contracting, and providing labor services, and other partnerships. Economic ties have been built with different countries across the globe instead of concentrating only on a few friendly nations, particularly after the Cold War ended. This book is a study of China's multi-faceted economic relations and the implications on the global economic and political landscape.

The team studying this topic had collected their academic inquiries to publish the first edition of the book *China External Economic Relations* in 1999, which was also a book of teaching material. That first edition discussed China's economic relations with various countries, noting the course of development, the achievements, the problems, and the future prospects. It received positive feedback and was selected as a textbook by many universities and schools at various levels. The earlier book also earned the first class award for publication excellence from the China Foreign Affairs University and the recognition of Beijing Municipal Higher Education Teaching Material Project. The first edition is now out of print and outdated. Therefore, we have decided to publish a revised edition, which inherits the strengths of the first edition but adds updates and adjustments, especially in terms of showing the mutual benefits and global implications of China's external economic relations.

In preparing this book, we have reviewed academic literature and online information authored by academics both in China and overseas, as well as websites. Here we would like to express our sincere gratitude to these academics.

Professor Liu Saili is the chief editor for this book and for this series of teaching materials. She outlined the framework for the book, reviewed, and coordinated the manuscripts and wrote the foreword and chapters 1 and 9. The deputy editor Professor Zhou Lin assisted with the review of manuscripts and wrote chapters 2 and 5.

Other contributors include (in no particular order):
- Zhu Caihua, assistant professor, and Xie Huajun (Chapter 3)
- Feng Xingyan, assistant professor (Chapter 4)
- Fan Ying, professor (Chapter 6)
- Zhu Caihua, assistant professor (Chapter 7)
- Jiang Ruiping, assistant professor, and Chang Sichun, lecturer (Chapter 8)
- Hu Zaiyong, assistant professor (Chapter 10)
- Lü Fengyong, researcher (Chapter 11)
- Zhang Cuizhen, assistant professor (Chapter 12)
- Tan Jijun, professor (Chapter 13)
- Yang Guang, lecturer (Chapter 14)

China's external economic relations make up a rapidly developing and broad subject that requires a deep understanding of policy and technical economics. It is a multi-discipline, academic subject that allows for the exploration and studying of systems, substance, theory, and practice. The information and analysis presented here are limited by the authors' and editors' perspectives and backgrounds. Should there be any gaps of knowledge or inadequacies in this book, we welcome the comment and criticism from experts, academics, and readers in general.

Edited by the China Foreign Affairs University

1

Chapter

The External Economic Relations of China and the Global Implications

China is the world's second largest economy and the country with the world's largest population. Its economic growth has been extraordinary amidst the volatility in the global economy. At the same time, the nation is acutely aware of the need for continuing its economic reforms. In order to achieve sustainable economic growth, China strives towards efficient and equal distribution of resources and economic opportunities within the country. It wants to improve labor productivity and upgrade the industrial and economic structure. It is taking steps to unleash the potential of the domestic market and tap into overseas markets. The breadth and depth of China's external economic relations today are a clear indication of how far the Chinese economy has come in opening itself to global opportunities. This chapter traces the development of China's external economic relations, and puts these relations into the context of the simultaneous forces of competition and cooperation in the globalized world.

Overview of the Development of China's External Economic Relations

Foreign invasion and occupation in modern history

Foreign invasion features prominently in the modern history of China, and forms part of the backdrop for China's current economic relations with the rest of the world. Its diplomatic, economic, and cultural relations with foreign countries flourished as early as the Han and Tang Dynasties, when China had sent ambassador Zhang Qian to the western regions, the Buddhist monk Xuan Zang to India, and monk Jian Zhen to propagate Buddhism in Japan. However, this nation with a glorious past experienced in modern history the occupation of Chinese coastal areas, the granting of concessions to foreign powers, the forced opening of trade and the plundering of resources. The foreign invasion and occupation, which ended only after the Second World War, injured the national pride of the Chinese people. Some still maintain cautiousness and suspicion when encountering foreign influences. This mentality could create obstacles to a full embrace of foreign economic relations.

Convoluted path since the establishment of the People's Republic of China

The Cold War affected the early economic relations of the People's Republic of China (PRC). Trade sanctions and the embargo from the Western bloc led by the United States meant that China's main trading partner was restricted to the

Soviet Union. China also provided development aid to North Korea, Vietnam, Mongolia, and some African states as part of the assistance to Communist friendly nations. A major shift took place in the early 1960s when China and the Soviet Union parted ways. Technology cooperation between the two countries stopped, with the Soviet Union withdrawing its scientists and demanding debt repayment from China. China became an essentially isolated economy as trade with the Soviet bloc evaporated. There were no external economic relations to speak of until the early 1970s.

After the PRC was re-instated to the United Nations in 1971, the country's development aid to third-world countries increased significantly, with some aid going to aid in "anti-American conflicts" underway in Vietnam, Cambodia, and Laos. Providing the large volume of aid was disproportionate to the real economic power of China at the time, but this aid served to boost China's power in international affairs. China's economic cooperation with Western powers also began to move forward. In 1973, China used a delayed payment arrangement to import complete sets of technologies from the West, mainly in petrochemicals, metallurgy, and energy sectors.

In the 1960s and 1970s, when other Asian economies such as South Korea, Singapore, Thailand, Hong Kong, and Taiwan had attracted foreign investment to boost their economic development, China was mired in the Cultural Revolution from 1966 to 1976. Some of those in power at the time (such as Lin Biao and Jiang Qing who were later vilified as anti-revolutionaries) insisted on "self-sufficiency" of the Chinese economy, branded all foreign trade as "treachery" and foreign technology import as "philosophy of foreign slaves." China was therefore a closed economy which lost numerous opportunities to develop and modernize.

The above events restricted the external economic relations of China, limiting the scale and modes of its trade and economic engagement. During this time, the technology gap and economic gap between China and the Western developed countries widened even more.

Adopting an open-door policy

A few years of soul-searching took place before China officially adopted an open-door policy at the 1981 National People's Congress. This policy indicated that the country would open its economy to the rest of the world and strengthen international economic and technological exchange. In December 1981, the opening of the economy was written into the Chinese constitution.

The significance of opening the Chinese economy became apparent after the

Cultural Revolution ended with the fall of the "Gang of Four." Government officials at the national and local levels had formed delegations to visit foreign economies. After a May 1978 visit led by then vice premier Gu Mu to Western Europe, including France, Germany, Belgium, Denmark, and Sweden, meetings took place within the Politburo and the State Council, at which key officials agreed to explore opening foreign economic relations. Their rationale was that, first, there are parts of the capitalist world that China could learn from. Second, they acknowledged that the gap between China and the advanced capitalist countries had widened during the years of China maintaining a closed economy. Third, the advanced countries would welcome cooperation with China because of its vast market for trade and investment. Therefore, China would explore the different facets of international economic exchange, including compensation trade, cooperative production, and attracting foreign investment.

"China has closed its doors for 300 years if we count from the middle of the Ming Dynasty to the Opium Wars," said Deng Xiaoping, the chief architect of China's opening of the economy. "There were 200 years if we count from Emperor Kangxi of Qing Dynasty. This long period of closed doors has made China impoverished, backwards and ignorant."[1] The central party leaders also found support in Marxist theory.[2]

The global economy at the time offered empirical evidence to support China's decision of opening its economy. The post-Second World War reconstruction of Japan and Germany was successful because these countries used the capital and technology imported from other countries, and opened economic, technical, and cultural interactions with the rest of the world. China also recognized that trade was not the only component of economic relations, and was willing to embrace foreign investment, opening to foreign capital markets, international technology transfer and exchange, international contracting, and provision of labor services, and tourism. It was Deng Xiaoping who advocated that reforms to open the economy would help China attain international competitiveness, thereby supporting China's reconstruction and modernization.[3 and 4]

The economic reforms in China are generally considered as having been launched at the December 1978 3rd Plenary Session of the 11th National Congress of the Chinese Communist Party. Three concrete goals were agreed upon:

1. China's GDP should be doubled by 1990 compared to 1980, allowing people to have a basic standard of living.
2. From 1990 to 2000, GDP should double again, building a moderately prosperous society.

3. By the middle of the 21st century, China's GDP per capita should be equivalent to a moderately developed country.

China also declared the objective of modernizing the economy so that it could catch up in 100 years to what developed capitalist countries had achieved in 300 years.

At the end of the 1970s, China also built diplomatic relations with the United States, signed a peace and friendship treaty with Japan, and improved its relations with the Soviet Union and other Western countries.

The Opening of the Chinese Economy

Main content

Economic reforms covered the following areas in order to institute new systems, policies, laws, and regulations to develop external economic relations in the following ways:

- External economic cooperation
- Foreign capital and technology
- International tourism
- The "Go Global" strategy, including encouraging Chinese firms to invest overseas, breaking down trade barriers in foreign markets, transfer production over-capacity from China to other markets, and invest in foreign markets by cooperating with the host country's investors.
- Full liberalization of the energy and transportation industries, and of the service sectors of commerce, foreign trade, finance, insurance, and telecommunications, in accordance with the protocol of accession to the World Trade Organization (WTO).

Stages of development

The opening of the Chinese economy took place in three stages:

First steps of opening coastal areas, 1979–1991

As a kick-start to opening the Chinese economy, the status of "special economic zone" (SEZ) was first granted to Shenzhen, Zhuhai, Shantou, and Xiamen in 1980. These four cities were located in Guangdong and Fujian Provinces, the two provinces most open to interaction with foreign economies at the time. They were sufficiently far away from the center of power in Beijing so that any risks of social disharmony or concerns about negative foreign influences would not affect the capital city. These SEZs were designed to attract foreign investment and introduce market forces into the Chinese economy. Investors were given favorable terms on taxation, land use fees, and import and export procedures. The SEZs were to become "windows" opened to the world economy, as the first experiments of the economic reforms.

When success was achieved by the first four SEZs, 14 more cities on the eastern and southern coast of China were further opened in April 1984. They include Dalian, Qinhuangdao, Tianjin, Yantai, Qingdao, Lianyungang, Nantong, Shanghai, Ningbo Wenzhou, Fuzhou, Guangzhou, Zhanjiang, and Beihai. These cities were granted more autonomy to run their economic affairs and to put in place policies to attract foreign investors and import foreign technologies.

Further opening of the coastal areas took place in 1988, when the opening of the economy was extended to the Pearl River Delta, Yangtze River Delta, Southeast Fujian Delta, Eastern Liaoning Peninsula, and the Shandong Peninsula. Hainan Island also became the largest single SEZ in China.

The New Pudong District in Shanghai was further opened and developed in June 1990, together with a group of other cities in the Yangtze River Delta.

These special economic zones were early experiments that allowed China to accumulate experience, improve systems, and train its human capital for the further opening of the economy. The success was particularly apparent in Shenzhen, which became the grounds for various policy experiments and improvements in administration, financial regulation, corporate governance, labor conditions, wages, and price controls. It became a typical practice in China's economic reforms to apply new liberalization policies to a selected few cities first, and then expand the coverage more widely once the earlier experiments had proven successful.

Exploring integration with the world economy, 1992–2001

Deng Xiaoping made his Southern Tour in 1992 to reassert the reformist agenda, visiting Guangzhou, Shenzhen, and Zhuhai, and spending the Chinese New Year in Shanghai. At the 14th National Congress of the Chinese Communist Party, Deng Xiaoping proposed the building of a "Socialist market economic system" and garnered support for the economic opening to extend to the inland cities and provinces.

In 1992, 13 inland and border cities were also granted the same status of economic development zones as the coastal areas. These included: Wenzhou, Kunshan, Weihai, Fuqing, Wuhan, Changchun, Harbin, Shenyang, Hangzhou, Wuhu, Chongqing, Xiaoshan, Huizhou Daya Bay, and Nansha District,

Guangzhou. In 1994, the Beijing and Urumqi development zones were approved. As of the end of 1996, China had established five special economic zones, 32 national economic and technology development zones, 52 national high technology development zones, and more than 1,000 other economic development areas at the local levels, opening the economies of more than 900 cities, municipalities, and counties. In terms of geography, the Chinese economy was fully opened.

There were also discussions of modernizing state-owned enterprises and implementing corporate governance reforms at the 15th National Congress of the Chinese Communist Party in 1997. Diversifying ownership structures of national assets and constructing systems of shareholding in stock corporations were discussed.[5] The objective of the economic reforms is to improve the international competitiveness of the Chinese economy and strengthen China's national power. Exploring the integration of the Chinese economy with the global economy and adjusting the Chinese system to the global rules of the game were considered essential steps forward.

In 2000, China raised the "Go West" strategy of encouraging foreign investment in the development of the western regions. The western regions included the provinces and municipalities of Gansu, Guizhou, Ningxia, Qinghai, Shaanxi, Sichuan, Tibet, Xinjiang, Yunnan, and Chongqing, covering two-thirds of China's land mass and almost a quarter of the Chinese population. The western regions possesses abundant mining resources, energy, and water resources, potential for tourism, and ample land. This region has 18,000 km in river shorelines and shares a 3,500 km land border with a dozen countries. The national plan for developing the western regions also includes the provinces of Inner Mongolia and Guangxi in addition to the above.

Full opening after WTO accession in 2001

China's WTO accession on December 11, 2001, started a new era of trade liberalization and further integration of China with the world economy.[6] WTO accession and the continued economic development also prompted further domestic economic reforms. In 2002, the role of the non-state sector in Chinese economic development was recognized, and China stated its intention for corporate governance reforms through introducing non-state ownership in state-owned enterprises and restructuring state-owned enterprises into stock corporations.

The WTO accession also prompted China to take steps to unleash the potential of its existing trading partners and sources of investments. The *Closer*

Economic Partnership Agreement (CEPA) with Hong Kong and Macau went into effect in January 1, 2004. This is a free trade agreement that eliminates tariffs and non-tariff barriers for particular products and service sectors, and facilitates bilateral investment.

A more equal distribution of wealth and the fruits of development has become a central theme of reforms in the 2000s. In 2003, China announced plans to revive the old industrial base in the northeastern regions and to support the sustainable development of cities that have been built around mining and resources. In 2006, China announced a strategy to accelerate development of the central regions, addressing the gap of per capita GDP between the central regions, and the eastern coast, and proposing solutions to the problems of rural development and agricultural industry and labor.[7]

In the decade following accession to the WTO, the Chinese central government pledged ambitious growth targets and a more equal distribution of wealth. In 2007, the 17th National Congress of the Chinese Communist Party touted the development of a moderately prosperous society (*xiaokang*) and revised the growth target announced in the previous congress—from quadrupling GDP to quadrupling per capita GDP. This was generally considered a new policy focus in which the quality of economic growth was emphasized. The rapid economic growth and simultaneous social inequalities had been obvious. The emphasis on per capita GDP growth was an attempt to link the growing economic power and international status of China to the improvement in the everyday lives of the population.

Main Features of Chinese External Economic Relations

Gradualism and experimentalism

The opening of the Chinese economy and the economic reforms have been largely marked by gradualism and experimentalism. The open-door policy first started with a pilot of four cities and was eventually broadened over a period of 15 years to cover the entire eastern and southern coast, and then the inland provinces and cities. The gradualism and experimentalism are usually attributed to the fact that the economic reforms have been unprecedented in history and the government leaders wanted to preserve stability and ensure political consensus as much as possible. At a practical level, the gradualist approach also allowed for adjustments in government policies as they see the results of the reforms.

From regional opening to sectoral liberalization

The opening of the Chinese economy started with a relatively monolithic sector of export-oriented processing. After expanding the reforms to all geographical areas, and prompted by the WTO accession commitments, the liberalization of sectors and services followed. Today, China's integration into the globalized world has extended beyond economic relations, into science, technology, culture, and education. There is even cooperation with foreign political parties, civil society, and parliaments.

The development of laws, regulations, and the market economy

A comprehensive legal and regulatory framework forms the foundation of a market economy system. Between 1978 and 2004, the legislative body of China passed 220 laws, the State Council issued over 670 administrative regulations, and the local people's congress passed nearly 10,000 local regulations, and the autonomous regions passed nearly 500 autonomous rules and regulations.[8]

Independence and sovereignty

China has maintained its independence and sovereignty while developing an open economy and liberalized trade. Foreign investment enters China only within the legal framework specifying the sectors, industries, and the mode of ownership allowed.

Alignment with diplomatic relations and global status

China has adopted a diversified strategy in foreign diplomacy, building diplomatic relationships with countries around the world instead of only engaging countries with similar political ideologies. Since the late 1980s and early 1990s, China has also launched a strategy to diversify markets. China has participated in multilateral and regional organizations both to enhance its political and economic power.

Main Achievements and Issues of China's External Economic Relations

Main achievements

Three decades of economic reforms have brought about significant changes in the economy, society, and culture in China. Quality of life has improved significantly, with the general population now aspiring to building a moderately prosperous household instead of merely surviving.

Strengthened national power

The unprecedented economic growth increased the political clout and raised the international status of China. From 1978 to 2007, China maintained over 9% annual economic growth for 30 years. The size of the economy reached USD3.13 trillion in GDP in 2007, from a base of USD216.5 billion in 1978, an average annual increase of 9.8%.[9] Table 1.1 shows that China was the world's fourth largest economy by 2004. Table 1.2 shows that China will continue its rapid economic growth and maintain its important status in the world economy.

Table 1.1. China's total GDP and per capita GDP, 1980–2007

Year	Total GDP (USD1 billion, current price)	Per capita GDP (USD, current price)
1980	307.60	311.63
1981	291.03	209.82
1982	279.77	275.22
1983	300.38	219.61
1984	309.09	296.19
1985	305.26	288.39
1986	295.48	274.85
1987	321.39	294.05
1988	401.07	361.24
1989	449.10	398.48
1990	387.77	339.16
1991	406.09	350.61
1992	486.05	412.26
1993	613.22	517.41

(Con't)

Year	Total GDP (USD1 billion, current price)	Per capita GDP (USD, current price)
1994	559.53	466.60
1995	727.95	601.01
1996	856.00	699.41
1997	952.65	770.59
1998	1,019.48	817.15
1999	1,083.29	861.21
2000	1,198.48	945.60
2001	1,324.81	1,038.04
2002	1,453.83	1,131.80
2003	1,640.96	1,269.83
2004	1,931.64	1,486.02
2005	2,243.69	1,715.93
2006	2,644.64	2,011.93
2007	3,250.83	2,460.79

Sources: According to data retrieved from the International Monetary Fund (IMF) database in April 2008. The 2007 data was provided as a projection by an IMF expert.

Table 1.2. GDP of selected countries as a percentage of global GDP, 2007 (%)

Country	Purchasing power parity (PPP)	Current prices
Brazil	2.81	2.42
China	10.83	5.99
France	3.17	4.72
Germany	4.34	6.12
India	4.58	2.02
Italy	2.76	3.88
Japan	6.61	8.08
Russia	3.18	2.38
United Kingdom	3.30	5.11
United States	21.36	25.51

Source: IMF database.

China has amassed one of the world's largest foreign exchange reserves, from USD167 million in 1978 to USD1.528 trillion in 2007. Its foreign exchange reserves exceeded Japan in February 2006 to become the world's largest (see Table 1.3).

Table 1.3. Foreign exchange reserves held by China, 1978–2007 (USD1 billion)

Year	Foreign exchange reserves
1978	0.17
1979	–0.84
1980	1.30
1985	2.64
1990	11.09
1995	73.60
2000	168.60
2001	217.40
2002	286.41
2003	403.30
2004	609.93
2005	828.90
2006	1,066.30
2007	1,528.20

Sources: 1978–2002 data from the National Bureau of Statistics website, August 1, 2005, http://www.safe.gov.cn/Statistics/AnnualReport_02.files/AnnualReport_02.htm#31; 2003-2007 data from the National Bureau of Statistics, *China National Economy and Social Development Statistical Report 2007*, February 28, 2008.

Shifts in foreign trade and related systems

The new system of foreign trade and a robust regulatory framework was successful in increasing foreign trade and making trade a driver in economic growth. China's trade volume grew from USD20.6 billion in 1978 to USD2.174 trillion in 2007. In 2007, China had the third largest trade volume in the world, and was the third largest importer and second largest exporter. While the global trade volume increased six-fold between 1978 and 2007, China's total foreign trade during this time increased by 104 times. The number of trading partners increased from a few dozen in 1978 to over 220 countries in 2007.

China's trade as a proportion of global trade increased from 32nd in 1978, to 16th in 1990, 8th in 2000, 4th in 2003, and 3rd in 2004, ranking only after the U.S. and Germany.[10] According to the IMF's *World Economic Outlook*, China's trade as a percentage of world trade increased from 0.86% in 1980 to 8.8% in 2007.[11] From 2006 onwards, the trade volume of China, the EU, the U.S. and Japan were each above USD200 billion. China, therefore, became one of the largest trading nations in the world. China also fulfilled its WTO commitments, including allowing foreign-invested banks to operate renminbi business in China since December 11, 2006. The general import tariffs of industrial products into China has decreased from 15.3% in 2001 to 9.8% in January 2008.[12] China has also liberalized its service sectors to an extent that almost matches the openness in developed nations.

Fruitful use of foreign direct investment

Between 1965 and 1980, China was without any foreign or domestic national debt, and received no foreign investment or foreign assistance. China's share of global foreign investment went from zero in 1980 to 10.39% in 2000. In 2002, China had been the world's largest recipient of foreign direct investment (FDI), receiving USD50 billion that year. By 2007, FDI that year reached USD74.77 billion. Foreign-invested enterprises contributed to national economic growth and to foreign exports. The cumulative actual utilized foreign investment from 1979 to 2007 was USD747.1 billion, placing China as the largest developing country destination for FDI for a consecutive fifteen years.[13]

An increasing number of foreign technology companies have placed research and development (R&D) centers in China, with 1,160 foreign-invested R&D centers in operation as of November 2007. The foreign companies include Microsoft, IBM, Motorola, Siemens, Nortel Networks, Dupont, General Electric, General Motors, Volkswagen, P&G, Honda, and Hitachi. Already, 490 of the Fortune 500 companies have set up businesses in China. The top automakers and top information technology firms have all entered China. As of the end of 2007, FDI had contributed 40% of China's GDP, and foreign-invested enterprises employed 30 million people, accounting for 10% of the urban employed population. Foreign management practices and concepts also contributed to changing the traditional mentality and corporate governance of Chinese firms.

China's outbound foreign investment has also developed. Chinese investors in overseas markets concentrated at first on the sectors of construction, engineering, and contracting, catering, tourism, transportation, and general consulting. Later, they also entered sectors including resource development, processing and assembly, high technology, and manufacturing. China is conscious of its rapidly depleting resources in fishery, forestry, mining, and petroleum, and therefore had encouraged Chinese firms to invest in exploration and acquisition of such resources overseas. As of the end of 2007, Chinese outbound investors had set up over 10,000 non-financial companies in over 200 overseas countries and regions, investing USD70 billion in total.

Developing international contracting and development aid

International contracting has been built from scratch and has become an important part of China's economic cooperation. As of 2007, China has over 2,000 licensed people to provide international contracting and labor services, of which 400 perform these services as their main business. These companies are growing in scale, professionalism, and international experience. As of March 2008, Chinese international contractors have had a cumulative revenue of USD215.7 billion, and have sent Chinese labor to almost 200 countries and regions, to serve in manufacturing, primary industries, transportation, and construction.[14]

Meanwhile, China has worked closely with various United Nations agencies to provide development assistance to developing countries.

Facilitating a re-balancing of economic progress in China

Economic development in China has enabled the country to develop its inland regions. Campaigns such as the western development, revival of the northeastern industrial region, and the central region development strategy have achieved mixed results. Nevertheless, the development of the inland regions helps break down administrative barriers within China, and enables each region to use its competitive advantage and participate in the economic progress.

Cooperation on bilateral and multilateral platforms

China has been an active contributor to East Asia cooperation through its participation in the ASEAN Plus Three mechanism. The negotiations leading up to the WTO accession and subsequently China's new membership in the WTO have provided opportunities for bilateral negotiations and dialogues that forge closer economic ties and avoid future conflicts. As of 2008, China has built 12 free trade areas with 29 countries in Asia, Australasia, Latin America, Europe, and Africa.[15] High-level dialogue mechanisms with China's major trading partners—for instance with the U.S., Japan, the EU, and ASEAN—have also been crucial to avoiding friction and maintaining positive economic relations.

International exchange of political parties, legislature, and civil society

China's economic power and its global status have risen hand in hand. It becomes even more important for close political and cultural ties to be built between China and the rest of the world, in order to create a favorable international environment for China's economic growth. To this end, the Chinese Communist Party has regular exchanges with over 400 political parties and organizations in 160 countries.[16] The National People's Congress (NPC), the Chinese legislature, maintains relations with the parliaments and legislatures of 178 countries, and has set up official exchange mechanisms with the NPC's counterparts in the U.S., Russia, France, Germany, Canada, Italy, Ukraine, the Philippines, and the EU.[17] The Chinese People's Political Consultative Conference (CPPCC), the political advisory body, also has friendly relations with 211 national organizations and 12 international bodies and regional organizations in 121 countries. It has also hosted the "21st Century Outlook Forum" since 1996 where dozens of countries' representatives discuss issues of regional security, economic cooperation, and other challenges of the time.[18]

Social and cultural ties with foreign countries have also been built at a civil society level.[19] Starting from Tianjin and Kobe, Japan forming the first pair of friendship cities, 1,401 pairs of friendship cities have been formed between Chinese provinces, regions or cities and locations across 120 countries in five continents.[20]

Main issues

There are still undeniable gaps between the Chinese economy and the developed countries, whether viewed in quantitative or qualitative terms:

Per capita GDP

Although it was an achievement for China to increase its GDP from USD307.6 billion in 1980 to USD3.25 trillion in 2007, it is still a much smaller economy compared to the United States, whose 2007 GDP was USD13.98 trillion. The gap between China and the major developed countries is even larger if we look at the GDP per capita (see Table 1.4).

In 2007, China's GDP per capita was only 1/20 of that of the United States. China ranked 143th in the world for GDP per capita in 2005, which improved to 128th in 2006 and 104th in 2007. Although the speed of improvement is impressive, this ranking is still very low. According to the World Bank's classifications, China is a mid to low income country. In other words, it is a poor nation that still struggles on the path of economic development.

Table 1.4. Comparison of GDP per capita in China and major developed countries

Country	GDP per capita (USD, current prices)
Canada	43,404
China	2,460
France	41,511
Germany	40,415
India	977
Italy	35,872
Japan	34,312
Russia	9,075
South Korea	19,750
United Kingdom	45,574
United States	45,845

Source: IMF, World Economic Outlook database, April 2008.

Quality of GDP

Heavy reliance on foreign economies

Foreign trade and foreign investment are the major drivers of the Chinese economy, which has maintained an external dependence of over 60% since 2003. The growth in imports from China to foreign markets has led to a surge in anti-dumping, technical barriers, and protectionist measures. Currently, China is the subject of 14% of all WTO anti-dumping investigations. The fact that China's "full market economy" status has not been recognized by the U.S. and the EU means that there may be some unfair results in the anti-dumping investigations. Some in China fear that the anti-dumping and trade protectionist actions could negatively impact the Chinese economy which is so heavily dependent on supplying Chinese exports to fulfil foreign consumer demand.

There has been a surplus in China's current account and capital account every year since 1994. The enormous foreign trade surplus has become one of the main focuses of China's external economic relations. The surplus (USD262.2 billion in 2007)[21] and the foreign exchange reserves (USD1.9 trillion in September 2008)[22] have exerted pressure for the Renminbi to appreciate, inviting speculation in the Chinese currency. This has negative consequences both for macroeconomic development and for the foreign trade relations of China.

The longstanding deficit of service trade

China's foreign trade in goods is ranked the third largest in the world, and yet its service trade is only eighth in the world and is in a longstanding deficit. From 1982 to 2006, although the service trade volume has increased 37-fold, service trade has always accounted for less than 10% of the total trade volume of China, which is only half of the international average.[23]

Limited scale of outbound investment

By 2007, China's outbound investment was a fraction of its inbound foreign investment. The campaign to encourage Chinese enterprises to achieve international competitiveness by investing in overseas markets seems to be still at a rudimentary stage. Chinese enterprises lack understanding of foreign policies, laws, markets, cultures, and customs, and may not have the ability to distribute and sell products in those foreign markets. The Chinese government could support through improvements in laws, taxation, credit, and loans, insurance and personnel training specifically in the area of outbound foreign investment.

Low competitiveness of the financial sector

Five years after joining the WTO, China has fully liberalized the banking and finance sector in accordance with accession commitments. However, the Chinese banks are still lagging behind foreign banks in their capital, asset quality, and profitability. Bad debt is rampant. The low competitiveness of the banking sector and financial system compromises the Chinese government's ability to use macro controls to influence the economy, and challenges the administration of foreign exchange. Because of these weaknesses in the Chinese banking system, foreign-invested banks may have an advantage when competing against Chinese banks. The banking sector is a strategic sector that relates to the everyday lives of people as well as national financial security and national production. China's continued economic development would require further efforts to improve its banking sector and financial systems.

Problems in the domestic economy

The structure of the domestic economy is unbalanced. Problems have been manifested in a wide urban-rural income gap and unresolved issues of the agricultural sector.[24] In economic terms, there is an over-representation of the primary sector, an over-representation in the low value-added manufacturing sector, and an under-developed services sector. There is over-investment and surplus production capacity, but insufficient domestic demand. In terms of social policies, the social security system is inadequate to provide healthcare and pensions for the aging population. These economic and social issues are intertwined as one generates opportunities that are unevenly distributed and exacerbates inequalities. Despite the remarkable economic growth, there are 22 million in impoverished population in China, and another 56 million people who are just at the poverty line.

A shortage of human capital

China has a shortage of professionals in diplomacy, foreign trade, and finance. These need to be people who understand economics and the international rules of the game in a globalized world. These professionals are required for China to master the rules in the WTO and other international economic organizations, as well as to help familiarize China with the laws and regulations in the European Commission.

The above issues, combined with global uncertainties such as trade protectionism, ethnic conflicts, volatility of oil prices and depreciation of the U.S. dollar, could hinder and challenge the long-term development of China's economic relations.

The Global Implications of the Rise of China

It is no surprise that many countries see China as a threat. China is the world's largest developing economy. It is showing robust growth rates when some of the world's most advanced economies are suffering from deep economic recession. It is engaging in proactive efforts to secure energy and other resources to fuel its future growth. All these factors contribute to a "China threat" belief. There are others who want to pressure China into taking a larger role in international affairs, by proposing a "China responsibility" theory.

In face of these global reactions to China's extraordinarily growth, China emphasizes the idea of "peaceful development," which was first articulated in 2005 by President Hu Jintao at the 60th anniversary of the United Nations.[25] China believes that its economic development generates growth opportunities for the rest of the world. According to one World Bank report,[26] China's accession to the WTO has brought an annual economic benefit of USD40 billion to China, and another USD75 billion to the rest of the world. An IMF report also ranks China as the world's top contributor in global economic growth. It was estimated that China contributed to 33% of world economic growth in 2007 by purchasing power parity. It ranked the second largest contributor in the world in contributing 12.5% of world economic growth by market prices, second only to the U.S.[27]

China has now developed its economic relations to a more mature stage, using bilateral relations, regional platforms, and multilateral organizations to engage other countries in diplomacy, politics, and economy. As of March 2007, China has established diplomatic relations with 166 countries, set up more than 240 diplomatic organizations as its overseas outposts, and has developed economic and trade relationships with 222 countries and regions. Its dialogue mechanisms with the United States and with the European Union have seen stable development. The strategic cooperative partnership with Russia has also moved forward at various levels of government. China uses regional platforms such as the Shanghai Cooperation Organization, the Asia-Pacific Economic Cooperation (APEC), the Association of Southeast Asian Nations (ASEAN), and the South Asian Association for Regional Cooperation. China has also engaged in friendly and generally cooperative relations with its neighbors including Japan, India, North Korea, South Korea, Pakistan, and Vietnam. Instead of engaging in conflict over border disputes and territorial disputes in the South China Sea, China has generally advocated joint development of the mining or energy resources while the conflict could be put on hold.

The economic development of China has directly benefited the least developed countries in Africa as China has become a major source of aid. As of April 2006, China has funded over 2,000 aid projects for 110 countries or regional organizations, and waived USD20 billion in debt for 44 developing countries.[28] Since 2002, China has assisted developing countries to construct 29 landmark projects such as convention centers, highways, bridges, schools, and hospitals.[29] China's efforts help the African countries towards achieving the Millennium Development Goals. Although its motives in Africa could be debatable—China might have accepted the "China responsibility" theory as a leading developing country or it is motivated by an agenda of energy security[30]—China's contribution to development in Africa helps ensure peace and stability.

The trade figures show very clearly the global implications of Chinese economic development. China imports nearly USD1 trillion a year to fuel its economic production and fulfill consumer demand. The import demand is estimated to create 10 billion jobs overseas. The large volume of affordable Chinese exports has benefited the end consumers in advanced countries by reducing the pressure of inflation. In 2007, China had over USD200 billion in bilateral trade with the U.S., the EU, Japan, and ASEAN.[31]

When alleged to be a threat, China has always responded by saying that even when it was at its historical height of economic power, it was still a peaceful nation. In the peak of the Ming Dynasty 600 years ago, China represented one-third of the world's GDP. By 1978, China had declined to the extent that it only represented 1.7% of global GDP. Three decades of reforms returned China to 5.99% of the global GDP. International Monetary Fund (IMF) managing director Rodrigo de Rato praised China for its economic achievements which Rato attributes to marketization of the economy and China's integration in globalization.[32]

As the Chinese economy made significant progress in the last three decades, so have China's economic relations with its major trading partners. This book will present how the economic relations have changed. In some cases, such as the United States, trading partners that have been plagued by frequent trade friction have eventually set up regular dialogue to resolve issues. With others such as India, political rivalries are apparent as the world's largest developing economies compete for oil. Meanwhile, less developed countries in Latin America and in Africa offer promising opportunities for economic cooperation with China, in a new era where diplomacy is less determined by military might than by economic prowess.

2 Chapter

The Foreign Trade of China

Foreign trade is an important aspect of China's external economic relations. Trade development has accelerated China's economic relations and Socialist modernization, especially since the economic reforms of the late 1970s. Therefore, understanding the role and impact of Chinese foreign trade, and analyzing its development, characteristics, and problems, is significant for further advancement of China's economic relations.

Supporting National Economy and International Relations

Foreign trade, which includes import and export, refers to a country's activity of exchanging goods and services with other countries. Foreign trade plays an intermediary role in Marxist social reproduction theory. Social reproduction is a process that consists of production, distribution, exchange, and consumption of goods and services as four essential stages. Production is thus seen as the beginning and the stage that sets this process into motion, consumption as the end, and distribution and exchange as intermediaries. Trade (exchange) is determined and impacted by production, but as an essential bridge between the first and last stages, trade can also impact production itself.

In this chapter we concern ourselves mainly with foreign trade as opposed to domestic trade. Both foreign and domestic trade are playing the important intermediary role noted above, and they are both components of social reproduction. However, the impact of domestic trade is limited to domestic production and consumption, whereas foreign trade involves a much wider and more complex influence. Foreign trade is a process by which China's commodities circulate in the global market, in exchange for resources required by the domestic economy, thereby connecting domestic production in China with foreign consumption, and connecting foreign production with domestic consumption in China. Foreign trade, therefore, has a special status in social reproduction theory that cannot be replaced by domestic trade. It is not only the bridge between production and consumption within a country, but also a bridge linking one country's economy with the global economy.

Prior to China's economic reforms which started in 1978, historical, political, and economic factors had limited China's understanding of the important strategic role of foreign trade for national economic growth. China had viewed foreign trade merely as a supplementary tool that could adjust for excesses and shortages in domestic production. As a result, before 1978 China's foreign trade trails far from reaching its full potential.

The Chinese Communist Party (CCP) decided the 3rd Plenary Session of the 11th CCP Central Committee in 1978 to open the domestic market and embrace the global markets, thus launching China's economic reforms. It gradually became apparent that foreign trade is an important component and catalyst of national economic growth, as well as a bridge that engenders international understanding. China's economic development was then accompanied by unprecedented growth in foreign trade.

Foreign trade has several important functions in the economic modernization of China: First, foreign trade is an important measure to achieve balanced growth in the national economy. Because of limitations in natural resources and technical skills, it is impossible for a country to possess the capability to produce all the goods it needs, or the wealth to invest in building such a capability. Even if a country can leverage the strengths of some of its regions to compensate for the weaknesses of other regions, this would lead to low-quality economic growth and would not enable the country to achieve its full potential. Therefore, an international exchange of goods could re-balance the strengths and weaknesses of a country's production, expand the scale of social reproduction and build a stronger foundation for economic growth.

Second, importing advanced technology and equipment can help upgrade the technological level of the domestic economy. Since the end of the Second World War, technology is increasingly traded across countries. Imported advanced technology and equipment have served to accelerate domestic development of economically important technologies and to close the gap with other more advanced countries. Since the 1950s, China imported whole sets of equipment and technology from Soviet Union and Eastern Europe, building the early foundation for industrialization. After the economic reforms, China imported a large amount of advanced technology and equipment from around the world so as to elevate China's own technological capabilities.

For example, in the five years between 1999 and 2003, China imported USD75.2 billion worth of foreign technology, which represents 42% of technology imported since the economic reforms. The large amount of imported technologies helped propel the structural adjustment and improvement of China's industrial sector. Traditional industries were upgraded, leading to higher quality of gross domestic product (GDP) growth. In 2003, sales revenues of China's information technology sector reached RMB1.88 trillion. China has become one of the world's largest producers of color televisions, stored program control (SPC) exchange systems, monitors, and DVD players. The design and manufacturing of computers, digital communication equipment, satellite communication equipment, automotive and heavy machinery have gradually developed. Several renowned brands such as Lenovo, Founder, Haier, and Changhong have emerged rapidly as global players once they developed their own intellectual property and established their competitive advantages. At the same time, technology content and value-added in traditional products have increased, with products such as textiles, clothing, shoes, bicycles, and sewing machines gaining a stronger position against international competitors.[1]

Third, foreign trade can build the financial resources of a country by increasing tax revenues and foreign currency income. Foreign trade expands the sources of tax revenue and increases the absolute amount of tax in the form of import and export duties, enterprise income tax resulting from export revenues, commodity tax, and tax on imported raw materials used for domestic production. During the 10th Five-Year Plan (2002–2007), customs tax revenue experienced enormous growth. From 2001 up to September 2005, the cumulative tax income was RMB1.74 trillion, one of the fastest-growing source of revenues for the central government. In 2007, customs duties and import linkage tax reached a total of RMB758.46 billion.[2] Developing export trade also increases the foreign currency income. In the first 10 years of economic reforms, China's USD292.97 billion worth of export income enabled the import of important goods for domestic use and supported China's economic development. As of 2007, China's foreign currency reserves, which mainly comes from exports, reached USD1.5 trillion.

Fourth, foreign trade development opens the door to global and domestic markets, increases the supply of consumer goods and enhances people's quality of life. Since the establishment of the People's Republic of China (PRC), China imported raw materials, technology, equipment, and household goods, increasing the availability of all kinds of commodities in the domestic markets. Imports continue to grow since the economic reforms, and the types of imported goods diversified. These imports improved the quantity and quality of commodities available in the domestic market and raised the standard of living in China.

Fifth, foreign trade increases employment. Employment can be a sensitive issue in many countries, and has been a concern in China during the economic reforms. Foreign trade provides direct employment opportunities to domestic labour. Statistics point out that every RMB100 million of exports creates 12,000 job opportunities. Using the export figures in recent years, we estimate that the export of industrial products employs about 40 million people in China. At the same time, according to the rule of thumb estimating 8,000 jobs created per RMB100 million in cost of domestic industrial production, imports in China has also provided employment for 30 million people.

Sixth, foreign trade accelerates the development of external economic relations. The various aspects of external economic relations—international economic and technology cooperation, the use of foreign investment, import and export of technology, providing economic aid to developing countries, and external contracting and labour cooperation—are all closely related to foreign trade. If there are no goods or technology required by another country, then there would be no economic cooperation. When engaging foreign investment, a typical consideration is to evaluate the country's ability to pay off national debt through exports. In addition, in practice, a country often develops foreign trade as a first step to opening external economic relations. Therefore, foreign trade is a foundation and a stepping stone towards stronger and wider external economic relations.

Seventh, foreign trade based on the principles of equality and mutual benefit can help the development of friendly relations with other countries, creating a positive external environment for the building and development of a country. China's modernization requires a peaceful global environment. Apart from trade, China's political, economic, and cultural ties with the rest of the world are also essential to build positive international relations. As peace and development have become priorities around the world, economic diplomacy has been valued by many countries. Therefore, strengthening foreign trade can help China establish normal, peaceful, and friendly relations with the rest of the world.

Measures and Principles of China's Foreign Trade Relations

The command economy formed the foundation of China's foreign trade relations. Then from 1979 onwards, China started reforming its foreign trade system and made a series of adjustments to its trade policies.

Reforms of China's foreign trade system

After the 1949 establishment of the PRC, China abolished the various privileges of foreign imperial powers, took back sovereign control of customs, confiscated import and export companies owned by large private capital, and set up state-owned external trading companies. This created a trade system driven by central government and dominated by state-owned enterprises. Policy adjustments made between 1974 and 1978 did not alter the centralized administration of foreign trade.

During this time, the Ministry of Foreign Trade would formulate a nationwide plan for export activities that is implemented through the state-owned trading companies after coordination with provinces, municipalities, government departments, and state planning agencies. Each trading company followed the export sourcing plans handed down by the Ministry of Foreign Trade, and signed contracts to purchase products from relevant supply departments or production units in China. On the other end, trading companies also handled the transaction with the foreign buying party and signed the export contract according to the government's export plan. An import plan was formulated by the State Planning Agency and handed down to the trading companies, whose headquarters are responsible for negotiations with foreign entities and signing contracts for imports.

This highly centralized, government-driven system has several advantages. The unified national policy, plan, and principles for external engagement were maintained. The system balanced the interests of various stakeholders and took long-term and short-term issues into consideration. The centralized system also allowed for effective coordination between external economic activities and diplomatic concerns. Due to these advantages, this system has been credited for allowing China's foreign trade to develop during the 1950s and 1960s despite economic sanctions and embargoes from the West.

But the disadvantages of the system were also apparent. It was too centralized. Industry and commerce were detached from each other, and so were manufacturing and sales. There was a lack of clear differentiation between politics and enterprise, so that simple economics of profit and loss were ignored. This trade administration system became increasingly unsuitable for China's foreign trade as the geopolitical and domestic conditions changed. Reforms of China's trade system started in 1979 in an exploratory mode, and gradually deepened.

First phase: Exploratory stage (1979–1987)

The first step was to decentralize and delegate the power to engage in foreign trade. The authority to manage and operate foreign trade was decentralized to different levels of government. Local governments and departments started having greater authority to manage their own foreign trade (1979–1983). However, due to weak macro controls, some trading companies exploited the opportunity to purchase goods at extremely high prices from domestic buyers and to export at extremely low prices in order to compete successfully in foreign markets. Foreign trade was thus more tightly regulated. Centralized control of foreign trade was given to the Ministry of Foreign Trade and Commerce, which offered more unified decision-making and specialized management (1983–1984). Tightened controls stopped trading firms from blind competition and running exports at high loss. But trading firms lost incentives, resulting in a drop in exports.

These issues prompted the Ministry of Foreign Trade and Commerce to launch comprehensive reforms of the foreign trade system in 1984. Trading companies became separate entities from the Ministry, thus separating government and commerce. An agent system was started. The scope of foreign trade that was governed by policy was reduced. Independent accounting and auditing were introduced, and the trading companies' financial performance and the government's budget and finances were separated from each other.

Despite initial results, these reforms failed to eliminate the deep-seated problems of centralization. Reforms did not completely change the system of centralized issuing of budgets and collection of revenues, because these practices had lasted for several decades. Even though the government and enterprise became separate entities, their respective responsibilities were not clarified. Trading companies were not yet professionally managed as companies, and lacked effective self-discipline. Moreover, macroeconomic controls were still weak in implementation.

Second phase: Fully implementing the foreign trade contracting system (1988–1990)

Based on the State Council's *Decision on Several Questions of Accelerating and Deepening the Foreign Trade Reform*, issued in February 1988, the foreign trade contracting system was fully implemented. Trading companies at all levels contracted with the central government regarding their export earnings, the proportion of earnings to be turned over to the central government, currency exchange costs and export profit or loss. Those companies that performed well against these indicators enjoyed higher retention rates on their foreign currency earnings.

Except for a small number of commodities which were still put under unified management, the majority of commodities were open for import and export. An export agent system was set up to encourage both industry and commerce to respond more effectively to market demand and supply signals. The export tax rebate system was established. As for imports, most commodities enjoyed a gradual reduction in tariffs as the national policies for domestic industrial production were adjusted during this period. Foreign trade was managed by specialized bureaux and departments at different levels of government.

The above reforms resulted in substantial improvement in export. Local governments and departments were allowed to take greater initiative in promoting foreign trade. Trading companies and exporting producers were keen to capture new market opportunities.

Third phase: Deepening reforms, and a trade system of international standards (1991–present)

Between 1991 and 1994, the reforms focused on making trading companies self-sufficient and responsible for their own profit and loss. Foreign trade was put on a path of healthy development, which featured more open and fair competition, fiscal responsibility for profit and loss, stronger ties between industry and commerce, and the export agent system. These reforms were launched following the promulgation of the *Decision on Several Questions Concerning Further Reforming and Improving the Foreign Trade System* by the State Council, December 9, 1990.

As part of the reforms, export subsidies were abolished and trading companies were allowed better access to foreign currency. Uniform export earnings retention ratios were introduced for main categories of commodities, replacing the previous system of having different ratios for different geographical regions. There was a stronger system for the collection of export earnings. Trading companies had greater decision-making power in their commercial decisions and enjoyed wider access to foreign currency. This benefited imports and allowed increased inflows of foreign goods into the China market.

A new round of reforms in foreign trade took place in 1994. The dual-track exchange rate system was abolished, uniting the official exchange rate and swap exchange rate. A single, managed floating exchange rate was introduced. New macroeconomic controls were imposed for imports and exports. The export tax rebate system was improved while import subsidies were abolished. There was a gradual opening of import and export trade. There was an attempt to restructure state-owned trading companies using modern corporate methods. There were pilot projects for issuing shares. Trading companies were encouraged to set up international structures and group structures. Chambers of commerce was given a larger role. There was increasing transparency in foreign trade policy, as seen in the new *Foreign Trade Law of the People's Republic of China* which went into effect in 1994. These reforms paved the way for further rule of law in this area, and brought China's foreign trade governing system closer to international standards.

After accession into the World Trade Organization (WTO) in 2001, China devised and revised a series of laws, regulations, and related policies in foreign trade, in accordance with its accession commitments. Tariffs were substantially reduced, non-tariff measures were continuously decreased and standardized. In a step that signifies further opening of foreign trade, the approval system for import and export of commodities and technology was abolished and replaced by a registration system from July 1, 2004.

China's foreign trade system today stands in stark contrast to foreign trade at the beginning of the economic reforms. The highly centralized system was completely overhauled, making it possible for a wide variety of trading companies to take advantage of market opportunities in various modes of operation. Macroeconomic controls on foreign trade were improved, and the government's control of foreign trade went from using direct administrative means to the more indirect economic and legal means. It is widely believed that China's foreign trade system following this series of reforms has become more suited to the country's Socialist market economy and is more aligned with the standards on the international market.

The instruments for regulating foreign trade in China

As global trade develops, a country would gradually shape its own set of foreign trade regulations and administrative controls based on its political and economic self-interests and the specific needs to regulate its trade activities. The same applies to China's administration of its foreign trade, which consists of an evolving set of laws, regulations, and policies that stemmed from its macroeconomic interests and domestic policy needs. As the Chinese economy has become increasingly integrated with the rest of the world, its regulation on foreign trade activities are also more in line with global standards and laws.

Regulatory system of trading companies

Under these regulations, companies were legally required to complete a registration system before they can engage in import or export activities.

Between 1949 and 1979, when the central government had the sole authority to engage in foreign trade, import and export enterprises were regulated through an approval process. Trade reforms after 1979 meant that the authority to control trade was gradually decentralized. New trading companies were set up at all levels of government—apart from the specialized trading companies under the supervision of the Ministry of Foreign Trade and Commerce, new trading companies were set up by the national ministries and provincial, municipal, and autonomous regions governments. State-owned enterprises were also allowed to engage in foreign trade.

Three types of foreign invested enterprises, including joint ventures, cooperatives, and wholly owned foreign enterprises, were allowed to engage in import and export activities that were related to their production.

In 1992, China granted 100 science and technology research institutes in the country the right to engage in import and export activities.

In 1996, the Ministry of Foreign Trade and Commerce issued the *Pilot Temporary Measures for the Establishment of China-Foreign External Trading Companies*, starting with Pudong District, Shanghai, and with Shenzhen. Under these pilot schemes, the right to operate foreign trade was extended to foreign enterprises.

In early 1997, the Ministry of Foreign Trade and Commerce issued the *Provisional Measures for Automatic Registration of Import and Export by Production Enterprises in Special Economic Zones*. This was a precursor to an automatic registration system on a national scale. Starting July 1, 2004, the registration system fully replaced the approval system. The number of entities engaging in foreign trade increased exponentially as the right to operate foreign trade became increasingly open.

In 1978, China had only a handful of specialized import and export companies. By 1986, the number of enterprises that were allowed to engage in foreign trade reached 1,200. This number reached 23,000 in 2008.[3]

A new landscape of Chinese foreign trade is now being shaped by all kinds of trading companies, production enterprises, commercial materials enterprises, research institutes, and foreign invested enterprises that have become players in import and export activities.

The import and export licensing system

A licensing system for import and export is a common regulatory instrument employed by numerous countries around the world. The government issues licenses or permits in order to regulate the flow of imports and exports.

From May 1951 to 1956, China implemented a licensing system that governed all commodities in import and export. From 1957 to 1979, trading companies under the supervision of ministries used the cargo certificates and the national plan issued by the Ministry of Foreign Trade and Commerce in lieu of the license for foreign trade.

The import and export license system was re-initiated from October 1980 onwards, and has been revised many times since then. After accession to the

WTO, China reduced the scope of goods covered in the license system and standardized the system's procedures in several rounds of legal adjustments in fulfilment of its accession commitments.

Currently, the Ministry of Commerce and the General Administration of Customs issue the annual *Catalog of Commodities under the Import and Export License Management*. Import and export licenses are approved and issued by the Ministry of Commerce, Ministry of Commerce's resident representative offices, or the departments of commerce and trade in provinces, municipalities, and autonomous regions.

China's import licensing system treats all trading partners equally and is not restricted to certain countries or regions. In 1995, China amended some aspects of the licensing system, including import quotas and licensing management, in order to align Chinese regulations with international practice. By 2005, three categories of goods were under the scope of the import licensing system, a total of 83 eight-digit codes under the Harmonized Commodity Description and Coding System (HS). From January 1, 2005, the import quota licensing system was abolished for automotives and related key components, and for compact disc production equipment. In the same year, the export licensing system covered 47 categories of products, a total of 316 eight-digit HS codes.

Apart from regulating the trading of a limited number of commodities essential to its national interests, China is likely to continue to reduce the scope of its import and export licensing system in the foreseeable future.

Foreign currency control system

The Foreign Currency Control System is a system in which an appointed or delegated official body regulates the foreign currency revenue, expenditure, utilization, movement, foreign currency market activities, and changes in exchange rates. Regulation tools include the use of legal decrees, systems, measures, or temporary measures. The principle of "centralized management, unified operation" governs China's foreign currency control system.

Centralized management refers to the supervision of the People's Bank and the State Administration of Foreign Exchange (SAFE) in all foreign currency–related activities. "Unified operation" means that a specialized foreign exchange bank—Bank of China—will be the single entity that handles the income and expenditure, savings, the purchase and sales and re-allocation of China's foreign exchange and foreign exchange reserves. Other financial institutions and foreign-invested banks may operate in some areas of the foreign exchange business after obtaining necessary approvals.

Regulating exchange rates and the foreign exchange income and expenditure are the focus of China's foreign exchange controls. These controls are wide in scope, covering trade foreign exchange, non-trade foreign exchange, and capital inflow and outflow. Also controlled is foreign currency of individuals, of China representative offices of foreign organizations, and of foreign invested enterprises. In addition, cross-border capital flow is monitored and controlled.

The economic reforms that started in the late 1970s included changes in the foreign exchange control system. Procedures and policies for foreign exchange earnings retention was put in place from August 1978. In October 1980, foreign currency swap centers were set up around the country, allowing companies to buy and sell foreign currencies at the prescribed rates and amounts. Major reforms took place in 1994, when China united the official exchange rate and swap exchange rate. A managed floating exchange rate was introduced, which better reflected market demand of the Renminbi. At the same time, a new foreign exchange settlement and sales system was established. Foreign exchange transactions between banks were allowed, replacing the swap market. This year also saw the abolition of the foreign exchange earnings retention system. These were breakthrough reforms that supported China's market economy, and helped China on its quest to become further integrated with the global economy.

Another significant step in reforms took place in 1996. From December 1, 1996 onwards, China accepted Clauses 2, 3, and 4, Article 8, of the *Agreement of the International Monetary Fund*, allowing the Renminbi to be convertible under revenue accounts.

The State Administration of Foreign Exchange (SAFE) again adjusted and liberalized foreign exchange controls for organizations and individuals in 2001 after China's WTO accession. This was intended to encourage exports and support Chinese companies going overseas. In July 21, 2005, China started a floating foreign exchange system that uses a basket of currencies as reference and is based on market demand.

In August 6, 2008, new *Regulations on the Administration of Foreign Exchange* were issued, a piece of regulation that had not been revised for 11 years. One of the most important highlights of the new regulation was that it advocated balanced management of the inflow and outflow of foreign currency, requiring that foreign currency income and expenditure in the revenue account must be supported by genuine, legal transactions. It changed the requirement for repatriation of foreign currency income derived offshore, by laying out more liberal conditions under which such income is allowed to stay offshore.

This latest regulation addressed the current situation and new issues in China's currency administration, and responded to recent developments in the international economy.

Customs management system

The supervision of imports and exports by customs is an important aspect in enforcing foreign trade policy. One important function of customs is to monitor and inspect cargo shipments.

Customs ensure that the cargo is in accordance with the national policies and regulations, and monitor the timely, correct, and safe loading, exchange, transportation, and storage of cargo at the ports. Import and export licenses and approval documents from legal authorities form the basis for customs' daily tasks.

The supervision of trade activities include:

1. *Customs declaration*: All goods imported and exported must have customs declaration, a bill of lading for imports and a shipping order for exports. They should be completed by the recipient, sender, or the agent.
2. *Inspection of cargo*: Customs will inspect all goods imported and exported, except the exempted goods.
3. *Releasing the cargo*: Once determined that the imported or exported goods adhere to relevant regulations, customs will approve the release of goods on the waybill.
4. *Monitoring the loading and unloading of cargo*: Customs will send representatives to monitor the loading and unloading of cargo into transport.

Checking for smuggling activities is another essential function of customs. The illegal transport, carrying, and mailing across borders of any goods, currency, gold and silver, negotiable instruments, and monetized securities are forbidden. It is also forbidden to import goods for which one does not have permission or licenses to sell in the domestic market.

Tariffs on imports and exports are collected by customs. Tariff policies allow China to regulate the flow of trade, to protect the domestic market, and to retaliate against the discriminatory tariffs imposed on Chinese exports by foreign countries.

China's tariff policy is independent, self-determined, and aims to protect domestic industries. Tariff rates are based on the nature and use of commodities, the state of domestic production, and domestic and international markets. China determines the tariff rates for imported goods using the following principles: imported materials for further production enjoy lower tariffs than consumer goods; essential consumer goods enjoy lower tariffs than luxury goods; tax rates for those machinery, equipment, parts, and components that China does not have domestic manufacturing capabilities for are lower than those rates for entire sets of machinery; tariff rates are charged for goods that compete with important domestic industries.

Two tariff rates are applied by Chinese Customs: common tariffs and most-favored-nation (MFN) tariffs. The common tariff rate is applied to imports from countries with no bilateral trade agreements with China. The most-favored-nation tariff is applied to imports from countries with bilateral trade agreements with China.

Since 1980, Chinese Customs has lowered import tariffs several times in significant proportions. In 1991, tariffs were lowered for 265 taxation items. At the end of 1992, tariffs were reduced for more than 3,000 taxation items. From April 1, 1996, China substantially reduced import tariffs for 4,000 types of products by an average reduction of 30%. Import tariffs were then reduced from an average of 35.9% to 23%. Since then, in October 1, 1997, China reduced its tariffs again, lowering the average tariff rate to 17%. Tariffs were further lowered after China's WTO accession in 2001, and by 2005, average tariffs were reduced to 9.9%.

Import and export commodity inspection

The commodities inspection system is responsible for ensuring that the quality, quantity/weight, and packaging of imports and exports meet the statutory technical standards and quality requirements. The system safeguards China's national reputation in relation to foreign trade and protects the legal right of consumers and buyers. Two pieces of legislation laid the foundation of this system: the *Regulations on the Inspection of Import and Export Commodities* promulgated in February 1984 and the *Law on Import and Export Commodity Inspection* promulgated in February 1989 (hereafter referred to as *Commodity Inspection Law*). The legislation improves the system and strengthens the legal basis for inspection and supervision efforts.

According to the *Commodity Inspection Law*, the General Administration of Quality Supervision, Inspection and Quarantine (AQSIQ) is the implementation agency for commodities inspection. Each province, municipality and autonomous region has set up its own Entry-Exit Inspection and Quarantine Bureau (CIQ). The functions of AQSIQ are summarized as follows:

1. *Statutory inspections*: Inspections are mandated for important imports and exports. The importer or exporter is required to make a declaration in advance and to complete the inspection process. The import or export can only take place after clearance is given by the relevant CIQ.

2. *Supervision and administration*: Through administrative measures, CIQs

facilitate and organize relevant departments to perform inspections on import and export goods.

3. *Verification and certification*: As an independent third party, CIQs and the China Certification and Inspection Group (CCIG) perform verification and certification as requested by relevant parties in the import or export process. In addition, the Generalized System of Preferences (GSP) certificate of origin used in exports are also approved and issued by the CIQs.

Over the years, there have been continuous reforms to the commodity inspection system. The *Catalog of Entry-Exit Commodities Inspection and Quarantine* have been revised several times.

In 2002, wide-ranging amendments were made to the *Commodity Inspection Law of 1989*. The amended law placed greater emphasis on stronger execution of the inspection and supervision procedures, instead of laying only a legal framework. Whereas the commodity inspection system used to be understood as only protecting the interest of those parties directly involved in foreign trade, after the amended law of 2002 includes safeguarding the interest of the general public as one of its main objectives.

Moreover, the *Catalog of Entry-Exit Commodities Inspection and Quarantine* also has broadened and clarified objectives. Justifications for commodities to be included in the *Catalog* now include the following: to safeguard the health and safety of mankind; to protect the life and health of plants and animals; to protect the environment; to prevent fraud; and to defend national security. Previously, the catalog was based on the needs of foreign trade policy.

It is generally believed that the commodity inspection system enabled the smooth development of China's economic and trade relations in recent years. From 1992 to the first half of 2005, a total of 6,164 shipments of import and export commodities were inspected by the Bureau. They were valued at USD2.6 trillion and represented 37.5% of the import and export goods in the same period. Among these goods, there were 480,000 batches valued USD47.3 billion that were deemed not to have met the standards.[4]

The principles for foreign trade of China

The foreign trade of China is based on the principles of equality and mutual benefit. According to these principles, there should be mutual respect for the sovereignty and aspirations of trading partners, which are considered as equals regardless of the relative size or economic strength of the countries. The trading partners attain mutual benefit from trade relations through rational international division of labor, in accordance with the needs and possibilities of each country.

The principles of equality and mutual benefit manifest themselves in the foreign trade of China in the following ways:

1. *Respect of sovereignty*: The two parties in foreign trade enjoy equal status and rights. They should respect each other's sovereignty, and insist on the equality of their sovereign status. China opposes unfair conditions or unreasonable demands, where foreign countries use excuses or attach political conditions to achieve political or economic privileges.

2. *Voluntary basis*: Foreign trade transactions should be done on a voluntary basis, and, in accordance with the needs and possibilities of each country. There should not be coercion, where a country is forced by another to accept goods that are not needed, or forced to supply goods that it does not have the capacity to produce.

3. *Reasonable pricing*: Pricing of goods in foreign trade should be based on fair competition and should use global market prices as reference points.

4. *Importance of contracts*: Contracts should be regarded as an important part of credibility and integrity in foreign trade. Both parties should strictly execute the trade agreements and commercial contracts that are signed. Pledges and commitments should be kept. There should not be breach of contract.

5. *Equality in procedures*: There should be equal rights and responsibilities between the two parties in relation to commodities inspection, customs, transport, insurance, arbitration, and other procedures of foreign trade.

6. *Equality in conflict resolution*: Should conflict arise in foreign trade, negotiation and resolution should take place on the basis of equality.

Here we should note the inter-relationship between politics and economy, for two reasons. First, the foreign trade development of China should be evaluated not only on its contribution to economic growth but also on its political impact. The metrics of evaluation should include the following: whether foreign trade has strengthened the cultural and political ties between people in China and in other nations; or whether it has supported developing countries and oppressed peoples in achieving independence and building their economy; and how trade has benefited world peace and the advancement of mankind, or the opposition of hegemony.

Second, the relationship between diplomacy, which reflects political interests, and foreign trade, which represents economic interests, is worth noting. Economic diplomacy is now increasingly emphasized among many countries. Strong diplomatic relations between two countries can create a positive environment to support the smooth development of foreign trade, and vice versa. Meanwhile, if a country has not opened channels for foreign trade, then diplomatic relations would be hindered because there would be no benefit to the economic interests of any of the countries involved.

Foreign Trade in China Since the Economic Reforms

Foreign trade developed gradually since the PRC was established in 1949, and has been accelerated since the economic reforms from the late 1970s onwards. Foreign trade has been further expanded since China's accession to the WTO in 2001, making China now one of the most influential trading powers in the world.

The development of foreign trade

Changes in the global and domestic political and economic conditions brought dramatic fluctuations in China's trade in the decades since the establishment of the PRC.

Stage 1: Establishment and recovery of foreign trade (1950–1957)

Government agencies and state-owned enterprises were set up to administer and engage in foreign trade, in order to push for recovery in the domestic economy and to counter the trade embargo imposed by foreign imperial powers. The first priority was the import of essential daily goods and industrial raw materials, and the export of agricultural by-products and processed goods.

Trade partners included politically friendly countries and individuals, and entrepôts were used. In 1953, China reversed its trade deficit, which had lasted for 73 years. Foreign trade developed rapidly and the country entered a period of large-scale economic construction. By 1957, China had established trade relations with several dozens of countries and regions, and signed inter-governmental trade agreements with 24 countries. The first Chinese Export Commodities Fair (also known as the Canton Fair) was held in Guangzhou in 1957. Foreign trade grew rapidly between 1950 and 1957, with an average annual growth rate of 15.4%. The first few years of this recovery period saw a high growth rate in foreign trade at 30.8%, while the First Five-Year Plan (1953–1957) saw an average annual growth rate of 9.8% in foreign trade.[5]

Stage 2: Huge fluctuation in foreign trade (1958–1966)

Due to "leftist" ideology which was detached from the reality of the national economy, there was a mistaken policy direction of expanding import and export as much as possible. This resulted in huge fluctuations in foreign trade. Initially, trade volume rose to USD4.38 billion in 1959, a 41.2% rise from 1957.

Difficulties then hit and made it impossible for China to execute some of the trade agreements signed in 1959. Foreign trade decreased significantly from 1960 onwards. In 1962, trade volume had dropped to USD2.66 billion, which is the same as 1954 levels. After 1961, policy changes prompted a slight recovery. Between 1963 and 1966, foreign trade grew 14.7% per year, and by 1966, trade volume reached USD4.6 billion.

During this time, China mainly imported goods that were in short supply in the domestic market, including important raw materials, large high-tech equipment, food, and sugar. Main exports included agricultural products and industrial and mineral products. In 1965, China's industrial and mineral products accounted for over 40% of total exports. There were also over 100 countries that have established trade relations with China.

Stage 3: Decrease and stagnation in foreign trade (1967–1977)

During the Cultural Revolution, there was enormous damage to the national economy, resulting in the decrease and stagnation of foreign trade. Trade volume decreased from USD4.62 billion to USD4.16 billion in just one year from 1966 to 1967. By 1969, it dropped to USD4.03 billion, which was a 12.7% decrease from 1966. Improvement came after 1972, as trade volume rose to USD10.97 billion in 1973 and USD14.8 billion by 1977, which was more than twice the trade volume in 1966 according to the Ministry of Commerce statistics

Stage 4: Rapid growth in foreign trade (1978–2001)

After October 1976, when 10 years of national chaos ended, China entered a new historic era. Foreign trade underwent substantial development after the 11th Plenary Session of the Central Committee of the Chinese Communist Party (CCP) in 1978, which set the national agenda for economic reconstruction and provided a basis for stable national economic growth. In 1978, China's trade volume was USD20.64 billion. By 2001, it had increased to USD509.77 billion—a 23 times increase in 23 years, according to the Ministry of Commerce statistics.

Stage 5: Foreign trade adjustment and development (2001–present)

Since the WTO accession in December 2001, China has comprehensively adjusted or revised trade-related policy and regulations so that they are better integrated with the global trade system so as to create strong momentum for rapid growth of foreign trade.

Customs statistics show that China's foreign trade experienced over 20% compound annual growth for six consecutive years since accession to the WTO.

In 2007, trade volume exceeded USD2 trillion for the first time and reached USD2.17 trillion, which is a fourfold increase since 2001. At the same time, China's trade surplus increased at a much faster rate than its trade volume. Trade surplus increased over 11 times between 2001 and 2007, and reached a historic high of USD262.2 billion in 2007, making China the country with the highest trade surplus in the world.[6]

However, rapid development of trade also brought problems. The trade structure is over-dependent on low value-added, export-oriented growth. Low value-added manufacturing has resulted in environmental pollution and resource wastage. The issue of trade imbalance has led to conflicts between China and other countries. In the face of changing political and economic conditions internationally and domestically, China would need to continue to reform its trade policies and to find a path that leads to sustainable growth of foreign trade under a multilateral global trade system.

Special features of foreign trade development since the economic reforms

The importance of foreign trade to China became apparent after 1978, so there was a welcoming attitude towards opening China to trade relationships since then. The key attributes of trade in this period are as follows:

Trade developed rapidly and expanded in scale

From USD20.64 billion in 1978, trade volume grew fourfold to USD102.78 billion in 1988. From 1978 to 1998, there was a 14 fold increase, when trade volume leaped to USD323.93 billion. By 2007, it grew to USD2.17 trillion. If we compare the trade volume in the 30 years between 1978 and 2007, it grew more than 100 times, with an average annual growth rate of 16.8% according to Ministry of Commerce statistics

China's rapid foreign trade development since 1978 outstripped the growth of domestic production and outshone global growth in trade. The status of China among the world''s leading trading nations rose through these years. In 1978, China ranked 32nd in the world by international trade volume. It jumped to 11th in 1998 and ranked 3rd in 2004. China's export volume as a percentage of world exports also increased from 0.75% in 1978 to 3.3% in 1997, and 8.8% in 2007. China's exports reached USD1.22 trillion in 2007, and ranked just behind Germany, the world's largest export nation, whose export volume stood at USD1.33 trillion and accounted for 9.5% of world exports.[7] China has undoubtedly risen in its status and enjoys increasing influence in global trade.

The structure of import and export commodities improved

Prior to the economic reforms, China's export goods were predominantly primary products, with very low representation of industrial products, according to categorization by Standard International Trade Classification (SITC) of the United Nations. In 1952, primary goods represented 83.4% of total exports, while industrial products represented only 16.6%. Since the economic reforms, China's economic and technical levels were higher and the industrial sector structure was adjusted. Industrial goods as a proportion of total exports continued to rise. The economic reforms enabled China to become an exporter of predominantly industrial goods, as by 1981, industrial goods accounted for half of China's total exports, at 53.3%, with primary goods decreasing to 46.7%. In 1997, industrial goods represented 86.9% of exports, valued at USD158.77 billion, while primary goods represented 13.1%, valued at USD23.93 billion.[8]

China has rapidly integrated with the global production and sales chain, which allows it to further increase the production and export of industrial products requiring higher technological skills. Currently, industrial goods represent 94% of total exports, with machinery and electronics products comprising 56%. Advanced technology products rose from 17.5% of exports five years ago to 28% today. Meanwhile, industrial products that are energy-intensive, polluting, and resource-intensive continue to decrease as a proportion of exports.[9]

Imports were dominated by industrial raw materials for a long time. Before 1960, industrial raw materials accounted for 91.9% of imports. After 1961, China started to import large quantities of basic consumer commodities such as food and sugar. After the economic reforms, according to the United Nations'' SITC, industrial goods became the main import into China. Chinese economic growth meant a rising demand for raw materials, machinery, and equipment. Industrial final products as imports had the fastest growth rate. The proportion of industrial final products was at 65.2% in 1980, and was raised to 72.8% in 1983. From 1984 onwards, it was maintained at over 80%.[10]

There may be small differences in the data contained in the tables, because the statistics in this book have been drawn from various sources. There will be no further explanation in the later data tables in this book (see Table 2.1) in relation to the slight decrease in recent years.

The number of China's trading partners increased, and China is trading with wider regions of the world

For a long time, China's main trading partners were the Soviet Union and Eastern European countries due to being constrained by an embargo and other

Table 2.1. China's import and export goods structure

Category	2005			2006			2007		
	Volume (USD100 billion)	Percentage of total (%)	Growth rate (%)	Volume (USD100 billion)	Percentage of total (%)	Growth rate (%)	Volume (USD100 billion)	Percentage of total (%)	Growth rate (%)
Primary goods									
Export	490.4	6.4	20.9	529.3	5.5	7.9	490.4	5.1	16.3
Import	1,477.1	22.4	26.0	1,871.4	23.6	26.7	1,477.1	25.4	29.8
Industrial goods									
Export	7,129.6	93.6	29.0	9,161.5	94.5	28.5	7,129.6	94.9	26.2
Import	5,124.1	77.6	15.4	6,044.7	76.4	18.0	5,124.1	74.6	18.0

Source: "Customs statistics," in Han Xiushen 韓秀申, "2007 nian Zhongguo duiwai maoyi zongshu" 2007年中國對外貿易綜述 (Summary of China 2007), July 15, 2008, http://www.caitec.org.cn/c/cn/news/200807/15/news_1172.html.

restrictions imposed by foreign powers in the 1950s. Since then, more countries and regions around the world have traded with China as the global political situation changed and China became an important international power.

In 1950, China had trade relations with only 46 countries or regions, but that number increased to 174 by 1980. After the opening of the Chinese economy in 1978, China started implementing a strategy of diversification of markets and began establishing new trade relations with many countries. In recent years, China's strategy of diversification of markets achieved further success. There are currently 227 countries and regions that have trading relations with China, with the main trading partners being the European Union, the United States, Japan, and Hong Kong.

Recent years have brought more changes in China's export markets. China set up a free trade zone with APEC since 2005, resulting in strong growth in exports to APEC countries. In 2007, Chinese export volume to APEC countries increased 32.1%. These exports to APEC now represent 7.7% of total Chinese exports. Emerging markets, such as Russia and India, are increasingly important as China's export markets. Russia has surpassed Taiwan and has become the seventh largest market for Chinese exports. India has replaced Australia to become one of the top 10 markets for Chinese exports. In 2007, Taiwan and Canada rose to the top eight of markets for Chinese exports (see Table 2.2).

Table 2.2. China's main export markets

Category	2005			2006			2007		
	Volume (USD100 billion)	Percentage of total (%)	Growth rate (%)	Volume (USD100 billion)	Percentage of total (%)	Growth rate (%)	Volume (USD100 billion)	Percentage of total (%)	Growth rate (%)
APEC	553.7	7.3	29.1	713.1	7.4	28.8	941.8	7.7	32.1
Australia	110.6	1.5	25.2	—	—	—	—	—	—
Canada	116.5	1.5	42.8	155.2	1.6	33.1	194	1.6	25.0
European Union	1,437.0	18.9	34.1	1,819.8	18.8	26.6	2,451.9	20.1	34.7
Hong Kong SAR	1,244.0	16.3	23.4	1,553.9	16.0	24.8	1,844.3	15.1	18.8
India	—	—	—	145.8	1.5	63.2	240.2	2.0	64.7
Japan	839.9	11.0	14.3	916.4	9.5	9.1	1,020.7	8.4	11.4
Korea	351.1	4.6	26.2	445.3	4.6	26.8	561.4	4.6	26.1
Russia	115.5	1.5	45.2	158.3	1.6	19.8	284.9	2.3	79.9
Taiwan region	165.5	2.2	22.2	207.4	2.1	25.3	234.6	1.9	13.1
United States	1,629	21.4	30.4	2,034.7	21.0	24.9	2,327.0	19.1	14.4
Total	7,620	100.0	28.4	9,690.7	100.0	27.2	12,180.1	100.0	25.6

Source: "Customs statistics," in Han Xiushen 韓秀申, "2007 nian Zhongguo duiwai maoyi zongshu" 2007年中國對外貿易綜述 (Summary of China 2007), July 15, 2008, http://www.caitec.org.cn/c/cn/news/200807/15/news_1172.html.

Some Problems in the Development of Foreign Trade

China would need to proactively resolve some problems that have arisen from the rapid development of foreign trade.

Low value-added goods form a high proportion of exports

Currently, a significant percentage of China's exports are still resource-intensive primary products and low value-added, low technology content, industrial products. There are concerns of over-reliance on natural resources and the poor efficiency of utilization. Severe wastage, environmental pollution, and unsustainable growth have also been identified as urgent problems. To a certain extent, the more China exports, the more serious the wastage of resources and environmental pollution.

Moreover, the most internationally competitive goods among Chinese exports are still mainly traditional, labor-intensive products. These include textiles, apparel, shoes, and hats, toys, and daily consumer goods. These goods have short product cycles and low value-added. Currently, among the 10 largest categories of Chinese exports, nine of them are labor-intensive manufactured goods.

Despite some success in increasing exports of Chinese electronic products, these exports tend to target a low market segment, have limited technology content, and low added value. This is because the production of these electronic products has traditionally relied upon export processing trade and foreign-invested enterprises. There is a lack of Chinese developed market-leading products. High technology products, especially those where China possesses the core technology and domestically developed intellectual property, account for only 15% of exports. This is a very low proportion compared to 40% of exports among the world's top 10 export nations. In addition, most of these high-tech products exported from China are produced by foreign-invested enterprises.

For a long time, China's service exports have concentrated on traditional services. China is much less competitive in modern services and has low

Table 2.3. Top 10 nations in the world in service exports, 2007

Country	Export			Import		
	Volume (USD100 billion)	Percentage of total (%)	Growth rate (%)	Volume (USD100 billion)	Percentage of total (%)	Growth rate (%)
China	127	3.9	—	129	4.2	—
France	130	4.0	11.0	120	3.9	12.0
Germany	197	6.1	18.0	245	8.0	15.0
Ireland	87	2.7	27.0	93	3.0	18.0
Italy	109	3.3	12.0	117	3.8	19.0
Japan	136	4.2	11.0	157	5.1	9.0
Netherlands	91	2.8	13.0	89	2.9	13.0
Spain	127	3.9	21.0	97	3.2	24.0
United Kingdom	263	8.1	17.0	193	6.3	13.0
United States	454	13.9	14.0	336	11.0	9.0
World	3,260	100.0	18.0	3,060	100.0	16.0

Source: WTO Secretariat, http://www.wto.org/english/news_e/pres08_e/pr520_e.htm.

capability in exporting them. These modern services include banking, insurance, telecommunications, law, accounting, and information services. As a result, China's service trade ranking is lower than its global ranking for the trade of commodities (see Table 2.3).

Over-concentration of trading partners and imbalanced development

China has tried to diversify its import and export markets since the early days of the economic reforms, but its trade today is still concentrated with certain nations and regions. Trading partners are still mainly in Europe, Asia, and the Americas, and are limited to a few particular partners, such as the top three: the European Union, the United States, and Japan. These three account for half of China's trade, while China's trade with Russia is relatively lagging behind.

For example, China-U.S. trade reached USD262.68 billion and accounted for 14.6% of China's global trade in 2006, which was almost eight times the China-Russia trade. China's trade with Japan was USD207.36 billion, which was 11.8% of China's global trade. Even China's trade with the Netherlands reached USD34.51 billion, at 2%. In comparison, Russia accounted for only 1.9% of China's global trade. Export to Russia accounted for 1.6% of China's global exports, and imports from Russia accounted for 2.2% of China's global imports.[11] The over-concentration of trade on certain countries or regions can create frequent trade frictions, and may cast China in a passive role where it becomes over-dependent on some countries.

3

Chapter

Foreign Investment and the "Go Global" Strategy

Foreign direct investment (FDI) is generally considered to have accelerated China's economic development. Over the course of more than 30 years, FDI has created jobs, made up for scarce domestic capital, supported the marketization and globalization of China, and aided in technological innovation and industrial upgrading. An International Monetary Fund (IMF) study indicates that foreign investment contributed 3% of the 10.1% annual GDP growth rate of China in the 1990s.

Apart from attracting inbound FDI, the Chinese government has taken an important initiative of encouraging outbound investment, in order to help domestic firms adapt to the globalized economy and foreign competition. This is part of China's "Go Global" strategy. Today, there are an increasing number of Chinese firms that have sought opportunities beyond China's borders.

Global Trends in Foreign Direct Investment

In recent years there are a few global trends in foreign direct investment (FDI):

Advanced countries are still the main source of FDI, but developing countries are catching up

According to statistics from the United Nations Conference on Trade and Development (UNCTAD), global FDI recovered to rapid growth after the recession between 2001 and 2003 (see Table 3.1). FDI grew 31.6% in 2004, 27.4% in 2005, 38.1% in 2006, and 12.9% in 2007. In 2006, global FDI exceeded USD1 trillion, reaching USD1.31 trillion, an increase of 131.5% since 2003.

Developed countries are the driving force in foreign investment, both as the investor and the recipient. Developed countries receive two-thirds of global FDI,

Table 3.1. Global FDI flow

Year	2002	2003	2004	2005	2006	2007
FDI Activity						
Global FDI Volume (USD100 million)	6,220.0	5,640.8	7,421.4	9,458.0	13,058.5	14,747.0
Growth rate (%)	–27.1	–9.3	31.6	27.4	38.1	12.9

Note: Projected data is shown for 2007.

Source: World Investment Report 2006 and 2007, United Nations Committee on Trade and Development (UNCTAD).

while developing countries receive only one-third. In 2006, a total of USD857 billion in FDI flowed into developed countries, representing a 45% year-on-year growth, which was faster growth than in the previous two years.

But developing countries are increasingly important, judging from the declining proportion of inbound and outbound foreign investment accounted for by advanced countries since 2006. In 2006, FDI inflow to developing countries increased 21% to USD379 billion, marking a historic high. FDI flowing into Eastern Europe, Southern Europe, and Russia rose 68%, reaching USD69 billion. Asia receives roughly 70% of all foreign investment to developing countries. In terms of FDI originating from the developing world, sovereign wealth funds from developing countries have expanded foreign investment activities and become a recognized force in global direct investment.

The rise of transnational mergers and acquisitions

In the 1990s, transnational mergers and acquisitions (M&As) became the dominant mode of foreign direct investment carried out by multinational companies. Transnational M&As are seen as an efficient, time-saving path to market entry.

Gaining ownership and control of a company in the host country is seen as a rapid, time-saving path to market entry. Synergies in competitive advantage, convergence, and brand enable multinational companies to lower costs in their global expansion. M&As can also eliminate competition for resources and market share.

The year 2000 saw a peak in multinational consolidation activities, with M&A transactions reaching USD1.14 trillion. Multinational M&As then experienced a sharp decrease to USD297 billion in 2003. A revival was seen from 2004 onwards, and by 2005 there was a total USD716 billion of M&A transactions, rising 88% on a yearly basis. According to the *World Investment Report 2007* by UNCTAD, M&As worth USD880.8 billion represented 67% of global FDI in 2006. Of this, developed countries initiated 85% of these transnational M&As.

According to Beijing-based Zero2IPO Research Centre, a consultant in the venture capital and private equity industry, a total of 84 transnational M&As took place in China in 2007. The 63 transactions that were publicly disclosed had a value of USD18.67 billion, which represented a 105.4% increase from USD9.09 billion in 2006.

M&As in this period were marked by several new trends. First, there was an increasingly large proportion of massive deals. Second, collective investment capital became an increasingly active participant, mostly in the form of private equity and other funds. There were increasingly diverse modes of M&As. These included the following: direct purchase of shares; private placement of convertible bonds; reverse merger of core assets; indirect acquisition through the parent company; indirect acquisition through the bond market; third party acquisition; buyout; and leveraged buyout.

Rapid increase of service outsourcing

Service outsourcing has become an important force in the globalized service industry. It is estimated that global businesses outsourced nearly 15% of daily operations in 2001, and this was increasing at a nearly 20% annual growth rate. According to statistics from International Data Group (IDG), an American technology, media and events company, the global software outsourcing market was worth USD100 billion in 2004. By some projections, the United States will outsource employment in the next 15 years' worth USD136 billion, or 3.3 million jobs, in the service industry to lower-cost countries.

The developed world drives the demand for service outsourcing. The United States represents two-thirds of this demand, while the European Union and Japan represents the remaining one-third. The developing world is the main supplier of service outsourcing, with India claiming 60% of market share. This is followed by China and Association of Southeast Asian Nations (ASEAN) countries. Meanwhile, Ireland and Eastern Europe receive much of the service outsourcing business originating from Europe, while Brazil serves Latin America as an outsourcing destination. In recent years, some advanced countries such as Canada and Australia have also competed to become outsourcing destinations.

In China, service outsourcing was a USD11.8 billion business in 2006, in which IT service outsourcing accounted for USD7.56 billion, while business process outsourcing accounted for USD4.27 billion. Offshoring represented 12.2% of the outsourcing market, while domestic outsourcing represented the remaining 87.8%.

India, China, and Russia possessed an advantage in human capital in the growing outsourcing market. This is especially true for India, which was ahead of China and Russia in offering software outsourcing and other technical services, and has since become a widely recognized world outsourcing hub. The service outsourcing market is expected to grow rapidly in the coming years, due to burgeoning international demand and favorable government policies.

Global companies have become the main investor

Multinational companies (MNCs) have now become the main foreign investor in China. An increasing number of MNCs are re-positioning themselves to shed their national identity. The national identities of MNCs are diluted as a result of their efforts to globalize and localize.

The national identity of a multinational company can be defined by several criteria:

1. *Roots of development*: The country where the MNC was first formed, nurtured, and strengthened, and the country where the company eventually crossed the borders to become a multinational.

2. *Headquarters*: National identity lies in the country where the MNC makes operational and financial decisions, and where the MNC keeps key activities such as research and development and production.

3. *Rights and interests*: The main owners and managers of the company come from a particular country, so that the country benefits the most from the MNC's success.

For example, IBM is an American company by all of the above criteria. Although, thus far, MNCs usually have national identities, they are increasingly positioning themselves to be simply global companies without a home nation.

Social responsibility of foreign investment under scrutiny

Corporate social responsibility is an increasing focus, particularly for multinationals from the developed world that have direct investments in the developing world. Environmental protection and consumer rights are often seen to be at odds with the profit maximization motive of multinational corporations.

When first opening the door to foreign investment, a developing country would offer super-national treatment to lure foreign investors. Corporate social responsibility is brushed aside as an issue. As the host country gains more experience with the market economy, and as consumers become more conscious of their rights, the corporate social responsibility of multinational corporations is increasingly scrutinized. Should they ignore corporate social responsibility, multinationals would be risking their revenues and reputation.

It is now common for multinationals to emphasize their corporate social responsibility of direct investments. Some have even issued social responsibility reports, together with their annual reports, in order to show that they are achieving social, environmental, and cultural objectives while also maximizing their profits.

Foreign Direct Investment and the Economic Development of China

Foreign direct investment in China

At the beginning of economic reform in China, foreign investment was limited. Between 1979 and 1982, China had only 965 foreign investment projects, with the foreign investment contracts and actual utilized foreign investment at only USD4.97 billion and USD1.79 billion, respectively (see Table 3.2). In 1992, the Southern Tour of Deng Xiaoping prompted a small peak in foreign investment. Since then, there were fluctuations in the generally growing trend of foreign investment.

FDI in China increased significantly after accession to the WTO. The number of foreign investment projects grew to 41,081 in 2003 and 41,473 in 2006, when the actual utilized foreign investment reached USD69.88 billion. In 2007, FDI increased to USD78.34 billion, an increase of 12.11% from 2006.

China's experience with foreign investment can be reviewed in five stages, based on the volume of foreign investment.

First stage: Early steps (1979–1986)

Between 1979 and 1980, policies to attract foreign investment were formulated in the special economic zones of Shenzhen, Zhuhai, Shantou, and Xiamen. These early attempts were marred by inadequate experience and incomplete legislation, which failed to alleviate the concerns of foreign investors. During this period, foreign investment was guided by the *Law of Chinese-Foreign Equity Joint Ventures of the People's Republic of China*.

The ineffectiveness of the early policies prompted the State Council to convene the first National Foreign Investment Work Conference in 1983, which resulted in improved legislation. Fourteen coastal cities including Shanghai, Guangzhou, and Dalian, were opened to foreign investment, which quickly flowed into the Chinese economy.

Between 1979 and 1986, there was a total of USD19.43 billion in foreign investment contracts and USD8.22 billion in actual utilization of foreign investment, representing an annual average of USD1.03 billion. Despite the improved flow of investment, it would be useful to note that the main source of foreign investment was from Hong Kong and Macau. The main regions in China receiving foreign investment were Guangdong and Fujian Provinces, and some coastal cities. Industries that received foreign investment were the labor-intensive processing industry, as well as hotels and related facilities.

Table 3.2. Foreign investment in China, 1979–2007

Year	Number of projects	Foreign investment contracts (USD100 billion)	Actual utilized foreign investment (USD100 billion)
1979–1982	965	49.74	17.88
1983	638	19.17	8.16
1984	2,166	28.75	14.19
1985	3 073	63.33	19.56
1986	1,498	33.30	22.44
1987	2,233	37.09	23.14
1988	5,945	52.97	31.94
1989	5,779	56.00	33.93
1990	7,273	65.96	34.87
1991	12,978	119.77	43.66
1992	48,858	694.40	192.00
1993	83,595	1,232.70	398.60
1994	47,648	937.60	432.10
1995	37,184	1,032.10	481.30
1996	24,646	815.10	421.40
1997	21,001	551.90	523.90
1998	19,846	549.40	479.20
1999	17,101	436.39	421.69
2000	22,532	641.88	420.90
2001	26,140	711.28	488.24
2002	34,171	847.51	550.11
2003	41,081	1,169.01	561.40
2004	43,664	1,565.88	640.72
2005	44,001	1,925.93	638.05
2006	41,473	—	698.76
2007	37,871	—	783.39

Note: The above foreign investment data refers to non-financial sectors.
Sources: *China Ministry of Commerce Yearbook* for data between 1979 and 2005. Data for 2006 and 2007 came from China Investment Guide website, http://www.fdi.gov.cn.

Second stage: Continued development (1987–1991)

The State Council issued the *Regulation For Encouraging Foreign Investment* to boost foreign investment, including expanding special economic zones and developing the Pudong District of Shanghai for foreign investment. There was a general improvement of the environment for foreign investors, which resulted in faster growth in FDI figures.

Between 1987 and 1991, there was a total of USD33.18 billion in foreign investment contracts and USD16.75 billion in actual utilized foreign investment. This represents an annual average investment of USD3.35 billion, which was a significant improvement from the annual average in the first half of the 1980s.

Taiwan was the new blood among foreign investors during this period. Geographical areas and industries that attracted foreign investment also expanded. Foreign investment that went into manufacturing and export-oriented enterprises, which laid the solid foundation for Chinese products to reach the global markets.

Third stage: Rapid development (1992–1995)

There was a new landscape in China's economic reforms in 1992 after Deng Xiaoping's Southern Tour. Cities along the coast, along major rivers, and other important cities and inland provincial capitals were opened during this time, resulting in a full acceleration in the opening of the economy and significant development in foreign investment utilization.

Between 1992 and 1995, there was a total of USD389.68 billion in foreign investment contracts and USD150.4 billion in actual utilization of foreign investment. This was an annual average of USD37.6 billion, a 36 times increase from the annual average of only USD1.03 billion in the early 1980s.

Also worth noting is the significant changes in the structure of foreign investment. There were an increasing number of Western multinationals entering China, and geographical areas receiving foreign investment were no longer limited to the coastal cities. Central and western China launched their efforts in attracting foreign investment. The industries for foreign investment also changed from labor-intensive industries to capital and technology intensive areas, such as large petrochemicals, electronics, services, and infrastructure projects.

Fourth stage: Adjustment (1996–2001)

Many problems were exposed from 1992 onwards as the volume of foreign investment increased. Foreign capital was still coming from only particular countries or regions. The distribution of foreign investment was unbalanced across different parts and sectors of China.

From 1992 onwards, the large volume of foreign investment that flowed into China's economic construction exposed many problems. The source of foreign capital was relatively concentrated on certain countries or regions. There was an imbalance of regions and industries receiving foreign investment. Some foreign investors were noncompliant with Chinese laws and regulations. The rise of foreign investment also created a difficult competitive environment for state-owned enterprises.

In view of these problems, China entered a period of policy adjustment from 1995, seeking to be selective in attracting higher-quality investment that has positive long-term economic and social impact. New policies attempted to align foreign investment with the Chinese government's objectives for developing certain industries or sectors.

Since 1995, in an effort to abolish or adjust some of the preferential treatment granted to foreign investors, the Chinese government issued regularly the *Catalog of Industries for Guiding Foreign Investment*. The catalog sought to regulate the sectoral direction of FDI inflow. Foreign-invested projects were categorized into encouraged, allowed, restricted, and forbidden. The Chinese government intended to speed up the restructuring of China's industrial sectors, and to improve overall productivity.

These new policies prompted a slowdown in foreign investment from 1995 onwards. The flow of foreign capital into China also slowed down because of the Asian Financial Crisis of 1997 and the strong growth in Europe and the United States, which required MNCs to invest in their home markets.

In December 1997, the State Council convened the Second National Foreign Investment Work Conference, where a new strategy was devised to expand and strengthen foreign investment policies. Some preferential measures for foreign investors that were abolished just a few years earlier were reinstated. As a result, the growth rate of foreign investment recovered in 1998 and 1999. In 1998, there was a total of USD54.94 billion in foreign investment contracts and USD47.92 billion in actual utilized foreign investment. In 1999, there was a total of USD43.64 billion in foreign investment contracts and USD42.17 billion in actual utilized foreign investment.

Fifth stage: Rapid, steady growth since 2002

There was a steady increase in FDI since China joined the WTO. Policies for market entry and national treatment of foreign investment were strengthened, and industrial and regional policies were improved.

In 2002 and 2003, China's actual utilized foreign investment reached USD55.01 billion and USD56.14 billion respectively. This figure reached USD64.07 billion in 2004, experienced a 0.4% drop to USD63.81 billion in 2005, then jumped to USD69.88 billion in 2006 and reached USD78.34 billion in 2007. Despite small fluctuations, there was a generally increasing trend in foreign investment in China.

Forms of foreign investment in China

Since the late 1970s, China has implemented policies that try to either encourage or regulate particular forms of foreign investment that are deemed suitable for the Chinese economy. These forms of foreign investment can be classified into three categories: external borrowing, foreign direct investment, and other foreign investment. See Table 3.3 for details.

Table 3.3. Forms of foreign investment in China (Actual utilized foreign investment) (USD100 million)

Form	2000	2001	2002	2003	2004	2005	2006	2007
External borrowing	1,457.30	1,848.00	1,863.30	2,087.60	2,474.90	2,810.40	3,229.90	3,736.20
Foreign government credit	246.10	237.00	244.20	254.20	322.10	271.90	276.70	300.60
International Monetary Fund credit	263.50	275.70	277.00	264.70	251.00	267.90	278.10	283.70
Buyer credit	132.30	130.50	124.00	112.50	118.90	92.80	89.80	75.10
Credit from foreign banks and other financial institutions	202.20	334.90	317.30	424.00	437.60	491.80	585.20	546.10
External bond issue	122.90	126.70	107.90	111.70	133.30	130.10	142.20	163.30
Others	490.30	743.20	792.90	920.50	1,212.00	1,555.90	1,857.90	2,367.40

(Con't)

Form	2000	2001	2002	2003	2004	2005	2006	2007
Foreign direct investment	407.70	468.78	527.43	535.05	606.30	603.25	658.21	747.68
Sino-foreign joint venture	145.80	157.39	149.92	153.92	163.86	146.14	148.30	155.96
Sino-foreign cooperative	65.01	62.12	50.58	38.36	31.12	18.31	19.88	14.16
Foreign wholly owned enterprise	191.30	238.73	317.25	333.84	402.22	429.61	485.6	572.64
Foreign investment shareholding	1.08	5.28	6.97	3.28	7.77	9.18	4.35	4.92
Joint development	4.36	5.11	2.72	0.33	1.09	0.00	0.00	0.00
Others	—	0.15	—	5.31	0.24	0.00	0.00	0.00
Other foreign investment	—	19.47	22.68	26.35	34.43	34.8	40.55	35.72
External issuing of stocks	—	—	—	2.75	6.95	1.60	13.55	4.02
International lease	0.34	1.04	1.31	1.29	0.38	1.08	0.36	1.80
Compensation trade	0.11	0.03	0.04	0.07	0.05	0.16	0.21	0.18
Processing and assembly trade	12.73	18.39	21.33	22.25	27.25	31.96	26.43	29.72
Total	1,865.00	2,336.30	2,413.40	2,649.00	3,115.60	3,448.45	3,928.70	4,519.60
Growth rate (%)	–3.86	25.30	3.30	9.76	17.60	10.60	13.90	15.00

Sources: External borrowing data came from State Administration of Foreign Exchange (SAFE). Data from after 2000 is in accordance to international statistics standards. Other data came from Ministry of Commerce's direct investment statistics.

External borrowing

According to SAFE regulations, there are 11 categories of external borrowing: foreign government credit; credit from the International Monetary Fund; credit from foreign banks and other financial institutions; buyer credit; borrowing from foreign exporters, enterprises, and individuals; external bond issue; trade credit; overseas private deposit; international leasing; debts that are repaid in cash in compensation trade; and others. The first five categories above are the main sources of external borrowing.

Table 3.3 shows an increase in external borrowing as the overall foreign investment increased. At the end of 2000, there was a total of USD145.73 billion USD in external borrowing. At the end of 2007, it increased to USD451.96 billion, which was more than double the amount in 2000.

Foreign direct investment (FDI)

FDI refers to foreign investors directly investing capital, assets, technology, and/or management to attain part or all the power to operate a company in the host country. There are five main forms of FDI in China: Sino-foreign joint ventures; Sino-foreign cooperatives; wholly owned foreign enterprises; foreign-invested shareholding corporations, and joint development.

FDI has been the main form of foreign investment in China. In 2000, FDI reached USD40.77 billion, which increased to USD52.74 billion in 2002. FDI increased steadily since the WTO accession, reaching USD74.77 billion in 2007, an impressive 42% increase from 2002.

Other foreign investment

International lease, compensation trade, and processing and assembly trade are other forms of foreign investment in China. Compensation trade refers to foreign investors providing technical equipment, and the Chinese party paying back through revenues generated by the equipment. These forms of investment represent a smaller proportion of foreign investment in China. In 2007, there was USD3.57 billion in other foreign investments (0.79% of total foreign investment).

China today has more than 30 years of experience with foreign investment. In the early days, foreign investments were driven mainly by external borrowing, especially by credit from foreign banks, governments, and international monetary authorities. FDI took over as the largest single source of foreign investment, and has remained important ever since.

The positive impact of foreign direct investment on the Chinese economy

Foreign direct investment is generally considered to have achieved significant success in China. As of the end of 2007, China has utilized a cumulative foreign investment of USD770 billion. In 2007 alone, foreign-invested enterprises had a trade volume of USD1.25 trillion, representing 57.7% of China's trade. Foreign-invested enterprises paid more than USD990 billion in taxes, accounting for 20% of national tax revenues. Of the Fortune 500 companies, 480 have invested in China, which contributed to China becoming an international manufacturing hub. Foreign investment has made an impact on the Chinese economy in several ways:

Foreign investment compensated for the scarcity of domestic capital

Foreign investment has played an important role in solving the problem of scarce domestic capital, and has helped spur on China's transition from an agricultural to an industrialized economy.

During the 8th Five-Year Plan (1991–1995), foreign investment accounted for 13.7% of all fixed asset investment in China and increased at an average annual rate of 70.9%. This is much higher than the average annual growth rate of 36.1% in domestic capital. In the coastal areas, foreign capital represented a higher proportion of fixed assets investment. In Guangdong and Fujian Provinces, 35% and 51.6% of fixed asset investment came from foreign capital.

In 1996, foreign-invested enterprises produced USD1.33 trillion in industrial output, a year-on-year increase of 24.28%. This is significantly higher than the growth in national industrial output, which was 14.07% in the same period of time. Foreign-invested enterprises also produced 13.3% of the national industrial output. The large volume of foreign direct investment was therefore an important engine for China's economic growth.

Foreign investment brought advanced skills and management experience into China

Table 3.4 shows that FDI has mainly supported secondary industries, followed by tertiary industries. Only a very small proportion of FDI went into primary industries.

From 2000 to 2006, tertiary industry has been receiving an increasing amount of foreign investment. This was most apparent in 2006, when tertiary industry accounted for 40% of foreign investment, helping China to move toward a more balanced industrial structure.

Table 3.4. Proportion of foreign investment in three sectors of the Chinese economy, 2000–2006

Actual foreign investment	2000	2001	2002	2003	2004	2005	2006
National actual foreign investment (100 million USD)	407.20	468.80	527.40	535.10	606.30	603.30	694.68
Primary industry (%)	1.66	1.92	1.95	1.87	1.84	1.19	0.86
Secondary industry (%)	72.63	74.23	74.83	73.22	74.98	74.08	61.19
Tertiary industry (%)	25.69	23.85	23.23	24.90	23.18	24.72	37.95

Source: Statistics on Foreign Direct Investment, Ministry of Commerce.

Foreign investment has catalyzed the growth of China's secondary sector, particularly in the processing industry in manufacturing. Foreign-invested enterprises account for one-third of the processing trade in China. This includes both light and heavy processing industries, which use other industrial products as raw materials. In comparison, foreign-invested enterprises account for only 10% of raw materials manufacturing in China. FDI has helped China develop its manufacturing capabilities that involve high levels of processing.

Technology intensive industries in China have also been supported by FDI. Foreign-invested industries generally possess superior equipment, better technology, and stronger management. Many industries in China have raised their technology level through competing against foreign-invested enterprises and cooperating with domestic enterprises. FDI can be credited for filling the blank slate in China's technology-intensive manufacturing industries, namely in the production of integrated circuits, remote transformers, color televisions, and automobiles. With the support of FDI, China departed from its original course of dependence on imports for technology-intensive goods. Foreign investment laid the early foundation for China to develop homegrown manufacturing and product development capabilities, and helped diversify the supply of goods in the domestic market.

FDI has also been credited for improving the quality of China's industries and helping to restructure the economy. After successfully attracting foreign investors, new enterprises sprung up and old enterprises were reformed in older industrial bases of Shanghai and Tianjin. Regions such as Guangdong and Fujian Provinces which used to have weaker industrial foundation managed to accumulate capital and skills, and significantly increased their production capabilities. FDI had, to a large extent, reversed the imbalance between heavy and light industries in China.

FDI also pushed forward the growth of tertiary industries in China. Since the 1990s, foreign investment has aided the growth of real estate and social services, which are accounting for an increased percentage of the tertiary sector in China. Foreign investment has also supported and helped improve the transportation, storage, and postal communication industries in China.

Foreign investment boosted foreign trade and improved China's current account

FDI is an important driving force in expanding foreign trade. Most foreign-invested enterprises produce export-oriented products and are closely linked to international markets. They also import technology, equipment, and intermediary products in China.

Data from the Ministry of Commerce in 2007 shows that FDI from multinational companies has risen in importance in Chinese foreign trade in the last three decades. Between 1986 and 1990, the trade volume, export and import of foreign-invested enterprises represented 9.48%, 6.41%, and 12.4% of China's national trade, respectively. In contrast, between 1991 and 2000, these percentages rose to 39.94%, 34.41%, and 46.06%. Between 2001 and 2006, these percentages became 55.71%, 55.1%, and 56.39%. Therefore, more than half of China's foreign trade can be attributed to foreign-invested enterprises. The large volume of exports increases foreign exchange reserves and improves the current account balance of China.

Foreign investment encouraged improvements in large and medium state-owned enterprises

The management practices and international operations of foreign multinational companies have influenced the marketization and globalization of Chinese industries. They have also set an example for China's corporate governance reforms. For example, over 90% of foreign-invested projects in Jiangsu Province are alliances with state-owned enterprises.

Foreign investors have brought new technology, industrial skills, and the use of new materials, mindsets, and methods of modern management. This prompted state-owned enterprises to incorporate these new resources and ideas into their operations, changing outdated management practices. In this process, corporate governance reforms and asset restructuring were accelerated, and a new generation of management and technical skills was groomed. There are several internationally competitive Sino-foreign joint ventures, including Shanghai Alcatel-Lucent, Shanghai Volkswagen, TCL and Tianjin Otis that involve state-owned enterprises working with foreign investors in this process of upgrading.

In summary, foreign investment has enhanced productivity and strengthened the Chinese economy over the last 30 years. It has increased the quality of life of Chinese people and benefited foreign trade. Foreign investment may be expected to further contribute to the Chinese economy, as the quantity and quality of foreign investment continue to improve.

The negative impact of foreign investment in the Chinese economy

Foreign investment has brought some challenges to the sustainable growth of the Chinese economy, and has unsettled the security in China's domestic industries. This is manifested in the following areas:

FDI increased the difficulty of China improving its industrial structure

In China's quest to balance its industrial structure, foreign investment can be seen both as part of the solution and as part of the problem. Because FDI has overwhelmingly focused on secondary industries, while paying relatively less attention to primary or tertiary industries, the imbalances of the whole industrial structure of China become even more intractable.

Data shows that the primary industries of China receive less than 2% of FDI, and tertiary industries less than a quarter. In contrast, secondary industry received about three-quarters of FDI. In 2005, agriculture, forestry, and fishery received an actual utilized foreign investment that represents only 1.19% of all foreign investment. This low percentage fails to mirror the importance of primary industries in the Chinese economy.

Among secondary industries, foreign investment has only minimal involvement in the industries that China urgently needs to develop. One example is mining extraction, which only attracted 0.58% of FDI in 2005. In the same year, FDI in the manufacturing industry was very high, at 70.37%. Within the tertiary sector, real estate has been the biggest area of investment and attracted about 9 to 10% of FDI in recent years. However, in areas of high technology content, such as scientific research and integrated technical services, there was very minimal foreign investment.

It is believed that these imbalances in foreign investment have worsened the imbalance in China's industrial structure, leading to duplication in the industrial structure, oversupply, and deflation.

Moreover, foreign investors are perceived to seek only market share and profits in the Chinese market, neglecting the social impact of their investments. Macro-economic controls in China may have been weakened by foreign investment, because multinational companies are backed by the governments of advanced countries. The political background of multinational companies adds a layer of complexity making it necessary for China to consider political consequences when it seeks to adjust its economic policies relating to foreign investment.

Foreign investors' unfair market share squeezing out domestic players

To a certain extent, FDI has brought positive and healthy competition to domestic enterprises. For instance, competition has brought about technical upgrade, innovation, more advanced management practices, and stronger brands in domestic enterprises. In theory, foreign investors would help domestic brands become stronger, by helping them upgrade their technology and marketing. In addition, Chinese enterprises should be able to learn from foreign investors about product development, branding, management, and marketing, through the processes of technology transfer, indirect technology spillover, or simply the foreign company acting as an exemplary. Indeed, a handful of Chinese brands including Changhong, Haier, Chunlan, Konkai and Lenovo have emerged in the sectors of electronics and home appliances, where fierce foreign competition exists.

When evaluating the criticism that foreign investment is squeezing out domestic enterprises, we should also be aware that many foreign-invested enterprises have Chinese shareholding. A market share of foreign-invested enterprises is not equal to a foreign-controlled market share, because there is significant Chinese shareholding in many of these foreign-invested enterprises. Moreover, foreign investors have made other contributions that are usually not quantified—they created new demand, and introduced new markets or market segments which did not use to exist in China, such as mobile phone market.

However, foreign investment is also seen to have the negative effect of squeezing out domestic competition: First, FDI ties up domestic capital and other production factors. This tends to create a monopoly in the domestic market and block the sustainable increase of domestic capital. A UNCTAD (1999) report[1] states that foreign investment can put negative pressure on the domestic market in two ways. First, foreign investment negatively affects local enterprises' products and services, and their process of learning and growth, thus squeezing out local enterprises and local investment. The second way is in the factor market, where foreign investment affects domestic enterprises' ability to obtain capital, labor, and other production factors, or increase the cost of obtaining these production factors.

Second, imbalances in the direction, source, and technology level of FDI directly translates into the negative effects. Foreign investment has mainly gone into the processing industry in China, which has low technology intensity. Small and medium enterprises from Hong Kong and Macau regions account for a large proportion of FDI. At the same time, foreign and domestic investment are structurally very similar, with some estimates indicating that 94% of the time they are investing in similar industries.[2]

Therefore, foreign and domestic investments are not complementary to each other, and instead often compete for the same market, with the result being that foreign investment squeezes out the domestic competitor. Foreign investors also have a tendency to enter into sectors that they know they can exert this negative competitive pressure on the domestic enterprises.

In addition, unfair competition between foreign and domestic enterprises has undermined the efficiency of various sectors. Sectors opened to FDI are usually more marketized or highly competitive. The preferential policies enjoyed by foreign enterprises have exacerbated the pressure FDI brings to domestic enterprises.[3]

This is especially true when there are foreign-invested enterprises with low production efficiency that have enjoyed super-national treatment in the domestic market. After they build their advantage, they were able to push out those domestic enterprises that operate at higher efficiency. Overall efficiency of that industry is therefore undermined.

Foreign-invested enterprises have occupied an absolute advantage in several pillar industries and emerging industries in China. They have 68% market share in the automotive sector, 70% of the elevator market, 65% of the color television market, and 62% of the machine tools market. In the cleaning agent market, Sino-foreign joint ventures account for 40% of national output.[4]

The sales of products from foreign-invested enterprises have risen significantly, representing an increasing proportion of national sales. Foreign-invested enterprise products account for 31.55% of national sales in 2005, compared to 19.11% in 1995.[5]

Lastly, foreign brands have often shown a dominating market share in the Chinese market, especially in industries where foreign-invested enterprises have a high market share. This is true in many industries including cleaning agents, cosmetics, beverages, beer, light sensitive materials, home appliances, and electronics.

In the cleaning agent market, Proctor and Gamble from the U.S., Unilever from the UK, Kao from Japan, and Hanko from Germany are the big four cleaning agent companies that have dominated the majority of the domestic market. In the beverage industry, seven of the eight largest domestic beverage companies in China have joint ventures with either Coca-Cola or Pepsico, and have simply become workshops for bottling the beverages of these foreign companies.

According to the Most Competitive Brands of China 2004 report, conducted by *V Marketing* magazine and market research firm Sinomonitor, of the 32 industries surveyed, many foreign brands ranked number one in the minds of Chinese consumers. These foreign brands were: Epson, Sony, Nokia, Rejoice, Olay, Master Kong, Kentucky Fried Chicken, Nike, Shell, and Uni-President. Master Kong and Olay were ranked number one in two categories. Foreign brands occupied second and third places in consumer consciousness in the industries of cosmetics, digital cameras, mobile phones, beverages, and shampoo.

In the same 2004 report, customer loyalty for foreign brands was found to be stronger than for domestic brands in the high-end consumer products market. The top three brands in mobile phones were Nokia, Motorola, and Samsung. In the digital camera industry, they were Sony, Olympus, and Canon. In cosmetic products, the top three were Mabelline, L'Oreal, and Avon. In daily skin care and bath products, Olay as a foreign brand overtook the domestic brands of Dabao and Liushen.

A threat to the host country government

The largest multinational enterprises have acquired super-national power through their enormous industrial systems, advanced technology, and ability to obtain financing. This super-national power makes them direct rivals to sovereign countries. The policies of a developing country pertaining to foreign investment often become bargaining chips between multinationals and sovereign powers in the game of international relations.

In decision-making on foreign investment policies, the government needs to balance efficiency, equity, and sovereignty. If there is an over-emphasis on efficiency of economic growth and the importance of FDI, this may result in a compromise in sovereignty and in equitable allocation of resources. On the other hand, if the sanctity of sovereignty is upheld at all costs, it would lead to many missed opportunities for development. As the government seeks an equilibrium or second-best option in balancing these factors, commercial opportunities are created for the multinational companies.

For example, it was widely anticipated that the Chinese government would merge the two tax systems for foreign-invested enterprises and domestic enterprises. *It is believed that foreign-invested enterprises enjoy many tax exemptions, which result in a lower overall tax rate than that paid by domestic enterprises.* It was widely expected that this issue will be resolved in the 2005 annual legislative sessions of the National People's Congress (NPC) and the China People's Political Consultative Conference (CPPCC). However, before these legislative sessions, 54 foreign multinational companies jointly lobbied the Chinese government, making it clear that they were sensitive to an increase in taxation.

Risk of over-dependence on foreign investment

The Chinese economy has become increasingly dependent on the burgeoning influence of foreign investment. Unfortunately, this reliance undermines stability in the Chinese economy, and exposes it to the volatile international environment.

China pays the high cost while foreign companies reap the benefits

Foreign-invested enterprises have enjoyed an impressive return on investment in China, which rose from 9.5% in 1995 to 10%–15% in 2000. According to some experts, this is the highest return on investment obtained by multinationals anywhere in the world. The article "China Takes Off" in the journal *Foreign Policy*[6] stated that the return on investment of American companies in China, with USD70 billion in foreign investment contracts, was much larger than that in any other developing country. On the other hand, China's benefit from FDI has been very limited if one takes into account the depletion of national resources, the environmental pollution, and the cost in labor protection. It is possible that the net benefit of FDI to China is, in fact, negative.

Certain industries have lower productivity

Although the shareholding percentage of the foreign investor has a positive correlation with the productivity of the joint venture, the benefits of the increased productivity are usually not kept within the joint venture, according to Aitken and Harrison (1999).[7] In fact, the domestic investor would have to bear the cost of overall decline in total factor productivity (TFP).

This is also supported by the research of Lu (2003),[8] which looked at China's role in providing low cost labor to the international value chain of foreign multinationals. The more multinationals drive labor-intensive activities in China, the more they are adhering to the principle of competitive advantage and achieving greater efficiency in allocating their resources globally. However, the TFP in China decreases as a result.

This has created a vicious cycle for China, as it stays at the low end of the global division of labor, and the more it tries to utilize FDI, the more it is trapped into providing low cost labor. According to this theory, China does not gain foreign technology by opening its markets. Instead it falls into a trap: China needed foreign investment because its economy was lagging behind, but foreign investment caused the economy to lag behind and thus China requires more foreign investment.[9]

Risk of imbalance in China's external economy

The inbound flow of FDI has brought huge surpluses in China's current account and led to the skyrocketing of foreign exchange reserves. There is now an oversupply of foreign exchange reserves, which has caused an imbalance in China's external economy which affects the stability of the Renminbi.

The Significance and Achievements of the "Go Global" Strategy

Proposal of "Go Global" and its significance

Given the unstable international economy and the continued restructuring of the domestic economy, it is an appropriate time to review the Go Global strategy. We will evaluate whether it is suited to China's economic development and how it can help resolve some of the problems faced by the Chinese economy.

Articulating the "Go Global" strategy

The Go Global strategy can be traced back to 1992, but the real launch and implementation was in the 10th Five-Year Plan (2001–2005). The Go Global strategy which encourages Chinese companies to enter the overseas market is seen by the Chinese government and the Communist Party as a political and economic policy that helps China integrate with the rest of the world.

The outline of the Go Global policy was first sketched in the 14th Chinese Communist Party (CCP) Congress in 1992. A report by General Secretary Jiang Zemin first suggested the proactive expansion of overseas investment and operation of Chinese enterprises as a strategy that should run parallel to the better utilization of foreign investment in China. In September 1997, a policy to encourage outbound investment in order to showcase the competitive advantage of China was confirmed at the 15th Central Committee of the CCP.

The policy was further articulated in 1998: China pledged to organize and support state-owned companies that possess capabilities and competitive advantage to enter overseas markets, mainly in Africa, Central Asia, the Middle East, Central Europe, and Latin America. They were to set up factories and build export-processing industries in these new markets, which in turn would expand Chinese exports and transfer China's mature industrial skills to these markets.

The Go Global policy was increasingly portrayed in China as a necessary strategy for the future of development. It was compared to the Go West policy which encouraged foreign and domestic capital to invest in western China.

By 2002, there was another renewed push for Chinese companies to go global. A report from the 16th CCP Congress pointed out that Go Global and attracting foreign investment should be combined strategies that allow China to utilize the opportunities offered by WTO accession and the globalized economy. The document also encourages international economic and technological cooperation in new fields and at higher levels.

The development and implications of "Go Global"

Go Global has been understood as a globalization strategy at the firm level and at the national level. It is complementary to China's policy of attracting inbound foreign investment.[10] Some academics categorize Go Global into exporting goods and exporting capital, with the latter category—in which firms are able to become foreign direct investors—a superior stage of development. This means that a firm would start with the first stage, in which it trades goods, services, technical skills, and contracted labor with a foreign market. Then it develops to the stage where it has the capability to export capital, mainly in the form of FDI, to build factories and operations overseas.

In addition, there are broad and narrow definitions of Go Global. The broad definition refers to all aspects from export of goods, services, and labor, to international capital raising, international travel, and Chinese companies' financial investments in foreign multinationals. Meanwhile, the narrow definition only focuses on the FDI of Chinese companies, and how they enter competition and cooperation in the international markets. This section is concerned with the narrow definition of Go Global.

Development and significance of "Go Global"

Stages of development in "Go Global"

It was after 20 years of economic reform and experience with receiving foreign investment that China believed the conditions were ripe for the country to pursue the Go Global strategy. Apart from encouraging outbound FDI, Chinese companies were also encouraged to contract with foreign markets for construction projects and labor services.

Before the official articulation of the Go Global policy, a small number of Chinese enterprises had already gone overseas to set up representative offices or companies, but most of them suffered losses due to unfamiliarity with the international market and inadequate management skills. There were, however, some lessons learned during this time, which formed the foundation for the later Go Global strategy.

The Go Global strategy can be understood in the following stages:

First stage: Prototype (1984–1992)

China started a preliminary structure for administration of outbound investments, with the 1984 and 1985 regulations, *Circular concerning approval authorities and administrative principles for setting up non-trade joint venture overseas and in the Hong Kong and Macau regions* and *Trial Regulations Regarding the Approval Procedures and Administration Methods of the Setting Up of Non Trade Enterprises Overseas*. These regulations set up standard approval procedures so that Chinese companies investing overseas would not need to be approved on a case-by-case basis.

Second stage: Strengthened regulations (1993–1998)

Further regulations were issued during this time that laid the legal and administrative foundation for Go Global. In 1993, Ministry of Foreign Trade and Economic Cooperation (MOFTEC) drafted the *Regulation for the Administration of Overseas Enterprises,* and appointed specialized departments for approving overseas investments. In 1997, MOFTEC issued the *Administrative Procedures for Overseas Trading Companies and Representative Offices.*

Third stage: Full implementation (1999–2001)

In February 1999, the State Council office issued the *Opinion on Encouraging Enterprises to Develop Processing and Assembly Business Overseas with*

Imported Materials, drafted by MOFTEC, National Commission for the Economy and Trade, and the Ministry of Finance. This document contained detailed measures and policies to support Chinese enterprises in the processing trade overseas. The importance for Chinese companies to gain international competitiveness was further emphasized by Jiang Zemin in the 3rd Plenary Session of the 9th National People's Congress (NPC) in March 2000. Various bodies under the State Council devised concrete supporting measures. A foreign trade fund was set up to support small and medium-sized enterprises going into international markets. An information platform was established for enterprises going overseas. Some overseas economic cooperation zones were also opened in key overseas markets.

Fourth stage: Taking "Go Global" to the next level (2002–present)

After China's accession to the WTO, foreign investors gained more open access to the Chinese market. In order to maintain the competitiveness of domestic enterprises, the Chinese government strengthened policies and mechanisms to support the overseas business activities of Chinese enterprises. As a WTO member, China gained further access to foreign markets for its domestic enterprises. The Chinese economy grew at more than 10% for a consecutive five years after WTO accession. We should attribute this success not to inbound foreign investment but also to China's Go Global strategy.

Significance of "Go Global" strategy

The Chinese economy is increasingly affected by the volatility in the world economy and by the challenges in its own economic restructuring. In the early years of economic reforms, inbound foreign investment helped China face some domestic challenges, whereas in the later years of reforms, Go Global was the necessary buffer against external volatility.

The significance of the Go Global strategy can be understood in the following ways:

Helping China take full advantage of globalization

A proactive policy for outbound investment ensures a better global allocation of resources and helps to promote sustainable development in the Chinese economy. Outbound foreign investment allows China to apply its natural and economic competitive advantages. It enables China to obtain natural resources that may be scarce in the domestic economy but available at cheap prices in foreign markets. It enables China to import advanced technology and management expertise.

"Go Global" signifies China's enhanced national power and firm capabilities

A national push for outbound investment was made possible only after the Chinese economy established its national power and Chinese firms cultivated their competitive advantage. The foundation was built through two decades of economic reforms and receiving inbound FDI.

While most countries in the world have policies to attract inbound foreign investment, few have proactive policies to encourage outbound foreign investment. China's Go Global strategy requires the government to use diplomatic and economic measures to create a favorable outbound investment environment for Chinese firms. It also requires domestic firms to compete internationally. One could argue that the Go Global strategy, when successfully implemented, serves to further enhance China's national power and strengthen the capabilities of Chinese firms.

Strengthening China's position in the international division of labor

The Go Global strategy can improve China's industrial structure, increase exports, open overseas markets, and deepen international economic cooperation. All these effects help build a stronger position for China in the international division of labor, by allowing China to tap into foreign resources based on its domestic development needs and, in turn, improve the country's competitive edge.

Safeguarding national security

The economic policies of each country are, to a certain extent, influenced by external factors. If a country's economy is dependent on only a few industries, this would attract the attention of multinational enterprises that might want to take advantage of the dependency. If the country's domestic policies are inadequate, these key industries might be acquired by foreign multinationals, which will threaten national security.

The Go Global policy enables those Chinese enterprises with international competitiveness to compete in the international arena. It is a strategy that considers the needs of the domestic economy and takes a long-term view of sustainable development and national security for China.

Achievements of the "Go Global" strategy

The Go Global strategy enabled Chinese companies to invest in opportunities in foreign markets, providing new fuel for China's economic growth. Outbound investment has grown from a negligible base to large scale, high profile investments today, and has kept a fast-growing trend in recent years. In 2007 alone, China's non-financial outbound investment reached USD18.7 billion, a 6.2% growth from 2006. As of the end of 2007, China's cumulative non-financial outbound investment reached USD93.7 billion. There were 12,000 overseas Chinese enterprises in 172 countries and regions approved by, or registered with, the Ministry of Commerce.

Rapid growth in outbound investment

China's outbound investment started to increase steadily in the 1990s, after 20 years of attracting inbound foreign investment. Following the official launch of the Go Global strategy in 1998, outbound investment grew much faster from 2000 onwards. Between 2000 and 2007, China's non-financial outbound investment enjoyed an average annual growth rate of nearly 50%.

As of the end of 2006, 5,000 Chinese entities had set up nearly 10,000 enterprises overseas, spread across 172 countries or regions, with a cumulative investment of USD90.63 billion. In the year 2006, there was USD21.16 billion in net investment, USD5.17 billion in additional share capital, representing 24.4%. There was USD6.65 billion in re-invested profits, representing 31.4%, and other investment at USD9.34 billion, and representing 44.2%.

In 2007, China made a total of USD18.72 billion in non-financial outbound investment, a 6.2% increase year on year (see Fig. 3.1). We would expect this rising trend to continue as Chinese enterprises become stronger.

Diversified structure of enterprises in outbound investment

The types of companies making outbound investments are changing in recent years. State-owned enterprises and limited liability companies (LLCs) may be seen as the leading investors, followed by stock corporations and private enterprises, while other types of enterprises take the smallest role.

Prior to 2005, state-owned enterprises (SOEs) were the largest participants in outbound investment. In 2005 and 2006, the proportion of outbound investment made by LLCs exceeded SOEs for the first time. In these two years, LLCs accounted for a respective 32% and 33% of the outbound FDI, while SOEs accounted for a respective 29% and 26%. See Table 3.5.

In the near future, LLCs and stock corporations will likely become the largest participant in outbound FDI.

Fig. 3.1. The volume of China's outbound investment, 1990–2007

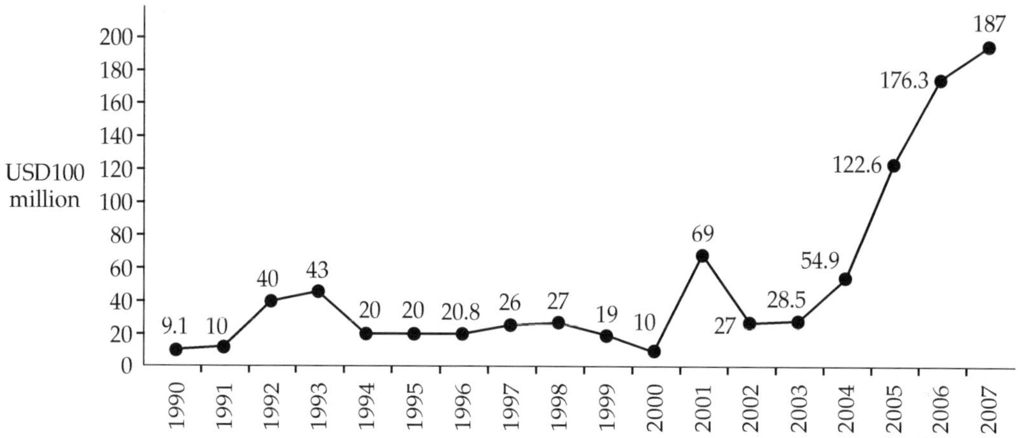

Sources: 1990–2001 data from UNCTAD World Investment Report; 2002–2007 data from Ministry of Commerce statistics.

Table 3.5. China FDI overseas main entities, by company registration categories (%)

Mode of company	2003	2004	2005	2006
Affiliated enterprise	1	1	1	1
Collective enterprise	2	1	2	2
Foreign-invested enterprises	5	5	4	4
Hong Kong, Macau, and Taiwan invested enterprises	2	2	2	2
Joint stock cooperative enterprise	4	3	4	9
Limited liability companies	22	30	32	33
Private enterprises	10	12	13	12
State-owned enterprise	43	35	29	26
Stock corporations	11	10	12	11
Total	100	100	100	100

Source: Ministry of Commerce China Outbound FDI statistics.

Outbound investment is spread across wide geographical regions

Ninety percent of the USD90.63 billion outbound investment from China went to Asia and Latin America, as of the end of 2006, according to statistics from the Ministry of Commerce. Hong Kong, Cayman Islands, and the British Virgin Islands received 81.5% of the investment..

In 2006 alone, China made USD17.63 billion in non-financial outbound investment, in which USD8.47 billion went to Latin America, representing 48%, mainly to Cayman Islands and the British Virgin Islands. Asia as a destination received USD7.67 billion of the investment, mainly going to Hong Kong, Singapore, and Saudi Arabia. Other regions such as Europe, Africa, North America, and Australasia play a much smaller role in the portfolio (see Table 3.6). But as China's outbound investment continues to expand, there will be continued changes in the overall geographical spread of the investments.

Table 3.6. China outbound FDI top 10 recipient countries (or regions)

Rank	1992	1993	1996	1998	1999	2003	2004	2005	2006
1	Canada	Australia	Australia	The U.S.	The U.S.	Hong Kong	Hong Kong	Cayman Islands	Cayman Islands
2	Australia	Canada	Canada	Canada	Canada	Cayman Islands	Cayman Islands	Hong Kong	Hong Kong
3	The U.S.	The U.S.	The U.S.	Australia	Australia	British Virgin Islands	British Virgin Islands	British Virgin Islands	British Virgin Islands
4	Hong Kong	Hong Kong	Hong Kong	Hong Kong	Hong Kong	Hong Kong	Sudan	Korea	Russia
5	Russia	Russia	Thailand	Peru	Mexico	Denmark	Australia	The U.S.	The U.S.
6	Thailand	Thailand	Russia	Russia	Russia	Thailand	The U.S.	Russia	Singapore
7	Singapore	New Zealand	Peru	Thailand	Thailand	The U.S.	Russia	Australia	Saudi Arabia
8	Macau	Singapore	New Zealand	Macau	South Africa	Macau	Indonesia	Germany	Algeria
9	Malaysia	Malaysia	South Africa	South Africa	Macau	Russia	Singapore	Sudan	Australia
10	Japan	Japan	Macau	New Zealand	Indonesia	Indonesia	Nigeria	Kazakhstan	Mongolia

Sources: *China Foreign Trade and Economy Yearbook*; Ministry of Commerce foreign direction investment statistics, http://www.mofcom.gov.cn.

Investing in diversified industries and sectors

As early as in the 1990s, China's outbound investment was already diversified across primary, secondary, and tertiary industries. With the accession to the WTO, China's outbound investment increased in volume and the types of firms engaged in outbound investment diversified. This has led to a further diversification of the industries that are attracting Chinese investment.

Table 3.7 shows that diversity. Commercial services, mining, finance, and wholesale and retail industries represent about 70% of the investment. In 2006, outbound direct investment in mining was USD8.54 billion, representing 40.4% of total investment. This mainly went into the mining of petroleum and natural gas, and the mining and processing of ferrous metals. Leasing and commercial services received USD4.52 billion, or 21.4% of the investment. The finance sector received USD3.53 billion, or 16.7% of the investment.

Table 3.7. China's outbound FDI by industry, 2004–2006 (USD10,000)

Industries	2004	2005	2006
Accommodation and catering	203	758	251
Agriculture, forestry, animal farming, and fishery	28,866	10,536	18,504
Construction	4,795	8,186	3,323
Culture, sports and entertainment	98	12	76
Education	—	—	228
Electricity, coal-fired gas, water production and supply	7,849	766	11,874
Finance	—	—	352,999
Hydro, environment, and public facilities management	120	13	825
Hygiene, social security, and social welfare	1	—	18
Information transmission, computer service and software	3,050	1,479	4,802
Leasing and commercial services	74,931	494,159	452,166
Manufacturing	75,555	228,040	90,661
Mining	180,021	167,522	853,951
Public administration and social organization	4	171	—
Real estate	851	11,563	38,376
Residents services and other services	8,814	6,279	11,151
Scientific research, technical service, and geo surveying	1,806	12,942	28,161
Transport, storage, and mail	82,866	57,679	137 639
Wholesale and retail	79,969	226,012	111,391
Total	549,799	1,226,117	2,116,396

Source: Ministry of Commerce China Outbound FDI statistics.

Meanwhile, manufacturing received only USD907 million, or 4.3% of the investment. This was mainly in the manufacturing of telecommunications equipment, computers and other electronics equipment, textiles, electronic machinery, transportation equipment, and general machinery, as well as in the processing of forestry products and the smelting and pressing of ferrous metals. However, manufacturing will become a main focus in outbound investment, because of the appreciating Renminbi, constraints in the domestic economy and adjustments in the industrial structure.

Challenges and Future Development of "Go Global"

Challenges for "Go Global"

It is inevitable that the implementation of Go Global has encountered obstacles. The main problems are summarized in the following sections.

Uncertainties in the external environment

There is currently a lack of emergency mechanisms for the government to support Chinese firms facing political and economic risks when investing in other countries. The firms' capability to tackle such crises is also inadequate. The Chinese government and Chinese firms often have to make policies and decisions without getting up to speed on the latest developments in the changing international environment. Even when new decisions are made in response to changes in the international market, there may always be unforeseen political or economic risks.

Government and administrative constraints

Macroeconomic control and coordination of outbound investment is complicated by the varied understanding and involvement of different levels of government. Currently, there is no unified department or government organization responsible for outbound investment. Various departments have the authority to manage some aspect of outbound investment, leading to uncoordinated actions, undermined efficiency, and weakened administrative power.

In addition, there is weak holistic planning of outbound investment and unclear guidance on industrial development. There is also no policy that synchronizes Chinese outbound investment with China's foreign trade policies. Moreover, there is a lack of transparency in some outbound investment policies, which runs counter to the intentions of WTO accession which emphasizes transparency of laws and regulations.

Last but not least, to this day China is missing a complete legislative structure for outbound investment. The legal status, property rights, taxation, and the protection of other rights for enterprises are not clearly defined. The lack of coordination in these foundational elements of the Go Global policy could become a constraining factor in outbound investment.

Problems at the firm level

In making investment decisions in an international market, the Chinese enterprises may make decisions based on inadequate understanding or due diligence in the overseas market. They might become over-optimistic in the investment project, which eventually leads to failure.

Other firm-level problems involve inadequate systems in management. China's outbound investors might not have adapted to the demands of international markets and competition. The parent company sometimes makes the mistake of over-managing or severely restraining the overseas subsidiary, or giving it too much freedom, or not paying enough attention. These behaviors are all unfavorable to the Go Global policy.

Inadequate supply of talents

The scarcity of high quality talents has become a bottleneck. Go Global can be considered a complex and systematic project that is demanding on the human capital of the domestic economy. The success of Chinese enterprises going global often depends to a large extent on procuring talents who possess skills, foreign language abilities, management experience, and an understanding of international commerce.

Chinese enterprises have been under the influence of traditional corporate structures, and have little experience in managing multinational business risk. They may lack the concept of quality, knowledge of legal systems, or the adaptability to the commercial demands, and the law of international commerce. In addition, compensation packages and training programs for the talents in Chinese enterprises are lagging behind the enterprises in the foreign markets. This results in a brain drain, which in turn creates more risk for Chinese enterprises venturing overseas.

Solutions and the future of "Go Global"

Despite its problems, the Go Global policy is widely considered a long-term strategy that will pay dividends to Chinese economic development. Below are a few possible solutions to the challenges mentioned above:

Reforms on government administration regarding outbound investment

The approval process for outbound investment needs to be streamlined. The functions of various government departments pertaining to outbound investment needs to be re-defined or clarified on a legal basis. Ideally, there should be a one-off approval with a single line of administration. The government should have a comprehensive plan for international business, a clear direction for industrial development, and a system that integrates legal protection, and international policy on outbound investment.

China should speed up its legislative effort on outbound investment, and synchronize outbound investment with international policies, in order to provide better protection for Chinese enterprises.

In addition, the government should set up or delegate a specialized organization to collect and provide information on investing in overseas markets. This information should not only include politics, economy, law, social customs, market, industries, and products of the overseas markets, but also highlight the foreign country's investment environment, investment criteria, procedures, policies, and legislation, the types of contracts permitted, as well as potential investment partners and projects. The government should be responsible for building bridges that link domestic enterprises with overseas markets.

Chinese enterprises should continue to raise their management capabilities and international competitiveness

While elevating the skill levels and encouraging innovation within their companies, managers of Chinese enterprises that are venturing overseas also need to update their business mentality, master modern management thinking, familiarize themselves with international regulations and customs, and improve their corporate structures. Chinese companies can improve their international competitiveness through expanding their capabilities and scale, protecting their intellectual property, and emphasizing the ways they are attracting high-quality talents. They can also innovate and apply new technologies, manage their own professionalization and diversification.

Cultivate versatile talents

China's Go Global strategy would be empty talk without the right talents. Go Global requires talents with versatile abilities. This includes talents with knowledge of the international finance sector; talents in business intelligence and information; those who know about international commerce and have technical skills; people who know international economic and trade laws and have expertise in negotiations under international rules; and those who are familiar with technology, foreign languages, management, international commerce, and with the politics, economy and culture of overseas markets.

Globalization has created a lot of opportunities for China and has allowed for an expansion of its outbound direct investment. After evaluating the pros and cons of China's outbound investment, the future of the Go Global strategy is clear. As government policies on outbound investment improve, Chinese enterprises will find a better environment for outbound investment. High tech industries will most likely attract more outbound investment. Industries where there is an oversupply in the domestic market will also see more outbound investment. Private enterprises will start to replace state-owned enterprises as the driving force among outbound investors. In terms of geographical areas receiving investments, developed countries will be the new focus. There is also a trend that the mode of outbound investment will evolve from the current joint venture and new-build into mergers and acquisitions. All signs point to China enjoying greater success through a full implementation of the Go Global strategy.

4

Chapter

International Contracting and Foreign Labor Service Cooperation

Foreign economic cooperation involves the international transfer of production factors, ranging from the tangible flow of capital and equipment, to the intangible transfer of patents, trademarks, and specialized technical skills and management. This chapter focuses on foreign economic cooperation in terms of international contracting and labor services.

International contracting can be defined as an economic exchange activity in which the contractor provides integrated technical skills in a foreign country, typically for engineering and construction projects. The process of international contracting starts with a request for bids, followed by the bidding and negotiation activities. When agreement is reached on price and other conditions, the contractor as the service provider then signs a contract with the project owner. The contract governs the capital, labor, management, equipment, and materials to be supplied by the contractor. Upon completion, the project owner would inspect to ensure compliance and that conditions for quality, quantity, and time have been met, and finally makes a payment to the contractor.[1]

International cooperation on labor services is a form of labor export in which authorized companies arrange and provide manpower to a foreign country in exchange for salaries paid by the project owner in the foreign country. This is the dominant form of labor export from China. Having received government approval to engage in labor export, labor service cooperation companies sign and execute an international labor service contract, select and dispatch workers abroad so that the workers can obtain salaries. This type of labor export is known as "cooperation" for its potentially positive effect on trade and diplomatic relations between countries. It reduces labor shortage in the host country using the competitive advantages in the labor of the exporting country.

The Current State of International Contracting in China

International contracting is a major component of China's foreign economic cooperation, and it plays an important role in accelerating GDP growth and economic development. The 30 years of economic reforms improved the competitiveness of Chinese industry, thus allowing China the capability to export its labor.

Main features of international contracting in China

Increasing scale of Chinese international contractors

China entered the international contracting market in 1979, when it signed USD33 million in contracts and set up four state-owned enterprises (SOEs) for this purpose. The SOEs were: China State Construction, China Road and Bridge Engineering Corporation, China Civil Engineering Construction, and China National Complete Plant Import and Export Corporation.

International contracting took off in 1989 and has since been a burgeoning industry. Contract value increased exponentially, from USD1.78 billion in 1989 to USD77.6 billion in 2007. Turnover also showed remarkable growth, from USD1.48 billion in 1989 to USD40.6 billion in 2007. As of the first quarter of 2008, the industry recorded a cumulative contract value of USD350.76 billion and a cumulative turnover of USD215.73 billion. See Table 4.1 for details.

Table 4.1. Statistics on international contracting and labor services cooperation of China, 1976–2007 (USD100 million)

Year	International Contracting		International Labor Service Cooperation	
	Contract value	Turnover	Contract value	Turnover
1976–1988	89	50	17	11
1989	18	15	4	2
1990	21	16	5	2
1991	25	20	11	4
1992	53	24	13	6
1993	52	37	16	9
1994	60	49	20	11
1995	75	51	20	13
1996	77	58	23	17
1997	85	60	26	22
1998	92	78	24	23
1999	102	85	26	26
2000	117	84	30	28
2001	130	89	33	32
2002	151	112	28	31
2003	177	138	31	33
2004	238	175	35	38
2005	296	218	42	48
2006	660	300	52	54
2007	776	406	67	68

Sources: *China Statistics Yearbook 2006*, National Bureau of Statistics, and data from Ministry of Commerce Department of Outward Investment and Economic Cooperation.

Diversifying markets for Chinese contractors

Asia and Africa are still the staple markets for China's international contracting industry, but Chinese contractors have also entered more than 180 other countries. Europe, North America, and Latin America can be considered new markets for Chinese contractors. The contractor China Harbor Engineering Company was a pioneer in entering the Latin American market, and has since led other contractors to follow. In 2006, Chinese contractors signed contracts worth USD5 billion with Europe, representing a year-on-year increase of 19.3%. However, the staple markets of Asia and Africa still account for 80% of revenues of Chinese international contractors. Asian markets include Indonesia, Hong Kong, the Philippines, Thailand, Malaysia, Singapore, and Pakistan, while those African countries possessing abundant natural resources are the ones with the largest market potential for the Chinese contractors.

Breaking into the markets of Europe, North America, and Australasia remains a challenge for Chinese contractors as they currently occupy only 1% of the market share in these regions. The world's largest construction market, the

Fig. 4.1. Market share of China international contracting and labor service cooperation, 2006

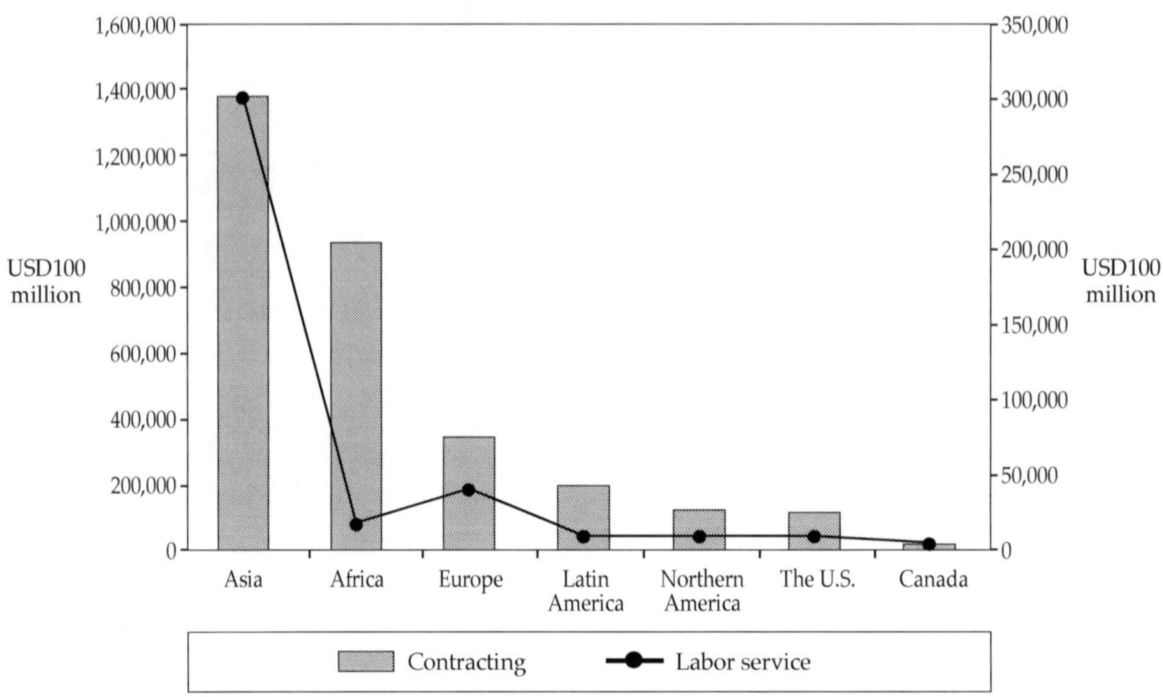

United States, is also the one where China faces the toughest competition. Since 2003, China State Construction led a consortium of Chinese contractors to win road and subway renovation projects in New York City. This sparked the hope that more Chinese contractors would be able to break into the U.S. market.

Chinese contractors become stronger industry players. Several Chinese contractors that were created by the government as specialized firms to undertake international contracts have now become global giants. China State Construction has been the industry leader for a long time. In 2007, Huawei Technologies overtook China State Construction for the first time by turnover. That year, Huawei recorded a turnover of USD4.88 billion and became China's largest international contractor. The top four Chinese international contractors each had a turnover of over USD1 billion.[2] In third and fourth place were Shanghai Zhenhua Heavy Industries and Sino Hydro Group.

An increasing number of Chinese contractors have entered the Top 225 International Contractors ranking by *Engineering News-Record* (ENR), a New York-based industry publication. The ranking is based on contracting revenues from projects outside the companies' home countries.

In the 2007 ranking, 49 Chinese contractors were ranked among the Top 225, including China Communications Group, China State Construction, and Sino Hydro Group. Mainland Chinese companies have 14 places in this ranking, which increased by 2 places from the previous year (see Table 4.2). The 49

Table 4.2. Top 10 Chinese contractors in the world's top 225 international contractors

Name of company	Rank in top 225 2006	Rank in top 225 2007
China Civil Engineering Construction Corporation	76	82
China Communications Construction Company	45	14
China National Chemical Engineering Co. Ltd.	94	88
China National Machinery Industry Corporation	50	55
China Petroleum Engineering and Construction Corporation	60	70
China Railway Construction Corporation Ltd.	73	83
China Railway Group Limited	67	67
China State Construction	20	18
Shanghai Construction Group	64	73
Sino Hydro	68	51

Source: Construction, Building & Engineering News, *Engineering News-Record,* August 2007.

Chinese contractors had a turnover of USD16.29 billion, representing a 62% increase compared to 2006. The turnover figures were at a historic high, as it was twice the total international revenue of *mainland Chinese contractors* from three years ago.[3]

These 49 Chinese contractors signed USD186.9 billion worth of international contracts in 2007, an increase of USD54.76 billion (29%) compared to 2006. The Chinese contractors had global operating revenue accounting for 8.6% of the Top 225 International Contractors, compared to 7% in 2006.

Contracted projects become massive in scale

Overseas contracts undertaken by Chinese contractors have increased in quantity and quality, indicating the industry's growing capabilities. The international contracting industry grew from having nine contracts worth USD100 million in 2000, to 138 contracts exceeding USD1 billion in 2007. The largest contract in 2000 was worth USD500 million. This figure jumped to USD8.3 billion by 2008.

In 2005, China Railway Construction won a USD1.27 billion contract to build a high speed railway in Turkey, creating a historic record for the largest single project. In 2006, Chinese enterprises won seven projects with contract values over USD1 billion. A joint bid by CITIC and China Railway Construction won a USD6.25 billion contract to build the Algerian highway.[4]

The turnkey project again broke the record as the largest international contract for China by contract value, and remains one of the highest-valued in the global contracting industry.[5]

Developing towards higher end contracting services

As a contractor, China started out focusing on relatively low-end construction and civil engineering projects, developing from providing the construction manpower to sub-contracting and finally to contracting.

In a move to upgrade the industry, the Chinese government allowed more than 100 engineering design institutes to enter the international market. In 2007, China's foreign design consulting services had a turnover of USD490 million, an increase of 48.5% year-on-year. New contracts worth USD1.03 billion were signed, a year-on-year increase of 151%. By the end of 2007, the Chinese design consulting industry had a cumulative overseas turnover of USD2.22 billion and total overseas contract value of USD3.78 billion.[6]

Entering the field of international engineering design consulting helped Chinese enterprises move upwards in the value chain of international contracting. More Chinese enterprises started to provide higher end and more upstream services such as project planning, exploration, design, and management. The mode of contracting and cooperation was also significantly changed, with Chinese firms moving towards the Engineering, Procurement, and Construction (EPC) contracting. Another new mode of cooperation has been for China to provide engineering services in exchange for resources.

In the foreseeable future, it would be the objective of the Chinese international contracting industry to move towards high-end projects and high-end markets. Chinese contractors will continue to experiment with different paths to attain greater success and capture the higher end segment of the growing global contracting market.

Problems with the development of international contracting in China

Despite its growing scale and international competitiveness, the Chinese international contracting industry would need to overcome some obstacles in order to maintain sustainable growth.

Most enterprises are small scale, limiting the size of the market

Extraordinarily large multinationals occupy the ranks of ENR's Top 225 International Contractors. For example, the French contractor Vinci Group France has 2,500 subsidiaries across the world, supporting 250,000 projects in more than 80 countries. Overseas operating revenues of the top 10 international contractors represent 50% of that of the world's top 225. Europe, the Americas, and Asia are their largest markets, accounting for 67.7% of the top 10 companies' operating revenues, at USD78.9 billion. A total of 168 contractors are focused almost exclusively on Europe and the Americas as their markets. It is projected that Europe and North America will remain the largest markets for international contracting, with the United States continuing its lead as the world's largest construction market.[7]

Although there are a handful of specialized contractors in China that have attained international success—they were typically part of the central government ministries, or set up by fast developing provincial or municipal governments—most Chinese contractors tend to be small. They have to cope with inadequate capital and difficulties in obtaining financing, and do not have the prowess to compete internationally. Of the more than 2,000 companies in China that have received government approval to engage in international contracting, most are small firms.

As project size increases in the international market, and as services required expand beyond construction to include design and project management, smaller firms may become unable to meet market demand. There are a limited number of contractors from China that can obtain projects worth over USD50 million. Chinese contractors have also been limited in their ability to develop new markets. They remain dependent on Africa and Asia as their markets and have difficulties breaking into Europe and North America.

Financing difficulties

Chinese contractors in general are weak in their ability to obtain financing, and this has become a bottleneck constraining their international competitiveness. Their sources of financing are limited. Chinese state-owned banks, in the absence of guiding government policies, consider the Chinese contractors as high risk debtors because of their low capital and high debt ratio. The banks would only provide large loans to contractors with substantial collateral or guarantees.

About two-thirds of the world's large-scale projects are built by the contractor's own capital. Possessing abundant capital and the ability to obtain financing becomes an important factor for winning the contract, as the mode of contract nowadays has moved towards providing full services ranging from design and procurement to project management and operation.

As a general rule of thumb, the cost of financing for large enterprises is usually around 10% and for small to medium enterprises about 20%–30%. Currently, Chinese banks offer a 3.8% interest rate in their loans to contractors in overseas projects. Although this is lower than the borrowing interest of 5.8% for other state-owned enterprises, it is much higher than the 1% interest that international contractors from other countries can obtain.[8]

Vicious competition and the lack of market order

Chinese contractors tend to launch cut-throat price wars instead of cooperating with each other. In order to gain market share, some Chinese contractors enter an unreasonably bidding price that does not cover their costs. This practice seriously damages the interest of the industry as a whole, and the interest of the Chinese economy.

Entering unreasonably low bidding prices raises concerns from competitors from other countries. It is seen as unfair and inappropriate, and it potentially leads to a low-quality outcome on the project. Moreover, the project owners themselves may be alarmed by the unreasonably low prices, and would rather ensure high quality than necessarily award the contract to the lowest bidder.

The low-price tactic ends up damaging opportunities for future cooperation. The vicious competition among Chinese contractors may also lead to action by the international multilateral trade community. Government regulations and policy guidance may be needed to establish market order in the international contracting industry in China.

Market entry barriers and technical barriers

China has a set of its own standards for design, equipment, materials, and a system of related laws. These have not been integrated with the global system. Meanwhile, Europe and North America have implemented professional licensing systems or standards for qualifying contractors, personnel registration, and qualification. Compliance is expected from contractors from other countries that participate in projects in these regions.

Advanced countries and their multinational companies have sought to influence the establishment of international standards, so that their patented methods become the international requirement, creating a technical barrier and maximizing the gains of advanced countries. New market entry barriers will be erected in the coming years as there is a continued effort to standardize the international service trade by imposing requirements on service delivery and quality. In addition, some countries have restricted contractors with a state-owned background in bidding for projects.

International risk factors

The growing market for international contracting has brought both opportunities and risks. First, market demand has outgrown the growth in management capacity, causing a shortage of experienced engineering management personnel and technical personnel. This poses the question of how to ensure quality in a rapidly growing market. Contractors now have to balance between seeking the growing market opportunities and tackling a shortage of qualified personnel.

Second, the price of construction materials such as concrete and steel has continued to rise, adding pressure on contractors.

Third, there is an increasing number of turnkey projects with contract value in the order of several times USD100 million. The risk in these projects has been mostly transferred onto the contractor, thus challenging the management capacity in the industry.

Lastly, there are personnel safety problems in some regions. Since 2006, there have been several personnel attack incidents in Afghanistan, Pakistan, Nigeria, and Iraq. These incidents created further difficulties for the contractor.

Development trends in the international contracting market

As the world economy becomes more diversified and globalized, each country's enterprises have sought to restructure, to expand international operations, and to innovate in order to seek greater opportunities in the world market. Enterprises that proactively participate in the international value chain and engage in international cooperation will be able to take advantage of these opportunities.

The landscape of the international contracting market

Positive market outlook

According to a research report by Davis Langdon & Seah International,[9] the global contracting market reached a size of USD4.6 trillion in 2006. The top three markets were the United States, Japan, and China, while Central and Eastern Europe, the Middle East, and Asia were classified as emerging markets.

The same trend of positive market outlook is shown in the statistics from ENR's 2007 ranking of the Top 225 International Contractors. In 2006, the top 225 contractors had a total turnover of USD224.43 billion. This represented an increase of 18.5% year on year, which was higher than the growth rate of 13% for the previous year.

In terms of the growth of contracting by sector, manufacturing and petrochemicals are the two sectors with the fastest growth for international contracting, whose contract value increased 54.7% and 34.6%, respectively, from 2005 to 2006. This is most likely due to global industrial growth and a widespread energy shortage. Other sectors such as electric power, telecommunications, and hydro have also experienced rapid growth.

Due to a round of recession in the housing market in the United States and Western Europe in 2006, that year's international contracting projects in the housing construction sector rose only 4.2%, which was much lower than the 18.5% average rate of the other sectors. Even so, the housing construction market still recorded a revenue of USD54.8 billion. Transportation sector and petrochemicals each recorded a revenue of USD58.93 billion and USD45.08 billion. These three sectors form 72.9% of all international contracting work globally (see Table 4.3).

European and American contractors in leading position

In 2006, European and American companies have dominated the international contracting market. The 105 European or American companies in the ENR

Table 4.3. Markets and sectors of the world's Top 225 International Contractors, 2006

Sector	Revenue (USD 1 million)	Market share (%)	Country or regional market	Revenue (USD 1 million)	Market share (%)
Electricity	14,441.2	0.4	Asia Pacific	40,185.2	17.9
Hazardous waste	606.3	0.3	Canada	7,990.7	3.6
Housing construction	54,843.9	26.5	Caribbean	2,247.1	1.0
Hydro	5,803.3	2.6	Europe	71,858.2	32.0
Industries	11,780.8	5.2	Latin America	13,622.8	6.1
Manufacturing	7,516.0	3.3	Middle East	41,380.8	
Petrochemicals	45,084.3	20.1	North Africa	75,158.0	3.3
Sewage/ Environmental Protection	2,849.1	1.3	Southern/ Central Africa	10,395.4	4.6
Telecommunications	2,900.2	1.3	United States	29,130.1	13.0
Transport	58,927.6	26.3	Others	101.6	0.1
Others	15,086.9	6.7			

Source: Construction, Building & Engineering News, *Engineering News-Record,* August 2007.

Top 225 rankings have been responsible for 74.8% of the projects. The United States has a market share of 17.1%, a slight decline compared to previous years. However, the United States remains a very strong competitor in the international contracting market. Its market share in Canada has even reached 76%.

Overall, the market share of European contractors had a slight decline, but it is still solidly strong, with a market share of 57.7%. There were 28 European contractors in the top 50 global ranking. In projects within Europe and in the United States, European contractors have a market share of 78.4% and 86.9%, respectively.

Compared to contractors from Europe and the United States, those from China, Japan, Korea, Turkey, and other countries are much weaker. In 2006's Top 225 rankings, these countries had a combined market share of 21.3%, which is only slightly higher than the market share of the United States.

However, if we look at the speed at which contractors from these countries are gaining market share, China, Korea, and Turkey are the emerging powers as international contractors. Their market share grew 61%, 167%, and 64%, respectively. In 2006, 49 Chinese companies were ranked within the world's top 225, with a turnover of USD16.3 billion for international contracts.[10]

Development trends of international contracting

Changes in the investment hotspots

There are an increasing number of high value-added, high technology content and integrated projects. In the area of technical contracting, information technology, new materials and new industrial crafts are commonly used. Due to the international energy shortage, the petrochemical industry is likely to be the fastest growing sector, with an annual growth rate of 34.6% in 2006.

As discussed previously, the three sectors of housing construction, transportation, and petrochemicals represent 72.9% of all international contracting work (see Table 4.3). Other sectors such as electric power, telecommunications, and hydro have also experienced rapid growth.

Diversification of the mode of international contracting

The types of investors in contracted projects changed in recent years. International financial institutions experienced slow growth, while the number of government projects decreased since the Asian Financial Crisis. The proportion of private capital investment increased.

The mode of contracting has also changed significantly. The traditional contracting has been replaced by a combination of integrated methods including EPC (Engineering, Procurement, Construction), international investment, project finance, international credit, equipment trade, technology transfer, BT (Build and Transfer), BOT (Build, Operate, Transfer), and BOOT (Build, Own, Operate, Transfer).

At the same time, the scale of single projects has increased in size. These trends all raise the demand for contractors to attain a better ability to obtain finance.

Frequent international alliances, mergers and acquisitions, and consolidation

The role of contractors has broadened from being simply the supplier of services to extending their involvement to include financing and operation of the project.

This applies especially to large and super-large projects, which place high demands on the capital, human resources, technical skills, and management of the contractor. The contractor needs to allocate and combine its resources and capabilities—something that the average contractor finds difficult. This has led many contractors to form alliances, and others to restructure internally, as the industry seeks to secure new sources of financial and technical support and to meet the new demands of the international market.

Recommended Solutions for the Sustainable Development of the Chinese International Contracting Industry

Developing the international contracting industry was listed as one of the sectoral objectives in the 11th Five-Year Plan (2006–2010). Improvements that could help the industry can be classified into two categories. First, there should be a restructuring of the industry itself and the service cluster supporting the industry. Second, there needs to be improved legislation, regulations, and policies to form a protection and risk management system to ensure healthy development of international contracting.

Further restructuring of international contracting

The Chinese international contractors have planned to move towards winning contracts with higher value-added, higher technology content, and higher profits. Despite the success of its largest contractors so far, China considers itself a latecomer to international contracting and believes that moving towards the higher end of the business is part of the catching-up process.

It is recommended that China support international contracting in those industries that can have a positive spillover effect on other parts of the Chinese economy. For example, the contractors' involvement in some industries is more likely to boost exports in Chinese-produced equipment and materials. These industries include petrochemicals, hydro and electric power, railway, chemical industries, mining and processing, and mine construction. Of course, these industries also increase Chinese exports of management, technical skills, and labor.

In order for China to catch up with other countries in the international contracting field, there needs to be better access to financing and import and export licenses for Chinese contractors. Also, China needs to further develop its design consulting services in order to establish the position of Chinese contractors in the world market.

Improving the service cluster for international contracting

Reforms in the foreign trade system, foreign exchange, and the financial system would need to be accelerated in order to improve the overall environment for Chinese international contracting and foreign labor service cooperation. For instance, an effective system for obtaining financing and guarantees, and an insurance system for personnel dispatched abroad in labor service cooperation, would be required to maximize opportunities and reduce risk.

International contracting is an important component of Chinese firms going global. Relevant government departments need to maintain a united front, and provide policy guidance, supervision, and support to the industry. The government's coordinated support and service provision to the international contractors can help them improve their competitiveness. The government should provide services to assist Chinese contractors, such as resolving problems with bureaucratic procedures for dispatching personnel or exporting equipment, or complying with insurance obligations and paying insurance premiums. The government should also be prepared to use diplomatic channels and multilateral trade negotiation platforms to seek opportunities for Chinese companies in international contracting.

Strengthen the capacity of international contractors

Many large Chinese contractors have recognized the importance of building their own capacity in order to allow them to obtain capital-intensive, management-intensive, and technology-intensive projects. They also aim to perform equally well in all processes in the project, from design to construction to obtaining investment.

In order to target the sectors of petrochemicals, telecommunications, and electric power, and in turn to increase the export of Chinese produced equipment and raw materials, Chinese contractors would need to raise their own capabilities in technology and be more responsive to market needs. They may need to develop their own patented techniques and raise the technology content in their projects. Moreover, Chinese contractors may consider improving their human resources development and management skills which are suited for multinational operations and focus on cultivating versatile skill sets within the company.

Another necessary initiative is to strengthen cooperation among Chinese contractors. Alliances among contractors can be strengthened so that company resources are allocated more effectively. Alliances may also include banks and trading companies, in order to resolve problems of inadequate capital and the high cost of financing and to smoothly handle repayment in kind and compensation trade.

Chinese contractors also need to have better awareness of risk management. Project decisions should be taken only after an evaluation of safety and risks. Mechanisms for improving safety, preventing risk, and managing crises need to be set up.

At the same time, Chinese contractors need to keep in mind the mutual benefit attained from cooperation and avoid vicious competition.

International contractors should observe the laws of other countries, protect the environment, respect local customs and show social responsibility. They need to adopt the mentality of building localized operations instead of a Chinese operation planted overseas. Instead of merely chasing economic gain, Chinese contractors should consider combining social interests with economic interests because it would help the whole industry to gain more commercial opportunities in the long term.

Using industry associations to ensure market order

The China International Contractors Association (CHINCA) should be encouraged to provide services, to reflect industry demands and concerns, and to regulate the contractors' behavior.

More research conducted by CHINCA may be necessary to help explore opportunities for Chinese international contractors and to help guide the industry's development towards providing higher end services and entering higher end markets.

CHINCA can also coordinate regulations within the industry in a way that respects the rules of the market and the status of contractors. An industry-wide credit system and other mechanisms to encourage self-discipline can be set up through the industry association.

Other services that CHINCA should provide may include improving the international contracting database and providing expert committees and consulting services for contractors.

Further improving the risk management system

International contractors can benefit from expanded channels to obtain financing, a new risk assessment system to evaluate overseas investments and a credit guarantee system for multinational operations. Insurance companies should be encouraged to provide tailored insurance services to Chinese international contractors, so that contractors are protected from financial loss, especially when they develop business in destabilized regions affected by war, political conditions, and nationalization. A contract can be signed between the insurer and the contractor, giving the insurer the right of subrogation. In other words, the insurer has the right to seek compensation from a third party on behalf of the Chinese contractor. The insurance company will compensate the Chinese contractor first should an insured risk occur, and then seek compensation from the foreign party. The Chinese government should also use bilateral investment protection agreements to protect the legal rights of Chinese enterprises overseas.

An international contracting risk management fund should be set up in China, following the example of Korea's foreign economic cooperation fund which has an interest rate of 1.5%. The fund can be operated by the industry association, and the funding will be taken from a certain percentage of the net income of enterprises. That part of the firms' revenues should be tax exempt. The central government will provide a corresponding amount of funding from the central coffers.

Foreign Labor Service Cooperation of China

Foreign labor service cooperation is a new industry that is a beneficiary of 30 years of economic reforms and an important component of the Go Global strategy.

Main policies

The Chinese government has issued policies and procedures for foreign labor service cooperation in order to ensure compliance and smooth operation of the industry. The Ministry of Commerce (MOFCOM) has the designated authority to carry out these policies and procedures:

The qualification and approval procedures

1. Companies can only commence their foreign labor service cooperation activities after they are registered in China, obtained qualification and approvals from MOFCOM, and possess the Certificate for the Operation Qualification of Foreign Labor Service Cooperation.

2. Foreign entities and their legal entities, persons or representative organizations cannot hire workers in Chinese borders for foreign labor service cooperation. This is according to Chinese government regulations.

3. MOFCOM manages the flow of foreign labor service cooperation and

imposes penalties for non-compliance. Enterprises committing mild offenses may receive warnings or penalties, or have their qualification to operate labor service cooperation suspended. Criminal offenses will be referred to the relevant legal departments.

Project approval

MOFCOM's departments at the provincial level will inspect the labor cooperation projects in their geographical areas. They inspect whether contracts signed between the labor cooperation enterprise, the foreign employer, and the Chinese workers are in accordance with Chinese law and the laws of the host country; and whether the workers are suitably trained.

Project verification

The Chinese embassy or consulate's commerce unit in the host country will verify the labor cooperation project. They will check whether the project actually exists, and whether the import of Chinese labor by the foreign employer has in fact been approved by the local authorities.

Clear payment standards

According to Chinese government regulations, foreign labor cooperation companies can charge a service fee from the Chinese workers. The service fee is capped at 12.5% of the salary specified in the contract signed between the worker and the foreign employer.

Also, the Chinese worker has to bear the cost of obtaining his or her passport, visa, medical check, training, and contract notary fee. More fees will be generated if the worker requires assistance from the labor cooperation company for these services. The fees may also be determined by the bilateral agreement between China and the host country, if one has been signed.

Training of dispatched labor

The foreign labor cooperation enterprise must arrange for workers to attend suitable training before they are sent overseas. The workers should be arranged to participate in exams at the overseas labor test center, in order to obtain the *Training Certificate for Laborers Working Abroad*. The training educates workers to follow the law of the foreign country, respect local customs, understand the basics of the foreign language, strictly adhere to the contract terms, and cooperate with the foreign employer.

Features and development trends in external labor cooperation

China's foreign labor cooperation industry has shown healthy development, especially since the 1990s when the number of workers sent overseas increased rapidly. Geographical regions and industries receiving Chinese workers have also diversified.

Increasing service volume

Table 4.1 shows the development of China's international labor cooperation since the economic reforms, indicating sustainable growth of foreign labor service cooperation over the last 30 years and rapid growth since the 1990s. As of June 2008, China's foreign labor service cooperation has a cumulative turnover of USD51.47 billion, cumulative contract value of USD56.04 billion, and a total of 4.38 million workers have been sent overseas.[11]

The majority of workers serve traditional industries

After 30 years of development, China's foreign labor cooperation efforts are mainly in the areas of manufacturing, construction, primary industries (including agriculture, forestry, animal rearing, and fisheries), transportation, and catering. Among these, construction, textiles, and fisheries workers represent over half of the dispatched workers (see Table 4.4). Meanwhile, there is a growing minority of workers in higher end services, including design consulting, IT services, science, education, culture, hygiene, and sports.

China has now become an important source of labor for construction, textiles, and seafaring. According to 2007 data, construction and manufacturing were the main sectors using Chinese workers, accounting for 67.3% of dispatched workers.[12]

Overseas low-wage jobs in traditional, low-end industries have become less attractive to Chinese workers in recent years as the Chinese economy has grown and offered ample job opportunities. However, there are now an increasing number of highly skilled workers being exported. In recent years, Shanghai and Jiangsu saw a rapid increase in demand for skilled workers in high end sectors. Thirty percent of workers sent from these areas are skilled professionals such as software engineers, senior chefs, and doctors.

Asia as the largest market, Africa and Latin America as emerging markets

China currently engages with more than 180 countries in labor service cooperation. Asia is the largest market and it remains a fast-growing one. China

Table 4.4. Ranking of key countries/Regions engaged in labor cooperation with China, as of the end of 2007

Rank	Construction		Manufacturing		Primary industries		Transportation	
	Country/ region	Number of workers	Country/ region	Number of workers	Country/ region	Number of workers	Country/ region	Number of workers
1	Singapore	39,378	Japan	110,142	Korea	22,118	Hong Kong	18,391
2	Algeria	32,023	Singapore	29,388	Japan	13,805	Singapore	8,076
3	United Arab Emirates	19,703	Korea	19,662	Russia	9,177	Taiwan	6,854
4	Russia	16,866	Macau	16,145	Taiwan	4,472	Japan	3,754
5	Macau	14,537	Vietnam	10,402	Singapore	3,405	Korea	2,524
6	Japan	9,780	Jordan	9,891	Argentina	2,855	United States	1,727
7	Saudi Arabia	8,460	Mauritius	6,377	Mexico	2,340	Thailand	1,332
8	Israel	8,378	Saudi Arabia	5,985	Burma	1,848	Germany	1,272
9	Burma	6,637	United States	3,496	Trinidad and Tobago	1,756	Panama	1,265
10	Qatar	5,959	Russia	2,884	Spain	1,697	Malaysia	929

Source: China International Contractors Association.

has maintained since 1995 a 70% market share in the Asia market for foreign labor. This was increased from 1990, when China sent 58,000 workers abroad, 46.9% or 27,000 of which were to Asia. In recent years, an increasing number of Chinese workers were sent to Japan, Korea, Singapore, and Hong Kong in foreign labor service cooperation arrangements.

Africa, Europe, and Latin America are new and growing markets for Chinese exported labor. China has signed bilateral cooperation agreements with Russia, Bahrain, Malaysia, Mauritius, Britain, and Jordan. Dispatched labor has also been sent to Germany, Austria, Norway, Sweden, the Netherlands, and Australia.

Foreign labor service cooperation enterprises have become stronger

There are an increasing number of companies in China involved in foreign labor service cooperation. The number of companies in this industry increased from 70 in the 1980s to over 1,600 in 2003.

A new administrative system for companies to qualify for operating foreign labor service cooperation was implemented from November 2006 onwards. Under the new system, 399 companies attained qualification for foreign labor service cooperation, while another 1,608 companies obtained approval to operate both international contracting and foreign labor service cooperation. As the number of industry players continues to increase, there is higher competitive pressure for the companies involved (see Table 4.5).

Table 4.5. The largest Chinese companies in foreign labor service cooperation by turnover, 2007

Rank	Company Name	Turnover (USD10,000)
1	China International Intellectech Corporation (CIIC)	189,906
2	Shanghai Foreign Services Co. Ltd. (SFSC)	32,035
3	Guangdong Xinguang International Group (GDIG)	27,809
4	Beijing Foreign Enterprise Service Group Co. Ltd (FESCO)	19,956
5	China Shandong International Economic and Technical Cooperation Group	10,618
6	Weihai International Economic and Technical Cooperative Co., Ltd	9,627
7	Shenzhen Foreign Enterprises Services Co., Ltd.	9,461
8	Jiangsu Suzhong Construction Group Co., Ltd.	9,350
9	China Guangzhou International Economic and Technical Cooperation Company	8,769
10	Yantai International Economic and Technical Cooperation Co., Ltd.	8,470

Source: China International Contractors Association website, http://www.chinca.org.

Global Development Trends in International Labor Cooperation

International labor cooperation can be seen as a type of service trade that is linked to the flow of the world's population, employment, and economic forces. This section covers some global trends in this important industry.[13]

Rising international demand for labor

There is an increasing demand for foreign labor, due to the growth in global investments and service industries. Currently, there is an annual flow of 30 to 35 million foreign workers globally, a 50% increase from 20 million workers in the 1980s.

Developed countries have seen an economic slowdown, and slower or even negative rates in population growth. Many face the problem of an aging population. As their working population shrinks, driving up the cost of labor, the demand for foreign labor increases. For example, in order to maintain the ratio of working population to retired population from 1995 in Germany, France, Britain, and Italy—the four largest countries in the European Union—there is a need to import 1.1 million foreign workers per year.

It is unrealistic to open the doors to immigration at such a large scale, which leaves importing foreign labor the only alternative. One may expect the wage gap between developing countries and advanced countries to continue in the foreseeable future, thus making job opportunities in advanced countries attractive to those in poorer countries.

Demand for technical skills increases while export of unskilled workers may be restricted

According to the International Labor Organization, jobs that are dirty, tiring, and dangerous are still the main types of work for migrant labor, many of them come from developing countries and possess only primary or secondary education. However, due to technological advances and global industry restructuring, a higher number of technically skilled and specialized personnel will be required for fields such as information industry, biotechnology, environmental engineering, computer software and hardware, telecommunications, insurance, and commerce.

In OECD countries, there is a much higher proportion of foreign labor with advanced degrees and conversely a much smaller proportion of foreign labor with low education levels.

Specialized professionals who possess advanced education would be more welcomed by developed countries. Europe, Australia, the United States, and Canada all have policies to attract highly educated foreign professionals to take up employment in their countries. These measures include preferential quotas, expedited approval processing, longer right of abode terms, and permission for their spouses to obtain employment. In the last five years, foreign professionals entering the U.S. increased 14% per year, whereas the increase was 35% in the U.K.[14]

In contrast, countries are increasingly restricting unskilled labor. According to the United Nations' data on international migration, in 1976 18% of advanced countries and 3% of developing countries had policies and measures in place to restrict migrant labor. By 2001, this had increased to 44% of all countries. These restrictions are mainly applied to junior ranking laborers with low technical skills or professional levels. Restrictions come in the form of the scope of market, specified industries, quotas, a strict visa and work permit process, and maximum time limits for the work duration.

Increased competition and downward pressure on salaries of non-technical labor

Developing countries encourage the export of migrant labor because of their labor surplus and low economic development. Labor export allows them to increase employment, increase the quality of life for the people, and develop their economies. But these migrant workers can be easily substituted, as they have low education levels and are sent to do labor-intensive work with low technology content.

The market for migrant labor is generally a buyer's market where there is intense competition that drives down the cost of labor. Unskilled foreign workers in the Gulf region had a monthly wage rate of USD500 in the 1970s. This has decreased to USD150 in recent years. In other countries, this downward trend in wages is manifested in a lower proportion of wages paid by foreign currency, or fewer benefits for workers and lower standards of accommodation.

More jobs in medicine, hygiene, and home care

Because of low birth and death rates, developed countries have an aging population. Between 2000 and 2050, the population over 65 will increase from 15% to 28% in the population of Europe. Japan's population over 65 will increase from 17% to 36%.

In the next 20 years, Hong Kong, Korea, and Singapore will also experience an aging population. By 2025, the population over 60 in Hong Kong will reach 28%, a dependency ratio of 3.3; in Korea and Singapore, these figures will reach 24% and 30%, respectively, with a dependency ratio of 4.0 and 3.0. The aging population will generate a higher demand for medical and nursing personnel.

Concerns about illegal immigrants

The term "irregular workers" refers to those who are illegal or unregistered in their entry to another country to work. It is estimated that in the U.S. and Western Europe in 2000, there were over 7 million and 3.3 million such laborers, respectively. The European Commission states that every year 500,000 undocumented workers enter the EU. Russia estimated that there were

1.5 million illegal migrant workers in the country in 2003. Asian and Latin American countries are also seeing an increase in irregular migrant workers.

The problem of irregular immigrant workers raises concerns of social problems such as public security, protection of rights, and racial or ethnic conflicts. Due to concerns about terrorism, some countries have become increasingly nationalistic and xenophobic, resulting in more conservative and restrictive labor import policies.

Recommendations for the Future Development of China's Foreign Labor Service Cooperation

Problems in foreign labor service cooperation

The industry of foreign labor service cooperation has experienced problems that have constrained its development. As a result, Chinese export of migrant labor is much lower in numbers compared to other Asian countries, considering the vast labor resources available in China. Problems facing the industry are discussed below.

Market entry barriers

Restrictions on labor import have been put in place in many countries because of the need to protect domestic employment, safeguard social order, and prevent illegal immigration. The restrictions usually limit the quantity of imported labor or the sectors that allow imports. The restrictions have made it difficult for China to expand the markets for its unskilled labor, especially since 70% of the labor exported from China is unskilled. Japan, Russia, North America, and Australia, and most developed countries have currently closed their markets to unskilled labor from China.

Although developed countries generally encourage the import of mid to high technically skilled personnel, their requirements for professional qualifications and education are often very harsh. Some countries have discriminatory treatment against Chinese workers, including extremely complicated approval procedures and excessively long waiting times for visas.

The market for Chinese exported labor is further constrained by economic cooperation bodies such as the *North American Free Trade Agreement* (NAFTA) and the eastern extension of the EU, where North America and Europe relaxed labor import policies from neighboring developing countries. China's main labor export market remains in Asia, especially East Asia and Southeast Asia. In these markets, India, the Philippines, Indonesia, Thailand, and Vietnam are

China's main competitors, and their workers hold language and education advantages compared to Chinese workers.

Backwards legislation and duplicated government administration

There are many legal difficulties in the foreign labor service cooperation industry. Because there is no unified legislation in China on foreign labor service cooperation, there is a lack of legal basis when some government departments make decisions affecting the industry. When companies have to participate in labor arbitration or legal disputes in relation to workers dispatched overseas, they sometimes find unclear laws in this area. There are duplicating authorities that govern different aspects of labor cooperation because in the absence of a unifying set of laws, departmental regulations have to be applied to resolve the issues regarding foreign labor service cooperation.

In the current administration system, the Ministry of Commerce is responsible for macro management of the industry, while its departments and the local governments oversee labor cooperation activities in their own regions. Industry associations should function to coordinate and encourage discipline in the industry. Government representatives based in foreign countries have a front-line administration role, with joint responsibilities with their counterparts in the labor-importing countries.

One shortcoming in this system is that the labor department does not get involved to protect the rights of the workers. The multiple external-facing departments and multiple lines of decision making also lead to the wastage of resources and this affects effective policy planning to support the Go Global effort of foreign labor service cooperation.

Low technical skills of labor

In recent years, unskilled labor has represented a lower proportion of the global labor export market, and moderately to highly skilled labor is increasing in representation. According to a report by the OECD, workers with tertiary education represent over 60% of foreign labor imported into OECD countries, while workers with a primary education only account for 10%.

Against this trend of growing demand for highly skilled labor, China sees many missed opportunities. The Chinese labor surplus is mostly excess rural labor and unemployed workers with low education, low technical skills, limited foreign language capability, and limited experience in communicating in a foreign environment. Most of these workers are in manufacturing, construction, and primary industries. These workers represent over 70% of Chinese labor dispatched overseas. In contrast, the proportion of highly skilled workers exported from China is relatively low.

Relevant authorities in the United States asked to import 200,000 nurses from China, but China could not meet the demand because there were not enough qualified nurses who had passed the relevant examination. In the global computer software service sector, the market share of Chinese exported workers is only 0.1%.[15] Also, China does not have sufficient reserve labor in the areas of computer technical skills, surveying and design supervision, management, and seafaring.

Inadequate service cluster to support foreign labor service cooperation

The Chinese government has made some effort in support of the foreign labor service cooperation industry. This includes signing agreements on labor cooperation with foreign governments, in streamlining approvals for Chinese workers going overseas, in setting up an insurance system for overseas workers, and in creating preferential policies of granting loans and waiving fees.

However, some problems still exist:

- The entry and exit procedures for managers and workers in foreign labor cooperation should be further simplified and the processing time shortened.
- Government departments do not have mechanisms to safeguard market order and to protect the legal rights of the companies operating labor exports.
- There is no market information network where companies or workers can obtain information about employment in various countries. There is limited access to information about the legal environment in foreign countries.
- There is inadequate legislative support, so that when there are disputes overseas with foreign parties, legal aid, or practical assistance is often unavailable.
- Chinese workers sent overseas receive very little assistance from the Chinese government, which allocates limited fiscal expenditure on labor export and provides limited support or protection for dispatched labor.

Management and market development abilities need to be upgraded

Chinese companies engaged in labor export are typically small, with low management skills. They lack a long-term view in their operations, focusing on short term projects and existing markets instead of developing new opportunities and new markets.

The narrow focus on existing markets created overcrowding in some markets, leading to severe competition based on price and labor substitutability, thus disturbing market order. Also, because of low management skills, some labor cooperation companies fail to grasp the significant changes that have occurred in the international market, and fail to fully understand the foreign country's policy or industry standards. They may be easily deceived or defrauded by false information, or inadvertently fail to follow policies and regulations. These companies also do not have enough risk management capabilities to brace against changes in a volatile external environment.

Competition by price wars and a lack of market order

Other than the enterprises approved by MOFCOM to engage in labor cooperation, there are other government departments and government-backed enterprises that are also engaging in labor export, creating a lack of market order. MOFCOM and the industry association have tried to install market order by establishing industry regulations and by implementing coordinated measures and minimum wages for different markets, but this effort has proved insufficient to ensure market order.

A small number of companies have failed to follow the relevant policies and industry regulations after they attained their qualification to operate labor export. They engage in competition by cut-throat prices, and create chaos in the market.

Recommended policies and measures

The 11th Five-Year Plan projects that China would send a total of 1.5 million workers overseas between 2006 and 2010. By 2010, the total of workers sent overseas is projected to reach 720,000. This is an opportune time for China to capture the growing demand for foreign labor generated by global demographic and economic trends.

Speed up legislation and streamline the administration system

A unified set of laws would provide the legal basis for developing the labor export market and ensuring market order. In order to protect the rights of both parties, there needs to be a clearer definition of the legal relationship between the workers and the company operating foreign labor service cooperation.

Government oversight and policy support for the foreign labor cooperation industry could help reduce the burden on labor export companies. Improvements in the administrative system can encourage firm-level innovation and strengthen the competitiveness of the whole industry. Processes should be streamlined and favorable policies should be created.

China needs to reform the current administrative system which results in multiple agencies being involved in decision making on foreign labor service cooperation. In this aspect, China could learn from the Philippines, a country that exports its labor on a large scale. The Philippine Overseas Employment Administration is the designated department focused on promoting labor export. China can consider setting up a similar agency to coordinate and supervise labor cooperation activities, as well as implement and improve relevant policies and regulations.

Strengthen external engagement, creating a positive environment for labor service cooperation

The government and the industry association should join hands to create a better international environment for Chinese labor exports.

The Chinese government should be ready to integrate tactics of politics and economics in its engagement with foreign countries and to use bilateral and multilateral negotiation platforms to help the labor cooperation industry. It can help break down regulatory barriers for Chinese labor by pushing for international labor cooperation agreements and by opening exchange and cooperation with countries with a strong demand for imported labor.

As the industry association, the China International Contractors Association (CHINCA) should proactively open cooperation with its counterparts overseas, opening markets in Europe and the Americas and promoting the export of Chinese seafarers and chefs. CHINCA can strengthen services that educate members about relevant laws, market demand, and practical labor export mechanisms. Representing its members' interests, CHINCA should strengthen its communication with overseas government agencies and coordinate efforts to protect the interest of the companies and dispatched workers.

Establish labor service cooperation centers and improve the quality of labor

International competition in the labor market is fundamentally based on quality. Investing in training for workers is an important long-term strategy to support the labor cooperation sector.

In areas with ample labor resources, governments at the county level or above collaborate with labor cooperation companies to recruit and train the workers known as "foreign labor service cooperation centers." Because these are targeted efforts involving public and private collaboration, it helps to develop specialized services to support labor export which helps to improve the management capabilities of the companies. Their economies of scale make it easier for the centers to seek support and investment by higher levels of government in terms of budget, tax, legislation, and credit. It is also easier for these centers to set up risk management mechanisms. The centers should provide high quality technical education for the workers, encouraging them to observe the law, respect their contracts, and understand their rights.

The administration of these centers may need to be improved, with clearer regulations and standards for the setting up of these centers. The effectiveness of these centers should be evaluated, with a mechanism to maintain the effective ones and downgrade those which are not meeting requirements.

Improve supportive policies and risk management system

Dispatched workers require some services that cater to their needs, such as medical services and pensions, which have a significant impact on their motivation in taking overseas jobs. They also need assistance in finding employment in China when they return. They may also require legal or psychological assistance.

A supportive set of policies for the foreign labor cooperation companies would also be important. An information platform on foreign markets can help companies improve business development and risk management knowledge and skills. Tax rebates, preferential policies, and legal services that help companies protect their legal interests would also help strengthen the industry.

In order to help labor export companies in dealing with international political and economic risks, the government may consider setting up a mutual insurance fund for Chinese workers dispatched overseas. The reserve fund for labor cooperation should be abolished so that companies can have better cash flow. Instead, companies could contribute a small fixed percentage of the workers' wages to the mutual insurance fund. Interest earned in the fund can be used on initiatives to protect the rights of the workers and to support business development.

Increase firm capabilities and emphasize corporate social responsibility

Foreign labor cooperation requires people who know commerce, management, and foreign languages. Stronger management capabilities are required in this sector so that Chinese exported labor can stay competitive in Asian markets and also break into new markets in Western Europe and North America.

Service outsourcing is a new global mode of commerce and a market worth over USD350 billion a year. Improved capabilities of Chinese labor cooperation companies and their recruitment of highly skilled labor will help China capture opportunities in the sectors where outsourced labor is in demand, such as telecommunications, finance, software service sectors, and manufacturing.

As the labor export companies interface with China's rural surplus labor and the unemployed, these companies should have a strong awareness of their corporate social responsibility. There should be government guidance, mechanisms, and supervision to encourage companies to pay attention to their corporate social responsibility. Foreign labor cooperation has so far played an important role in providing employment opportunities for surplus labor in Western and Central China, lifting the workers from poverty and promoting local economic development. As the middleman between foreign employers and Chinese workers, the labor export companies in China need to be aware of their role in ensuring harmonious labor relations.

5

Chapter

Economic Relations between China and the United States

Economic relations between China and the United States are not only important to these two nations themselves, but they also have enormous implications for the global economy. Sino-U.S. economic relations have developed on a convoluted and sometimes turbulent path. However, significant progress has been made as the two nations both recognize the importance of taking a long-term view, seeking common ground, and tolerating differences. This chapter focuses on the economic relations between the largest developing country and the largest developed country in the world.

The Development of Sino-U.S. Economic Relations

Sino-U.S. relations before establishment of the PRC

The long history of trade relations began shortly after the United States gained independence. American merchant vessel Empress of China set sail from Boston in February 1784, and reached Canton in August that year, opening direct trade between the two countries. Trade volume grew over the years. By 1931, bilateral trade reached USD165 million. The U.S. accounted for 19% of the imports into China and became China's second largest trading partner. By 1946, Sino-U.S. trade grew to USD558 million and the U.S. became China's largest trading partner, accounting for 57.2% of imports into China, at USD465 million, and 38.7% of exports from China, at USD93 million.[1]

In the few years before the establishment of the PRC, Sino-U.S. trade had a slight decline, but the U.S. remained China's largest trading partner. Imports from the U.S. included rice, flour, cotton, petroleum products, textiles, pharmaceuticals, cigarettes, canned food, matches, glass, and silk stockings. Exports from China included tung oil, pig bristle, tungsten powder, wool, raw silk, woven fabrics, feather, carpets, and musk. The U.S. was also China's largest foreign investor, accounting for 80% of foreign investment, mostly in the transport and textiles sector.

Disruption and recovery of Sino-U.S. relations (1949–1978)

When the PRC was first established, Chinese exports to the U.S. were at a small volume but had already exceeded Chinese exports to West Germany, France, and Japan. In 1950, trade volume reached USD238 million, which included USD143 million in imports and USD95 million in exports.[2]

However, the Korean War set off anti-American sentiments in China and Sino-U.S. trade suffered. A period of enmity and distrust followed, as the

U.S. took a series of actions to contain the Communist bloc that eventually resulted in a complete trade embargo against China. On July 20, 1950, the U.S. Department of Commerce rescinded export permits that were already granted for American exports to China. On December 17, President Harry Truman declared a national emergency in relation to the Korean War. The U.S. Congress then passed the Foreign Assets Control Regulations, freezing all Chinese property and capital in the U.S. In May 1951, the United Nations was persuaded by the U.S. to pass a resolution on an embargo against China. The *Battle Act* was then passed by the U.S. Congress in October 1951 to stop foreign aid to any country that did not follow the embargo. In September 1952, the Coordinating Committee of the Paris Consultative Group of Nations (COCOM) set up a sub-committee focused on enforcing the embargo against China. From 1954 to the late 1960s, economic ties between the U.S. and China were completely severed.

The two countries reached a more conciliatory phase in the late 1960s, as the U.S. pursued rapprochement with China. Travel restrictions were relaxed on July 21, 1969, when six types of Americans (congressman, journalists, academics, students, scientists, and medical and Red Cross personnel) were allowed to travel to China and bring small amounts of Chinese products back to the U.S. The trade embargo was partially lifted on December 19, 1969, and further relaxed in April 1971, when a list of American products including primary products, tobacco, fertilizer, coal, rubber, textiles, and household goods were again granted export licenses for sale to China.

The formal ending of the 21-year embargo came on June 10, 1971, when the U.S. permitted trade with China on a long list of nonstrategic items. In terms of export control, China was re-classified in February 1972 along with most Eastern European states in a less restrictive category of countries.

The *Shanghai Joint Communiqué* signed on February 28, 1972 on President Nixon's visit to China marked a new era in Sino-U.S. trade relations. Nixon's visit followed the preparatory visit by Henry Kissinger. The *Shanghai Communiqué* was a milestone document in which both countries pledged to normalize trade relations. With Sino-U.S. trade standing at USD12.88 million that year, the *Shanghai Communiqué* opened the way towards a gradual recovery of the trade relationship.

The U.S.-China Business Council was established in March 22 the following year, and made its first visit to China in November. The U.S. and China each set up a semi-governmental liaison office in each other's countries in June 1973. In 1975, a delegation of Chinese foreign trade enterprises and China Council for the Promotion of International Trade (CCPIT) visited the U.S. Later that year, President Gerald Ford visited China.

Also worth noting was the allegation from the Work Glove Manufacturers Association (WGMA) to the U.S. International Trade Commission (USITC) on December 15, 1977 that imports of Chinese-made cotton gloves were disrupting market order based on Article 406 of the *Trade Act of 1974*. This allegation became an inadvertent push forward to Sino-U.S. trade when hearings of the USITC decided against the WGMA.

The 1978 trade figures give a glimpse of the recovery of Sino-U.S. trade. Bilateral trade reached USD990 million, a jump of nearly 240% in one year.

Development and adaptation of Sino-U.S. economic relations (1979–2001)

The establishment of diplomatic relations on January 1, 1979 between China and the United States further supported the normalization of economic relations. The *China-U.S. Technology Cooperation Agreement* was signed on January 28, 1979 when Vice Premier Deng Xiaoping visited the U.S. The China-U.S. Joint Economic Committee (JEC) was set up. In February 1979, the U.S. and China drafted a claims agreement in which frozen China assets on U.S. soil would be unblocked. This was officially signed three months later. Resolving the issue of frozen assets was a milestone that paved the way for starting direct flights, opening banking services, organizing conventions and exhibitions, and negotiating trade agreements between the two countries.

Further normalizing of trade relations came with the signing of the *Agreement on Trade Relations* on July 7, 1979, in which the two countries granted most-favored-nation treatment to each other. Going into effect in February 1980, the agreement simplified procedures for tariffs, customs declaration, and other processes for import and export. China also agreed to relax requirements for U.S. financial institutions opening representative offices in China, and to grant easier access to foreign currency and banking services.

The first meeting of the Joint Economic Committee (JEC) was held in September 1980, during which the U.S. and China signed a consular treaty and several agreements on civil aviation, sea transport, and textiles. They also signed agreements on industrial technology, fisheries and avoidance of double taxation, which became important legal documents guiding the closer interaction in economic cooperation and trade between the countries. The JEC meeting provided a platform for discussion of issues and solutions in Sino-U.S. trade. The JEC has generally been considered an effective early mechanism for improving economic relations.

Beginning in 1981, the Reagan administration adopted a policy towards

Taiwan that led to a stalemate in U.S.-China relations. Bilateral trade suffered for two years. This was the first episode of conflict that occurred since the establishment of diplomatic relations in 1979.

A friendlier and steadier phase quickly followed, with the Chinese Vice Premier visiting the U.S. in January 1984 and with President Reagan visiting China in April that year. U.S. export controls on China were relaxed in December 27, 1985 as the green zone was expanding to include 27 types of products. Further adjustments to U.S. export control were made in 1987. The relaxation of export control was a direct factor in the increase in Sino-U.S. trade during this period.

However, in 1989, the U.S. started a series of trade sanctions and once again tightened export controls towards China. Trade suffered.

Sino-U.S. relations thawed in the winter of 1993, but not for long. When the U.S. permitted the entry of Taiwan's leader Lee Teng-hui, U.S.-China relations soured and trade once again dropped.

Economic relations took a more positive turn from 1996 onwards. The *Sino-U.S. Joint Statement* was signed between Chinese President Jiang Zemin and U.S. President Bill Clinton on October 29, 1997, during Jiang's visit to the U.S. The statement acknowledged a constructive strategic partnership between the two countries. This was one of the most important Chinese state leader's visits to the U.S. since Deng Xiaoping's visit in 1979, and it is considered to have lasting positive implications for Sino-U.S. cooperation in economic, political, military, and cultural arenas. President Clinton then visited China in June 1998, which was the most important U.S. presidential visit to China since George Bush's visit in February 1989.

Maturing and rapid development of Sino-U.S. economic relations (2001–present)

Before China joined the WTO, there was constant friction between China and the United States, often pushing the two countries to the brink of a trade war. After the WTO accession in 2001, China and the U.S. were able to use the bilateral and multilateral frameworks to tackle problems, and thus ensure steady growth of

Table 5.1. China-U.S. trade volume, 2001–2007 (USD100 million)

Year	2001	2002	2003	2004	2005	2006	2007
Trade volume	804.8	971.8	1,263.3	1,696.3	2,116.3	2,626.8	3,020.8

Source: Compiled from Ministry of Commerce statistics.

trade. Between 2001 and 2007, trade volume grew 280% from USD80.48 billion to USD302.08 billion, at an annual growth rate of 24.7% (see Table 5.1).

Main Features of Sino-U.S. Economic Relations

Although there are still occasional conflicts and tensions, trade between China and the United States has shown healthy, steady growth in recent years. Compared to the early years when trade relations were newly established, economic cooperation between the two countries expanded from the trading of goods to other forms of economic cooperation.

Continuous growth of bilateral trade

In the span of 28 years from 1979 to 2007, trade between China and the U.S. grew 119 times. It rose from a low base of USD2.5 billion in 1979, eventually to USD302.08 billion in 2007. The rapid growth rate was maintained in recent years.

Between 1979 and 1995, the U.S. was consistently the third largest trading partner of China. In 1996, it became China's second largest trading partner. As of 2007, the U.S. still maintained this second place, following the European Union which is China's largest trading partner (see Table 5.2).

Exports from the U.S. increased since the 1990s. Between 1990 and 1996, U.S. exports to China had an average annual growth rate of 16%, which was much

Table 5.2. Trade volume with China's top 10 trading partners, 2007

Rank	Country/region	Trade Volume (USD100 million)	Year-on-year increase (%)	Percentage of total trade (%)
1	European Union	3,561.5	27.0	16.4
2	United States	3,020.8	15.0	13.9
3	Japan	2,360.2	13.9	10.9
4	ASEAN	2,025.5	25.9	9.3
5	Hong Kong	1,972.5	18.8	9.1
6	Korea	1 599.0	19.1	7.4
7	Taiwan	1,244.8	15.4	5.7
8	Russia	481.7	44.3	2.82
9	Australia	438.5	33.1	2.0
10	India	386.5	55.5	1.8

Source: Compiled from Ministry of Commerce statistics.

higher than the growth rate of all U.S. exports over the same period of time. The growth rate of exports to China is among the highest when ranked against other U.S. trading partners. In 1980, China was the 24th largest trading partner of the U.S. By 1995, it had risen to fifth place. In 2004, China ranked third, after Canada and Mexico. From 2006 onwards, China and U.S. were the second largest trading partners for each other. China was the fastest-growing export market for the U.S. for five consecutive years, at a growth rate of 24% per year, which was three times the rate of the U.S.' export growth globally (see Table 5.3).

Table 5.3. U.S. trade volume of goods with major trading partners (USD100 million)

Export											
Country	1996	1997	1998	1999	2000	2001	2002	2003	2004	2005	2006
Canada	1,326	1,501	1,541	1,639	1,768	1,633	1,608	1,697	1,892	2,118	2,305
Mexico	568	714	790	870	1,119	1,012	975	976	1,109	1,203	1,343
China	120	128	143	131	163	192	220	285	347	419	553
Japan	675	657	579	575	654	575	514	521	544	555	597
Import											
Country	1996	1997	1998	1999	2000	2001	2002	2003	2004	2005	2006
Canada	1,597	1,713	1,779	2,014	2,329	2,199	2,135	2,272	2,598	2,923	3,078
Mexico	741	871	961	1,111	1,376	1,327	1,359	1,395	1,579	1,728	2,005
China	544	658	751	878	1,077	1,093	1,333	1,630	2,106	2,602	3,058
Japan	1,180	1,243	1,251	1,349	1,508	1,296	1,244	1,210	1,334	1,422	1,523

Source: Compiled from WTO international trade statistics, 2007, http://www.wto.org/english/res_e/statis_e/its2007_e/its07_appendix_e.htm.

According to U.S. statistics, there was rapid growth in U.S.-China trade in 2007. Trade in goods reached USD386.7 billion, which grew by USD43.7 billion or 12.8%. American exports to China reached USD65.2 billion and imports from China reached USD321.5 billion, which increased 18.2% and 11.7%, respectively, year-on-year. China remained the second largest trading partner for the U.S., accounting for 12.4% of all U.S. trade, second only to Canada. That year was also when China overtook Canada to become the largest source of imports for the U.S., accounting for 16.5% of all U.S. imports (Canada accounted for 16%). The gap between China and Mexico, the U.S.' third largest trading partner, widened from USD10.73 billion in 2006 to USD39.41 billion in 2007. At the same time, China also overtook Japan to become the third largest export market for the U.S., accounting for 5.6% of American exports.[3]

The types of goods traded between China and the U.S. have changed significantly over the years. Before the 1990s, Chinese exports to the U.S. were mainly textiles, apparel, shoes, toys, leather and leather goods, petroleum and chemical products, metals and minerals, and processed agricultural products. Textiles used to be the largest category of Chinese exports by value, representing one-third of exports to the U.S. China was the largest source of textiles for the U.S.

After the 1990s, the increasing technological level of Chinese industries was reflected in a different and more diverse portfolio of exports to the U.S. Exports of electronic products increased significantly. Currently, Chinese exports to the U.S. are mainly electrical products and consumer products such as textiles, apparel, toys, furniture, shoes, and suitcases. Machinery, electric and electrical equipment exports account for 43.8% of Chinese exports to the U.S. and have a value of USD140.77 billion. If we add to this number the exports of automobiles, auto parts, and optical and medical equipment, the total value becomes USD152.42 billion and this can account for 47.4% of the value of Chinese exports to the U.S. Exports of textiles reached USD31.19 billion, accounting for 9.7%. Toys accounted for 8.1%, furniture for 6.3%, and shoes for 4.4%.

Details of the top 10 categories of goods exported from China to the U.S. are shown in Table 5.4:

Table 5.4. Top 10 categories of goods exported from China to the U.S.

Rank	Categories	Export volume (USD1 billion)	Growth rate (%)
1	Electric, electrical, and audiovisual equipment	76.70	18.3
2	Reactor, boiler, machinery, and parts	64.00	2.8
3	Toys, games, sporting goods and related parts	26.10	25.0
4	Furniture, lights, and mobile houses	20.40	5.2
5	Shoes, boots, leg protective gear, and related goods	14.10	1.79
6	Non-knitted and non-crocheted garments and related accessories	13.40	13.7
7	Knit or crocheted garments and related accessories	10.60	31.9
8	Steel and metal products	9.77	16.7
9	Plastic and plastic products	8.26	10.6
10	Leather goods, suitcases, and casings	7.20	5.8

The major Chinese exports are, in turn, important sources of those goods for the U.S. According to 2007 figures by value, Chinese products account for 30.8% of the imports of electric, electrical, and audiovisual equipment into the U.S.

China also accounted for 25.6% of imported reactors, boilers, machinery, and parts; 31.4% of imported textiles; 49.7% of imported furniture; and an almost monopolistic market share of 84.1% in toys, and 72.8% in shoes.[4]

There were also significant shifts in the types of goods that were exported from the U.S. to China since the late 1970s. The early American exports were food, cotton, and timber. Between 1979 and 1982, U.S.-exported agricultural products accounted for over 50% of American exports to China. In the late 1980s, American agricultural products to China declined while electrical machinery exports increased, including electric power equipment, aircraft and parts, industrial chemicals, agricultural chemicals, chemical production machinery, machine tools, mining equipment, computers, auto parts and service equipment. Since the 1990s, there was an increase in the technology content of American exports to China. Some examples of high tech exports included powered aircraft, space shuttle launch and transportation equipment, manned vehicles, radio telegraph transmitters, and cameras.[5]

The top 10 product categories of American exports to China in 2007 were as follows:

Table 5.5. Top 10 categories of goods exported from the U.S. to China, 2007

Rank	Categories	Export volume (USD1 billion)	Growth rate (%)
1	Electric, electrical, and audiovisual equipment	10.66	4.8
2	Reactor, boiler, machinery, and parts	8.86	14.9
3	Aircraft, spacecraft and related parts	7.20	18.2
4	Oil seeds, nuts, plants for industrial and medicinal use and feedstock	4.18	61.6
5	Plastics and plastic products	3.60	32.6
6	Optical, photo imaging, medical equipment, and related parts	3.31	12.7
7	Steel	2.23	25.2
8	Copper and copper products	2.16	21.9
9	Organic chemicals	2.10	48.0
10	Wood pulp and other cellulose mixture	2.05	39.3

The above products accounted for 78.8% of all American exports to China. Most of them were equipment and raw materials that supported the growth of heavy and light industries in China. The top three categories, which account for USD26.72 billion in value and 41% of total American exports to China, can be considered electrical products. Other exports such as agricultural products, steel, plastics, and pulp also account for a significant portion. In addition, USD3.31 billion of precision instruments and equipment and USD1.97 billion of automobiles and auto parts were exported to China. Base metal and related products account for 11.5% of American exports to China, with a value of USD7.53 billion. Exports of steel, copper, and related products exceeded USD2 billion. Plastics and plastic product exports exceeded USD3.6 billion, whereas timber and paper pulp exports reached USD2.63 billion. Among agricultural exports, oil seeds, nuts, plants for industrial and medicinal use, and feedstock reached USD4.18 billion, and cotton exports reached USD1.48 billion.[6]

Rapid increase in direct investment

Foreign direct investment (FDI) from the U.S. started in 1980, and fell short of USD400 million in the early 1990s. Since then, American FDI has increased rapidly in China. As of the end of 2006, there were 52,211 American-invested enterprises in China, with foreign investment contracts of USD124.16 billion and actual utilized foreign investment of USD53.96 billion. As a percentage of total FDI in China, the U.S. accounted for 8.78% of the number of enterprises, 8.39% of foreign investment contracts, and 7.87% of actual utilized investment. See Table 5.6. The U.S. placed fourth in terms of actual utilized foreign investment, after Hong Kong, Japan, and the Virgin Islands.[7]

As of April 2008, there were a cumulative total of 55,466 American-invested projects in China, with an actual utilized investment of USD57.9 billion. The U.S. had therefore become one of the largest foreign direct investors in China.[8]

U.S. companies invested in a diverse range of sectors in China. Manufacturing and service industries, including finance and insurance, have been the main focus. Before the 1990s, American investment was primarily in the service and energy sectors, and later entered into electronics, machinery, metallurgy, and aviation. From the 1990s onwards, investments have focused on industries that are capital-intensive and technology-intensive, such as computers, electronics, electrical equipment, and telecommunications equipment. Industry leaders in microelectronics, such as Hewlett-Packard, IBM, and Intel, set up manufacturing plants in China. Currently, capital-intensive investments account for 80% of American investments in China's manufacturing sector, while the service sector increasingly becomes the new focus of American investors. In 2001, there was a cumulative total of USD1.59 billion in American investment in the Chinese service sector, such as finance, insurance, and real estate industries, representing 15.1% of total American FDI in China. By 2004, the percentage increased to 18%.[9]

Table 5.6. U.S. investment in China, 1986–2006

	Number of projects			Foreign investment contracts (USD10,000)			Actual utilized foreign investment (USD10,000)		
Year	The U.S.	Total	Proportion (%)	The U.S.	Total	Proportion (%)	The U.S.	Total	Proportion (%)
1986	102	1,498	6.81	54,148	333,037	16.26	32,617	224,373	14.54
1987	104	2,233	4.66	34,219	370,884	9.23	26,280	231,353	11.36
1988	269	5,945	4.52	37,040	529,706	6.99	23,596	319,368	7.39
1989	276	5,779	4.78	64,052	559,976	11.44	28,427	339,257	8.38
1990	357	7,273	4.91	35,782	659,611	5.42	45,599	348,711	13.08
1991	694	12,978	5.35	54,808	1,197,682	4.58	32,320	436,634	7.40
1992	3,265	48,764	6.70	312,125	5,812,351	5.37	51,105	1,100,751	4.64
1993	6,750	83,437	8.09	681, 275	11,143,566	6.11	206,312	2,751,495	7.50
1994	4,223	47,549	8.88	601,018	8,267,977	7.27	249,080	3,376,650	7.38
1995	3,474	37,011	9.39	747,113	9,128,153	8.18	308,301	3,752,053	8.22
1996	2,517	24,556	10.25	691,576	7,327,642	9.44	344,333	4,172,552	8.25
1997	2,188	21,001	10.42	493,655	5,100,353	9.68	323,915	4,525,704	7.16
1998	2,238	19,799	11.30	648,373	5,210,205	12.44	389,844	4,546,275	8.58
1999	2,028	16,918	11.99	601,611	4,122,302	14.59	421,586	4,031,871	10.46
2000	2,609	22,347	11.67	800,089	6,237,952	12.83	438,389	4,071,481	10.77
2001	2,606	26,140	9.97	751,487	6,919,455	10.86	443,322	4,687,759	9.46
2002	3,363	34,171	9.84	815,647	8,276,833	9.85	542,392	5,274,286	10.28
2003	4,060	41,081	9.88	1,016,147	11,506,969	8.83	419,851	5,350,467	7.85
2004	3,925	43,664	8.99	1,216,516	15,347,895	7.93	394,095	6,062,998	6.50
2005	3,741	44,001	8.50	1,351,150	18,906,398	7.15	306,123	6,032,469	5.07
2006	3,205	41,473	7.73	1,204,364	19,372,734	6.22	286,609	6,302,061	4.56

Source: Compiled from Ministry of Commerce foreign investment statistics.

From the 1990s onwards, numerous American multinationals have entered the China market and increased their direct investment in China. Kodak invested USD1.3 billion to build a manufacturing base of film, developing liquid, and digital cameras, and has a chain of retail stores in more than 700 cities in China. Intel, the world's largest maker of chips, announced in 2007 an investment of USD2.5 billion to build a wafer fabrication facility in Dalian, to be completed in the first half of 2010.

More than 200 of the Fortune 500 companies have invested in China. This includes DuPont, General Motors, Chrysler, Ford, IBM, Motorola, American Bell, AT&T, United Technologies, Ingersoll Rand, and Xerox. American investment projects have spread across more than 20 provinces, autonomous regions, and municipalities. The modes of investment have included joint ventures, cooperatives, wholly owned, joint development, leased, and compensation trade. In recent years, some American companies have acquired shareholding of Chinese companies and participated in the corporate reform process in China. Compared to the average company from other countries, American companies and, in particular American multinationals, tend to have large-scale investment projects that feature high technology levels, strict management, sound operations, and high efficiency.

Chinese direct investment in the U.S. has been small compared to American FDI in China. However, some Chinese companies have set up trading and non-trading arms in the U.S. In the first half of 1996, there was USD430 million in Chinese direct investment in the U.S., with nearly 500 companies set up. By the end of 2006, Chinese investment in the U.S. had risen to USD960 million, with over 1,100 companies set up. By the end of 2007, Chinese FDI in the U.S. had almost reached USD3 billion.[10]

Chinese FDI has mainly entered sectors including industries, technology, apparel, agriculture, food and beverage, food processing, tourism, finance, insurance, transportation, and contracting. The trend of increasing FDI in both directions shows that there is common interest and vast potential for the U.S. and China to develop trade and investment.

Expanding economic cooperation

Sino-U.S. economic cooperation has expanded into various sectors and industries in the last three decades. This section provides an overview of the economic cooperation in each sector.

Banking

In 1978, the First National Bank of Chicago was the first American bank to establish an office in China. There are currently more than a dozen American banks with subsidiaries in China, and their operations are expanding.

Export-import financing

On May 21, 2007, the export-import banks of the U.S. and of China signed several cooperation agreements, providing financing and loans to facilitate American exports to China. The export-import banks of the two countries will provide financing to American investment projects in China that exceed USD20 million in value.

Insurance

The AIA Insurance Group was the first American insurance company to enter the China market, when its entry was approved in 1992. AIA has since set up operations in eight cities including Shanghai, Beijing, Guangzhou, Foshan, Shenzhen, Dongguan, Jiangmen, and Suzhou. In May 2006, AIA received approval from the China Insurance Regulatory Commission to provide group insurance policies through its branches in China.

Retail

American retailers have successfully expanded since they entered the Chinese market. Wal-Mart entered China in 1996 when it first opened a Supercenter and a Sam's Club in Shenzhen. In the following decade, it opened 73 stores in 36 Chinese cities including Shenzhen, Dongguan, Kunming, Dalian, Shantou, Fuzhou, Shenyang, Xiamen, Harbin, Changchun, Changsha, and Beijing. These stores include Supercenters, Sam's Clubs and community stores. Wal-Mart has so far invested a total of RMB1.7 billion and created 36,000 jobs in China.

Transportation and infrastructure

In the transportation and road sector, China and the U.S. have engaged in cooperation in engineering consulting, design, supervision, and personnel training. In 1984, the first China-U.S. engineering design joint venture, Chelbi Engineering Consultants, was established. Many American companies have since then participated in the engineering consulting, design, and supervision of projects including the Beijing-Tianjin-Tanggu, the Chengdu-Chongqing, and Jinan-Qingdao highways.

American Presidential Lines (APL) and Sea-Land were the first wholly-owned foreign sea cargo companies in China. Currently, American companies are involved in transport in sea, land, and air in China.

The Civil Aviation Administration of China (CAAC) and the U.S. Department of Transportation signed the *U.S.-China Aviation Liberalization Agreement* on May 22, 2007, in Seattle. Between 2007 and 2012, flights between the U.S. and the eastern part of China would be increased to 70 flights per week. The central regions of China, including Anhui, Hunan, Hubei, Jiangxi, Henan, and Shanxi Provinces, would be fully open to American direct air transportation. Chinese airlines would also have no more restrictions in entering the China-U. S. aviation market. The U.S.-China air cargo market would also be fully open in 2011. Between 2004 and 2010, the number of airlines approved to fly routes between the two countries would increase from four to nine. The number of flights between the U.S. and China would increase from 54 to 249 per week, which included 111 cargo flights and 84 passenger flights. This agreement was a breakthrough in civil aviation for both countries, and is set to bring enormous commercial opportunities to both sides.

Agriculture

Sino-U.S. agricultural cooperation was boosted in 2002 when an agricultural technology cooperation agreement was signed between the Chinese Ministry of Science and Technology (MOST) and the U.S. Department of Agriculture. A joint working group on agricultural science and technology was established, coordinated by both governments and experts on both sides. The working group focused on seven areas of cooperation: natural resources management, water conservation, processing of agricultural products, agricultural biotechnology, food safety, milk production and processing, and bio energy. Six working group meetings were held, seven joint R&D centers were built, several exchange programs, academic seminars, and personnel training sessions were held. The 2002 agreement was then renewed in 2011 to ensure continued cooperation.

The spirit of cooperation was reiterated in the July 8, 2008 meeting of the joint working group where a seminar was held on using agricultural technologies to mitigate climate change. Representatives from both sides stated that China and the U.S. should expand their cooperation in this field in order to tackle global issues such as food security, climate change, and energy shortage.

Energy

The U.S. and China have long cooperated in the energy sector, particularly in nuclear power. The *Agreement for Peaceful Uses of Nuclear Technology* was signed between the U.S. Department of Energy and China's National Development and Reform Commission in 1998. The agreement, which renewed a similar document signed in 1985, outlined cooperation in the areas of export control of nuclear technologies, the handling of nuclear crises and safety issues, and the handling of radioactive waste. The International Atomic Energy Agency (IAEA) would support the enforcement. The efforts of cooperation culminated in the signing of the U.S.-China Memorandum of Understanding, which paved the way for American company Westinghouse to export AP1000 nuclear technology to China.

In 2005, the first China-U.S. Energy Policy Dialogue (EPD) was held in Washington, D.C. The second EPD followed in Hangzhou, China. The two countries agreed to focus their cooperation efforts on increasing energy efficiency and developing alternative energy and renewable energy. In the Third China-U.S. Strategic and Economic Dialogue (S&ED) in 2007, a memorandum of understanding (MoU) was signed for joint development of biofuels. Increasing efficiency in the use of coal and developing clean energy also became the new highlights of China-U.S. energy cooperation.

Labor

A joint statement to strengthen U.S.-China cooperation in labor and social security was signed in September 13, 2006 by Chinese Minister of Labor and Social Security Tian Chengping and U.S. Secretary of Labor Elaine Chao. Each side pledged to promote understanding of each other's labor laws, to jointly tackle labor issues, and to respect the domestic regulations on compensation and working hours, taking action based on international principles on labor. The cooperation would also cover the broad areas of pensions, administration, legal education, employment training, and labor statistics. Under the agreement, exchange programs of government officials and experts, joint seminars and conferences, as well as other technical cooperation would be organized.

Small and medium-sized enterprises (SMEs)

The U.S.-China Business Matchmaking Conference, which targets small and medium-sized enterprises, has been held annually since 2001 in alternate locations in China and the U.S. This conference is a platform for promoting economic cooperation in SMEs and in the mid-size to smaller size cities in the two countries. It is organized by the U.S.-China Exchange Association, the U.S. Small Business Administration, the U.S. National League of Cities, and various Chinese government departments. As of the end of 2007, a total of 39 matchmaking conferences were held in the American cities and states, including New York, Boston, Newark, NJ, Rhode Island, and Philadelphia, and in the Chinese cities of Shanghai, Hangzhou, Beijing, Changsha, Guangzhou, Qingdao, Nanning, Chengdu, Chongqing, and Harbin. These events served more than 8,000 Chinese and American companies in business matchmaking, with over USD1.2 billion in contracts signed. They also facilitated the signing of economic cooperation agreements between 42 pairs of American and Chinese cities.

Food safety

The *U.S.-China Cooperation Agreement on Food and Feedstock Safety* was signed on December 11, 2007, launching a food safety reporting mechanism for the first time. It was agreed that a food safety issue would be reported to the other country within 48 hours when the issue is determined to threaten public health, or is related to product safety, conditions of production and product recalls, or involves serious fraud against consumers. The other side would respond within five days and provide the contact information of the relevant company or organization.

Tourism

A MoU was signed in December 11, 2007 to facilitate Chinese tour groups visiting the U.S. This was the first time the U.S. officially became a destination for Chinese tourists. Developing tourism between the two countries is considered to have had a positive effect on commerce, cultural exchange, and aviation.

Sources of Conflict and Issues in Sino-U.S. Economic Relations

Several intractable problems have constrained the healthy development of Sino-U.S. economic relations. Tackling and resolving these issues will be essential to further improving and maximizing the benefits of this important relationship.

Regarding Taiwan

The issue of Taiwan is a fundamental political issue considered to be the most sensitive and potentially destructive factor in Sino-U.S. relations. Serious difficulties and crises occur when the interests of the U.S. and China clash over Taiwan. Sino-U.S. relations can enter periods of stagnation or deterioration when U.S. actions seem at odds with China's priorities for Taiwan.

The Taiwan issue has been a long-standing critical issue. In 1950, the U.S. Seventh Fleet entered the Taiwan Strait. *A Mutual Defense Treaty* was signed with Taiwan in 1954. The U.S. military presence and the treaty were considered escalation by the U.S., from a rhetorical interference of Chinese domestic policy to using military means to prevent the unification of China.

In the *Shanghai Joint Communiqué* signed in 1972, the U.S. acknowledges that Taiwan is part of China. In 1979, when China and the U.S. established formal diplomatic relations, the U.S. again recognized China's stance that "there is only one China, and Taiwan is part of China." However, the U.S. continued to maintain a special relationship with Taiwan. Within 100 days of establishing diplomatic relations with China, the U.S. Congress enacted the *Taiwan Relations Act*. Subsequently, the U.S. set up a representative organization in Taiwan. In 1980, the U.S. announced arms sales to Taiwan worth USD280 million, including tanks and anti-ballistic missiles. Conflict over this issue subsided after laborious negotiations when the U.S. signed the *817 Joint Communiqué* with China on August 17, 1982.

Sino-U.S. relations soured again in September 1992, when U.S. President George Bush ignored protests from China and announced the sale of 150 F-16 jet fighter aircraft to Taiwan, valued at USD5.9 billion. In June 1995, the U.S. permitted Taiwan President Lee Teng-hui to visit the U.S. and give a lecture at Cornell University asserting the independence of Taiwan. This incident created tension that resulted in a standoff and posturing between the two countries. The U.S. deployed two aircraft carrier battlegroups to the Taiwan Strait, while the People's Liberation Army staged military exercises in the East China Sea and South China Sea. This historic low point of Sino-U.S. relations highlighted the sensitivity required to discuss the important issue of Taiwan.

A détente came two years later. During Chinese President Jiang Zemin's 1997 visit to the U.S., both countries acknowledged that the delicate issue of Taiwan was key to the prosperous development of Sino-U.S. relations. In a joint press briefing, U.S. President Bill Clinton announced the "Three No's policy" of the U.S. on Taiwan, meaning that the U.S. does not support the independence of Taiwan, does not support United Nations membership of Taiwan, and does not support policies commonly labelled "Two Chinas" or "One China, One Taiwan." When Chinese President Hu Jintao visited the U.S. in April 2006, U.S. President George Bush reiterated that the U.S. maintains a "One China" policy, and does not wish to see Taiwan unilaterally changing the status quo in the Strait of Taiwan as such action would seriously affect U.S.-China relations.

The issue of Taiwan is linked to the core interest of China. If the Taiwan issue can be smoothly resolved, we believe that the biggest obstacle in Sino-U. S. relations would be eliminated, and economic relations between the two countries can more steadily and sustainably move forward.

Trade imbalance and currency

We now discuss the direct economic issue of the United States' long-standing trade deficit with China. The U.S. believes that the huge trade deficit is created by unfair competition, dumping of cheap Chinese products, export subsidies, and an artificially low valuation of the Renminbi (RMB). The U.S. exerts pressure on China in various occasions, making repeated demands for RMB appreciation. In 2005, U.S. Congressmen Charles Schumer and Lindsey Graham even proposed imposing a penalizing tariff of 27.5% on imported goods from China if China does not further adjust its currency upwards against the U.S. dollar.

The trade imbalance between China and the U.S. is an objective reality. According to U.S. statistics, there was a trade surplus from 1979 to 1982, followed by a trade deficit from 1983 onwards. From the American point of view, the deficit expanded since then and persisted until today. In 2003, China overtook Japan to become the country with which the U.S. runs the largest trade deficit. The U.S. estimates that in 1983 the U.S.-China trade deficit was USD320 million. The deficit increased over 700 times by 2006, reaching USD232.5 billion and accounting for one-third of the U.S. trade deficit with all overseas markets. In 2007, the deficit grew to USD256.27 billion, an increase of 10.2% within a year which represented 31.4% of the U.S. total trade deficit that year. The size and growth rate of the trade deficit were record-breaking for the U.S.

However, according to statistics compiled by the Chinese, China had run a trade deficit against the U.S. between 1979 and 1992. The Sino-U.S. trade surplus only started in 1993, and did not expand to such a size as calculated by the U.S. According to Chinese statistics, China-U.S. trade ran a surplus of USD58.63 billion in 2003. This increased to only USD114.2 billion in 2005. Thus, there is an enormous gap between the statistics calculated by each side.

There has been disagreement between China and the U.S. regarding the size of the trade imbalance and the reasons behind it. The authors believe that the U.S. had exaggerated the size of the trade imbalance due to statistical errors and American policy towards China.

In order to understand this gap in calculation, the Joint Commission on Commerce and Trade (JCCT) set up a bilateral Statistics Working Group in 1994 to study this topic. The working group issued a report after a year which indicated that U.S. statistics had overestimated Chinese exports and underestimated Chinese imports. This is because the U.S. ignored the entrepôt trade and the value-added from entrepôt trade, resulting in an overestimation of imports from China. Incomplete export data also caused the U.S. to underestimate its exports to China.

Because of the above reasons, in 1992 and 1993 the American calculation of the trade deficit was inflated by USD8 billion and USD9.6 billion, respectively. If we apply the same ratio, the U.S. trade deficit with China in 1996, as calculated by the U.S., was also inflated by about USD16 billion.[12]

We can explain the U.S.-China trade imbalance by several factors:

First, there is a technical problem in using the country of origin to calculate imports. The judgment of the origin of imported goods is usually based on

Table 5.7. Comparing U.S. and Chinese statistics on bilateral trade in goods, 1984–2005 (USD million)

Year	U.S. trade with China (Based on U.S. statistics)			Chinese trade with the U.S. (Based on statistics from China)		
	U.S. Export	U.S. Import	U.S. Balance	Chinese Exports	Chinese Imports	China Balance
1984	3,004	3,381	–377	2,313	3,837	–1,524
1985	3,856	4,224	–368	2,336	5,199	–2,863
1986	3,106	5,241	–2,135	2,633	4,718	–2,085
1987	3,497	6,910	–3,413	3,030	4,836	–1,806
1988	5,017	9,261	–4,244	3,399	6,633	–3,234
1989	5,807	12,901	–7,094	4,414	7,864	–3,450
1990	4,807	16,296	–11,489	5,314	6,591	–1,277
1991	6,287	20,305	–14,018	6,198	8,010	–1,812
1992	7,470	27,413	–19,943	8,599	8,903	–304
1993	8,767	31,183	–22,416	16,976	10,633	6,343
1994	9,287	41,326	–32,039	21,421	13,977	7,444
1995	11,749	48,521	–36,772	24,744	16,123	8,621
1996	11,978	54,409	–42,431	26,731	16,179	10,552
1997	12,805	65,832	–53,027	32,744	16,290	16,454
1998	14,258	75,190	–60,932	38,001	16,997	21,004
1999	13,118	81,786	–68,668	41,946	19,480	22,466
2000	16,253	100,063	–83,810	52,104	22,363	29,741
2001	19,234	102,280	–83,046	54,300	26,200	28,100
2002	22,053	125,167	–103,115	69,959	27,227	42,731
2003	26,806	151,620	–123,960	925,410	33,882	58,628
2004	34,721	196,699	–161,978	124,973	44,652	80,321
2005	41,836	243,462	–201,626	162,938	48,734	114,204

Source: U.S. data from the U.S. Department of Commerce. Data on China from the General Administration of Customs and Global Trade Atlas cited from Thomas Lum and Dick K. Nanto, "China's Trade with the United States and the World," CRS Report for Congress, updated on August 18, 2006. In turn cited from Wang Yong 王勇, *Zhong Mei jingmou guanxi* 中美經貿關係 (Sino-U.S. Economic and Trade Relations), (Beijing: China Market Publishing, 2007).

the declaration by importers. Goods determined as originating from China are recorded as imports from China, regardless of whether they are actually exports via an intermediary location and whether the goods have acquired added value in that intermediary location. Some imports which have been recorded by the

United States as imports from China should in fact be recorded as imports from other third countries or regions. Due to the nature of today's globalized economy, this country of origin method may be outdated and it is partially responsible for creating the statistical discrepancies in the U.S.-China trade imbalance.

Second, foreign-invested companies in China are responsible for increasing Chinese exports to the U.S. A *Business Week* article pointed out that 65% of the growth in Chinese exports from 1994 onwards come from foreign-invested enterprises in China, many of which are American companies.[13] Foreign-invested enterprises use the cheap labor and low-cost resources of China to manufacture goods that were mostly or partially exported to the U.S. and to other countries. Statistics show that most companies in China engaged in the export of goods involve foreign investment. The percentage of exports accounted for by foreign-invested enterprises reached a peak of 58.5% in 2005. When multinational companies relocate their operations to China, a part of the trade surplus from their home countries is also relocated to China. This phenomenon may account for the decreasing trade deficit that the U.S. has with Taiwan, Singapore, and Japan.

Third, American export control policies have restricted U.S. exports to China. Since the opening of the Chinese economy, China has tried to increase imports from the U.S., but has encountered many difficulties. Since the establishment of diplomatic relations, the U.S. moved China from the restrictive "Y" category to the more relaxed "P" and "V" categories in its export control policy. However, in practice, China does not enjoy the treatment of V category countries. In 1989, the U.S. used human rights issues as a justification for imposing a series of sanctions, including export controls that restrict China from importing high technology products from the U.S. Thereafter, the U.S. has yet to relax its export control policy for China. For example in 2001, China wanted to purchase from the U.S. high tech equipment for constructing a chip manufacturing plant, but President Bush froze the export license issued by his predecessor's administration. China then had no choice but to procure the equipment from Sweden. New and tightened regulations were issued on June 19, 2007, which added 31 types of merchandise that had potential military use and which required an export license. The new regulations also expanded requirements for the Chinese Ministry of Commerce to submit details about the final users of the technology.

Such discriminatory policies have restricted the export of U.S. technology intensive products, causing many American companies to lose commercial opportunities in the Chinese market. When we compare the statistics of 2001 and 2006, American high technology exports as a percentage of total U.S. exports to China dropped from 18.3% to 9.1%. If the percentage had been kept at 18.3%, U.S. exports to China would have been USD70 billion higher during this period. This would also explain why the growth rate in American exports to China between 2001 and 2006 was 287% lower than U.S. exports to Germany, and 100% lower than U.S.-exports to Japan.[14]

A more sympathetic view of China came from respected economist and former Morgan Stanley Asia non-executive chairman Stephen Roach. Roach pointed out that between 2004 and 2006,[15] the inflation-adjusted savings rate of American individuals, companies, and the government was only 1% on average, which was the lowest among developed countries. As the U.S. aspires to maintain economic growth despite low domestic savings, it must attract deposits and capital from foreign sources. According to Roach, an operating budget deficit and trade deficit are tools for attracting foreign capital.[16] Based on Roach's argument, it would appear that the U.S. itself needs to take steps to increase its domestic savings in order to reach an ultimate solution to its trade deficit with China.

On the issue of RMB appreciation, we would argue that although the exchange rate can affect the price of goods traded, it is not responsible for creating the U.S. trade deficit. Any attempt to pressure China into allowing RMB appreciation does not help to resolve the problem and may, in fact, damage the interests of both countries.

In conclusion, the issue of the trade imbalance between the U.S. and China requires both countries to adopt a calm and pragmatic approach, and the blame does not rest solely with either country.

Intellectual property rights

The issue of intellectual property rights (IPR) has been a source of friction between the U.S. and China since the 1990s. On several occasions, the U.S. has invoked Section 301 of the *Trade Act* to threaten retaliatory action on China and this has pushed the two countries to the brink of a trade war. The issue of IPR protection is the second most important source of conflict in the economic relations between China and the U.S., according to Peterson Institute of International Economics fellow Fred Bergsten.[17]

A few American companies started to complain about a lack of IPR protection in China since the 1980s. They alleged that China needed to improve its protection for computer software, chemical formulae, and the publications of American companies. During the 1990s, the U.S. placed China on the "watch list" of its annual *Special 301 Report* in three instances, in 1990, 1991, and 1996, and threatened trade sanctions against China. After China's accession to the WTO in 2001, the U.S. still maintained that China's efforts in IPR protection were insufficient.[18]

In April 29, 2005, the U.S. placed China on its "priority watch list" in the *Special 301 Report*, and took the issue to WTO litigation. On May 25 of that year, International Intellectual Property Alliance chairman Eric H. Smith presented to the Senate Judicial Committee on Intellectual Property Rights an estimate of losses of U.S. trade incurred by piracy in China (see Table 5.8).

In April 2006, the U.S. Office of the Trade Representative (USTR) issued the report *U.S.-China Trade Relations: Entering a New Phase of Greater Accountability and Enforcement*, which articulated a revised U.S. trade policy towards China. Out of the six priority goals listed, five of them emphasized the importance of encouraging China to implement IPR protection.

Table 5.8. Estimated trade losses due to copyright piracy, 2000–2004

	2000		2001		2002		2003		2004	
Year	Loss (USD million)	Level of Piracy (%)	Loss (USD million)	Level of Piracy (%)	Loss (USD million)	Level of Piracy (%)	Loss (USD million)	Level of Piracy (%)	Loss (USD million)	Level of Piracy (%)
Books	130	NA	130	NA	40	NA	40	NA	50	NA
Business software	765	94	1,140	92	1,637	92	1,787	92	1,465	90
Entertainment software	NA	99	455	92	NA	96	568	96	510	NA
Motion pictures	120	90	160	88	168	91	178	95	280	95
Records and music	70	93	47	90	48	90	286	90	203	85
Total	1,085	—	1,932	—	1,893	—	2,859	—	2,508	—

Source: International Intellectual Property Alliance, "2005 Special 301 Report, People's Republic of China," http://www.iipa.com/rbc/2005/2005SPEC301PRCrev.pdf.

In fact, China has always been dedicated in its efforts to protect intellectual property rights, especially from a legislative point of view. A *Trademark Law* was drafted in March 1979 and promulgated in August 1982. The *Detailed Rules for the Implementation of the Trademark Law* was issued in March 1983. This was the first foundation of China's legal structure for IPR protection. A series of other legislations followed, especially after WTO accession: *Patent Law* (2000), *Copyright Law* (2001), *Regulation on Computer Software Protection* (2001), *Measures for the Copyright Registration of Computer Software* (2002), *Provisions for the Recognition and Protection of Well-Known Trademarks* (2003), and *Regulation for the Customs Protection of Copyright* (2003). The enforcement of these laws was also stepped up, and Chinese and foreign plaintiffs were treated equally and fairly. Between 1986 and 1993, the courts at different levels in China handled a total of 3,505 IPR cases, including 1,168 cases related to copyright, 1,783 on patents, and 554 on trademarks.[19]

Based on these statistics, the authors believe that the judicial system has sufficiently protected the legal rights of IPR owners.

Between September 2004 and August 2005, a one-year national campaign on IPR protection was launched and later extended until the end of 2005. In order to promote coordination between government departments related to enforcing IPR protection, an IPR protection working group was formed in 2004, led by Vice Premier Wu Yi which consisted of 12 government agencies. In 2006, the working group was expanded to involve 17 government agencies.

China also actively participates in international cooperation for protecting intellectual property rights. China joined the United Nations' World Intellectual Property Organization (WIPO) in 1980, and the Paris Convention for the Protection of Industrial Property in July 1985. It joined the Madrid Protocol for International Registration of Marks in 1989, and signed the *Treaty on Intellectual Property* in respect to Integrated Circuits the same year. In 1992, China signed the *Berne Convention for the Protection of Literary and Artistic Works* and the *WIPO Copyright Treaty*. China applied for membership of the *Patent Cooperation Treaty* on September 15, 1993, and became a member from January 1, 1994, onwards. The State Intellectual Property Office of China became one of the receiving offices for the implementation of the *Patent Cooperation Treaty*, responsible for international searches and preliminary reviews.

While the U.S. and China have both occasionally threatened trade sanctions over IPR disputes, the two countries also engaged in negotiations and dialogue. An annual Roundtable on Intellectual Property Protection was started in 2003 upon the suggestion of the U.S., which averted escalation of trade conflicts in several instances. At the fourth meeting of the Strategic and Economic Dialogue in Annapolis, Maryland in June 2008, both sides agreed that having an innovative society was key to the interests of both countries, and that intellectual property protection will promote innovation. The two countries agreed to tackle the IPR issue at a senior level and provided guidance for the JCCT to continue to play a role on this front.

We expect that the issue of IPR will continue to be a source of conflict between China and the U.S. The legislative action, enforcement efforts, and cooperative dialogue taken by China show its determination to tackle intellectual property rights issues. But we must realize that due to a lower level of economic and technological development, improvement of IPR protection is going to be a long process for China.

Market access issues

The U.S. and China have challenged each other on market access issues throughout the development of economic relations. The U.S. has been dissatisfied with China's market entry barriers, and blamed them for creating the U.S.-China trade deficit and the vast foreign exchange reserves amassed by China. From the American point of view, the Chinese market for services remains closed. On the other hand, China believes that the U.S. unfairly employs anti-dumping, anti-subsidy and protectionist measures against Chinese exports. These issues have caused several disputes over the years.

In the 1980s, the U.S. sought more open market access from China in order to balance its trade deficit. U.S.-China negotiations in Beijing fell apart in May 1992, after the U.S. made harsh demands that China was unwilling to meet. The U.S. then threatened retaliatory tariffs on a list of USD3.9 billion worth of Chinese goods, to which China responded with the threat of imposing tariffs on USD4 billion worth of American goods. This was a potential trade war that came shortly after a dispute over intellectual property rights. After tough negotiations, the two sides eventually signed a memorandum of understanding just before their self-imposed deadline of October 10, 1992. However, the U.S. has since then maintained that China did not fully implement the agreement to open market access.

Since China's accession to the WTO in 2001, the U.S. has scrutinized China's efforts in implementing its commitments made as a condition to accession. From the U.S. point of view, China has not yet completely accepted some principles of the WTO, including market access and non-discriminatory and national treatment. The U.S. alleges that China has industrial policies that restrict market access for service industries, non-tariff barriers in agricultural trade, and a lack of transparency in the regulatory environment. These criticisms were presented in a report by the U.S. Office of the Trade Representative (USTR) which was submitted to Congress on March 31, 2006.

In the March 2005 *National Trade Estimate Report on Foreign Trade Barriers* issued by the USTR, the U.S. identified market entry problems in China for 17 service industries. The report stated that entry barriers for banking, finance, and insurance were set too high. There remained obstacles to the smooth entry of American music and films into China, which indirectly encourages the sales of pirated CDs and DVDs. In March 30, 2006, the U.S. and European Union took to the WTO dispute settlement panel the issue of Chinese tariffs on imported auto parts. It was alleged that the Chinese tariffs were protectionist and that they restricted market access.

In fact, China has reformed its traditional economic and trade system over the years. In the U.S.-China negotiations on market entry, China made commitments on reforming its foreign trade system and adhering to international rules. After WTO accession, China has implemented its commitments in lowering import tariffs, liberalizing market entry, simplifying import procedures and documentation requirements, and increasing the transparency of policies. Due to these liberalization efforts, China became the world's third largest import market in 2006, importing goods worth USD800 billion. This was a leap from being the eighth largest import market in 2000.

China has sought to increase imports from the U.S., often through large scale procurement delegations. In 2006 alone, the delegations of Chinese businesses led by Vice Premier Wu Yi procured USD16.2 billion in American products. In May 2007, Wu Yi again led a delegation comprising more than 200 Chinese enterprises and visited 25 cities in 24 U.S. states. This resulted in 138 signed contracts and agreements, with a contract value of USD32.6 billion. The contracts were in the areas of agricultural products such as soybeans and cotton, nuclear power technology and equipment, coal and petrochemicals, aircraft engines, computer software, telecommunications, electronic equipment, automobiles and auto parts, railway parts, and medical instruments.[20]

During Wu Yi's visit to the U.S. in 2006, the China Council for the Promotion of International Trade (CCPIT) and the U.S. Department of Commerce signed the *Agreement to Fully Advance U.S. Exports to China*. This was the first such agreement China had signed with an individual country. U.S. exports to China have shown strong growth in recent years. Between 2001 and 2005, Sino-U.S. trade increased at an average annual growth rate of 27.4%, whereas American exports to China grew at 21.5% per year. American exports to China grew 118% from 2001 to 2005, nearly five times the rate of all American exports, according to data from Chinese customs.[21]

The Chinese market has become a driver in the growth of American exports. It became the fourth largest export market for the U.S. in 2006, up from the ninth largest in 2001. In 2007, China became the U.S.' third largest export market.

The U.S. market is generally considered open and free. The world's largest single market also offers a high degree of freedom in trade and investment, as well as low import tariffs at an average of 5%. However, the entry of Chinese products and companies into the U.S. market has met several obstacles, with the most intractable one being anti-dumping duties. Anti-dumping duties were used by the U.S. against Chinese products as early as the 1980s. China then became the main object of U.S. anti-dumping action in the 1990s. Due to U.S. concerns over a worsening trade deficit with China, the U.S. imposed anti-dumping duties on Chinese TVs and cathode ray tubes. It also decided that the Chinese furniture industry was engaging in dumping in the U.S. market. The furniture anti-dumping case was worth USD1 billion, the largest to date in the history of Chinese trade.

The U.S. is the country that has filed the highest number of anti-dumping suits against China. According to the U.S. Department of Commerce, between 2001 and 2007 a total of 31 anti-dumping suits were lodged against Chinese products, which represented 25% of all anti-dumping actions taken by the U.S.[22] Anti-dumping allegations have covered a wide range of more than 100 Chinese products, including printed cloth, cobalt chloride, ceramic kitchenware, electric fans, pencils, garlic, disposable lighters, and apple juice concentrate. Anti-dumping duties were imposed on about 80% of the cases that have received a decision.

The U.S. has also limited the Chinese exports of textiles and apparel through the special safeguard mechanism. The safeguard provisions and mechanism are laid out in Article 16 of *China's Protocol of Accession*. Until December 11, 2013, countries may impose safeguards against Chinese products in the event of a rapid increase in Chinese exports that disrupts market order. Textile-specific safeguards are stated under paragraph 242 of the *Report of the Working Party on the Accession of China Under the WTO Framework*. Countries have the authority to impose temporary safeguards on Chinese textiles between 2005 through the end of 2008.

The U.S. was the first country to launch the special safeguard measures against Chinese textiles, in order to protect what was already a sunset industry in the U.S. domestic economy. On November 18, 2003, the U.S. implemented quotas for Chinese knit fabrics, brassieres, and robes. In 2005, when the global textile quotas under the Agreement on Textiles and Clothing (ATC) ended, the U.S. announced quotas on Chinese knit shirts, underwear, and trousers on May 13, and then quickly added similar measures on four other types of goods six days later. China strongly protested against these U.S. measures. Between June and November 2005, the U.S. and China had seven rounds of talks and negotiations within half a year, and eventually averted a trade war by signing the *U.S.-China Memorandum of Understanding Concerning Textiles and Apparel.*

In recent years, the U.S. started using anti-subsidy measures to protect its home market. For instance, in March 30, 2007, the U.S. announced its decision to impose countervailing duty on Chinese coated free sheet paper products, after a preliminary investigation by the U.S. Department of Commerce indicated illegal subsidies. This was the first time the U.S. had imposed countervailing duties on imports from a "non-market economy."

China has met many obstacles as it expands direct investment in the U.S. This is seen in the attempt of China National Offshore Oil Corporation's (CNOOC) bid for Unocal, Lenovo's acquisition of IBM's personal computer unit, and the cumbersome process which Chinese financial institutions undergo as they set up branches in the U.S. These are all typical examples of the problems of market access in the U.S.

The Significance and the Future of Sino-U.S. Economic Relations

Economic relations between China and the U.S. carry strategic significance for the rest of the world. Over the years, Sino-U.S. relations have been marked by healthy development that was disrupted by tumultuous frictions and conflicts.

Exerting extensive influence on the world economy

China and the U.S. have become the dual engines of the world economy today, as they represent the largest economies of the world. The U.S. is the world's largest net importer of industrial goods, and a magnet attracting the largest inflow of foreign direct investment. American consumption drives growth in the manufacturing of consumer goods in many countries across the world. As for the Chinese economy, its appetite for energy, raw materials, and investments has propelled economic development in Asia, Australasia, Latin America, and Africa.

According to the World Bank statistics, the Chinese economy has contributed 13.8% of world economic growth, which is second only to the U.S.' contribution of 29.8%.[23] In recent years, China and the U.S. each contributed nearly half of the global economic growth.

Offering an important solution for global economic imbalances

The trade imbalance between China and the U.S. is a structural issue that involves not only Sino-U.S. trade but also broader trade patterns between East Asia and the U.S. Running trade deficits and capital deficits are common issues in particular phases of economic development. Resolving the Sino-U.S. trade imbalance is a key to addressing the broader issue of global trade imbalances, and is closely linked to the steady development and security of the world economy.[24]

Strengthening global market order

As a developing country, China participated in, and supported, the development of international systems after the Second World War. For instance, China participated in the drafting of the *Charter of the United Nations*, and was one of the 23 founding members of the *General Agreement on Tariffs and Trade* (GATT) in 1947. As these international bodies were improved and strengthened, they have been successful in restricting the behaviors of some Western advanced countries that contravene international economic order.

In today's globalized world, the United States and China are two of the most important economies. The U.S., to a large extent, plays the role of a protector of global economic order while China as an emerging economy is becoming increasingly vocal about the global economic order. The future improvement of global economic systems and the continued integration of the Chinese economy with the rest of the world depend upon a positive Sino-U.S. relationship. On the other hand, any deterioration of this relationship will lead to severe disruption in the multilateral systems of globalization.

So far, both the U.S. and China appear to be optimistic about the future of this important relationship. There are several reasons to be optimistic:

First of all, the relationship delivers strong complementarity and mutual benefits. The American and Chinese economies have contrasting capital levels, economic structure, technology levels, and consumer habits. These differences create complementarity. The sectors of high Chinese demand such as energy, telecommunications, electronics, and transportation are precisely the sectors where the U.S. has a competitive advantage. Chinese exports to the U.S. are typically low value-added products that do not compete with American manufacturing, such as textiles and apparel, shoes and toys. American exports to China are the capital and technology intensive products required for China's development, including aircraft, power systems, machinery, electronic equipment, telecommunications equipment, and petrochemical products.

Sino-U.S. relations have already been fruitful for both economies, resulting in employment opportunities and consumer choice. Morgan Stanley estimated that 4 to 8 million American jobs are created by trade with China, mainly through American retailers selling Chinese products. The low-priced Chinese products sold in the U.S. have reduced household expenditures for American consumers. In the 10 years prior to 2007, importing Chinese products allowed American consumers to save USD600 billion. The savings were estimated at USD100 billion in 2004 alone.[25]

The U.S. has also been the largest beneficiary of the liberalization of the Chinese service sector. Between 2002 and 2006, the U.S. accounted for 40% of foreign investment that flowed into the Chinese banking sector. Representative offices of American law firms account for nearly 45% of foreign law firms' representative offices by number and over 50% by revenue. American companies account for 55% of foreign-invested enterprises that are allowed to engage in direct sales in China. China imported 121 American movies through either buyout or revenue sharing, which is 52% of all imported movies.[26]

China offers very high returns as an investment destination. For example, American companies in 2004 were seeing an average global rate of return of 10.1%, and a declining rate of return from American investments in Canada and Europe. Yet in China, American companies reaped a 10.9% rate of return in 2000 and 19.2% rate of return in 2004.[27] This strong foundation of mutual benefit is likely to shield the two countries against future political turbulence.

Second, both countries recognize that the vast markets in the U.S. and China represent enormous opportunity. It is clear that American economic interests are closely tied to U.S.-China trade, and, therefore, the U.S. has an interest in seeing the continued modernization and rapid development of the Chinese economy. Several Chinese government policies are also likely to increase commercial opportunities for the U.S. These include China's initiative to increase domestic consumption, and the effort to encourage environmental protection, innovation, and efficient utilization of resources.

The U.S. has become an attractive market for China, as it is China's second largest trading partner and the top export destination. Growth in Chinese exports to the U.S. has even been compared to the "strategic deterrent" of military weapons, according to some international observers. In 2001, the U.S. procured USD1.24 trillion worth of products, which is 6% of the world's total procurement of USD21.4 trillion. This means that 6 out of 100 people in the world depend on American consumption for their livelihoods. China no doubt aims to have a meaningful share in the vast U.S. market.

Third, the U.S. and China have common strategic interests. Economic relations are the foundation for political relations, and vice versa. China is a nuclear power with one-fifth of the world's population, a member of the United Nations Security Council, and with enormous influence in the developing world. Therefore, China's cooperation and involvement is essential to the United States in achieving nuclear non-proliferation, campaigns against drug trafficking and international crime, and efforts to maintain the global balance of power and resolve regional conflicts. From China's point of view, friendly relations with the U.S. and other developed countries are essential to ensure a stable and peaceful external environment.

Fourth, effective bilateral mechanisms have been established to manage Sino-U.S. trade relations. As early as 1983, the China-U.S. Joint Commission on Commerce and Trade (JCCT) was set up to discuss and negotiate issues in bilateral trade relations. A stronger mechanism for dialogue known as the China-U.S. Strategic and Economic Dialogue (S&ED) was then set up in 2006. The format is for the top leaders of both countries to meet twice a year with the location alternating between Beijing and Washington D.C. The S&ED involves senior government leaders on both sides, and is historically the highest level dialogue on trade that has taken place between the two countries. The U.S. wishes to construct long-term, mature economic relations with China, similar to the relations between the U.S. and Europe. It is both countries' intention that direct dialogue would prevent misunderstanding, and ensure timely and result-oriented resolution of all kinds of issues.

Developing economic and trade relations between the U.S. and China is mutually beneficial and creates a win-win situation for the people of both countries. The *China-U.S. Joint Communiqué* issued in 1997 when President Jiang Zemin visited the U.S. announced the intention of both countries to focus on a constructive strategic partnership for the 21st century. This was reinforced in April 2006, when Chinese President Hu Jintao and U.S. President George W. Bush jointly confirmed the constructive and cooperative relations between the two nations.

6

Chapter

Economic Relations between China and the European Union

The Path of Development and Achievements

Economic relations between China and the European Union (EU) encompass trade, bilateral direct investment, and technical cooperation in finance and economy.

Historical overview

Diplomatic relations between China and the European Union were established in 1975. At that time economic relations were limited to bilateral trade, which was in the scale of USD2 billion only. With China's economic reforms and growth, combined with the EU's several rounds of membership expansion, bilateral economic relations flourished. This was especially true when the EU became a 27-member economically integrated organization, the largest of its kind in the world, after the enlargement in May 2004 and January 2007. Today, the EU has become China's largest trading partner and the largest source of technology imports, while China is the EU's second largest trading partner and fourth largest export market. Economic relations between China and the EU have a generally positive outlook.

Achievements in China-EU economic relations

Rapid development of bilateral trade

The fast pace of growth in bilateral trade

In the new millennium, especially after China's accession to the WTO, China-EU trade increased rapidly on an already large base, doubling once every three years. As of 2007, China-EU trade had reached USD356.2 billion, an increase of 147 fold compared to the USD2.4 billion in 1975. This is much higher than the average growth of 70 fold in China's total foreign trade during the same period of time (see Table 6.1). Today, products made in China are prevalent in the European markets. At the same time, China is now the second largest trading partner for the EU, second to the U.S. Between 2000 and 2007, China's imports from the EU more than doubled. In the 15 years up to 2007, the EU's exports to China increased 600%. This was much higher than the average growth rates in imports and exports for both countries. There is no doubt that China-EU trade has brought enormous economic opportunities to the EU.

Table 6.1. Trade between China and the European Union (1984 as base year)

Year	Export (USD billion)	Growth rate (%)	Percentage of total China exports (%)	Export (USD billion)	Growth rate (%)	Percentage of total China exports (%)
1984	2.36	—	9.04	3.55	—	12.96
1985	2.25	–5.00	8.25	6.06	70.70	14.34
1986	4.02	78.66	13.00	7.97	31.52	18.58
1987	3.62	–10.00	10.40	5.73	–28.10	17.20
1988	4.28	18.20	10.50	5.92	3.20	14.80
1989	4.35	1.60	10.00	6.12	3.50	15.60
1990	5.07	16.60	9.70	4.83	–21.10	14.60
1991	6.74	32.90	9.40	8.40	73.90	13.20
1992	7.60	12.80	8.94	9.81	16.70	12.17
1993	11.70	53.90	13.00	14.40	47.00	14.00
1994	14.60	24.70	12.00	16.90	17.40	14.60
1995	19.09	30.80	12.80	21.25	25.70	16.10
1996	19.83	3.80	13.10	19.87	–6.50	14.30
1997	23.80	20.02	13.02	19.20	–3.40	13.50
1998	28.10	18.10	15.30	20.70	7.90	14.80
1999	30.20	7.50	15.50	25.47	22.70	15.40
2000	38.19	26.40	15.30	30.84	21.20	13.70
2001	40.90	7.10	15.40	35.71	15.80	14.70
2002	48.10	17.60	16.10	38.62	8.15	13.30
2003	78.30	62.80	17.90	54.43	40.90	13.20
2004	107.20	36.90	18.10	70.09	28.80	12.50
2005	143.70	34.00	18.80	73.60	5.00	11.10
2006	182.00	26.70	18.80	90.32	22.70	11.40
2007	245.20	34.70	20.10	111.00	22.00	11.60

Source: General Administration of Customs.

Development of trade in services

There has been rising demand for European services in China. For instance, the Beijing Olympics National Stadium, the National Center for Performing Arts, and the Terminal 3 of the Beijing Capital International Airport have all been built with European engineering, design and technology. However, the expansion of trade in services in recent years has not matched the spectacular growth rates of the trade in goods mentioned above. China has a long-standing deficit in the service trade with the EU, and accounts for a very small proportion of the EU's foreign trade in services. This is incongruent with the enormous volume of the China-EU trade in goods, and incongruent with the EU's status as the largest service trade economy and the largest exporter of services. This shows that the China-EU trade in services is in a rudimentary stage and needs to be further strengthened.

Effective cooperation in bilateral investment

The EU is the world's largest source of FDI, and it has ascended in the rankings of China's top FDI contributors (see Table 6.2). As of the end of 2007, EU investors have set up 27,000 companies in China, with a cumulative total of USD60 billion in actual utilized investment. By actual utilized investment, the EU's direct investment in China ranks fourth just after Hong Kong, the U.S. and Japan. In terms of geographical spread of EU investments, apart from the coastal areas, EU investors have also supported the development of the western regions and the re-tooling of the northeastern heavy industrial base. Some EU companies are relocating their production and research and development facilities to the western and northeastern regions because of the lower cost of labor and land in those areas.

Several leading Chinese firms have started direct investments in the EU, including Huawei, ZTE, and Haier. The original one-sided EU-to-China investment has been revised into a more balanced picture. Chinese investment in the EU accelerated after the EU eastward enlargement. According to Chinese statistics, Chinese direct investment in the EU increased from USD150 million in 2003 to USD2.64 billion in 2006, but suffered a sudden drop in 2007 down to USD755 million.

However, China was a latecomer as an investor in the EU, so that Chinese investment in the EU lags significantly behind EU investment in China. For two countries with such a large bilateral trade volume, China's contribution to their bilateral investment pales in comparison. It is well-known that there is an imbalance in China-EU trade that is in China's favor, but there is also an imbalance of bilateral investment. China's investment in the EU has been also restricted to a handful of EU member countries such as Germany, the U.K., France, Spain, Denmark, and Italy. Although Chinese investors are getting involved in a greater variety of sectors, only a very limited number of Chinese companies are investing in heavy industries in Europe.

Fruitful economic technological cooperation

Technological cooperation started in the 1980s and it plays an important role in the strategic partnership between China and the EU today. For over 20 years,

Table 6.2. EU direct investment in China, 1979–2007

Year	Total number of FDI projects	EU Projects	Percentage of total (%)	Total FDI contract value (USD100 million)	EU FDI contract value (USD100 million)	Percentage of total (%)	Total actual utilized FDI (USD100 million)	EU actual utilized FDI (USD100 million)	Percentage of total (%)
1979–1985	6,797	134	1.97	160.83	9.80	6.09	60.60	6.50	10.73
1986	1,498	32	2.14	33.30	3.52	10.60	22.44	1.79	7.96
1987	2,346	42	1.79	37.09	4.23	11.40	23.14	0.53	2.28
1988	5,945	87	1.46	52.97	2.85	5.39	31.94	1.57	4.92
1989	5,779	78	1.35	56.00	3.33	5.94	33.93	1.88	5.53
1990	7,273	82	1.13	65.96	2.24	3.40	34.87	1.47	4.23
1991	12,978	163	1.26	119.77	7.59	6.34	43.66	2.46	5.63
1992	48,764	763	1.56	581.24	9.64	1.66	110.08	2.43	2.21
1996	83,437	1,726	2.07	1,114.36	31.82	2.86	275.15	6.70	2.44
1997	21,001	1040	4.95	510.04	42.29	8.29	452.57	41.71	9.22
1998	19,799	1,002	5.06	521.02	59.39	11.40	454.63	39.79	8.75
1999	16,918	894	5.28	412.23	40.96	9.94	403.19	44.79	11.11
2000	22,347	1,130	5.06	623.80	88.55	14.20	407.15	44.79	11.00
2001	26,140	1,214	4.64	691.95	51.53	7.45	468.78	41.83	8.92
2002	34,171	1,486	4.35	827.68	45.07	5.45	527.43	37.10	7.03
2003	41,081	2,074	5.06	1,150.70	58.54	5.09	535.05	39.30	7.35
2004	43,658	2,423	5.55	1,534.31	83.62	5.45	606.44	42.39	6.99
2005	43,988	2,846	6.47	1,890.65	115.30	6.10	724.06	51.94	7.17
2006	41,485	2,738	6.60	—	105.80	—	735.23	53.90	7.33

Note: EU25 data shown from 2004 onwards.

Sources: Compiled from *Statistical Yearbook of China External Trade* and the China Investment Guide website.

China participated in more than 100 EU technology research programs, while the quality and implementation of these cooperation programs are ever rising. The EU is the largest source of imported technology for China, accounting for 50% of the technologies imported into China. As of the end of 2007, China had imported a cumulative total of 27,000 technologies from the EU, with contracts of USD112.3 billion in value.[1] In 2007, the EU accounted for 40% of all of China's technological cooperation contracts by value, which is the combined value of technologies imported from Japan and the U.S. The EU is also the supplier of the most advanced technologies to China. Compared to American or Japanese companies, EU companies have shown themselves to be more willing to fulfil China's many technology needs, such as in the Airbus A320 assembly line project. This is especially true for relatively sensitive technologies. The EU's relative willingness on this front bodes well for China-Europe economic cooperation.

The satellite navigation program Galileo is the largest international technology cooperation program in which China has ever participated, and it therefore occupies a special position in China-EU technology cooperation. In recent years, there has been new interest in China-EU cooperation in tackling climate change through technology transfer, application, and dissemination of clean energy and technologies from the EU. The European Investment Bank (EIB) has also pledged to set up a EUR500 million loan to support China in tackling the challenge of climate change.

Currency and financial cooperation

Closer links in financial sector cooperation

As China has sped up its financial sector reforms, China and the EU have cooperated in this area, mainly in the following two aspects:

EU and China financial institutions set up in each other's countries

In banking, over 50 banks from the EU, most notably HSBC and Standard Chartered from the U.K., Société Générale from France, and Deutsche Bank from Germany have set up branches and representative offices in China. Meanwhile, the Industrial and Commercial Bank of China (ICBC), Bank of China, China Construction Bank, and Bank of Communication have also set up operations or representative offices in Frankfurt, London, and Paris.

In insurance, EU insurance companies such as AXA from France and General Reinsurance AG from Germany, have set up shop in China, while China Life Insurance and People's Insurance Company of China have set up subsidiaries and agents in the U.K., Germany, and Luxembourg. In securities, the EU has a dozen securities institutions that have set up nearly 20 representative offices. Securities trading firms and funds were also set up.

The role of Hong Kong

Strengthen cooperation through using Hong Kong's earlier liberalization in the banking sector. There are 167 licensed banks in Hong Kong including EU banks, such as BNP Paribas and Deutsche Bank. There are also over 100 licensed futures trading firms, consulting firms, and asset management companies in Hong Kong, of which several hundred are, in fact, European invested.

EU financial resources give it soft power

Capacity building for China's finance system

The EU has provided financial support to China for capacity building. Currently, the EU and its financial organizations have provided a cumulative total of USD20 billion in loans to China, accounting for over 40% of loans from foreign governments and governmental financial organizations. The loans from the EU are intended to support China in meeting challenges as a developing country. In the 2002–2006 China Strategy document of the EU, a USD250 million loan was pledged in order to support China in social and economic reforms, environmental protection and sustainable development, and to improve governance and the rule of law.

The role of the euro

EU officials have suggested that China purchase more euros for its foreign exchange reserves in order to reduce China's dependency on the U.S. dollar.[2] This was based on the strength of the strength of the euro against the U.S. dollar, as well as its international status, credibility, and stability. As China has reformed its exchange rate mechanism for the Renminbi, determining it based on a basket of currencies including the euro, it makes sense to buy in euros at a suitable level.[3] As a country that holds the highest amount of foreign exchange reserves, China could use the euro to diversify risk in its foreign exchange reserves, as well as to accelerate the internationalization of the Renminbi.

Main Features

Strong complementarity

China and the EU are complementary to each other's strengths. The EU is highly competitive in the high value-added sectors of advanced technology, high-end manufacturing, and modern services. Meanwhile the most competitive sectors in the Chinese economy have so far consisted of low-end to middle market manufacturing and labor intensive industries. There is strong complementarity between the economies, generating a high demand for trade. China-EU trade reflects the free flow of capital, labor, technology, and goods in a globalized world.

The asymmetry: China's greater reliance on the EU

The growth of bilateral trade

There is a level of asymmetry in China-EU trade. In the years after China's accession to the WTO, Chinese exports to Europe showed staggering growth at rates higher than China's overall average export growth (see Tables 6.3 and 6.4). Chinese imports from the EU increased more slowly than the average growth rate of total Chinese imports. However, China's reliance on exports to the EU is much higher than the EU's reliance on exports to China.

Bilateral trade as a percentage of total trade of China and the EU

The EU market is more important to Chinese exports than the China market is important to EU exports. As of 2007, 20% of Chinese exports are destined for the EU market, while only 7% of EU exports are for China.

Geographical spread

China's trade with the EU is concentrated in several European countries, namely Germany, France, the U.K., the Netherlands, and Italy, despite the uniform trade policies and openness across the member countries. The five countries account

Table 6.3. Comparison of the growth rates of China-EU Trade and China's total trade, 2000–2007 (%)

	Import growth rate		Export growth rate	
Year	China from EU	Total	China to EU	Total
2000	21.20	35.85	26.40	27.84
2001	15.80	8.22	7.10	6.78
2002	8.15	21.18	17.60	22.36
2003	40.90	39.84	62.80	34.58
2004	28.80	36.00	36.90	35.41
2005	5.00	17.58	34.00	28.42
2006	22.70	19.92	26.70	27.18
2007	22.40	20.80	29.20	25.70

Source: General Administration of Customs.

Table 6.4. China-EU bilateral trade as a percentage of the total import and export of China and EU, 1997–2007 (%)

	Export		Import	
Year	Export to EU as percentage of total Chinese exports	Export to China as percentage of total EU exports	Import from EU as percentage of total China imports	Import from China as percentage of total EU imports
1997	13.0	0.9	13.5	1.2
1998	15.3	0.9	14.8	1.4
1999	15.5	1.1	15.4	1.6
2000	15.3	1.3	13.7	1.5
2001	16.6	1.5	14.9	1.8
2002	16.1	1.5	13.3	2.0
2003	14.9	1.7	13.2	2.5
2004	18.1	1.9	12.5	2.8
2005	18.8	1.8	11.1	3.5
2006	18.8	2.0	11.4	3.9
2007	20.1	5.8	11.6	16.3

Sources: Compiled from data in *Statistical Yearbook of China External Trade*, 1998–2006, and the websites of WTO and UNCTAD.

for 70% of China-EU trade, with Germany being the largest trading partner accounting for 30% of China-EU trade. EU investments in China are mostly concentrated in the coastal area.

Mechanisms

China-EU economic relations are characterized by robust systems and mechanisms. As the EU is a large, regionally integrated body with advanced economies as its core members, its policy-making and its capacity to execute policy tend to be strong. The EU has a relatively comprehensive trade policy towards China, which is adjusted over time in accordance with the best interest of the EU.

In terms of institutions of cooperation, the EU-China trade and economic joint committee was first set up under the *European Communities-China Agreement on Trade and Cooperation* signed in 1985. The China-Europe High-Level Dialogue later became an important platform for both sides to discuss trade and economic issues, to coordinate their stance, resolve conflict, and forge cooperation. These mechanisms cover a very wide diversity of areas of cooperation, including: competition policy, customs, education, culture, energy, and nuclear energy, the environment, employment, the Galileo satellite navigation system, information technology, intellectual property rights, sea transport, industrial policy, healthcare, science and technology, space programs, and trade policy. Government officials of China and the EU at every level have maintained frequent contact and exchange which culminates every year in the China-EU Summit.

Complexity

The EU comprises 27 member countries with varying levels of economic development, each with their own complex issues. The economic structures and the portfolio of products traded with China vary, causing an internal debate among member countries in regards to EU trade with China. The internal differences within the EU add a layer of complexity to China-EU dynamics, because it could be less challenging for China to develop trade relations individually with each member nation instead of going through the European Union.

The Eastward Expansion of the EU and Its Effects on China-EU Trade

There were two recent rounds of EU enlargement, admitting 12 new members from Eastern Europe and the Mediterranean. In May 2004, the fifth enlargement added 10 states, namely Poland, Hungary, the Czech Republic, Slovakia, Slovenia, Estonia, Latvia, Lithuania, Cyprus, and Malta. In January, Bulgaria and Romania joined the EU. After the expansion, the EU covers a population of 490 million and a gross domestic product of USD14 trillion, forming the world's largest regionally integrated economy.

It is only natural to expect that the expansion of such an organization would affect the states both within the union and outside. China is therefore seeing both opportunities and challenges arising from this expansion.

China-EU trade after EU's eastward expansion

The expansion of the EU has a generally positive impact on China, manifested in the following trends:

Increase in importance as trading partners

The EU became China's largest trading partner and second largest export market after the 2004 expansion, and then it surpassed the United States to become China's largest export market after the 2007 EU expansion. China's exports to the EU rose from representing 16.5% of China's total exports in 2003 to representing 20.1% in 2007. At the same time, China also rose in the rankings of trading partners for the EU. Since 2006, China replaced the U.S. as the largest trading partner in goods of the EU. The correlation in EU expansion and rapid rise in these trade figures would lead us to believe that the EU expansion has enhanced cooperation and strengthened China-EU ties.

Table 6.5. Top 10 export markets of China as percentage of total export, 2003–2007 (%)

Rank	1	2	3	4	5	6	7	8	9	10
2003	The U.S.	Hong Kong	EU	Japan	ASEAN	South Korea	Taiwan	Australia	Russia	Canada
Percentage of total	21.1	17.4	16.5	13.6	7.1	4.6	2.1	1.4	1.4	1.3
2004	The U.S.	EU	Hong Kong	Japan	ASEAN	South Korea	Taiwan	Russia	Australia	Canada
Percentage of total	21.1	18.1	17.0	12.4	7.2	4.6	2.3	1.5	1.5	1.4
2005	The U.S.	EU	Hong Kong	Japan	ASEAN	South Korea	Taiwan	Russia	Canada	Australia
Percentage of total	21.4	18.9	16.3	11.0	7.3	4.7	2.2	1.7	1.5	1.5
2006	The U.S.	EU	Hong Kong	Japan	ASEAN	South Korea	Taiwan	Russia	Canada	India
Percentage of total	21.0	18.8	16.0	9.5	7.4	4.6	2.1	1.6	1.6	1.5
2007	EU	The U.S.	Hong Kong	Japan	ASEAN	South Korea	Russia	India	Taiwan	Canada
Percentage of total	20.1	19.1	15.1	8.4	7.7	4.6	2.3	2.0	1.9	1.6

Source: Compiled from data from the General Administration of Customs.

Continued growth in Chinese exports to the EU

The traditional theory of a customs union or free trade union states that, once formed, such a trade union would incentivize members to increase trade with each other, thereby reducing members' trade with countries external to the organization. However, this effect did not occur for China. This is unusual particularly because many of the new member countries in the EU are less developed economies, with goods produced that could compete with exports from China.

Contrary to the theory, Chinese exports to both old EU states and newly joined EU states have increased after the EU expansion. Export to the EU increased on an average of 30% every year between 2004 and 2007 (see Table 6.6), exceeding the growth in total Chinese exports and exceeding the growth rate of Chinese exports to the U.S. and to Japan.

Steady growth in EU direct investment in China

Again, it was projected that the advanced economies in the EU would reduce their direct investment in China after the 2004 and 2007 enlargement, because the new members would become their new focus in investment. However, there was steady growth in EU direct investment in China during this time, except for small declines in the years 2001 and 2002 which was most likely due to a global economic downturn. The transfer of new investment from China to the new EU member countries did not seem to have occurred (see Table 6.7).

Main reasons for the continued growth in China-EU trade after EU expansion

Benefits to non-members

China had already established close economic ties with EU countries before the EU's eastward expansion. China has been a global hub of the processing trade and occupies an important position in the supply chain of multinational companies from the EU. Much of the processing trade takes place when a foreign multinational enters another market to establish its own processing plant or to outsource the processing of parts, crafts, equipment, instruments, and after sales support. As the competitiveness of these multinationals is strengthened, the processing trade increases and the competitiveness of these global suppliers is also increased. In this way, China's processing trade has developed very strong advantages against newcomers from the Eastern European states. As the EU multinationals grow their business as a result of the EU expansion, Chinese enterprises that are part of the global supply network also enjoy the benefits.

Table 6.6. Trade with China as the European Union expands eastward

Comparison			2004	2005	2006	2007
Year-on-year increase (%)	Trade	EU25	33.40	22.60	25.30	27.00
		EU15	34.20	22.90	24.10	27.70
		New members	20.40	16.85	48.60	19.50
	Export	EU25	36.70	34.10	26.60	29.20
		EU15	38.40	35.10	25.40	30.90
		New members	17.40	21.10	46.00	14.60
	Import	EU25	28.70	4.90	22.70	22.40
		EU15	28.60	5.10	21.70	21.40
		New members	33.40	−1.60	60.90	50.20

Source: Compiled from data from the General Administration of Customs.

Table 6.7. Direct investment from the EU original members in China, 1998–2008

Year	EU Total		EU Original Members	
	Actual utilized foreign investment (USD100 million)	Year-on-year growth (%)	Actual utilized foreign investment (USD100 million)	Year-on-year growth (%)
1998	454.6	—	39.8	—
1999	403.2	−11.3	44.8	12.6
2000	407.2	1.0	44.8	0.0
2001	468.8	15.1	41.8	−6.7
2002	527.4	12.5	37.1	−11.3
2003	535.1	1.4	39.3	5.9
2004	606.4	13.3	42.4	7.9
2005	724.1	19.4	51.9	22.5
2006	735.2	1.5	90.0	73.4

Note: Original members of the EU were Belgium, Denmark, United Kingdom, Germany, France, Ireland, Italy, Luxembourg, the Netherlands, Greece, Portugal, Spain, Austria, Finland, and Sweden.

Source: Compiled from data from the China Ministry of Commerce.

China's WTO accession

At the same time of the EU expansion, the Chinese economy had established a foundation of successful economic reforms and was bolstered by the WTO accession. Trade liberalization resulting from the WTO accession had possibly mitigated any negative effect from the EU expansion.

EU's large markets

After the 2007 expansion, the EU had 480 million consumers and one-quarter of the world's GDP, making it a market larger than the U.S., Canada, and Mexico combined. As the new Eastern European members have a lower level of economic development compared to the old members, there is strong demand for a larger volume and wider variety of goods. From a lower base, the economic growth of these Eastern European states also creates opportunities for EU members and non-members alike. According to a report by the European Commission, the eastward expansion would bring an average annual GDP growth of 0.7% for all EU members between 2004 and 2009. The rising income and growing consumer demand in the new EU member states would undoubtedly drive export growth in China.

World economic growth and global FDI growth

The five years between 2003 and 2007 featured the fastest global economic growth since the 1970s. Data from the International Monetary Fund (IMF) showed the global real GDP growth to be at 3.6%, 4.9%, 4.4%, 5%, and 4.9% in those five years. At the same time, international direct investment was recovering after the downturn prompted by 9/11. In those years, international direct investment grew at over 30% per year from USD557.9 billion to USD1.5 trillion, exceeding the previous peak of USD1.4 trillion in 2000. This level of economic growth and FDI growth ensured that China did not experience any negative impact of the EU enlargement.

Renminbi depreciation against the euro

Since China's reform of the exchange rate adjustment mechanism in July 2005, the Renminbi had appreciated against the U.S. dollar but depreciated against the euro. In November 2007, the euro, and the Chinese yuan was at a 1:11 height, the highest since the euro's inception in 1999. According to calculations from Standard Chartered, from January 2006 to March 2008, the Chinese yuan appreciated 12.2% against the U.S. dollar but depreciated 16% against the euro.

The depreciated currency has been advantageous to expanding Chinese exports and increasing the Chinese trade surplus with the EU.

Underlying concerns of the eastward expansion

The concerns

The U.S. subprime crisis

The U.S. subprime crisis which started in mid-2007 had prompted many uncertainties in the global financial markets, affecting Europe and China. The depreciation of the U.S. dollar meant that commodity prices such as oil, mining products, and agricultural products have risen exorbitantly, increasing risks and inflation pressures across the world.

As the EU markets are closely linked to the U.S., the property markets in the U.K., Spain, Ireland, and France have been severely hit by the burst of the American property bubble. As the euro appreciated against the U.S. dollar, the competitiveness of major EU exports was undermined. Many European states have had to lower their forecasts of economic growth.

The Chinese economy will also be affected. An IMF report shows that for every 1% decrease in GDP in the U.S., Chinese exports may decline by 4.5% and its GDP may decline by 0.75%. The Chinese export market is heavily reliant on American and European consumer demand, since the U.S. and the EU accounted for 39.2% of Chinese exports in 2007. The recession that started as the subprime crisis resulted in lower consumer demand in Europe and the U.S. and therefore a reduction in Chinese exports. This was already seen in 2007 when many small and medium enterprises engaged in exports came under pressure. These forces of uncertainty in the global economy cast a dark shadow over China-EU economic relations.

Rising cost of "Made in China"

The Chinese economy has been largely driven by the export-oriented manufacturing sector, which was in turn supported by the low cost of labor and other production factors. However, the low-cost proposition is becoming invalid as China transitions into higher-end manufacturing, increases requirements for environmentally friendly and sustainable production, and puts in place a new labor law to protect workers. Those foreign multinationals who have come to China only because of the low-cost proposition would no longer find China an attractive location. This, combined with the rising oil prices, makes it increasingly expensive to transport goods from China to European markets. In the long run, it would not be surprising if European multinationals, especially in the lower-end, export-oriented manufacturing sector, relocated their investments and operations to the Eastern European EU member states.

Increased anti-dumping allegations

The EU policies on anti-dumping have been applied to the markets of the new members, which might have originally relatively relaxed policies on trade protection. Since these new members have a competitive relationship with China due to their relatively low level of economic development, they have stronger incentives to protect their homegrown industries. This resulted in a trend of increasing anti-dumping investigations after the EU's eastward expansion. Between 2003 and 2006, the EU's new cases of anti-dumping were 7, 30, 25, and 34. In terms of cases against China, new cases lodged were 9, 8, and 12 between 2004 and 2006, a significant increase from the 2 and 3 cases lodged in 2002 and 2003.

The solutions

Increase Chinese direct investment in the EU

Chinese companies should target the Eastern European new members of the EU and ramp up their direct investment in these new markets. Chinese direct investment overseas has been on the rise, but in terms of geography it has been relatively focused on Asia (63.9%) and Latin America (26.3%), with very little direct investment in Europe (3%). Even the existing direct investment in Europe is limited to the old EU members, while there is enormous potential to invest in the Eastern European markets where Chinese investment has been negligible.

In fact, these new EU members offer the advantages of low labor cost and low company profits tax (see Table 6.8). Their foundation for industrial development is superior to Africa and Latin America, and their laws and regulations, financial, accounting, and management systems are close to the rest of Europe and to the U.S. These Eastern European states have been undergoing a privatization process and are in need of foreign capital. Chinese companies should seize the opportunity.

Brand building and capturing more of the value chain

In producing and exporting low-end, low-technology products, China is only capturing the small margins of the "smiling curve," and leaving to the U.S. and

Table 6.8. Comparison of company profits tax revenue in selected original and new members in the European Union, 2005 (%)

	Country	Tax rate
Original members	Germany	38.6
	Italy	37.3
	France	33.8
	Greece	32.0
	The Netherlands	31.5
	Denmark	28.0
	Austria	25.0
New members	The Czech Republic	26.0
	Poland	19.0
	Hungary	17.5
	Romania	16.0
	Latvia	15.0
	Bulgaria	15.0

Europe the processes most capable of value creation, namely the upfront R&D and marketing and branding at the later stage. In order to capture the higher value of production, China needs to develop and market its own brands. This would allow China to maintain a competitive edge against the Eastern European states, especially in the face of rising labor cost that may drive the relocation of the low value-added industries.

Closer cooperation of small and medium-sized enterprises (SMEs)

SMEs are the main driver of economic activities. A vibrant SME sector could indicate the health and sustainability of an economy. Currently, SMEs in China and Europe may require government support when providing the platform to exchange information and open communication channels, in order to forge closer cooperation.

The Main Obstacles to the Development of China-EU Relations

China-EU economic relations have improved in breadth and depth over the years. Trade frictions and other issues may be more likely to arise as trade and economic ties continue to develop on an unprecedented scale. We discuss the major obstacles below.

Grievances from both sides

Grievances from the European Union

The EU has criticized China for its human rights record. As trade increases, the EU has also voiced grievances about unfair trade, intellectual property rights protection, and illegal immigration with China.

Grievances from China

China has its own grievances against the EU, which are that the EU has refused to recognize China's full market economy status, WTO new member status, and developing country status.

The worsening trade imbalance

The trade imbalance

According to Chinese statistics, the EU maintained a trade surplus with China up to 1996 (USD60 million). From 1997 onwards, the trade imbalance tipped in favor of China, mainly because of the 10 new EU members that joined in 1997. Using China's accession to the WTO as a baseline, in the prior five years (1997–2001), the EU had a relatively small deficit with China, at a maximum of just over USD7 billion. From 2002 onwards, EU's trade deficit with China continued to expand on a yearly basis (see Table 6.9).

China's trade surplus with Europe almost doubled every year since China's 2001 accession to the WTO. In 2007 it rose to a record high of USD134.2 billion. In the four years between 2004 and 2007, although Chinese imports from the EU grew at the fast pace of 32.3%, 4.9%, 22.7%, and 22.9%, respectively, the growth in Chinese exports to the EU was even faster, at the rates of 48.5%, 34.1%, 26.6%, and 34.7%. (Note that there were macro-economic controls imposed in 2005 to cool down the heated domestic investment environment, which caused imports to grow at only 4.9% that year.)

Similar to the debate over the trade deficit between China and the U.S., there are also statistical discrepancies between China and the EU in the calculation of the trade deficit. The EU categorizes re-exports through Hong Kong as an export from China. Therefore, from the European point of view, it runs an alarmingly

Table 6.9. Trade between China and the European Union, 1994–2007

Year	Trade Volume (USD100 million)	Year-on-year growth rate (%)	Export (USD100 million)	Year-on-year growth rate (%)	Import (USD100 million)	Year-on-year growth rate (%)	Imbalance (USD100 million)
1994	339.7	—	153.9	—	185.8	—	-31.9
1995	403.5	18.8	191.0	24.1	212.5	14.1	-21.5
1996	397.2	-1.6	198.3	3.8	198.9	-6.5	-0.6
1997	430.0	8.3	238.1	20.1	191.9	-3.4	46.2
1998	488.6	13.6	281.5	18.2	207.1	7.9	74.4
1999	556.8	13.9	302.1	7.3	254.7	22.7	47.4
2000	690.4	24.0	381.9	26.4	308.5	21.1	73.4
2001	766.4	11.0	408.9	7.1	357.2	15.7	51.7
2002	867.6	13.2	482.1	17.9	385.4	7.9	96.7
2003	1,252.2	44.4	721.5	49.7	530.6	37.7	190.9
2004	1,772.8	41.6	1,071.6	48.5	701.2	32.2	370.4
2005	2,173.1	22.6	1,437.1	34.1	735.9	4.9	701.2
2006	2,723.0	25.3	1,819.8	26.6	903.2	22.7	916.6
2007	3,561.5	30.8	2,451.9	34.7	1,109.6	22.9	1,342.3

Source: Compiled from data from the General Administration of Customs.

large trade deficit with China (see Table 6.10). Based on the EU calculation, its trade deficit with China started much earlier in 1992 as opposed to in 1997 in China's statistics. In addition, the size of the deficit is much larger based on the EU calculation, at USD217.8 billion as opposed to the Chinese estimate of USD134.2 billion. China alleges that the EU has purposely exaggerated the size of its deficit. This issue has become the main controversy between the two trading partners.

Main reasons for the trade imbalance

The development of China as a global manufacturing hub has played a key role in the profit maximization and cost minimization of Western multinationals. The multinationals have built a value chain such that production processes can be outsourced or allocated to different locations around the world where the factors of production are available at a lowest cost. As one economist put it,[4] China offers the unique combination of first-class infrastructure and third-rate labor, which enabled it to become a key participant in the globalized division of

Table 6.10. Differences in Chinese and EU statistics on bilateral trade balance, 1992–2007 (USD100 million)

Year	Balance based on Chinese statistics	Balance based on EU statistics	Difference
1992	–21.8	128.8	150.6
1993	–27.0	106.2	133.2
1994	–31.9	135.3	167.2
1995	–21.5	154.6	176.1
1996	–0.6	198.8	199.4
1997	46.2	242.1	195.9
1998	74.4	276.3	201.9
1999	47.4	322.9	275.5
2000	73.4	412.6	339.2
2001	51.7	451.6	399.9
2002	96.7	511.4	414.7
2003	190.9	717.0	526.1
2004	370.4	992.0	621.6
2005	701.2	1316.5	615.3
2006	916.6	1592.4	675.8
2007	1342.3	2177.6	835.3

Source: General Administration of Customs and EUROSTAT.

labor. Looking at the main Chinese exports causing the Chinese trade surplus, these are mainly office and communication equipment and textiles and apparel. In the fastest-growing export category of electrical goods and machinery, China is responsible for the low value-added processing and assembly, while the foreign-invested enterprises in China are the dominant players in those industries. (Two-thirds of China's exports are from foreign-invested enterprises and most of them are produced under foreign brands, see Table 6.11.

As a matter of fact, China is often only responsible for a low value-added process towards the end of manufacturing. Despite the ubiquitous "Made in China" label, China does not gain as high returns from manufacturing as some in the West might imagine. In contrast, leading advanced nations such as the EU nations, the U.S., and Japan have completed the high value-added R&D and organization of the supply chain. Therefore, the label should more accurately read "Made by the World" instead of "Made in China." The belief held by some countries that they are threatened by China, or that they should fear China, would seem to be unwarranted.

Table 6.11. The contribution of processing trade and exports of foreign-invested enterprises to China's trade surplus, 2000–2007

Percentage (%)	2000	2001	2002	2003	2004	2005	2006	2007
Surplus of processing trade as a percentage of total surplus	89.1	91.6	88.2	99.3	98.6	78.2	106.0	95.1
Surplus of foreign-invested enterprises' exports as a percentage of total surplus	63.6	67.9	70.1	74.1	77.8	81.0	48.3	54.6

Source: National Bureau of Statistics.

As many EU countries are welfare states, their consumption represent a higher proportion of GDP and require a large volume of industrial finished goods. China's low cost environment for this type of products creates a competitive advantage. This puts the EU in a strong position in its trade with China. According to estimates by the European Central Bank, there was a 16% decrease between 2001 and 2004 in the prices paid by European industries to import goods from China.[5] As a result, European consumers have stronger buying power. This is a positive development in the face of global inflationary pressures and a shortage of resources. In contrast, China is a low income country with limited buying power to purchase the high technology and high-end products exported from Europe. Where China wishes to buy high technology from the EU, the embargo on products for military use has been an obstacle.

Therefore, the EU's trade deficit with China is likely to continue as the conditions described above are unlikely to change in the near future. In fact, globalization and the global division of labor by the multinationals have also caused the trade deficit that China has with Japan, South Korea, Taiwan, and ASEAN. The trade deficit China has with Asian trading partners grew from USD40 billion in 2000 to USD171.2 billion in 2007. Meanwhile the trade surplus China has with the EU and the U.S. was USD297.6 billion. This means that China's surplus earned from trade with the EU and the U.S. is then transferred to the Asian trading partners in China's trade deficit. By these calculations, China believes that it is unfair for the EU and the U.S. to criticize China for its large trade surpluses. From China's perspective, the trade imbalances are a result of the way global supply chains are organized.

Furthermore, the discussion about the EU's trade deficit with China should

Table 6.12. Trade balance between China and its major trading partners, 2005–2007 (USD100 million)

Trading partner	2005			2006			2007		
	Export	Import	Balance	Export	Import	Balance	Export	Import	Balance
ASEAN	553.7	749.9	–196.2	713.1	895.3	–182.2	941.8	1,083.7	141.9
European Union	1,437.1	736.0	701.1	1,819.8	903.2	916.6	2,451.9	1,109.6	1,342.3
Japan	839.9	1,004.5	–164.6	916.4	1,157.2	–240.8	1,020.7	1,339.5	318.8
South Korea	351.1	768.2	–417.1	445.3	897.8	–452.5	561.4	1,037.6	476.2
Taiwan	165.5	746.8	–581.3	207.4	871.1	–663.7	234.6	1,010.2	775.6
The U.S.	1,629.0	487.3	1,141.7	2,034.7	592.1	1,442.6	2,327.0	693.8	1,633.2

Source: Compiled from data from the Ministry of Commerce in relevant years.

not neglect the vast profits of EU-invested enterprises in China. According to the *2006 World Investment Report*, developed countries' outbound FDI accounts for 83.11% of global FDI. While the foreign investment garners its return, part of the investment has replaced trade and therefore added to the trade imbalance. For example, a significant portion of the EU investment in China is to reach the Chinese market by placing production in China. This replaces the need to export EU-produced goods to China, and adds to the trade imbalance.

Foreign multinationals that have entered China during the past three decades have enjoyed a high return on their investments and many of them of called China their "second home." For example, the Dusseldorf, Germany-headquartered machinery producer in the steel industry SMS Demag stated

Fig. 6.1. Export of EU-invested enterprises in China

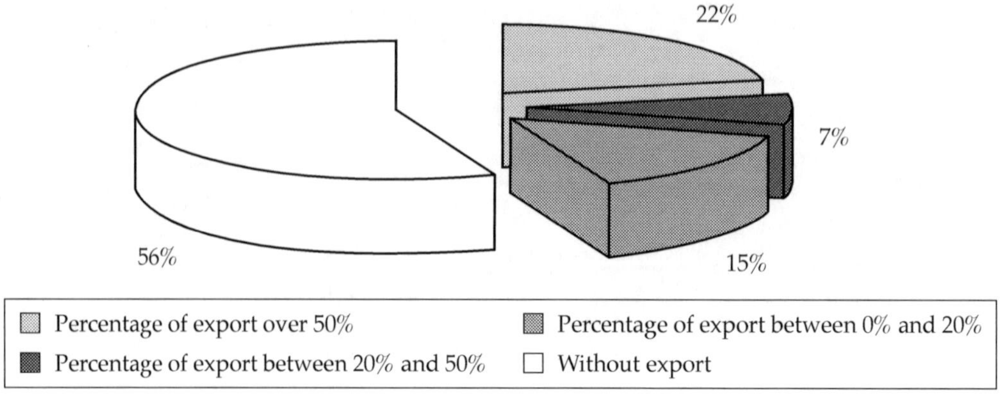

Source: A National Development and Reform Commission survey of 807 EU-invested enterprises in China.

that 40% of its revenues come from China.[6] Some foreign-invested enterprises also take a part of the slim profit margins made by the processing and assembly industry in China. These dynamics of foreign investment are not captured in the data regarding the trade balance. If we take the bigger picture, the Western multinationals are the true winners of the globalization process. Criticisms about China benefiting from a large trade surplus with the EU only serve to obscure the enormous dividends paid to EU multinationals for their investments in China.

The increasingly serious anti-dumping issue

Main features

Anti-dumping cases lodged by the EU against China have increased in frequency and in value, and have widened in products and sectors involved. From China's perspective, the EU has also put in place stronger discriminatory measures in the name of anti-dumping.

In regards to the increasing frequency of cases, China has been consistently the top country to be a subject of anti-dumping complaints lodged by the EU. In 2006, the EU raised 12 anti-dumping cases against Chinese exports, a 50% increase from the previous year. The EU is the WTO member that has raised the largest number of cases against China. However, as India and other developing

Table 6.13. Top 10 countries or regions in EU launched anti-dumping cases, 1995–2006

Subject country (or region)	Number of anti-dumping investigations	Percentage of total EU launched cases in the same period (%)
China	72	19.89
India	28	7.73
Indonesia	12	3.31
Malaysia	15	4.41
Russia	18	4.97
South Korea	26	7.18
Taiwan	21	5.80
Thailand	17	4.70
Ukraine	12	3.31
The U.S.	11	3.04

Source: WTO website, cited in *Shijie jingji yanjiu* 世界經濟研究 (World Economic Study) 5 (2008).

countries have started using the WTO mechanisms to raise anti-dumping cases against China, the EU has fallen a few notches since the 1980s in the ranking of countries that have taken anti-dumping actions against China.

Second, in regards to the widening products allegedly dumped, these are typically products for which China has a competitive advantage. Steel, electric machinery, chemicals, and textiles are the main sectors. Color TVs, auto parts, strawberries, garlic, and leather shoes have been the main products. As China attempts an industrial upgrade to shift its main exports from low value-added products to high value-added ones, the EU's anti-dumping cases seemed to cover both of these types of products.

Third, the value of these cases has increased. Among cases that involve more than USD100 million, the EU accounts for the largest number and shows an increasing trend.

In these cases, the EU typically uses the price of the goods sold in a third country to calculate the true price of the produce and the extent of the dumping. The EU has typically rejected information provided by the alleged dumping Chinese firms about the cost structures of their production in China, on the grounds that Chinese firms have enjoyed government subsidies. From the Chinese point of view, these are discriminatory measures on the part of the EU. Meanwhile, the EU maintains that the calculation of the true price is a technical issue, and because the anti-dumping cases account for only 0.5% of bilateral trade, they are by no means discriminatory.

The relevant authority in the EU to investigate anti-dumping cases has grown from a staff of seven people to over 200 people today. In response, China has also used WTO mechanisms including anti-dumping cases in order to protect its industries against unfair trade practices by other countries.

Reasons behind the anti-dumping conflict

Former EU Commissioner Peter Mandelson has stated many times that the EU will use anti-dumping duties against the trade barriers set up by China. On one hand, the Chinese perspective on this issue is that the EU has re-framed its concerns about the rising Chinese economy into allegations of anti-dumping.

First, allegations of unfair trade in China are in fact directed at the government and the public sector's involvement in Chinese companies. Second, these allegations are also a reflection of the general insecurities in Europe about the rising economy of China. As the Chinese industrial sector moves from low value-added production to providing higher value-added goods and services, some Chinese companies have tried to enter the EU market, specifically in the market segment of high-end, high quality brand name goods. This new force of competition has unsettled the EU. It therefore re-frames the issue into "unfair trade" and "dumping," and uses anti-dumping measures to curb the wave of Chinese products entering the EU. No wonder the German media had once said that "anti-dumping has become the largest trade barrier."[7]

On the other hand, Chinese exporters have often used low prices in order to enter a new market and gain market share. However, they have not realized that their extremely low prices would then invite anti-dumping allegations. Most unfortunately, some Chinese exporters have relied on low prices without understanding that their long-term competitive advantage could only be strengthened through better R&D, higher quality of products, better after-sale service, or innovative marketing and public relations. Instead, their insistence and eagerness for short-term gain has led to anti-dumping cases against their products.

Overall, anti-dumping cases and measures only account for a very small proportion of bilateral trade, although the number of cases lodged by the EU against China are bound to increase as Europe continues to be sensitive about China's strengthening economy. From a Chinese perspective, these anti-dumping cases may be a natural consequence of the growing volume of bilateral trade and the EU's comfort level with China, and therefore there is no need to make this issue over-politicized or exaggerated.

The controversy over China's "full market economy status"

Source of the controversy

In the course of negotiations for China's WTO accession, the U.S., EU, and Japan have insisted that China as a government-led trading entity should be considered a "non-market economy" in relation to WTO anti-dumping investigations. China eventually accepted the terms that in the first 15 years of WTO accession, China would be considered a "non-market economy" for the purposes of anti-dumping assessments.[8]

Definition by the European Union

Unlike the U.S., the EU has not devised criteria for classifying any country as a non-market economy. Instead, it simply lists out the countries. This is a pragmatic method that allows EU institutions to avoid any burden of explaining or proving any country's non-market economy status, and allows the EU greater freedom in its arbitration with these non-market economies.

In April 1998, the EU passed an amendment[9] to remove China and Russia from the list of non-market economy countries. However, their full market economy status was not immediately recognized, and instead they were added into the category of "special market economy countries."[10] In November 2002, the EU officially recognized Russia's full market economy status, removing all restrictions on non-market economies for Russia. Debate and tensions over the EU's refusal to recognize full market economy status for China are still ongoing.

The root causes of the EU opposition

General situation of recognition of full market economy status for China

Through economic, political, and diplomatic channels, China has sought "full market economy" status recognition from other countries. Since April 2004 when New Zealand was the first to recognize China as a full market economy, a total of 77 countries have done the same as of February 2008. Also, some countries have not officially recognized China as a full market economy but have, on a micro level, granted part of the full market economy treatment to China. In fact, the EU is a prime example.

The real reasons for EU's refusal to recognize the full market economy

Economic considerations

The EU runs a large trade deficit with China, which the EU attributes to unfair trade practices. The EU has continued to demand that China improves its implementation of WTO accession commitments, including strengthening its protection of intellectual property rights, further opening of the market, and eliminating sector-specific support and protection for its domestic industries. The "full market economy" status is a bargaining chip for the EU in negotiating with China.

Political considerations

The EU is also using the "full market economy status" to achieve political outcomes. As Willem van de Geest, director of the Europe Institute for Asian Studies, pointed out, the granting of full market economy status to Russia in 2004 was a typical politicization of an economic issue.[11] China has twice officially sought the European Commission to recognize the "full market economy" status of China and has been refused both times. Reasons given for the first refusal in June 2004 were that China lacked a complete accounting law and bankruptcy law; the export of resources in China are controlled by non-market systems; there is inadequate protection of intellectual property rights; and the financial system and capital-raising mechanisms are not up to market economy standards. China asserts that Russia did not have to prove these points when its full market status was recognized.

EU anti-dumping measures

The relationship between China's non-market status and EU anti-dumping cases

Whether a complainant WTO member can adopt anti-dumping measures against imports from the respondent country is determined by whether the "material damage" caused on the complainant is caused by the imports. There is arguably no relationship between China's non-market status and whether the EU will win or lose its anti-dumping investigations. The non-market status only determines whether a developed or developing country would be used to compare to China in the process of trying to assess the scale of the dumping activity. If a developing country is used, the extent of dumping tends to be exaggerated.

"Non-market status" would not reduce the number of anti-dumping cases

Between 1995 and 2005, South Korea and the U.S. were ranked second and third in being the subject of the most anti-dumping cases. Even though South Korea is recognized as a full market economy, it was the subject of almost as many anti-dumping cases as there were for China. Therefore, even after recognizing China's full market economy status, the EU would have the same mechanisms to raise anti-dumping investigations against imports from China.

The full market economy status does not resolve all China-EU trade friction

Even after China is recognized as a full market economy, there will be other sources of friction with the EU. These may be anti-subsidy measures, technical trade barriers, intellectual property rights protection, and product quality. Trade friction between China and the EU would not be resolved overnight.

The non-market economy status has not been the main reason for China losing anti-dumping cases

Chinese enterprises setting too low a price for their exports is the main reason. Many Chinese companies in fact wish to compete by cutting their prices, sometimes even to levels lower than their production costs. When such exports also meet the criteria of dumping, such as causing material damage to the importing country's economy, then there are grounds for anti-dumping cases.

The Chinese firms also have an inadequate capability to respond to the dumping allegations. The EU side has a high rate of success in its anti-dumping allegations against Chinese exporters because Chinese exporters have been particularly passive in responding and defending themselves. The usual practice is that, if the respondent has made a reasonable or proactive effort to respond, the anti-dumping duties awarded to the complainant would be a fraction of what was originally claimed.[12] However, if Chinese companies decline to respond it could result in a higher award of anti-dumping duties. In the long term, the Chinese companies would risk losing their market shares in the EU.

As political economist Susan Strange has said, international commerce cannot be explained by market dynamics and demand and supply. Instead, it is a mix of economic and political influences. Economics cannot be separated from politics.[13]

Therefore, the debate over China's full market economy status is conducted against a backdrop of global economics and politics. China's staggering economic growth makes the EU and other developed countries wish to use the international rules of the game to encourage China to further integrate its trade practices and regulatory environment with the rest of the world.

After more than 30 years of development, China-EU trade and economic relations have reached a stage of maturity and stability. Intractable issues and the occasional friction have not dampened the continued growth in bilateral relations. The two trading partners have built a strong foundation for cooperation and would be expected to find new and innovative ways of forging closer economic ties in the 21st century.

7 Chapter

Economic Relations between China and ASEAN

The Association of Southeast Asian Nations (ASEAN) was formed on August 8, 1967 by Indonesia, Thailand, Singapore, the Philippines, and Malaysia. The foreign ministers of the four countries and the deputy prime minister of Malaysia met in Bangkok and signed the *Bangkok Declaration*, the founding document of ASEAN. To date, ASEAN has included all 10 countries in Southeast Asia. Brunei joined in 1984, Vietnam in 1995, Laos and Myanmar in 1997, and Cambodia in 1999.

If ASEAN were a single entity, it would rank as the 9th largest economy in the world. The Southeast Asia region covers 4.5 million km^2 of land, 510 million in population, and a nominal GDP of USD1.8 trillion in 2010. The nations making up ASEAN have abundant natural resources provided by tropical geography, ocean, and forests. And they are the world's largest producers of rubber, palm oil, tin, and semul, and important suppliers of rice, petroleum, timber, manganese, and aluminum.

Because of the strategic geographical locations of ASEAN countries, the stability and prosperity of the region has political, economic, and security implications for the rest of the world. The region borders the Pacific and Indian Oceans, and is located between Asia and Australasia. The Straits of Malacca, which connects the two oceans, is on one of the world's most important shipping lanes. There are many islands and archipelagos in the region, involving complex shipping routes and several deep harbors, among which Singapore has emerged as a leading entrepôt in the world.

China and ASEAN are neighbors that have developed close relations since the end of the Cold War. Today, this relationship has entered a golden age.

Overview

China-ASEAN relations had a rocky start. When ASEAN was established in August 1967, China was at the height of the Cultural Revolution and in the midst of the Cold War between the American and Soviet blocs. ASEAN and China had ideological and political differences, and viewed each other with enmity. Indonesia, which had been the only ASEAN member with diplomatic relations to China, announced it would sever diplomatic ties with China just two months after ASEAN was formed. ASEAN countries then each implemented a trade embargo on China.

China adjusted its policy towards ASEAN when Sino-U.S. relations improved and the international geopolitical environment stabilized. In fact, China made it a priority to forge closer relations with neighboring countries. By 1991, all 10

ASEAN countries had established or resumed diplomatic relations with China. Since then, China engaged in closer cooperation with ASEAN, going from a consulting partner to a full dialogue partner and finally to a strategic partner (see Table 7.1).

Table 7.1. Seventeen years of China-ASEAN economic cooperation

Date	Event
July 1991	Chinese Foreign Minister Qian Qishen was invited to participate in the ASEAN Ministerial Meeting which began China-ASEAN dialogue
July 1992	China became a Consulting Partner of ASEAN
July 1996	China became a full Dialogue Partner of ASEAN
1999–2000	China and all ASEAN member countries signed and issued the *China-ASEAN Framework Agreement*
2000	At the 4th China-ASEAN Summit, China proposed the establishment of a China-ASEAN Free Trade Area
2001	China and ASEAN set up a new mechanism for cooperation: the China-ASEAN Business Council
November 2001	Consensus regarding the China-ASEAN Free Trade Area was reached at the 5th China-ASEAN Summit. The Free Trade Area will be completed in 10 years.
November 2002	At the 6th China-ASEAN Summit, the *China-ASEAN Framework Agreement on Comprehensive Economic Cooperation* was signed, forming the basis of the Free Trade Area. Negotiation on the establishment of the Free Trade Area started after the summit.
January 2003	Negotiation on the Free Trade Zone focused on concrete issues.
October 2003	Several milestone documents were signed at the 7th China-ASEAN Summit, including the *Joint Declaration on China-ASEAN Strategic Partnership for Peace and Prosperity*, the *Southeast Asia Cooperation Treaty* and a supplementary agreement to the *Framework Agreement for Comprehensive Economic Cooperation* were signed. A strategic partnership was started between China and ASEAN.
October 2003	The Early Harvest Program was implemented.
January 2004	The Early Harvest Program was fully implemented, opening the market for 500 types of agricultural products and reducing tariffs for 570 processed agricultural products and an additional 30 products.
November 2004	Two important agreements were signed at the 8th China-ASEAN Summit. They relate to cargo trade and dispute settlement mechanisms for the Free Trade Area.

(Cont'd)

Date	Event
July 2005	The cargo trade agreement went into effect. Tariffs were reduced to around 20% for the first group of 7,445 products. Average Chinese tariffs for the six ASEAN majors were reduced to 8.1%, a lower rate than the most-favored nation treatment by 1.8%.
2006	The *Joint Statement of the China-ASEAN Commemorative Summit* was signed to celebrate 15 years of dialogue between China and ASEAN.
January 2007	China and ASEAN signed the *Service Trade Agreement for the Free Trade Area*.
July 2007	The *Service Trade Agreement* went into effect after the legal review process in each country.
Planned for 2010	Zero tariffs for the majority of goods traded between China and six ASEAN majors.
Planned for 2015	Zero tariffs for the majority of goods traded between China and the other four ASEAN members.

Source: Yin Shengnan 尹聖男, "Zhongguo yu Dongmeng jingmou guanxi de fazhanqianjing" 中國與東盟經貿關係的發展前景 (The Future Prospects of China-ASEAN Economic and Trade Relations), *Heilongjiang duiwai Jingmou* 黑龍江對外經貿 (Heilongjiang External Trade) 9 (2007).

First phase, 1991–1996

The years 1991 to 1996 marked the foundation of economic and trade cooperation between China and ASEAN. In July 1991, China's Foreign Minister Qian Qishen was invited to attend the 24th ASEAN Ministerial Meeting in Kuala Lumpur. This was China's first official engagement with ASEAN. In July 1994, China became a founding member of the ASEAN Forum, a regional security mechanism. In 1996, China's status in relation to ASEAN was upgraded from Consulting Partner to Full Dialogue Partner. These developments allowed China to build closer economic and trade ties with the six early members and the four later or prospective members of ASEAN.

Second phase, 1997–2000

In the wake of the Asian Financial Crisis, a "10+1" mechanism for dialogue was established in December 1997. China and ASEAN members issued a joint statement to confirm their "neighborly partnership of mutual trust for the 21st century." Since then, every autumn, China and ASEAN hold a senior level summit to discuss economic, political, and security cooperation. New initiatives have been launched every year. In 1999 and 2000, China signed a framework agreement individually with the 10 ASEAN member countries, confirming bilateral cooperation and long-term, stable relations on a foundation of neighborly relations and mutual trust. Cooperation was further deepened in 2000 when China signed an agreement with ASEAN to mutually promote and protect investment in each other's countries.

Third phase, 2001 to present

In November 2011 at the 5th China-ASEAN Summit, consensus was reached on building a China-ASEAN Free Trade Area within 10 years. In 2002, a framework agreement for the Free Trade Area was signed. This was a historic milestone in China-ASEAN relations. In the same year, the Declaration on the Conduct of the Parties in the South China Sea was signed. In 2003, China joined the Southeast Asia Cooperation Treaty. A *Joint Declaration on a Strategic Partnership for Peace and Prosperity* was also signed in 2003. These steps provided political safeguards that enabled further economic cooperation.

Progress and concrete plans for setting up the Free Trade Area followed. A *Plan of Action* was signed in 2004, outlining cooperation projects and objectives for 2005–2010. A *Service Trade Agreement* was signed in 2007. These agreements formed the basis for effective cooperation in the Free Trade Area.

The China-ASEAN Free Trade Area

Background

The concept of an "East Asia Free Trade Area" was floated early in the 1994 ASEAN Summit. The ASEAN members had realized that Southeast Asia was only a subregional organization, and it would have to expand its economic sphere to include China, Japan, and Korea in order to ensure regional sustainable development. However, ASEAN had an unrealistic vision of the East Asia Free Trade Area, believing that ASEAN should take a dominant role in the region. The reality is that ASEAN cannot represent the political, economic, and security interests of the East Asian region of 13 countries and 2 billion people. Moreover, rivalry between Japan and Korea caused the abandonment of the East Asia Free Trade Area concept in its earlier form.

The idea of a regional free trade zone nonetheless persisted. Regional economic cooperation had become inevitable in globalization, and China's WTO accession raised concerns from ASEAN about Chinese competition in exports and attracting foreign direct investment. The China-ASEAN Free Trade Zone was born out of these considerations. Although it covers a smaller area than the earlier concept, it is believed to be more practical.

Main content

The China-ASEAN *Framework Agreement on Comprehensive Economic Cooperation* was signed in November 2002 at the "10+1" China-ASEAN Summit held in Phnom Penh, Cambodia. A framework for the Free Trade Area was outlined—free trade would take place between China and the six original members of ASEAN by 2010, and be extended to the four new members of ASEAN by 2015. The main content of the Free Trade Area includes the following:

Reduced tariffs

According to the level of economic development in each member country, different schedules of tariff reduction were devised.[1]

The latest date to start reducing tariffs for agricultural products was set for early 2004, and the completion date was set for the end of 2006, thus giving member countries at least three years for implementation.

Eliminating trade barriers

China and ASEAN pledged to gradually remove trade barriers. Trade facilitation measures would be implemented, including the simplification and coordination of tariff levying procedures, transport, and a certification and verification system. Trade protection policies towards non-members of the Free Trade Area would remain.

Allowing exception clauses

China had announced in 2001 privileged treatment in tariffs for Laos, Cambodia, and Myanmar, aiming to increase the export of Chinese goods into these three countries. It also offered most favored nation treatment to non-WTO members in ASEAN. Other favorable treatment was given to the less developed members of ASEAN, outlined in the Early Harvest Program of the Free Trade Area. Under the scheme, China provided USD5 million in financing for a sediment removal project in the Mekong River. As part of foreign aid, China was also the contractor that constructed one-third of the Laos section of the Kunming-Bangkok Highway.

Free trade of services

China and ASEAN would cooperate in the areas of finance, tourism, investment, agriculture, human resources development, industrial cooperation, intellectual property rights, environmental protection, forestry, and energy. Five main areas of focus were identified: agriculture, human resources development, information technology, investment, and development of the Mekong River region.

Results achieved

The 11-country Free Trade Area promotes economic integration in the region and creates a new emerging force in the global economy.

Negotiations for the liberalization of trade and investment have been conducted in earnest since the Free Trade Area was agreed upon in 2000. More concrete negotiations followed as the Early Harvest Program commenced, first applying to Thailand in January 1, 2004 and extended to other ASEAN members in September that year. Agreements on cargo trade and on the dispute settlement mechanism were also signed in 2004, the latter of which provided a legal basis for resolving disputes in the future.

The China-ASEAN Free Trade Area officially started to operate in 2005. Tariff reduction started on July 20, when the first batch of 7,445 types of goods enjoyed a roughly 20% reduction in tariffs. China lowered its tariffs to 8.1% for the six original ASEAN members, which was 1.8% lower than most favored nation treatment. By 2010, tariffs for the majority of products traded between China and the four new ASEAN members were reduced to zero.

Expanding cooperation beyond the trade in goods to cover free trade in services was a significant step in the China-ASEAN Free Trade Area. Based on WTO accession commitments, China liberalized market access for ASEAN countries in the areas of construction, environmental protection, transportation, sports, and commercial services. ASEAN companies were granted easier access in setting up wholly owned enterprises or joint ventures in China. Shareholding requirements for setting up companies in China were relaxed for ASEAN investors.

ASEAN countries also made new commitments based on their WTO accession conditions. Singapore liberalized the service trade in commercial services, distribution, education, finance, medicine, entertainment, sports and recreation services, and transportation. Malaysia made commitments in the sectors of commercial services, telecommunications, construction, finance, medicine, tourism, and transportation. For Thailand, the sectors included professional services, construction and engineering, education, tourism and transportation. For the Philippines, they were commercial services, telecommunications, construction and engineering, environment and tourism. Brunei's sectors were tourism and transportation, whereas Indonesia's were construction and engineering, tourism and energy. Other ASEAN countries including Cambodia, Laos, and Myanmar also pledged to open to different extents the sectors of commercial services, telecommunications, construction, finance, tourism, and transportation. The *Service Trade Agreement* has thus been a catalyst for liberalizing the service trade in the region.

Closer ties in the broader region also enabled other formats of cooperation between China and the individual countries in Southeast Asia. China and Vietnam have proposed the "two corridors and one circle" economic cooperation strategy, while the Asian Development Bank has proposed and supported the "Economic Cooperation of the Mekong River Subregion. The area between Nanning, Guangxi, and Singapore is also considered an economic corridor.

Negotiations on the free flow of investments are underway, based on the foundation of the agreements on cargo and service trade. At the same time, the agreement on the dispute settlement mechanism defines the rule of the game. These elements create a complete framework of the Free Trade Area.

The Role of China and ASEAN in the Economic Integration of East Asia

The role of China

Up until the 1990s, the regional cooperation of East Asia has been underdeveloped and it very clearly lags behind cooperation that exists in other regions. It was the Asian Financial Crisis in July 1997 that highlighted the extent to which the regional economy was already highly interlinked, and prompted the acceleration of frameworks including the "10+3" (including Japan and Korea), "10+1" (including China), the cooperation among China, Japan, and Korea, and ASEAN.

China started to adopt a much more proactive approach to regional cooperation, especially after WTO accession. At the same time, ASEAN became more interested in cooperation with China, as some member countries feared that a stronger Chinese economy would undermine their interests, and others wanted to take advantage of opportunities offered. This set off a competitive atmosphere in which various countries sought to participate or lead the regional economic integration. After China and ASEAN announced the Free Trade Area, Japan and Korea changed their previously lukewarm attitude and signed cooperation agreements with ASEAN.

In theory, China is best qualified for a leadership role in East Asia regional cooperation. China sits on the United Nations Security Council. China wields enormous influence in East Asia as it is the largest market in the region and is supporting the formation of the China-ASEAN Free Trade Area.

However, China does not wish to seek a leadership role in East Asia, and prefers to focus on domestic development instead. Japan has also objected to a Chinese leadership of regional economic integration. Therefore, China has chosen to adopt a practical and results-oriented approach towards the East Asia cooperation, the prime example of which is building the China-ASEAN Free Trade Area.

The role of ASEAN

Traditionally, East Asia and Southeast Asia were seen as different regions. Singapore's former prime minister Lee Kuan-yew had once stated that he defined East Asia as South Korea, North Korea, Japan, China, and Vietnam, whereas Southeast Asia was a different region with a hybrid of Chinese and Indian cultures. However, the Asian Financial Crisis of 1997 highlighted the interdependency in the East Asian and Southeast Asian region, when China, Japan, Korea, as well as Hong Kong and Taiwan were widely affected by the collapse of the Thai baht. ASEAN then realized that it would be wise to consider Southeast Asia as part of the East Asian region, and to take an active role in driving the development of the whole region.

ASEAN has since taken a formal leadership role in driving economic cooperation in the broader East Asian region. This is unusual for a subregional organization. We believe that this can be explained by the following three factors:

First, ASEAN's leadership role is a result of the geopolitical balance of power among China, Japan, and Korea. In terms of economic prowess, either China or Japan would be qualified as the leader of the region. Even if we take into account those who hesitate to see one nation dominating a region, it would still be safe to say that China and Japan should take joint leadership and joint responsibility in regional development. However, as discussed above, China does not wish to, and is not able to, take full leadership.

Meanwhile, Japan's credibility as a leader of East Asia would be challenged due to historical reasons, the Japanese attitude towards its historical legacy, and developments in its domestic politics. There have been concerns over Japanese nationalism that have been manifested in its economic policies, in particular when Japan requires harsh conditions in return for foreign aid. In terms of politics, Japan's alliance with the United States has raised concerns that the two countries may join efforts in obstructing China's peaceful development. In bilateral relations with China, Japan has refused to cooperate. In its plans for regional economic cooperation, Japan has put its relationship with China in the lowest priority. The lukewarm attitude towards China can be seen both in the 2002 *Japan Free Trade Agreement Strategy* issued by the Japanese Ministry of Foreign Affairs and the 2006 *Global Economy Strategy* issued by the Japanese Ministry of Economy, Trade, and Industry. These two strategy documents both advocate the integration of East Asia in which Korea, ASEAN, and India would be the main partners in free trade and economic cooperation, while closer relations with China would only be considered in the medium to long term. The attitude of Japan towards its historical legacy has seriously affected its political relations with China and Korea. When Japan sought a leadership role in East Asia regional cooperation, it was met with wide opposition from various countries in the region.

Due to the above reasons which bar Japan and China from taking the leadership role, and because Korea alone does not have the substantial power to take the helm of regional cooperation, the leadership responsibility naturally fell upon the 10 nations of ASEAN. Either Japanese or Chinese leadership could lead to turmoil, as Singaporean foreign minister George Yong-boon Yeo put it. The stability of East Asia could only be ensured with ASEAN in the driver's seat.

Second, ASEAN has proactively sought the leadership role in promoting East Asia regional cooperation. The mechanisms of "10+1," "10+3," and East Asian Summits (EAS) have been initiated by ASEAN, and constructed so that ASEAN is the host and the other participating countries are invited guests.

Indeed, the idea of East Asian regional integration was first raised by ASEAN. In 1990, Malaysian prime minister Dr. Mahathir bin Mohamad was one of the earliest proponents of an East Asia Economic Group, but the idea was met with American opposition. Mahathir later resurrected the idea as the East Asia Economic Caucus, but efforts were thwarted again by opposition from the U.S. and ambivalence from Japan. The idea gained traction only after the 1997 Asian Financial Crisis. At the meeting of East Asia heads of states at the First Informal Summit in Kuala Lumpur in December 1997, the frameworks of ASEAN Plus One and ASEAN Plus Three were formalized. China, Japan, and Korea would be invited to participate while ASEAN would remain the official host.

While the spirit of cooperation remained, the format and mechanism of engagement were wide open to debate, during which ASEAN fought hard and stood its ground for taking a leadership role in East Asia integration. The final report of the East Asia Study Group, an expert panel comprising representatives from the ASEAN Plus Three countries proposed the blueprint for the process of regional cooperation in 2001 and passed the following year. Then, at the 2004 ASEAN Plus Three Summit, debate ensued over the roles played by member countries participating in the first East Asian Summit (EAS), which was scheduled to be held in 2005 in Kuala Lumpur. The final report of the East Asia Study Group originally suggested that ASEAN Plus Three countries would participate on an equal footing, and the EAS would be held at different locations rotating among the member countries. However, ASEAN members, and in particular Malaysia, were concerned that if ASEAN did not assume leadership, the EAS would simply be dominated by one of the bigger countries and ASEAN would become a tool of a dominant power. There were also questions over further broadening of the membership of EAS, to include Australia, New Zealand, and India. The possibility of more large countries that may participate in the future then raised even greater concern over diluting the power of ASEAN in the new East Asian Summit.

Therefore, ASEAN believed it should take a leadership role, that ASEAN countries would take turns hosting the EAS Summit, and would also take turns in the chairmanship role. Conditions were proposed for EAS membership. EAS memberships should have concrete political and economic relations with ASEAN, members should be Dialogue Partners of ASEAN, and have joined the Southeast Asia Cooperation Treaty. ASEAN insisted to be at the helm of East Asia regional cooperation as part of its strategy for survival and long-term development.

Third, ASEAN has several advantages that enable its leadership position. The Southeast Asian region possesses abundant natural resources, shows the potential for rapid economic growth, and occupies an important strategic position in regional security. It has also accumulated substantial experience in regional cooperation, and has been recognized for its political, economic, and security achievements. Therefore, ASEAN as an important subregional organization is well placed to assume leadership here. The larger nations of China, Japan, and Korea are also more comfortable with ASEAN's leading role.

ASEAN has adopted a balance of power policy by proactively building strong relations with the larger countries within East Asia. This can be considered an ingenious maneuver that allows for ASEAN, an organization comprising smaller nations and economies, to lead regional development in a region that includes much larger political and economic players. ASEAN's strategy has created a favorable external environment for development in Southeast Asia.

Future Trends of China-ASEAN Relations

The outcome of economic and trade cooperation

Developing the breadth and depth of cooperation

China and ASEAN have become the fourth largest trading partners for each other. ASEAN is also the fifth largest export market and third largest source of imports for China. In 1991, the China-ASEAN trade volume was USD8 billion. This figure increased by about 20% per year since then. In 2007, bilateral trade reached USD 202.5 billion, which increased 25.9% compared to the previous year. The objective of reaching USD200 billion in bilateral trade was reached three years ahead of schedule.

At the same time, there has been a reduction in the China-ASEAN trade deficit (see Table 7.2). As China opened its market to ASEAN countries, trade deficit grew rapidly, from USD4.83 billion in 2000 to USD16.5 billion in 2003 and further to USD20.08 billion in 2004. This was partly due to the Early Harvest Program. This program went into effect on January 1, 2004, implementing zero tariffs for trade in nearly 600 categories of goods in the customs code. China happens to be less competitive in these categories of goods compared to the ASEAN trading partners. For example, Thailand exported USD185 million in plant products to China in the first five months of 2004, creating a trade deficit of USD146 million for China, which increased 926.7% year-on-year.

China's appetite for raw materials also led to an increase in imports. In the first five months of 2004, China imported from Indonesia and Malaysia USD200 million and USD260 million in timber and related products, respectively, creating a trade deficit of USD448 million. Importing mining products created a deficit of USD1.94 billion in the same five months, a year-on-year increase of 142%. The trade deficit has declined gradually in recent years but remains significant, dropping to USD19.6 billion in 2005, and USD14.2 billion in 2007.

The five founding members of ASEAN, namely Singapore, Malaysia, Indonesia, the Philippines, and Thailand, are the larger trading partners with China. China has run a trade deficit with Malaysia, the Philippines, and Thailand, and a trade surplus with Singapore and Vietnam (see Table 7.3).

Table 7.3. Trade between China and ASEAN countries, 2007

Country	Import and export (USD100 million)	Year on year change (%)	Export (USD100 million)	Year on year change (%)	Import (USD100 million)	Year on year change (%)	2007 Trade balance (USD100 million)	2006 Trade balance (USD100 million)
ASEAN	2,025.08	25.9	941.39	32.0	1,083.69	21.0	–142.30	–182.08
Brunei	3.55	12.7	1.13	13.1	2.42	12.5	–1.29	–1.16
Cambodia	9.33	27.3	8.82	26.4	0.51	45.6	8.31	6.63
Indonesia	249.97	31.2	125.99	33.3	123.98	29.0	2.02	–1.56
Laos	2.49	13.9	1.64	–3.0	0.85	71.3	0.79	1.19
Malaysia	463.98	25.0	176.90	30.7	287.07	21.8	–110.17	-100.38
Myanmar	20.57	40.9	16.86	39.6	3.71	46.9	13.15	9.55
Singapore	471.53	15.4	296.34	27.8	175.19	–0.8	121.15	55.16
Thailand	346.38	24.9	119.74	22.6	226.65	26.2	–106.91	–81.94
The Philippines	306.14	30.8	74.98	30.7	231.16	30.8	–156.17	119.36
Vietnam	151.15	51.9	119.00	59.4	32.16	29.4	86.84	49.79

Source: Ministry of Commerce website, http://www.mofcom.gov.cn.

The types of goods traded between China and ASEAN used to be mostly primary goods and light textiles as of 1991, but is now more focused on industrial goods, in particular machinery and electronic goods. The two trading partners are complementing each other as ASEAN exports rubber, industrial raw materials, and energy to China, and imports electronic goods from China. They compete against each other in the manufacturing of textiles, but China is a net exporter of textiles to ASEAN. In 2007, China exported USD10.87 billion in textiles to ASEAN countries, a year-on-year increase of 53.1%. The competition between China and ASEAN countries in the textiles industry is a well-recognized trend. Indonesia has projected that Chinese textile exports to Indonesia would increase 380% in the next five years, resulting in reduced production or the closing of many factories in the textiles, apparel, and shoe industries. Meanwhile, tropical fruits from ASEAN countries are competing against the fruits produced in southern China.

The increase in bi-directional investment

Direct investment between China and ASEAN has steadily increased. ASEAN is now an attractive destination for Chinese enterprises "going global," while ASEAN countries are also major foreign direct investors in China.

Chinese investments in ASEAN

Chinese investment in ASEAN has been relatively low and yet shows a trend of significant potential and rapid growth. In 1991, the cumulative investment from China to ASEAN was USD150 million. In that year, China invested USD1.25 million in ASEAN. This figure has grown as a result of the Go Global policy. In 2006, China had USD336 million in non-financial investments in ASEAN, and a cumulative investment of USD1.59 billion. The above figures only cover those investments that had received approval or been registered with the Ministry of Commerce in China. The true figure should be higher if we could count the investment activities of private enterprises and small to medium enterprises, which are not normally registered with the Ministry of Commerce. It is estimated that there are more than 1,000 Chinese-invested non-financial companies in ASEAN countries, in sectors ranging from smaller projects in processing and production, to larger ones in construction, hotels, electronic goods, mining, and transportation. The mode of investment includes direct investment and development, as well as balance of trade (BOT). The main investment destinations are Thailand, Indonesia, Cambodia, Singapore, and Vietnam, accounting for 85% of total Chinese investment in ASEAN. In Cambodia, China has been the largest foreign investor for several consecutive years.

ASEAN Investments in China

ASEAN countries started investing in China in the 1980s. The flow of investment grew steadily from the late 1980s onwards, reaching a peak between 1993 and 1995. In 1995, ASEAN countries had investment contracts of USD11 billion in China, with an increasing amount of actual utilized investment. However, the situation reversed after the 1997 Asian Financial Crisis. In 1999, the actual utilized investment from ASEAN showed a sharp decline of 22% compared to 1998. In 2000, it again dropped 4.4%. There was a small rebound in 2001. Between 2004 and 2006, ASEAN investment in China fluctuated around USD3 billion. It showed a more significant recovery in 2007, reaching USD3.9 billion.

ASEAN investment in China comes mainly from the five original members of ASEAN, with Singapore in the lead. The investors are typically companies owned by overseas Chinese in these countries. Investment focused on the sectors of manufacturing, hotels, and real estate. In terms of geographic spread, ASEAN investment mainly went to the eastern coastal regions of China. They also tended to be medium- to small-sized projects.

Chinese international contracting and labor cooperation in ASEAN

ASEAN is a key market for Chinese international contracting and labor cooperation. Chinese contractors built electric power stations, bridges, highways, airports, piers, factories, office towers, and residential buildings in ASEAN countries. In 2005, the contract value of Chinese contracted construction work in ASEAN was USD35 billion, with a turnover of USD23.2 billion. In that year, Chinese contractors raked in a turnover of USD1.17 billion from Singapore, USD309 million from Thailand, USD275 million from Vietnam, USD183 million from the Philippines, and USD123 million from Cambodia.

Broadening economic cooperation

China-ASEAN cooperation was narrowly focused on agriculture and hydro power in the early days, but has since broadened to include human resources development, finance, tourism, transportation, telecommunications, and energy. The development of the Mekong River region is one of the more well-known projects. In 2004, China announced river transport, agriculture, and public health cooperation projects with countries along the Mekong. China has also provided aid to the highway system and dams of Laos and Thailand. Other forms of cooperation are as follows:

Transportation

In response to the needs of different ASEAN countries, cooperation in transportation has broadened from land transportation to sea transportation in recent years. The cooperation is focused on facilitating transportation traffic, protecting the environment in the sea, and developing human resources.

Economic growth areas

China has sent delegations to visit Brunei, Indonesia, and the Philippines in support of the development of the East ASEAN Economic Area (EAGA). These countries will become more important destinations for Chinese enterprises' Go Global efforts.

E-commerce

The Ministry of Commerce of China has organized training courses in e-commerce for ASEAN countries.

Information Industry Cooperation

A MoU for cooperation has been signed, and China has held several training courses for participants from ASEAN.

Aid

China has run many foreign aid projects with Cambodia, Laos, Vietnam, and Myanmar.

Technology

China has organized training courses in biotechnology and remote sensing technology, which were met with overwhelming demand.

Agriculture

A MoU has been signed in November 2002. Agriculture is one of the main focus areas of China-ASEAN cooperation.

Tourism

China and ASEAN are putting effort into combining tourism, trade promotion, and investment promotion. This is part of the "China-ASEAN Center" concept proposed by an ASEAN Plus Three meeting of tourism ministers.

Customs

The simplification of customs procedures and other trade facilitation measures are particularly important as the Free Trade Area is being set up. A MoU has been signed on this topic.

Education

There are more than 13,000 students from ASEAN countries studying in China. A MoU in education cooperation has been signed between China and over half of the ASEAN countries. There have been exchange programs for university presidents, as well as joint training courses in distance learning and Chinese teaching.

The outlook for China-ASEAN Free Trade Area

The China-ASEAN Free Trade Area has become a milestone initiative for both China and ASEAN. This section presents in detail the opportunities and threats involved.

The China-ASEAN Free Trade Area covers a region of 1.8 billion consumers and 14 million square kilometers. The population of this free trade zone, at close to 30% of the world's total population, would exceed that of the European Union and the *North American Free Trade Agreement* (NAFTA). Covering 10% of the world's land mass, the China-ASEAN Free Trade Area would cover more land than the European Union and would be second only to NAFTA.

The solid foundation of the China-ASEAN Free Trade Area

The China-ASEAN Free Trade Area is a cooperation framework that emerged out of a favorable environment: China's success in economic reforms and ASEAN's recovery from the Asian Financial Crisis. The preparation for constructing a free trade zone has already led to deepening trust among the countries. A *Declaration on the Conduct of the Parties in the South China Sea* was signed in 2002 between China and ASEAN countries. The *Southeast Asia Nuclear Weapon Free Zone Treaty* was proposed by China in 2006 and was welcomed by ASEAN. Programs to cooperate in disease control and natural disaster response have also been successfully held.

The Free Trade Zone itself has brought concrete economic benefits to the region, breaking down barriers of mistrust that previously existed in the region. For example, the Philippines withdrew from the Early Harvest Program out of concern over competition from Chinese agricultural products, but re-joined after the program's proven success for Thailand and Vietnam.

China's accession to the WTO and the subsequent economic growth generated further opportunities for the Free Trade Area. Since 2003, the Chinese economy has been growing at about 10% per year. According to a World Bank report, China's over 10% annual growth rate in the five years leading up to 2006 has created a strong economic foundation for the region.

Lastly, ASEAN has implemented free trade within Southeast Asia and has seen the benefits. Under the Common Effective Preferential Tariff (CEPT) scheme, ASEAN has implemented free trade within the subregion earlier than originally scheduled. In addition, investment and service trade have been liberalized in ASEAN. With this foundation, ASEAN actively negotiated free trade agreements with the U.S., Japan, Korea, India, and Australia, becoming an important economic player in the East Asian region. At the ASEAN Summit in January 2007, ASEAN decided to implement the ASEAN Free Trade Zone five years ahead of schedule, moving the completion date of full economic, political, social, and cultural integration from 2020 to 2015. At the same time, the deliberation and drafting process of an ASEAN charter is under way. These steps in strengthening the subregional organization will no doubt support the future development of the China-ASEAN Free Trade Area.

Problems and uncertainties with the China-ASEAN Free Trade Area

Despite the vast potential for regional cooperation, China and the 10 nations in ASEAN are each at a different level of economic development. Their objectives in cooperation and the ability for each country to contribute are therefore varied. Given internal problems and external uncertainties, the path of China-ASEAN regional cooperation might not be a smooth one.

Internal issues

Low and mutually competitive bilateral trade and investment

China and ASEAN are currently not the top trading partners for each other. China's largest trading and investment partners are Japan, the U.S., and the regions of Hong Kong, Macau, and Taiwan. ASEAN's largest trading and investment partners are Japan, the U.S., and Taiwan, South Korea, Hong Kong, and Singapore. The trade volume between China and ASEAN is relatively low. China-ASEAN trade accounts for 11% of the total trade volume of ASEAN and only about 7% of the total trade volume of China. Both trading partners are heavily dependent on the markets of the U.S. and Europe. Also, in terms of the types of goods traded, over half of the exports from China to ASEAN are electronic goods. These electronic goods are in fact produced by foreign-invested enterprises or multinationals with manufacturing operations in China, adding a layer of uncertainty for trade.

There has also been occasional trade friction between China and ASEAN. Protectionism has emerged in ASEAN. The framework agreement for the China-ASEAN Free Trade Area launched in 2003 specified that emergency measures can be taken to protect the goods of ASEAN countries if their competitiveness was undermined by Chinese exports leading to financial losses. From 2004 to 2005, Malaysia invoked this provision and imposed anti-dumping duties on bicycles produced by mainland China and Hong Kong.

Bilateral investments have also remained at very low levels, although the liberalization of service trade has not been fully implemented. Chinese investment only accounts for 0.5% of the total foreign investment in ASEAN. Although the Go Global policy of China promises faster growth in Chinese outbound investment, some ASEAN markets have opaque and unstable investment environments. For example, Vietnam's foreign investment implementation regulations categorize mining exploration, development, and deep processing as sectors encouraging foreign investment. However, Chinese investors have found the approval process for these sectors to be excessively complex, time-consuming, and uncertain. Many Chinese investors themselves also do not have adequate foreign investment experience, making it more difficult for them to deal with the uncertain investment environment in ASEAN countries.

China and ASEAN also compete with each other in producing a range of exports and in attracting foreign investment from the rest of the world:

- China and several ASEAN nations are at a similar stage of industrialization and have an export-oriented economy. Their exports are typically resource and labor intensive, such as textiles and apparel, shoes, processed food, and electronic products, or primary goods such as resources, raw materials, and agricultural products. The product categories and their quality are similar. This is a constraint to increasing trade between China and ASEAN.
- Developed countries in the West are the main export markets for both China and ASEAN. Over 50% of ASEAN exports are destined for the U.S., Japan, and EU countries. These markets also account for around 50% of Chinese exports. China and ASEAN therefore compete against each other in these export markets.
- China and ASEAN countries compete against each other for foreign investment, as they both have strong demand for foreign capital to support their economic development.

Vast differences among ASEAN members

The 10 nations of ASEAN are at vastly different stages of economic development, featuring different economic structures. The most advanced ASEAN country is Singapore, whose GDP per capita has exceeded USD30,000. In contrast, GDP per capita in Vietnam, Myanmar, Laos, and Cambodia has yet to reach USD400. This is a difference of 70 times, which is much higher than the differences in GDP per capita of 16 times among EU countries and 30 times among the NAFTA countries. The economic policies of ASEAN nations would naturally be different. Taking into consideration the varying economic development in ASEAN, tariff reduction and the types of products included in free trade were laid out in a different plan and timeline for each country. However, the process of tariff reduction is still a sensitive one, especially for sectors that have been traditionally protected and those that will experience significant unemployment.

Some ASEAN nations have domestic political turmoil and unstable political situations. Vietnam invaded Cambodia in the 20th century, and the enmity between the two countries has persisted until today. There are territorial conflicts among Malaysia and Singapore. Indonesia, Malaysia, and the Philippines also have territorial conflicts over islands in the region. The governments in ASEAN countries often involve numerous political parties and constant conflict. Some are military governments, others have frequently changing cabinets, or are troubled by anti-government militants or terrorists.

ASEAN includes countries from different religious backgrounds. Malaysia, Indonesia, and Brunei are Muslim countries, while Thailand and Cambodia are Buddhist. The majority of Filipinos are Catholics. Religious differences sometimes lead to political clashes between and within countries.

ASEAN has a guarded attitude towards China

Some ASEAN countries have subscribed to the view that China is a threat to the region. China's rapid economic development, large-scale inbound foreign investment, and large volume of cheap exports to ASEAN have put pressure on some ASEAN countries. Other ASEAN countries have seen China as a possible military threat. Although China has engaged this region through diplomatic means and foreign aid, several ASEAN countries still view China with a guarded attitude.

Continued conflict over the leadership role

In East Asia cooperation, China has always supported the leadership of ASEAN. But ASEAN itself is a body of 10 nations, and as a subregional organization it has lacked a single country as a core coordinator. In similar mechanisms in the EU or NAFTA, there is always a single country that acts as the core leadership. The problem of lack of leadership and coordination within ASEAN was exposed in the Asian Financial Crisis, when the ASEAN countries scrambled to depreciate their currencies in order to protect their own economies, thus setting off detrimental consequences for the entire region.

The power struggle within ASEAN has, in fact, never ceased. In terms of population and land area, Indonesia is the largest country in ASEAN, but political chaos and economic doldrums have undermined its capability to be the leader. Malaysia and Singapore have both sought to be the leader. Yet, Singapore's close relations with the U.S. and Israel has raised concerns among other ASEAN members. Unless ASEAN becomes a more well-coordinated entity, it could not gain political or economic power on the world stage. Although

China is the largest country in the China-ASEAN Free Trade Area, and has the capability to lead the region, it is a delicate question whether ASEAN countries would accept the leadership of China. ASEAN has commenced free trade negotiations with India, Australia, and Japan, and has signed some free trade agreements with the U.S. These bilateral trade agreements can be viewed as ASEAN's endeavor to balance the influence of China.

Operation mechanism for the Free Trade Area

The Chinese government views Asia-Pacific Economic Cooperation (APEC)—the forum for 21 Pacific Rim countries promoting free trade and economic cooperation in Asia Pacific—as an advocate of unilateralism and loose, non-systemic cooperation. Several ASEAN countries are also APEC members. When China and ASEAN need to decide between an open free trade zone or a closed one, they need to first clarify the pros and cons of the APEC-style open regionalism. They also need to consider how the extent of openness of a free trade area could affect the interests of individual members.

On a separate note, territorial disputes in the South China Sea, drug trafficking, international terrorism are other issues that introduce uncertainty in the region, and may have potentially negative impact on China-ASEAN cooperation.

External uncertainties

Uncertainty over world economic growth

There has been a global economic imbalance. There are issues of the depreciating U.S. dollar, a pressured world financial system, soaring oil prices, a food crisis, highly mobile and excessive hot money, and insufficient consumer demand. Both China and ASEAN are export-oriented economies with heavy dependence on the U.S., Japan, and Europe, and are, therefore, exposed to the volatility of the global markets. Moreover, changes in regional security and the situation in the Taiwan Strait may also impact China-ASEAN cooperation.

Interference from the U.S. and Japan

China has become more influential in Southeast Asia because of its economic growth. Chinese exports in consumer goods and electronic products have successfully competed against American and Japanese exports in the ASEAN markets. The U.S. and Japan, which have been traditionally the dominant powers in ASEAN economies, are now intervening in China-ASEAN cooperation in order to maintain their political power and market share in the region.

Despite the challenges described above, the potential benefits of the China-ASEAN Free Trade Area are obvious. Stronger China-ASEAN political and economic relations create a win-win situation for both partners. Cooperation could shield both China and ASEAN from external volatility, prevent Chinese economic growth after WTO accession from negatively affecting ASEAN economies, and create new opportunities for trade and the resolution of conflicts such as in the South China Sea.

We believe in the opportunities offered by the China-ASEAN Free Trade Area. China should further strengthen political dialogue with ASEAN in order to promote mutual trust. It should continue to reform its economic structure, elevating the competitiveness of the whole region. Stronger cooperation in technology and in regional security would also be beneficial for both China and Southeast Asia.

Other important areas of cooperation

China should also strengthen economic cooperation with ASEAN in the following areas:

Strengthen cooperation in agriculture, energy, and tourism

The nations of ASEAN are abundantly endowed with mineral resources. Indonesia possesses an estimated 50 billion barrels in oil reserves and 7.3 billion cubic meters in natural gas, and is the largest producer of oil in ASEAN. Brunei and Malaysia also have considerable oil reserves. Vietnam possesses abundant bauxite, iron, and coal. The Philippines has confirmed mines in 13 metallic minerals and 29 non-metallic minerals, with its gold, copper, nickel, and chromium reserves are of high quality and have been ranked the world's third, fourth, fifth, and sixth largest reserves, respectively. These countries have underdeveloped industrial capability, while Chinese enterprises have the competitive advantage in resource development and processing. Therefore, China should more actively participate in the development of the mining industry in ASEAN.

The tropical and subtropical climate of Southeast Asia is conducive to agricultural crops. ASEAN produces 83% of the world's palm rattan, and exports large amounts of rubber, timber, and fruits. Thailand and Vietnam are large exporters of rice. Cambodia, Laos, and Myanmar have the potential for further agricultural development. Vegetable and fruits are produced in abundance in Thailand, Vietnam, and Myanmar. Again, due to the underdeveloped industrial capability in these countries, there are opportunities for Chinese enterprises to invest in factories, technology, and equipment so as to produce agricultural products that would be sold to China.

Both China and ASEAN have rich tourism resources. The 10 nations in ASEAN have all been opened to Chinese citizens for travel. In 2005, 3 million Chinese citizens have visited ASEAN, accounting for one-third of all outbound travel of Chinese citizens. More than 3 million ASEAN travelers also visited China, accounting for 20% of inbound visitors to China.

Strengthen cooperation in industry and international contracting

Several ASEAN countries, particularly Vietnam, Laos, Cambodia, Myanmar, and the Philippines, lack competitiveness in the industries of steel, automobiles, electronic goods, and medicine. Their need for advanced technology has created opportunities for China. China is now the fifth largest source of imported automobiles in Singapore, following Japan, Korea, Germany, and the U.S. Chinese sugar, paper, steel, concrete, and electronic goods are also competitive in the ASEAN market, and have served as the basis for cooperation. Vietnam, Laos, and Cambodia have also imported Chinese machinery for agricultural use, such as tractors, diesel engines, pumps, threshing machines, and drying machines, and have found these imports to offer superior effectiveness and cost efficiency.

As ASEAN countries recovered from the Asian Financial Crisis, its demand for infrastructure and foreign capital related to infrastructure has increased. China's international contractors have the technical capability to support the construction of electric power, telecommunications, and transportation projects in Southeast Asia. Thailand is already an important market for China in international contracting. Chinese contractors have won a variety of projects in real estate, highways, bridges, metallurgy, hydro, piers, dredging of navigation channels, and well drilling.

Singapore is the largest ASEAN trading partner for China, accounting for a quarter of the total China-ASEAN trade. As Singapore has planned large-scale civil engineering projects over the coming two to three decades, including subway and reclamation, there are ample opportunities for Chinese contractors.

Strengthen cooperation in logistics, service trade, and financial investments

China and ASEAN would each open their markets according to the *Service Trade Agreement* that became effective July 1, 2007. China would open the 26 industries within the five sectors of construction, environmental protection, transportation, sports, and commercial services. Meanwhile, ASEAN would open the sectors of finance, telecommunications, education, tourism, construction, and medicine. Chinese companies would be allowed to set up wholly owned enterprises or joint ventures in ASEAN, and the requirements for shareholding percentages in companies would be relaxed.

As a network of highways, railways, air transportation and sea transportation have been constructed between China and ASEAN, opportunities for logistics cooperation have emerged.

Singapore has the most advanced service industries among the ASEAN countries, as services account for 66% of Singapore's GDP. Its commercial services (including foreign trade), transportation, and telecommunications, wholesale and retail, and financial services are the major service sectors. When Chinese companies set up operations in Singapore, they can utilize the network with international markets, reaching not only the rest of Southeast Asia but also the rest of the world.

Guangxi and Yunnan are the two provinces in China bordering ASEAN countries. Guangxi's ports and the Nanning-Kunming railway form part of the highway, river transportation, air transportation, and infrastructure network that connects southwestern China with sea transportation. Yunnan's highway network allows cargo to enter other Chinese provinces or to reach the ASEAN countries. China has opened 103 aviation routes to connect to Bangkok, Singapore, Kuala Lumpur, Hanoi, Yangoon, Mandalay, and Vientiane. There are railway links between China and Vietnam. The Lancang River-Mekong River International Route, and the international highways linking Kunming to Laos have been opened. The highways between Kunming and Bangkok and between Kunming and Singapore are under construction. These transportation links will facilitate trade between southwestern China and the neighboring ASEAN countries.

As the China-ASEAN Free Trade Area is launched and the *Service Trade Agreement* and *Investment Agreement* are signed and implemented, China and ASEAN will fully open the markets for trade and investment. By 2015, the economic integration of East Asia will have been achieved earlier than original expectations. We expect relations between China and ASEAN to be further improved which will deliver benefits for the whole region.

8

Chapter

Economic Relations between China and Japan

Japan is the third largest economy in the world and the second largest economy in Asia after China. Japan is an important trading partner of China, a leading foreign investor and partner in technological cooperation. Both China and Japan play a crucial role in East Asia economic cooperation. A study of China's foreign economic relations would therefore inevitably include an attempt to understand China-Japan relations.

The Development and Evolution of China-Japan Relations

Economic relations between China and Japan, which gradually recovered after the establishment of the People's Republic of China (PRC), can be understood in four stages.

Before re-establishment of diplomatic relations, 1949–1972

Following the American lead in foreign policy, Japan had recognized the "Two Chinas" policy regarding Taiwan and also participated in economic sanctions and embargo against China until the Moscow International Economic Conference in April 1952. Three Japanese members of parliament—Koura Yutaka, Houashi Kei, and Miyakoshi Kisuke—visited China and commenced negotiations for civil trade. On June 1 1952, the Japanese representatives and the China Council for the Promotion of International Trade signed a privately negotiated trade agreement, under which a barter trade of 3,000 British pounds was pledged. Three more privately negotiated agreements were signed in October 1953, May 1954, and March 1958. Trade volume fluctuated and was kept at a small scale because of the bartering arrangement. In 1957, trade was estimated at USD115 million. For all other years during this stage, trade was kept below USD100 million.[1]

Meanwhile, the trade balance was favorable to China.

Due to the Cold War and opposition from Taiwan, these privately negotiated trade agreements were not fully implemented. The first agreement was 5.05% executed, the second one 38.8%. The fourth one was not executed at all, as an incident two months after it was signed involving two Japanese youths ripping down a Chinese flag in a Nagasaki department store in May 1958 brought all diplomatic and trade relations to a halt.

Both sides made efforts in normalizing relations. In August 1958 China requested that Japan would adopt three political principles—that Japanese policies should not see China as the enemy, should not create "two Chinas," and should not obstruct the normalizing of relations. Chinese Premier Zhou Enlai then proposed three principles in trade in August 1960 government agreement; civil contracts; and case-by-case basis. Bilateral trade relations recovered and expanded. Trade volume rose from a low base of USD23.45 million in 1960, to an increase by 31% in 1961, and 24% in 1962, and then by over 40% in 1963.

A semi-governmental trade coordination office was set up in August 1964 following a memorandum of understanding signed between businessmen Liao Chengzhi from China and Tatsunosuke Takasaki from Japan. This type of privately negotiated, government supported MoU helped facilitate trade between 1964 and 1972. Trade volume reached USD625 million by 1969.

After re-establishment of diplomatic relations, 1972–1980

China and Japan officially re-established diplomatic relations in 1972 with the *Japan-China Joint Declaration*. In 1978, further basis for stable political relations was confirmed with the signing of the *Treaty of Peace and Friendship between China and Japan*. The newly energized trade relations had the following features:

Expanding scale of trade

The first government-led trade agreement between China and Japan was signed in 1974. An eight-year trade agreement was then signed in February 1978, which eventually extended to 1990. Cooperation agreements were also signed in the sectors of sea cargo, aviation, fishery, trademark protection, technology, and investment protection. These documents formed a strong foundation for trade development thereafter. The bilateral trade volume grew six-fold from USD1.04 billion in 1972 to USD6.6 billion in 1979.

Diversifying trade

Apart from joint ventures and cooperatives, other forms of trade such as processing trade, compensation trade, partial orders, and appointed factory became more prevalent. Trade and investment expanded in a more balanced manner.

Financial sector cooperation

Bank of China became a correspondent bank of 31 Japanese banks in China by 1978. There were frequent exchanges and visits of bank personnel between the two countries. Every year more than 100 people visited each other. This early cooperation in the financial sector would later contribute to China's ability to secure investment capital from Japan.

Technology and complete equipment import

According to some accounts, as of the first half of 1979, China had 38 projects of Japanese technological imports worth 916 billion Japanese yen.

After the economic reforms of China, 1980–1990

China-Japan economic relations entered a new stage as China embraced market-oriented reforms and the Japanese economy developed in full throttle. The following trends were evident in this period:

China as an additional economic engine

In the early years after establishing diplomatic relations, Japan was the single economic engine in the Sino-Japanese relations. Only after the Chinese economy had a chance to recover from the Cultural Revolution and to start constructing a market economy that the situation changed. During this time, the Sino-Japanese economic relations gradually became a more equal, double-engine relationship.

Increasing economic strength in China

In comparison to Japan, China had a relatively weak economy before the economic reforms. It was running a substantial trade deficit with Japan, and was exporting primary goods and other goods with low value-added and low technology content. From 1981 onwards however, China reversed the trend in trade balance and starting running a surplus against Japan. From 1981 to 1990, China ran a surplus in six of those 10 years, which was a total surplus of USD11.15 billion.

Increasing Japanese investment in China

Japanese investment in China was marked by acceleration after a slow start. The first Sino-Japanese joint venture (named *Jinghe*) was established in November 1979, just months after a *Sino-Foreign Joint Venture Enterprise Law* was issued. There were four Sino-Japanese joint ventures by 1981, and nine by the first half of 1983. Japanese investment in China was then stimulated after the two countries signed a treaty to avoid double taxation. The investment environment continued to improve as an investment protection agreement was signed in July 1988, laying out regulations and procedures on national treatment, most-favored-nation treatment, and other issues such as compensation for requisition or nationalization. By 1990, there were 341 Japanese investment projects in China, with an actual utilized investment of USD500 million, accounting for 14.4% of all utilized foreign investment in China during that period.

Increasing Japanese development aid to China

In December 1979, Japan became one of the first developed countries to provide development aid to China. Since then, Japan continued to be one of the largest donors to China in Official Development Assistance (ODA). China has been the largest recipient of ODA every year. Between 1980 and 1985, China received assistance of 380.6 billion Japanese yen, which was increased to 546.8 billion yen in the next five years.[2]

The transition of China-Japan relations, 1990–present

China-Japan bilateral trade has become integrally important to the economic health of both countries. The unprecedented growth of the Chinese economy, which has now surpassed Japan to become the second largest economy in the world, has also significantly changed the dynamics of bilateral economic relations.

A reverse in comparative advantages

In comparing the economic power of the two countries, Japan had the upper hand over China for decades since the Second World War. However, these power relations fundamentally changed in the 1990s.

During the 1950s and 1960s, Japan was the fastest growing economy in the world, as its average annual economic growth rate was close to 10%. During this time, the Chinese economy was stagnant or even close to collapse. In the 1970s, despite the oil crisis that dampened growth rates, Japan was still in a leading position relative to the lagging economy of China. During the 1980s, the Japanese economy further strengthened, and had an impressive run between 1987 and 1991 by showing rapid growth over 51 months.

China started to reap the fruits of its economic reforms as early as the 1980s, but its achievements became more apparent by the 1990s, when Japan was steeped in a decade of recession. Since then, the comparative advantage in East Asian economic growth belonged to China.

In the decade between 1996 and 2005, Japan's real GDP increased only 1.5% on an average year, whereas China's increased 8.2%.[3] There were signs of recovery in Japan in 2002 and in the following five years, when its real GDP growth rate varied between 1.7% and 2.6% in 2003–2007. However, China's GDP growth rates were much more remarkable, varying between 10% and 11.4% during those years (see Table 8.1). It appears that China has now gained the upper hand in terms of the size of the economy and in sustained momentum of economic growth.

Table 8.1. Comparison of real GDP growth of China and Japan (%)

Year	1995	1996	1997	1998	1999	2000	2001	2002	2003	2004	2005	2006	2007
China	10.9	10.0	9.3	7.8	7.6	8.4	8.3	9.1	10.0	10.1	10.4	11.1	11.4
Japan	2.0	3.4	1.8	–1.0	–0.1	2.4	–0.3	0.2	1.7	2.3	2.6	2.4	2.1
Difference	8.9	6.6	7.5	8.8	7.7	6.0	8.6	8.9	8.3	7.8	7.8	8.7	9.3

Source: Ministry of Commerce website, http://www.mofcom.gov.cn.

Role reversal in inter-dependency

Initially, China-Japan relations were more important for China than for Japan. But in recent years there was a role reversal. China's rapidly growing economic prowess and its elevated status in the global economy meant that Japan increasingly recognizes China's importance to its external economy.

This role reversal can be seen from the statistics. Since 2000, trade with Japan is accounting for a decreasing proportion of China's total trade. Exports to Japan as a percentage of China's total exports dropped from 16.7% in 2000 to 8.4% in 2007. Imports from Japan as a percentage of China's total imports dropped from 18.4% to 14% in the same period. These two percentages had reached their heights in 1985, when they were 22.3% and 35.7% respectively (see Table 8.2). For a long time, Japan was the largest trading partner of China. That role was later occupied by Europe, and then surpassed by the U.S., so that Japan is now China's third largest trading partner.

Japanese investment as a proportion of total foreign investment in China has also declined. On one hand, it is encouraging that Japanese investment in China has shown a high growth rate in recent years, such as 32.2%, 43.6%, 22.2%, and 65% in the respective four years from 2000 to 2003. However, China's total foreign investment has expanded at an even faster rate, thus causing a decline in Japan's share. Japan's original position as the largest foreign investor in China was replaced by the United States as early as in 1999. At that time, Japan accounted for 7.4% of the total utilized foreign investment in China. This was already lower than the 10.5% contribution from the United States and the 11.1% from Europe that year. In terms of actual utilized foreign investment, Japan's share went from 14.4% in 1990 to 7.9% in 2002 and an even lower 6.6% in 2006.

In the other direction, China's share in Japan's total trade volume has become larger. As a percentage of the total trade volume of Japan, China accounted for 3.5% in 1990, 7.4% in 1995, 9.9% in 2000, and 17% in 2005. If we consider the increase in these percentages in every five-year period, from 1990–1995

Table 8.2. China-Japan trade volume as a percentage of total foreign trade of China (%)

Year	1980	1985	1990	1995	2000	2005	2006	2007
Exports to Japan as percentage of Chinese total exports	22.2	22.3	14.7	19.1	16.7	11.0	9.5	8.4
Import from Japan as percentage of Chinese total imports	26.5	35.7	14.2	21.9	18.4	15.2	14.5	14.0

Sources: Cabinet Office, Government of Japan, *World Economic Trends*, December 2005, p.212, 216; website of Ministry of Commerce of China, Trade Statistics; website of General Administration of Customs of China, Customs Statistics.

it was 3.9% growth, from 1996–2000 it was 2.5%, and from 2000–2005 it grew 7.1%. That means the highest growth in China's share of Japanese foreign trade took place between 2000 and 2005. During these five years, China accounted for 39.1% of the increase in total Japanese trade, and 39.3% of the growth in Japanese exports were goods sold to China. From 2002 onwards, China became Japan's largest source of imports. From 2006, China surpassed the United States to become Japan's largest trading partner. Trade with China as a percentage of total trade in Japan increased from 11.8% in 2001 to 17.5% in 2006. During the same period, the share of the United States dropped from 24.5% to 17.2%.

China also became a major foreign investment destination for Japanese enterprises seeking an increase in profits. In 2003, although Japan's total foreign investment dropped 9.2%, its investment in China rose 65%. This made China's share in Japan's total foreign investment rise by nearly 4% in a single year.

Equal footing and interactive forces

In the early development of China-Japan economic relations, Japan was leading and China was following. However, after Japan entered recession in the 1990s while China experienced staggering economic growth, the burgeoning consumer demand in China had become a major driving force of the Japanese economy. This was especially true because domestic consumer demand in Japan had evaporated, so the country's recovery almost entirely depended upon external forces. From 2000 to 2004, Japan's exports grew by 8.52 trillion Japanese yen, of which exports to China grew by 4.72 trillion Japanese yen. This meant that 55.4% of Japanese exports during those five years were sold to China.

China's economic growth also created business opportunities for Japanese companies, as these companies stepped up their investment in China to take advantage of the low-cost labor. Using China as a manufacturing base, from which the products were then exported to Japan, could increase consumer choice and improve general quality of life in Japan.

New specializations

At the beginning of the 1970s, Japan and China had contrasting structures and specializations in their economies. As a result, Japan exported goods with high technology content to China, while over 80% of Chinese exports were low value-added, low technology content products. However, after 30 years of development and partly due to the improvement in industrial production brought by Japanese investors, China has started exporting to Japan a much higher proportion of industrial products with high technology content. Currently, industrial products account for 80% of Chinese exports to Japan, and the largest category in these industrial product exports is machinery and transportation equipment which accounts for 39.4%.

Multiple forms of cooperation

In contrast to the Cold War legacy that hindered all forms of cooperation between China and Japan in the early 1970s, the China-Japan economic relations today are crucial to the success of regional cooperation. Since the 1990s, mechanisms such as the APEC, ASEAN Plus Three, and China-Japan-Korea trilateral meetings have been constructed to engender closer cooperation and interaction in the region.

Fair competition

In the early 1970s, China-Japan economic relations were characterized by unfair competition from Japan. China ran a significant deficit in trade with Japan. In 1978, the Chinese deficit was half the amount of the bilateral trade volume. A new level playing field had been created in the recent decade, as the Chinese economy advanced in size and industrial structure to catch up with Japan.

Main Features of China-Japan Economic Relations

The economic relations between China and Japan are characterized by the following features:

Stable growth

From the 1970s onwards, China-Japan trade encountered stable growth since it departed from the private trading ties in the 1950s and semi-governmental trade in the 1960s. Bilateral trade volume grew 15-fold between 1972 and 1990—from USD1.04 billion in 1972 to USD9.2 billion in 1980, to USD16.6 billion in 1990—with an average annual growth rate of 16.6%. However this was a fluctuating trend, with the actual growth rates fluctuating between negative double digits to over 50%. This was destabilizing for the economic growth of China at the time, because Japan had accounted for an average 20% of China's total foreign trade at the time, and even 25.8% of China's total foreign trade in 1975.

The growth in bilateral trade volume became more stable in the 1990s, when fluctuations were smaller and sudden dips were infrequent. Even in the year of the Asian Financial Crisis, the only year in the 1990s when bilateral trade slipped, the negative growth was only 4.8%. According to statistics from the Chinese government. In the first half of 1990s, bilateral trade grew rapidly, from USD20.25 billion in 1991 to USD57.47 billion in 1995, showing an average annual growth of just under 30%. In the decade that followed, bilateral trade enjoyed several years of record-breaking growth. In 2000, bilateral trade exceeded USD80 billion for the first time, reaching USD83.17 billion, with 25.7% year-on-year growth. In 2002, it exceeded USD100 billion for the first time, reaching USD101.91 billion, growing 16.2% year-on-year. In 2006, it broke the USD200 billion milestone, reaching USD207.36 billion. It reached even higher in 2007, to USD236.02 billion.

Table 8.3 shows the official data from the Japanese government, which showed the same trend. Before the stable growth of the 1990s, China-Japan trade could have a good year of 83% growth (in 1973) or 63.4% growth, then there were bad years of –19.9% (1976) and –18.2% (1986) setbacks. In the 1990s, apart from the negative growth in 1998, other years generally maintained about 30% growth. The pace of growth in bilateral trade was similar in the two periods of 1972–1990 and 1990–2003, except for the absence of rollercoaster fluctuations in the latter period.

Positive momentum

Bilateral trade and economic growth can be mutually reinforcing. Four trends in China-Japan relations illustrate this.

First, unprecedented economic growth in China drove demand for Japanese exports. In fact, during the global economic downturn of 2001–2002, China played a crucial role in absorbing Japanese exports while Japan's exports to

Table 8.3. Growth in China-Japan trade, 1972–2003

Year	Export (USD million)	Import (USD million)	Export minus import (USD million)	Trade volume (USD million)	Year-on-year growth (%)
1972	609	491	118	1,100	—
1973	1,039	974	65	2,013	83.0
1974	1,984	1,305	679	3,289	63.4
1975	2,259	1,531	728	3,790	15.2
1976	1,663	1,371	292	3,034	–19.9
1977	1,939	1,547	392	3,486	14.9
1978	3,049	2,030	1,019	5,079	45.7
1979	3,699	2,955	744	6,654	31.0
1980	5,078	4,323	755	9,401	41.3
1981	5,095	5,292	–197	10,387	10.5
1982	3,511	5,352	–1,841	8,863	–14.7
1983	4,912	5,087	–175	9,999	12.8
1984	7,217	5,958	1,259	13,175	31.8
1985	12,477	6,483	5,994	48,960	43.9
1986	9,856	5,652	4,204	15,508	–18.2
1987	8,250	7,401	849	15,651	0.9
1988	9,476	9,859	–383	19,335	23.5
1989	8,516	11,146	–2,630	19,662	1.7
1990	6,130	12,054	–5,924	18,184	–7.5
1991	8,593	14,216	–5,623	22,809	25.4
1992	11,949	16,953	–5,004	28,902	26.7
1993	17,273	20,565	–3,292	37,838	30.9
1994	18,682	27,566	–8,884	46,248	22.2
1995	21,931	35,922	–13,991	57,853	25.1
1996	21,890	40,550	–18,660	62,440	7.9
1997	21,785	42,066	–20,281	63,851	2.3
1998	20,022	36,896	–16,874	46,918	–10.9
1999	23,336	42,880	–19,544	66,216	16.3
2000	30,428	55,303	–24,875	85,731	29.5
2001	31,091	58,105	–27,014	83,196	4.0
2002	39,866	61,692	–21,826	101,558	13.9
2003	57,219	75,193	–17,974	132,412	30.4

Note: The above figures are official statistics of Japan.
Source: Japan External Trade Organization, http://www.jetro.go.jp/ec/j/trade.

other leading trading partners suffered. China's rapid real GDP growth in the five years between 1999 and 2003 was also accompanied by the high rate of increase in imports, averaging 24.7% per year.

Second, trade liberalization drove up China's foreign trade dependency. After China joined the WTO in 2001, its foreign trade as a percentage of GDP rose significantly. From 44.5% in 2000, it rose to 50.2% in 2002 and 60.3% in 2003. The percentage of imports to GDP also increased from 20.8% in 2000 to 23.9% in 2002 and 29.3% in 2003. Japan has been a major beneficiary of China's rising demand for imports, as the Japanese economy has become dependent on external demand instead of domestic consumption.

Third, China's efforts in industrial upgrade fueled its imports of high technology products, an area where Japan has strong specializations. In 2003, the fastest growing categories of goods among Japanese exports to China were digital cameras and television receptors, which grew 115% year-on-year. Several other fast-growing imported goods areas were also high-technology products: audiovisual products and parts grew 114%; auto parts grew by 105%; and construction and mining machinery grew 99.2%. These high technology products were also keys to the growth of exports in Japan. In 2003, 10.8% of Japanese exports to China were electronic components such as semi-conductors. Semi-conductors alone accounted for 4.8% of the growth in Japanese exports to China that year.[4]

Fourth, China's campaign to industrialize the western provinces and re-tool the heavy industries in the northeastern provinces created new business opportunities for Japan. Statistics show that Japanese direct investment and exports to China have also reflected moves westward and towards the northeast. The mega events of the Beijing Olympics in 2008 and the Shanghai World Expo in 2010 also generated increased demand for products and services from Japan.

From Japan's perspective, its trade with China has made a significant contribution to its economic recovery. According to estimates from the Cabinet Office of the Japanese government,[5] domestic demand accounted for only 0.4% of the real GDP growth of 1.2% in 2002. External demand (or net exports) contributed the other 0.8%, or two-thirds of the growth. Although the U.S. was still the largest buyer of Japanese exports at the time, accounting for a 28.2% share in total Japanese exports, the economic downturn in 2002 meant that the American contribution to Japanese GDP dropped 0.8% compared to the previous year. As the second largest buyer of Japanese exports, China accounted for 9.6% of Japan's total exports, but grew 28.2% in that year alone. If we also count the Japanese exports to Hong Kong, which grew 8.7% that year, China's significance as a trading partner and contributor to Japan's economic growth would be even more obvious.

China's trade deficit with Japan

China is now maintaining an increasingly large trade deficit with Japan. Table 8.3 has shown that the trade imbalance was increasingly favorable to China between 1988 and 2001. According to statistics from Japan, China had a trade surplus of USD27.01 billion with Japan in 2001, a 70-fold increase since 1988. However, from 2002 onwards, the balance tipped towards the other direction. The surplus of China (or deficit of Japan) shrunk to only USD17.97 billion in 2003, and by February 2004, the trade imbalance tipped in Japan's favor.[6]

The trade deficit of China started much earlier by the calculation in Chinese statistics, where the trade imbalance became favorable to Japan in 2002. Data from the China side shows the Chinese trade surplus to have shrunk to USD2.16 billion in 2001, which turned into a trade deficit of USD5.03 billion in 2002, enlarging to USD14.73 billion in 2003. In 2004, the Chinese trade deficit continued to rise, exceeding USD20 billion to reach USD20.86 billion. By 2007, the trade deficit had exceeded USD30 billion to reach USD31.88 billion, another historic high.

These differences in trade statistics are mainly due to the calculation of re-exports through Hong Kong. Those goods that are exported from Japan through Hong Kong to eventually enter the China market are accounted for in the Chinese statistics as imports from Japan, whereas the Japanese statistics categorize the re-exports differently. In 2003, Chinese statistics recorded USD74.15 billion in imports from Japan, while Japanese statistics recorded USD57.24 billion in exports to China, and USD29.8 billion in Japanese exports to Hong Kong. About 60% of Japanese exports to Hong Kong were then re-exported to China. If we take into account this difference in definition of re-exports via Hong Kong, the statistics from China and Japan in fact show a similar trend.

There are two reasons behind this growing Chinese trade deficit with Japan. First, China has experienced a much faster rate of economic growth compared to the relatively stagnant economy of Japan. This means that China has much higher demand for imports. Second, China as a new member of the WTO has a newly liberalized economy for trade and investment, whereas Japan has been an established WTO member whose economic opening and trade liberalization had already taken place decades ago. Table 8.4 shows the strong positive correlation between economic growth and imports. We can therefore expect that China's trade deficit with Japan will continue to rise for several years to come.

Competition

In the early years of trade relations, the Japanese and Chinese economies showed strong complementarity and limited competition. Japan exported high technology content and high value-added products to China, while China exported low technology content and low value-added products to Japan. C.H. Kwan of the Research Institute of Economy, Trade and Industry (RIETI) of Japan studied the changing relationship of complementarity and competition

Table 8.4. Comparison of growth in GDP and trade volume of China and Japan, 2000–2003

	Real GDP growth (%)			Growth in trade (%)		
Year	China	Japan	Difference	China	Japan	Difference
2000	8.4	2.4	6.0	35.8	23.3	12.5
2001	8.3	–0.3	8.6	8.2	–7.9	16.1
2002	9.1	0.2	8.9	21.2	–4.1	25.3
2003	10.0	1.7	8.3	39.9	13.3	26.6

Sources: Real GDP growth data came from National Bureau of Statistics of China, and Cabinet Office, Government of Japan. Trade growth figures came from Ministry of Commerce of China and Japan External Trade Organization.

by comparing Japanese and Chinese exports to the United States. Kwan pointed out that up to 2002, only about 20% of exports of Japan and China to the U.S. involved the two countries competing against each other, with the 80% majority of the exports being complementary to each other. He then concluded that it would be difficult to imagine China and Japan competing against each other in the field of high technology production, because Japan maintains a lead in that area.[7]

On the other hand, it may be argued that China has indeed made progress in closing the gap in high technology production, and has therefore become more capable of competing with Japan. In the same article by Kwan, the ratio of competing Chinese exports to the total Japanese exports to the U.S. was 3% in 1990, but increased to 8.3% in 1995, 16.3% in 2000 and 20.5% in 2002.[8]

This trend of strengthening capability of China in high technology manufacturing is also illustrated in Chinese exports to Japan. In the 1970s, 80% of Chinese exports to Japan were primary products. This percentage was reduced to 70% in the 1990s and 15.5% by 2003. In contrast, the percentage of industrial finished goods among Chinese exports to Japan grew to 84.5% in 2003, among which 35.6% were machinery and transportation equipment with high technology content.

Admittedly, much of these Chinese exports to Japan have come from Japanese-invested companies in China (about 50%). Japanese direct investment in China has brought about improvements at the industry and firm levels, and in turn changed the Chinese industrial structure such that there is greater competition between China and Japan in producing goods with high technology content. This increasing competition may increase trade friction in the future, and may require both countries to engage each other in multilateral and regional cooperation platforms.

Investment-led trade

The rising investment of Japanese companies in China has led to increasing trade and an increase in the value-added and technology content of the goods traded. Japanese investment in China started to rise in the mid-1980s, when the number of investment projects grew 36 fold from 94 in 1986 to 3,488 in 1993. Contracted investment value grew 27 fold from USD280 million in 1986 to USD7.59 billion in 1993. Actual utilized investment grew 16 times from USD260 million to USD4.33 billion. There was some fluctuation in Japanese investment in the late 1990s, when the number of projects dropped to 1,167 in 1999, while contracted value of investment decreased to USD2.59 billion in 1999 and the actual utilized investment was USD2.92 billion in 2000. These figures represented a decrease of 66.5%, 65.9%, and 32.6%, respectively, from the peak of Japanese investment in China.

Investment picked up again from 2005 onwards. In 2005, the number of projects doubled from year 2000, reaching a total of 3,269 projects. The actual utilized investment reached a new historic high of USD6.53 billion in 2005, representing a nearly 125% increase from 2000. According to statistics from Japan, Japanese investment in China increased by 21.5%, 78%, and 45.3%, respectively, in 2002, 2003, and 2004.

The reasons behind the new interest in investing in China include the strong economic growth in China, a newly liberalized trade and investment environment in China after WTO accession, and the recovery of Japanese companies making them more capable of overseas investments. At the turn of the century, Japanese companies suffered negative growth for six consecutive quarters. They entered a recovery mode in the third quarter of 2002, growing 8.4% that year, and subsequently 9.7% in 2003, and 10.5% in 2004.[9]

The rise in Japanese investment in China has two important effects for Sino-Japanese trade. First, major manufacturing and operations bases were relocated from Japan to China, which induces Japanese exports of large volumes of machinery, equipment, components, and parts that are not available in China. This is known as the effect of "induced exports." A 2003 study by the Japanese External Trade Organization (JETRO) confirms this phenomenon.[10] According to statistics from the Department of Foreign Investment Administration in the China Ministry of Commerce, in 2002 Japanese-invested enterprises in China recorded imports of USD35.95 billion, a 24.4% increase from 2001, and represented 67.2% of all imports from Japan to China.

Second, because the production capabilities of Japanese companies have moved to China, the domestic consumer demand in Japan has to be supplied by exports of Japanese-invested companies in China. This is known as "reverse imports." Statistics from JETRO show that Japan has increased its imports of machinery and home appliances from China, and growth is particularly high in personal computers and printers.[11] Statistics from China's Ministry of Commerce also show that in 2000, 2001, and 2002, the exports of Japanese-invested companies in China to Japan grew at the high pace of 32%, 13.1%, and 13.6%, respectively. In 2002, these reverse exports reached USD29.99 billion, accounting for 62% of Chinese exports to Japan, as shown in Table 8.5. These two effects of induced exports and reverse imports show the importance in bilateral trade and investment for both countries.

Table 8.5. Import from and exports to Japan by foreign-invested enterprises in China, 1992–2002 (USD100 million)

Year	1992	1994	1996	1998	2000	2001	2002	2002/1992
Import from Japan	41.6	141.8	195.0	187.7	284.2	289.0	359.5	8.64 times
Export to Japan	19.5	78.6	148.8	159.2	233.4	264.0	299.9	15.38 times

Source: Department of Foreign Investment, Ministry of Commerce of China.

Difficulties and Solutions for Sino-Japanese Economic Relations

Several historical and political issues re-surface every few years and interfere with the economic relations between China and Japan. This is often described as "hot economics, cold politics" in Sino-Japanese relations. The years of the Koizumi administration in Japan was a recent example of this dilemma. Although some level of "cold politics" are tolerated in the Sino-Japanese economic ties, over the long run these political differences are still destabilizing for the economy.

Difficulties

The cooling in politics around 2002 has affected Sino-Japanese economic ties in the following ways.

Slowing growth in China-Japan trade

After 2002, bilateral trade between China and Japan reached new historical heights in terms of trade volume. Trade volume grew from USD101.91 billion in 2002 to USD133.57 billion in 2003, USD167.89 billion in 2004, USD184.44 billion in 2005, and exceeded USD200 billion in 2006, reaching USD207.36 billion.

However, compared to the strong growth in the foreign trade of China, the growth in trade with Japan has been slow. Japan therefore decreased in importance as a trading partner for China. In the five years from 2002 to 2006, China's foreign trade grew at rates of 21.8%, 37.1%, 35.7% , 23.2% ,and 23.8% in the respective years. However, China-Japan trade only grew 16.2%, 31.1%, 25.7%, 9.9%, and 12.5%, which are much lower numbers than the average.[12]

This slower-than-average growth in China-Japan trade means that Japan's share in China's total foreign trade decreased from 16.4% in 2002 to 11.8% in 2006. This percentage was as high as 23.6% in 1985. Also, the growth rate of China's trade with Japan has slowed down in recent years, from 2003 to 2006, the growth rates were 30.4%, 26.9%, 12.7%, and 11.5%, showing an obvious trend of slowing down.[13]

Japanese investment in China decreasing in importance

Japanese investment in China has continued to grow, but its share of total foreign investment in China has shrunk. Japanese FDI in China decreased in the late 1990s and picked up again after 2000. In 1999, investment had dropped to 1,167 projects from 3,488 projects in 1993. Contracted investment also dropped from 1996 onwards, from USD7.59 billion in 1995 to USD2.59 billion in 1999. Actual utilized investment declined from 1998 onwards, and by 2000 it had shrunk to USD2.92 billion, from USD4.33 billion in 1997. The rebound came quickly thereafter, when actual utilized investment reached the historic high of USD6.53 billion in 2005. It tapered again to USD4.6 billion in 2006. Japanese statistics shows a continued increase since.

However, Japan's contribution has paled in comparison to the strong growth in FDI in recent years. In 2004, FDI in China (by actual utilized investment) increased 13.32% year-on-year while Japanese investment in China only grew 7.87%. This reduced the share of Japan in China's total FDI to drop from 9.45% to 8.99%. In 2006, Japanese investment in China dropped 21% by the number of projects, decreased 30% by actual utilized investment, and this reduced its contribution to total FDI in China to 6.62%.[14]

Sharp decrease of Japanese aid to China

Aid from Japan played an important role in energy development, infrastructure construction, and environmental protection in China, indirectly facilitating friendly trade and economic relations between the two countries. As of 2006, Japan had provided 3.58 trillion Japanese yen in Official Development Assistance to China, with over 90% in yen-denominated loans. However, from 2000 onwards, ODA was granted a multi-year basis instead of a yearly basis. ODA granted to China was also drastically reduced.

Yen-denominated loans stood at 214.4 billion yen in 2000. It was reduced to 161.4 billion yen in 2001 (–24.7%), to 121.2 billion yen in 2002 (-24.9%), and to 96.7 billion yen in 2003 (20.2%). The declining trend continued in 2004, when ODA loans dropped to 85.9 billion yen, which represented a 60% drop since 2000. In 2005 and 2006, it was reduced to 74.8 billion yen and 62.3 billion yen, respectively.[15] During that time, China had dropped from the top recipient to the third largest recipient of Japanese aid. Providing ODA to China, which already competes with the Japanese economy in many aspects, has been a controversial political issue in Japanese politics. It was originally planned that all Japanese aid to China would stop by 2008. The issue is still under discussion today.

Trade frictions

There has been a series of trade frictions between China and Japan in the recent decade. In April 2001, Japan imposed emergency tariffs on three agricultural crops imported from China. Currency exchange has become a hot-button issue, with China first criticizing Japan for a drastic devaluation of the Japanese yen, followed by Japan joining the U.S. in attempting to force China to allow the appreciation of Renminbi. Japan has also criticized China for "exporting deflation" to Japan. The two countries have also competed with each other for oil pipeline projects in Russia.

Laggard economic cooperation

One effective way to handle trade frictions is to construct mechanisms and platforms in order to avoid escalation of conflict and resolve any disputes. Both China and Japan have engaged in multilateral and bilateral platforms to this end. In recent years, Japan has actively sought to build closer economic ties and to liberalize trade with several of its major trading partners in Asia and beyond. Japan has signed bilateral free trade agreements (FTA) with Mexico and Singapore. It has engaged in FTA negotiations with several ASEAN members, and has concluded talks with South Korea regarding a free trade area. However, Japan and China have yet to create their own trade and investment liberalization mechanism.

Favorable factors for resolution of differences

The following factors will be favorable to resolving the problems in Sino-Japanese economic relations discussed above.

Japanese economic recovery

China's rapid economic growth in the 1990s has generated the theory that China poses a threat to Japan, especially because the Japanese economy suffered from recession during that time. According to estimates by the International Monetary Fund, between 1997 and 2006, China's economy grew at an average annual rate of 8.3% while Japan's only grew at 0.9%.[16]

However, the Japanese economy is recovering. The issue of bad debts in banks has been resolved—Koizumi's 2002 *Financial Resurrection Plan* has begun to reap results, as the bad debt ratio in the Japanese banking system was lowered from 8.4% in March 2002 to 2.9% in March 2005.[17] Deflation has subsided as the consumer price index rose 1.5% in 2004.[18] Unemployment has been reduced from 5.4% in 2002 (or 3.6 million in unemployed population) to 4.2% in 2005 (or 2.85 million unemployed).[19] After real GDP shrunk by 0.3% in 2001, the Japanese economy returned to a healthier 2.3% and 2.6% growth rate in 2004 and 2005. As Japan emerges from its recession, we would expect that the opinion that China poses a threat to Japan may subside.

Japan's policy to attract inbound investment

In January 2003, the Japanese government led by Prime Minister Junichiro Koizumi launched a plan to stimulate inward foreign investment. The plan had immediate practical results, doubling inward FDI by 2004, attracting USD37.46

billion in foreign investment.[20] This plan dovetails with China's "Go Global" plan of encouraging domestic enterprises to enter the international markets. Chinese outbound foreign investment is still in its rudimentary stage but it offers vast potential. In 2006, China's non-financial outbound investment reached USD17.63 billion, a year-on-year increase of 43.8%. According to Ministry of Commerce statistics, China's non-financial investment totals in Japan in the four years between 2003 and 2006 were USD73.7 billion, USD153 billion, USD171.7 billion, and USD394.9 billion, respectively. While Japanese investment in China has been a long-established trend, Chinese investment in Japan could become a new feature of bilateral economic relations.

Reform of Renminbi exchange rate mechanism

The currency issue has been controversial in China-Japan relations. After the Asian Financial Crisis, China criticized Japan for purposely devaluing its currency. Subsequently, Japan joined the G8 powers in persuading China to allow the Renminbi to appreciate. The fluctuations in the exchange rate over the years between the Renminbi and the Japanese yen have been damaging to trade and investment.

In July 2008, China instituted a new exchange rate mechanism in which a basket of major currencies would be included. The Renminbi immediately rose by 2%. Zhou Xiaochuan, head of the People's Bank of China, had already explained that the currencies of the United States, European Union, South Korea, and Japan would be included as these countries are China's major trading partners.[21] A clearer and more stable policy for the yen-Renminbi exchange rate is conducive to continued growth in bilateral trade relations.

East Asia regional cooperation

Closer regional cooperation is set to provide further momentum for growth in trade and investment between China and Japan. The importance in regional cooperation was made clear after the Asian Financial Crisis. Since then, China, Japan, and Korea have each signed free trade agreements (FTA) or economic partnership agreements (EPA) with ASEAN, and have set up Free Trade Areas with ASEAN in 2009, 2010, and 2012. Japan has also signed an EPA with Singapore and Indonesia, while its EPAs with Mexico, Malaysia, the Philippines, Thailand, Brunei, and Chile have already come into effect. Japan has started FTA or EPA talks with Korea, Vietnam, India, Australia, and the Gulf Cooperation Council. In terms of regional cooperation in finance, the 2001 Chiang Mai Mechanism was launched which moved relations towards greater currency liquidity. An Asia-wide bond market is also being constructed.

China-Japan cooperation critical to resolving global economic risks

Rising oil prices and foreign currency fluctuations are major economic risks for both China and Japan. Both China and Japan are highly dependent on oil imports. Due to staggering oil prices, in 2004 China's expenditure on importing crude oil and oil products rose 34.8% and 71.3%, respectively. In the same year, Japan's expenditure on importing crude oil and oil products also increased 22.6% and 28.7%.

Currently, China and Japan are the top two countries possessing the world's largest foreign currency reserves. In 2006, foreign currency reserves held by China and Japan were USD1.07 trillion and USD895.3 billion, respectively. The falling U.S. dollar has therefore generated severe losses for both countries.

China and Japan would need to seek solutions to cooperate on averting these risks. Instead of engaging in vicious competition to secure energy resources, as China and Japan did for the Russian oil pipeline project, the two countries would need to open channels for cooperation. Similarly, due to the falling U.S. dollar, the appreciation of the Renminbi would not in fact benefit Japan.

Possible solutions

There are several areas of cooperation that could help China and Japan strengthen economic ties:

Launch negotiations for a China-Japan Free Trade Area

The regional cooperation mechanisms set up so far in Asia have yielded impressive results. Because the economies of China and Japan are highly complementary, they would benefit from a free trade area which would lower transaction costs for trade and reduce trade frictions.

Strengthen financial sector cooperation

The currency valuation of the Renminbi was previously too focused on the U.S. dollar. Now that the currencies of Japan and Korea have been included in China's currency exchange mechanism, it is in the interest of the relevant countries to strengthen financial sector cooperation in Asia. China and Japan can consider coordination in exchange rate adjustment, currency exchange, and East Asia bond market construction. As China and Japan jointly possess nearly USD2,000 in foreign currency reserves, accounting for 40% of the world's foreign currency reserves, the two countries form a strong foundation for regional currency cooperation.

Set up a bi-directional investment mechanism

As discussed above, Japan's new policy to attract inbound foreign investment and China's policy of encouraging outbound foreign investment coincide to create new opportunities. The two countries can work together to close the gap between them in terms of the investment environment, investment policy, investment protection, and market entry. They may also consider reaching an agreement on bilateral investment or a regional investment framework in order to promote bilateral investment.

Cooperation in energy and environmental protection

In both the energy and the environment sectors, cooperation would seem to yield better results than competition. There may be merit in China and Japan considering a joint construction of a petroleum reserve system and the joint development of disputed areas that may contain offshore oil. The two countries also need to work together to ensure safety in the transportation of oil and in sharing the energy conservation technologies from Japan.

Economic Significance of China-Japan Strategic Relations

In the October 2006 visit of Japanese prime minister Abe Shinzo to China, the *China-Japan Joint Press Communiqué* was issued which stated that "mutually beneficial relations for strategic interests" would be the objective of China-Japan relations. In the April 2007 Japan visit of Chinese Premier Wen Jiabao, both sides issued another *China-Japan Joint Press Communiqué*, laying out the key content and initiatives of a new era of cooperation.

The "strategic interest" referred to in these documents covers political, economic, security, and cultural interests, as well as regional and international affairs. It should be noted that the promotion of economic interests is especially important as a catalyst to promote strategic interest in other areas.

Economic background

There is a political context to these declarations of a new era in cooperation. Abe Shinzo was newly elected as prime minister, and eager to break the ice in political relations with China. His predecessor's visit to the Yasukuni Shrine had created a stalemate with China. The proclamation of new "strategic and mutually beneficial relations" was simply an attempt to resume cordial political relations with China.

However, there is also an economic backdrop to these new initiatives. Apart from the "cold politics," there were also signs of cooling economic relations between China and Japan. Because of the economic growth of China and the recession in Japan, China has become an engine of recovery for the Japanese economy by generating demand for Japanese goods and services. However, Japan has decreased in importance to China as a trading partner and source of foreign investment. The *China-Japan Joint Press Communiqué* creates a new framework and generates new momentum to support and coordinate the economic relations between the two countries.

The year 2007 was the 10th anniversary of the Asian Financial Crisis. The economies of China and Japan have maintained their leading role in Asia, jointly accounting for 80% of the East Asian economy and 60% of the foreign reserves in Asia and 40% of foreign reserves in the world. The economic relations between these two countries would be clearly crucial to the stability and economic prosperity of the whole region.

Measures for economic cooperation

The strategic interests covered in the 2007 *China-Japan Joint Press Communiqué* cover political, economic, security, cultural, regional, and international affairs interests. The main initiatives included deepening cooperation in the areas of energy, the environment, finance, information technology, and intellectual property rights protection. The main content of this new China-Japan cooperation is discussed below:

Set up a China-Japan senior level dialogue mechanism

With the 2007 meeting between Wen Jiabao and Abe Shinzo, the China-Japan Senior Level Dialogue was launched. The three main features of this dialogue mechanism are: that macro-economic policy dialogue is enabled; that the dialogue would involve coordination of multiple government departments at several senior levels; and that the dialogue would enable the two countries to discuss regional and international affairs.[22]

Strengthen economic cooperation

Energy and Environment

Japan possesses world-class technology in energy conservation and environmental protection. China is in need of such technology and may need Japanese capital in support. A joint statement on China-Japan cooperation in the environment sector was issued during Wen Jiabao's 2007 visit to Japan, in which China pledged to implement commitments in the Kyoto Protocol, to tackle pollution and improve environmental protection, and to reduce emissions of air pollutants by 10% in 2010 compared to 2005. China invited Japan to participate in tackling water and sea pollution in the Yangtze River and Bohai Yellow Sea region.

An energy policy dialogue was started during the 2007 visit of Wen Jiabao to Japan. A joint statement on energy cooperation was issued. China would welcome Japan to bring its advanced energy conservation technology and management experience to China, and to open cooperation in new energy development and commercialization, in energy reserve systems, and in the security of energy transport. A ministerial level energy policy dialogue would become a regular mechanism for this kind of cooperation.[23]

Agriculture

China and Japan aimed to go beyond the trade of agricultural products and expand their cooperation to Japan who would share its modern agricultural technology and operation methods. The two countries could also cooperate in resolving some issues in the agricultural sector in Japan, including the aged agricultural workforce. China and Japan would coordinate their agricultural trade under the systems in the WTO.

Safeguarding intellectual property rights

Disputes in this area have directly affected trade and investment, especially in the technology transfer from Japan to China. There needs to be continued dialogue in this area, to elevate the understanding of the use and protection of intellectual property rights in China.

Small and medium-sized enterprises (SMEs)

Although large enterprises have been the main driver in bilateral trade and investment, small and medium-sized enterprises are playing an increasingly important role. Government support would be given to small and medium-sized enterprises to obtain capital, technology, and market access. According to the Ministry of Economy and Trade of Japan, there were 463 Japanese SMEs investing overseas in East Asia in 1995. This number increased to 725 in 2000 and 1,141 in 2004. Of these, 135 companies in 1995 invested in China (29.2%), 254 in 2000 (35%), and 483 (42.3%) in 2004.[24]

Information technology

China and Japan will cooperate in the areas of next-generation mobile communication and network technology.

Finance

China and Japan will strengthen their cooperation in the financial sector and in financial regulation. Japan would share with China its experience in financial sector reform, the construction of capital markets, safeguarding against financial risks, and strengthening financial regulations. China would also welcome Japanese financial institutions to participate in Chinese financial sector reforms, and strengthen exchange and cooperation in the financial sector.[25]

Coordinated efforts in regional economic integration and international economic affairs

China and Japan have pledged to cooperate in two initiatives in regional cooperation. One initiative is in fostering a better investment environment in East Asia. To this end, China and Japan have signed an investment agreement and devised an action plan together with South Korea. A second initiative is in economic cooperation, where both sides agreed to start joint development aid for third world countries.

Strategic and mutually beneficial economic relations

As Japanese Prime Minister Shinzo Abe and Chinese Premier Wen Jiabao made efforts in warming up China-Japan relations, we would expect a new era in bilateral economic cooperation.

Greater clarity

The economic relations between China and Japan need to be re-defined and clarified. Both sides have made efforts to dispel the theory of a China threat, and to steer economic relations towards an understanding of the mutual benefit involved. The positive contribution made by bilateral trade, investment, and economic cooperation to each other's economy needs to be properly understood.

Improvement in cooperation mechanism

We are hopeful about the new mechanism, the China-Japan High-level Economic Dialogue. The mechanism would have a macro focus, involving the highest levels of government as well as multiple ministries and sectors. Apart from aiming to expand bilateral trade and to engage in policy dialogue, both countries would have a regular mechanism to deepen their cooperation in regional cooperation and international affairs. China has already appointed Vice Premier Zeng Peiyan as the China chairman of this economic dialogue, with the Ministry of Foreign Affairs, Ministry of Commerce, National Development and Reform Commission, and Ministry of Finance engaged to coordinate cooperation activities with their Japanese counterparts.

Widening cooperation

There have been varied results in three areas of bilateral economic cooperation activities, namely trade, investment, and development assistance. While trade has grown, talks on a free trade agreement between the two countries have yet to commence. Bilateral investment is one-sided as Chinese investment in Japan has yet to be fully developed. Meanwhile, Japan's ODA to China has also been drastically decreased and may be completely eliminated.

Based on the *China-Japan Joint Press Communiqué*, the two countries will be strengthening cooperation in the following areas:

Trade

Promote systems, mechanisms, and regulatory frameworks for bilateral trade. Study the feasibility and practical implementation of a free trade area, including one that covers all the ASEAN Plus Three members.

Investment

Encourage bi-directional investment, mainly by improving the Japanese investment environment for Chinese companies.

Finance

Strengthen regulation of the financial sector, increase protection against financial risks, promote East Asia regional cooperation. China and Japan have been promoting regional cooperation under the ASEAN Plus Three framework. This is based on the Chiang Mai mechanism which offers a regional foreign exchange liquidity of USD80 billion.

Energy and environment

Implement projects included in the energy cooperation agreement. Increase the technical, equipment, and capital support for environmental protection projects.

Agriculture and small to medium-sized enterprises

Focus on promoting bilateral trade in agricultural products, support small and medium-sized enterprises in business matching, and improve the general business environment.

9

Chapter

Economic Relations between China and South Korea

The History and Current Status of China–South Korea Economic Relations

China and the Korean Peninsula have a long history of friendship, based on geographical proximity, shared cultural traditions and a history of trade dating back to China's Han Dynasty (206 BC–AD 220). In terms of geography, the closest point between the two countries is only 92 nautical miles from each other. The two countries remained in close political, economic, and cultural contact, with migration in both directions, which only came to a complete halt with the advent of the Cold War after the Second World War.

Before the establishment of diplomatic relations

The two countries built a healthy foundation of economic relations before they officially established diplomatic relations in 1992. By the end of the 1970s, tensions subsided between China and South Korea as the Cold War came to an end. Separated families were allowed to visit each other, and re-exports resumed via Hong Kong, Japan, and Singapore. At the beginning, bilateral trade volume was very low, standing at USD20 million in 1979. But it took off in the 1980s, fueled by both countries' desire for economic reconstruction. China's economic reforms, the brightening prospect of peace between North and South Korea, as well as the multilateral trade policy South Korea embraced following friction with the United States and other developed nations, all contributed to positive bilateral trade relations.

The mode of bilateral trade also changed from indirect to direct, with the trade volume reaching USD1.76 billion by 1988.[1] In 1990, China and South Korea established non-official trade representative bodies in each other's countries—the China Chamber of International Commerce and the Korea Trade-Investment Promotion Agency. These efforts in trade and investment promotion soon paid off. Direct trade continued to grow, accounting for over half of the total trade volume of USD3.25 billion in 1991. As for direct investment, there was a cumulative total of 32 projects of Korean investment in China by 1990. In contrast, in the year 1991 alone, there were 69 such projects involving USD42 million in investment.

Close ties since the establishment of diplomatic relations

China and South Korea established official diplomatic relations on August 24, 1992. China has always valued peaceful relations with its neighboring countries,

Table 9.1. China-Korea trade since 1991

Year	Total (USD100 million)	Year-on-year growth rate (%)	Export to Korea (USD100 million)	Growth rate (%)	Import from Korea (USD100 million)	Growth rate (%)	Deficit for China (USD100 million)
1991	32.50	67.0	21.80	72.7	10.70	55.8	11.10
1992	50.27	55.2	24.04	10.6	26.22	144.9	–2.18
1993	82.20	63.5	28.60	18.9	53.59	104.3	–24.99
1994	117.21	42.6	44.20	54.5	73.18	36.6	–28.98
1995	169.82	44.8	66.89	51.3	102.93	40.6	–36.04
1996	199.81	17.7	74.99	12.1	124.81	21.3	–49.82
1997	240.56	20.3	91.26	21.5	149.29	19.6	–58.03
1998	212.64	–11.6	62.68	–31.3	149.95	0.4	–87.27
1999	250.33	17.7	78.07	24.9	172.26	14.7	–94.19
2000	345.00	37.8	112.90	44.6	232.10	34.7	–119.20
2001	359.10	4.1	125.20	10.9	233.90	0.8	–108.70
2002	440.70	22.7	155.00	23.8	285.70	22.1	–130.70
2003	632.30	43.5	201.00	29.7	431.30	51.0	–230.30
2004	900.70	42.5	278.20	38.4	622.50	44.3	–344.30
2005	1,119.30	24.3	351.00	26.2	768.20	23.4	–417.20
2006	1,342.30	19.9	445.30	26.8	897.80	16.9	–452.50
2007	1,599.00	19.2	561.40	23.1	1,037.60	15.6	–476.20

Source: Compiled from the *China Customs Statistics Yearbook*, relevant years.

while South Korea pursued the "Nordpolitik" policy aimed at engaging China and the former Soviet Union in the hope that North Korea would be further isolated politically. Nordpolitik (also known as Northern Policy) became an important factor that marked a new era of friendly relations between China and South Korea.

The visit of South Korean president Roh Tae-woo to China in September 1992 made progress in bilateral political and economic relations. He met with his Chinese counterparts to discuss issues of international relations, especially in regards to North Korea. Economic cooperation agreements were signed in the areas of trade, investment protection, the setting up of a joint committee on economic, trade, and technological cooperation, sea transport, double taxation, the peaceful use of nuclear energy, aviation, and fisheries. These agreements formed the political and legal foundation for the growth of economic relations and technological cooperation thereafter.

A system of regular meetings was set up between Chinese ministries and their Korean counterparts. There were the National Development and Reform Commission, the Ministry of Commerce and the Ministry of Science and Technology on the Chinese side. The Korean ministries included the Economic Planning Board, the Ministry of Commerce, Industry and Energy, and the Ministry of Finance.[2] Channels of contact were also opened in the areas of customs, commercial inspections, patents, statistics, fishery law, and commercial arbitration. Economic relations developed smoothly as numerous representative offices and trade organizations cropped up in both countries representing various sectors and industries.

Bilateral trade advanced in stride

There was double-digit growth in bilateral trade for several years since 1992. The China–South Korea trade volume was USD5.03 billion in 1992. There was continuous growth since then throughout the 1990s except for a small setback in 1998 due to the Asian Financial Crisis. Rapid growth followed after year 2000, as the record-breaking trade volume exceeded USD100 billion for the first time in 2005, reaching USD11.93 billion. China and South Korea had originally agreed to drive their trade to pass the USD100 billion milestone within five years from July 2003, an objective that was reached three years early. By 2007, the China–South Korea trade volume reached USD159.9 billion, fast approaching the total South Korea-US and South Korea–Japan trade combined. This also represented a 31-fold increase compared to the trade volume in 1992, and an average annual growth rate of 25%. This is a much higher growth rate compared to other trading partners of China for the same period.

China and South Korea started to account for a larger proportion of each other's foreign trade. China–South Korea trade accounted for 5.5% of China's foreign trade in 2000. This percentage rose to 7.6% in 2006. From the South Korean perspective, trade with China had accounted for 10% of its international trade in 2000 (following 19% with the US, 16% with Japan, 11.9% with the EU, and 11% with ASEAN). The percentage increased to 16.6% in 2004.[3]

The types of products that were traded also evolved over time, from raw materials and primary products to manufactured goods, and from low value-added to high value-added goods.

China became South Korea's largest trading partner in 2002. It also surpassed the US to become the largest export market for South Korea in the same year. In 2007, China surpassed Japan to become the largest source of imports. At the same time, South Korea also became the fourth largest trading partner for

China, ranking only after Japan, the U.S. and the EU. The rapid rate and scale of trade development between China and Korea are rarely seen elsewhere.

Rapid development of South Korean investment in China

Compared to other countries investing in China, South Korea entered the market relatively late. The first Korean investment arrived in 1985, but only as indirect investment through Hong Kong or Japan. The first direct investment started in 1988 and increased rapidly since then, rising to 170 projects and an actual utilized investment of USD141 million in 1992, the year diplomatic relations were established. These investment figures exceeded the cumulative number of projects and cumulative value of investment from previous years.

The number of projects doubled from 1992 to 1993, reaching 381 projects, while the investment contracts increased to USD631 million, triple that of 1992.

Table 9.2. South Korean investment in China, 1998–2006

Year	Number of agreements	Agreed investment (USD1,000)	Actual number of projects	Actual utilization of investment (USD1,000)
1988	2	3,400	1	10
1989	12	9,770	7	6,360
1990	39	55,624	24	16,174
1991	112	84,722	69	42,468
1992	269	223,113	170	141,127
1993	631	631,281	381	263,682
1994	1,065	825,141	841	634,472
1995	884	1,280,585	751	841,763
1996	927	1,959,741	738	921,634
1997	751	916,974	631	738,658
1998	318	904,768	262	695,124
1999	553	494,173	459	365,321
2000	913	999,135	777	710,379
2001	1,137	997,065	1,047	653,380
2002	1,547	2,092,702	1,381	1,019,508
2003	1,838	2,805,453	1,679	1,642,358
2004	2,247	3,680,458	2,149	2,290,740
2005	—	—	2,242	2,781,000
2006	—	—	2,300	3,300,000

Sources: Data of 1988–2004 from the Export-Import Bank of Korea. Data of 2005–2006 from *Korea-China Trade* 3 (2007).

Actual utilized investment in 1993 reached USD264 million, almost double that of 1992. Korean investment in China showed staggering growth in the following years until the Asian Financial Crisis in 1997. FDI from South Korea to China grew from USD634 million in 1994 to USD921 million in 1996. Because of the Asian Financial Crisis, Korean investment in China slipped for two years in 1998 and 1999. The actual utilized investment from Korea dropped to USD365 million in 1999, which was less than half of that of 1997 (see Table 9.2).

However, the Korean investment projects in China tended to be small in scale. Around the landmark year of 1992, three-quarters of the investment projects were under USD1 million, and half were under USD500,000. By 1994, there were still fewer than 20 projects with an investment over USD5 million, and 90% of investment projects were in labor-intensive manufacturing industries. Investment in apparel, machinery and equipment, leather goods, and shoes accounted for 52.9% of the value of all investment projects. At that time, South Korea accounted for only 0.5% of foreign investment in China, ranking seventh.[4]

There was significant growth in South Korean companies' investment in China since 2000, and especially after China's accession to the WTO in 2001 and the liberalization in various sectors that followed. Investment projects were typically in light textiles and food products and services. In addition, Korean companies also tended to invest in industries in which China had attained a certain level of technical skills and production capacity. These industries included home appliances, apparel, shoes, and leather goods processing.

In terms of geography, the areas in China attracting Korean investment widened over the years. Before 1994, Korean investment in China focused on the three northeast provinces and the Bohai regions of Shandong, Beijing, Tianjin, and Hebei. This early pattern was formed partly because of geographical proximity and the absence of language barriers, and partly because the Bohai and Yellow Sea regions were opened to economic development relatively late compared to southern China, and they therefore offered lower costs for the investment projects.

Later, the geographical pattern of Korean investment in China moved inland, as Korean companies invested, set up production facilities, and pursued cooperation projects in Henan, Shanxi, Shaanxi, and Guangdong Provinces as well as in Shanghai. Due to the comparative low cost of labor and land in China, Korean investment quickly went beyond the early phase of testing the water. Instead, 10 companies that can be considered the giants of Korean industry including Hyundai, Samsung, and LG have invested in China, and their investments are large-scale, and capital and technology intensive.

South Korean investment projects in China reached a cumulative total of over 46,000 projects and USD39.99 billion in April 2008, according to the statistics of approved investment of the Ministry of Commerce.[5] According to the Korea International Trade Association, Korean companies have a cumulative 60,707 investment projects in China by the end of 2007, with a cumulative value of USD20.7 billion. China represents 50.3% of the number of projects and 25.3% of actual utilized investment of Korea.[6] Regardless of whether we consider the Chinese or the Korean statistics, China has become the largest destination for Korean outbound investment.

The first steps towards a China-Korea Free Trade Area

China and South Korea are in the process of setting up a free trade area. The two governments, joined by industry and academia, have started a series of discussions and negotiations after a preliminary study on the free trade area that was completed in the first half of 2007 by civil organizations. Discussions so far have focused on articulating the macroeconomic impact and industry level impact. More concrete issues of defining which sectors to cover and how to manage the trade of sensitive products are also being explored. The mode and timeline of implementing the free trade zone have also been discussed.

By the end of 2007, four conferences have been held, led by the two governments with industry and academic participation. The discussion took a sector-by-sector approach. Consensus was reached regarding manufacturing, country of origin, customs clearance, intellectual property, economic cooperation, and hygiene, inspection and quarantine. Agreement was reached in a total of 15 sectors. Major areas for future negotiations include the primary industries of agriculture, forestry and fisheries, government procurement, as well as the concluding agreements.[7]

Fruitful cooperation in the financial services sector

Financial sector cooperation between the two countries started with an agreement signed after diplomatic relations were established. China Construction Bank (CCB), the Industry and Commerce Bank of China (ICBC) and the Agricultural Bank of China (ABC) set up representative offices in Seoul, while the Bank of China (BOC) set up a branch there. As of June 2006, Korea set up 39 financial institutions in China. Eight Korean banks have set up 17 branches, four representative offices, and one legal entity in China. Korean investors also set up 11 insurance companies and four securities companies in the cities Beijing, Tianjin, Shanghai, Qingdao, Shenyang, and Dalian and in Guangdong Province.[8]

Also worth noting is the Economic Cooperation Development Fund (EDCF) set up by the South Korean government to provide assistance to developing countries. Assistance to China in the form of government loans started in 1994. As of 2008, funding of USD233 million had been provided for 22 projects. The loans contributed to sectors including airports, roads, ports, provision of water in cities, telecommunication, agriculture, and environmental protection.[9]

In the wake of the Asian Financial Crisis in 1997, China provided funding through an International Monetary Fund (IMF) bailout to South Korea in three instances, with a total amount of USD681.5 million.[10]

Continued momentum in industrial cooperation and investment

Architecture and construction have been among the sectoral focus of China-Korea cooperation. Based on an agreement signed January 8, 1993, Korean architecture companies have participated in the re-design of Chinese cities. Several dozen Korean companies have entered the Chinese market, contracted for projects in the order of over several million USD each year. Korean and Chinese companies have also cooperated to invest in design and construction projects in other countries. Korean companies contributed their capital and technical capability while Chinese companies contributed manpower.

The two countries also cooperated in the production of automobiles, mid-sized passenger aircraft, stored program control (SPC) switches, and HD television sets. These cooperation projects were laid out by the bilateral agreement signed on June 6, 1994, to set up an Industry Cooperation Committee. Another agreement on peaceful use of nuclear power was also signed on October 31, 1994, forming a basis for widening cooperation in developing civil use of nuclear energy.

Samsung, the largest Korean conglomerate, expanded its investment in China over the years. As of the end of 2007, more than 30 Samsung companies had invested a cumulative USD6.1 billion, set up 123 entities, and hired more than 63,000 people in China. These companies include Samsung Electronics, Samsung Electro-Mechanics, Samsung Telecommunication Systems, Samsung Life, Samsung Fire and Marine Insurance, Samsung Securities, Samsung Properties. Their involvement spanned the sectors of electronics, finance, trade, heavy industries, construction, chemicals, apparel, textiles, and advertising. In 2007, the Samsung business in Greater China recorded USD38.9 billion in revenue, including USD27.6 billion in revenue from mainland China. Also in 2007, 61% of Samsung's mainland China sales were exports to the international market.[11]

Another Korean conglomerate, the LG Group, also made China one of its priority markets in direct investment. As of the end of 2005, LG had built large production facilities in Changsha and Tianjin, and has mainly invested in semiconductors, oil refining, and petrochemicals. In 2006, its China businesses had a revenue of USD9 billion. Its rising profile in China has been visibly shown in its 40-storey headquarters building in Beijing, which was built before the 2008 Olympics.

The Beijing Hyundai Motor Co. Ltd. also showed impressive growth in China. The joint venture between Beijing Automotive Group and Hyundai Motor Company had a record-breaking year in 2007. The company produced 1 million vehicles in a short time frame of 62 months, the highest production rate for any Chinese automobile company. A second Hyundai factory is under construction, which when completed will increase the company's total production capacity in China to an annual 600,000 vehicles.[12]

China and Korea also had a track record of cooperation in postal and telecommunications. A joint venture Beijing Jingkoh Integrated Communication Equipment was set up by the Beijing Communications Administration and Kohap Group of Korea in March 1994, and this paved the way for other Korean telecommunication companies to enter China. Daewoo Group of Korea joined the Ministry of Space Industry of China to form a joint cooperative in Beijing with an investment of USD20 million to produce electronic switches. Daewoo also invested in Tianjin and opened a production plant manufacturing audio systems for automobiles. In addition, China and Korea cooperated in developing new telecommunication technologies.

Foreign labor service cooperation

The Korean labor market opened in 1994, when 8,000 Chinese workers were among the 20,000 foreign-imported workers imported in the first year, accounting for 40% of imported labor.[13] In 2006, China and Korea signed new labor contracts and international contracting contracts with a value of USD370 million, with a turnover of USD650 million.[14] As of March 2008, China had 53,000 workers in Korea, with a cumulative turnover of USD4.02 billion.[15] Because Korean economic development has been affected by the domestic shortage and high cost of labor, imported Chinese workers had become a solution.

Tourism, cultural, and education cooperation

Chinese citizens were permitted in 1998 to visit Korea as individual travelers. In 1999, Chinese citizens enjoyed visa free travel to Jeju Island, Korea. In 2006, more than 780,000 Chinese citizens visited Korea. In terms of number of visitors to Korea, China ranks second only to Japan.

China has also become the top destination for Korean overseas travel. In 2007, more than 477,000 Korean visitors went to mainland China, making China the destination attracting the largest number of Korean visitors.[16]

Among the foreigners living in mainland China, Koreans also form the largest community, and this is still growing by 60,000 to 70,000 people per year. In 2007, more than 700,000 Koreans lived in China, which is a population equivalent to a mid-sized city in Korea. One in three foreign students in China is from Korea. In Korea, the number of Chinese citizens living, working, and studying there has exceeded 530,000 and this number is still growing.[17]

Korean brands have been featured in China as parts of a fashionable trend, as demonstrated by the Daewoo and Hyundai cars on the road, Korean-produced laptops and mobile phones, and the Korean spas, modeling schools, and Korean soap operas and ads on TV. China has also become a popular subject in Korea, where studying Chinese has become popular. All 140 universities in Korea have a Chinese language department. The general population in Korea has shown great interest in studying Chinese and learning about Chinese culture.

The two countries have also maintained close cooperation in diplomacy, anti-terrorism, nuclear non-proliferation, and environmental protection.

Since the establishment of diplomatic relations in August 1992, the two countries have rapidly developed economic and trade relations on many levels. Their close and highly complementary relations were further boosted by China's accession to the WTO.

Favorable Factors for Rapid Growth in China-Korea Economic Relations

The main reasons behind the smooth and rapid development of China-Korea relations can be summarized as follows:

Positive political relations

China and Korea share the common interest in maintaining close and friendly neighborly relations, especially since both are important powers in Asia. China has supported peaceful engagement between North and South Korea, and advocated nuclear non-proliferation on the Korean Peninsula. South Korea has respected the "One China" principle and opposed Taiwan's claims to independence. It has also clearly stated that it will not get involved in any conflict in the Taiwan Strait. This mutual respect of independence, sovereignty, and core interest has supported positive diplomatic relations between the two countries. China and Korea are also united in their opposition to Japanese political leaders visiting the Yakusuni Shrine.

China and Korea have also effectively utilized the international platforms of political and security dialogue. Since the establishment of diplomatic relations, the two countries have maintained frequent contact, discussion, coordination and cooperation through the mechanisms in the United Nations, APEC, Asia-Europe Meeting (ASEM), ASEAN forums, and the East Asia Summit. There is a consensus for continued peace in the Korean Peninsula, in East Asia and in Asia Pacific. Both countries also recognize that regional growth in East Asia would lead to further opportunities for economic advancement for each individual country.

Regular visits of state leaders helped the two countries forge closer diplomatic ties. Upon Korean President Kim Tae-jung's visit to China in 1998, the two countries started their "cooperative partnership for the 21st century." A new stage of comprehensive cooperation was then started in 2000 with the visit of Chinese Premier Zhu Rongji to Korea. Bilateral ties became even closer as a comprehensive and cooperative partnership was declared in 2003 when Korean President Roh Moo-hyun visited China. In 2005, during the visit of Chinese President Hu Jintao, Korea recognized China's status as a full market economy. In May 2008, the relationship of the two countries was elevated to a strategic cooperative partnership.[18]

In August 2008, President Hu Jintao made an official visit to Korea, the third meeting of the two state leaders within three months. *The China–South Korea Joint Declaration* was announced, outlining long-term development and closer cooperation between the countries across various sectors.

Frequent exchange has also taken place at the regional level and in civil society in the two countries. Chinese consulates have been set up in Busan and Guangju in Korea, while Korean consulates have been set up in Shanghai, Qingdao, Guangzhou, Shenyang, Chengdu, Xi'an, Wuhan, and Hong Kong. Organizations of cultural exchange and trade facilitation have also been formed, strengthening economic and cultural ties at all levels of civil society. China has set up a China-Korea Friendship Association. Korea has set up the Korea-China Friendship Association, Korea-China Economic Association, and the 21st Century Korea-China Exchange Association. Moreover, Beijing, Shanghai, Tianjin, Shandong Province, and Liaoning Province have been paired with Seoul, Busan, Incheon, Gyeongsangnam-do and Gyeonggi-do, respectively, as sister cities or provinces. As of September 2007, the two countries had 85 provinces and cities that had established friendship ties with each other.[19] All these efforts have formed a comprehensive and multi-tiered foundation for economic cooperation.

Shared objectives

China and South Korea each makes economic development a priority in its long-term national strategy. Peaceful relations and stability in the region would be a prerequisite for economic growth. The two countries share a long history of friendly relations and have both experienced foreign invasion and occupation in the 20th century. This makes both countries desire continued peace, despite the fact that South Korea remains an ally to the United States, and has had some conflicts with China in recent history. Since the two countries are important economic powers in Asia, their closer exchange and cooperation would only bring greater prosperity to the region.

Cultural and geographical connection

China-Korea economic relations are supported by favorable factors in culture and geography. First, their historical ties can be traced back for over 2,000 years. The two countries share similarities in cultural traditions, customs, and mentality.

Second, there is a 2 million-strong Korean ethnic group in China [known as *chaoxianzu* in Chinese and *joseonjok* in Korean]. These Chinese citizens have strong ties to Korea, acting as a bridge in trade and investment promotion.

Third, transport and communication links between the two countries are well-developed because of the geographical proximity. China's Liaoning and Shandong peninsulas are separated from the Korean peninsula only by the Yellow Sea. Sea transport from Incheon and Kunsan in Korea to Qingdao, Weihai and Yantai in China take just over 10 hours. Since the cargo route for international consignments was opened in January 1994 between Lianyun Port in China and Busan in Korea, four other passenger and cargo routes were opened between the two countries. A sea route for postal delivery was also started in March 1994. Nearly 70 flight routes for passengers and cargo were opened between 30 Chinese cities and six Korean cities. There are 780 flights every week between China and Korea.[20] These transportation links have minimized the already short distance between the two countries, lowering cost, improving cargo delivery time, and creating more convenience for travelers.

Communication links have also been strengthened ever since the submarine fiber-optic cable system was officially launched in February 1996 between Qingdao, China, and Taean, Korea. The 550km system contains more than 15,000 cables.

Strong complementarity in the two economies

Both China and Korea are post-industrial economies. Korea's industrialization started earlier and developed faster. In 2007, the per capita GDP of Korea is USD19,485, which indicates that Korea is a developed country.[21] Yet, due to challenges in the international market, Korea has adopted multilateralism in its diplomacy and diversification in its economy and foreign trade. Its diplomatic policy sees the US and Japan as the core, and aims to advance its economic self-interest by expanding foreign markets and seeking transitional economies as emerging markets. These considerations have determined Korean relations with China.

China's industrialization started later and is still incomplete. It is still a developing economy. The two countries tend to specialize in producing different goods—Korea specializes in capital-intensive and technology-intensive products while China has so far specialized in labor-intensive products. There is a divergent gap in labor cost between the two countries. The average monthly wage in Korea is USD1,500, which is more than 10 times that in China. This complementarity has driven the growth in trade and the relocation of some Korean industries to China.

Problems in China–South Korea Economic Cooperation

Some unresolved issues in the economic relations between China and South Korea can be understood as follows:

Trade imbalance

South Korea is the country with which China has the largest trade deficit. The persistent and increasing trade deficit may affect the long-term stability in trade relations. Ever since the establishment of diplomatic relations in 1992, China has run an increasingly large trade deficit with South Korea. Customs statistics show that the trade deficit was approaching USD10 billion prior to 1999. It increased to USD23 billion in 2000, USD34.4 billion in 2004, and USD41.7 billion in 2005. In 2007, it increased to USD47.7 billion. In the first 15 years between 1992 and 2007, China had a cumulative total of USD239.4 billion in trade deficit with Korea.[22]

The deficit grew especially rapidly after China joined the WTO. In 2002, the trade deficit grew 34.4% compared to the previous year. It then grew 83.9% in 2003 and 52.3% in 2004. The size of the deficit has been recognized as an important issue on both sides, but it remains unresolved.

Although trade between China and Korea has changed from predominantly primary products to industrial finished goods, Korea still exports goods with high added value to China, such as electronics, chemicals, machinery, automobiles, steel, and telecommunication equipment. About 30%–40% of Chinese exports to Korea are still resources such as agricultural and mining products, with low added value and high labor intensity.

There was a surge in Korean exports to China after the bilateral trade agreement between the two trading partners. The rapid rise of Korean investment in China also accelerated the export of Korean machinery, raw materials, and parts to China. There has been an increase in anti-dumping cases launched against China by Korea, which citing protection of domestic industries as a reason, imposed tariffs and other discriminatory measures. This barred further expansion of Chinese exports to Korea and contributed to the growing trade deficit.

In addition, the Korean market is much smaller compared to China, and is therefore unable to absorb a large amount of primary goods or daily essential goods. At the same time, Korea has adopted a proactive policy to boost exports to China, but has been much more passive in increasing imports from China.

Investment imbalance and lack of Chinese investment in Korea

There has been over 5,000 Chinese investment projects in Korea as of June 2007, ever since a company was jointly set up by Sinotrans and Korea's Dongnama Shipping in Korea in January 1991.[23] Chinese companies have set up wholly owned businesses and joint ventures in transportation, catering, and trade. One of the high profile investment projects was the Shanghai Automobile Industry Corporation (SAIC) acquisition of SsangYong Motor Company in Korea. Also, Beijing Oriental Science and Technology acquired the LED screen business of Korea's Hynix company (formerly Hyundai Electronics). Chinese investment projects in Korea are increasing in scale, but are still predominantly small projects. In terms of the number of projects, Chinese investment in Korea accounts for 9.9% of foreign investment in Korea, surpassing the US and Japan. But in terms of contract value, these projects are much smaller, and the total Chinese investment does not even account for 1% of the value of foreign investment in Korea.

This imbalance in bilateral investment translates into a different magnitude of eagerness or need to develop economic cooperation. The smaller Chinese investment in Korea is partly because the "Go Global" policy has been launched relatively late in China. However, it is also partly due to an unfavorable investment environment in Korea. Although the Korean market has been internationalized since 1995, foreign-invested companies still face obstacles and discrimination when bidding for projects in Korea. High cost of labor, powerful unions, and incessant labor disputes have also raised the difficulty and risks of investing in Korea. Foreign workers in Korea encounter a complex process and stringent requirements when applying for multiple entry visas. All these factors have hampered the growth of Chinese investment in Korea.

Pre-existing problems in the countries

A certain level of suspicion and guardedness has developed between the people of China and Korea, indicating the need for further efforts in advancing mutual understanding. This is partly because of imperfect information. There is a limited amount of information in China introducing Korea, whereas the information available in Korea about China is often inaccurate and not comprehensive. The misunderstanding is illustrated in a 2007 global perspective survey conducted by the Pew Research Centre, which was at the time led by former US Secretary of State Madeleine Albright. When asked questions about who was perceived as the largest ally and the largest threat, 64% of respondents in Korea viewed China as the largest threat, whereas a negligible number of Chinese respondents saw Korea as the largest threat.[24]

From the Chinese perspective, trade and investment in Korea has lacked macro planning and controls. Numerous Chinese companies have started cooperation with Korean entities, sometimes occupying the same space in the market and causing vicious competition. The favorable terms offered to Chinese investors have not been well-coordinated, so that the different regions or government organizations are undercutting each other's advantages. There has been poor management of personnel on the part of Chinese companies in Korea, leading to a reduction in the actual income of workers, as well as disputes, escapes, injuries, and deaths.

Moreover, despite numerous trade promotion expos showcasing Korea and numerous delegations of Chinese companies visiting Korea, few Chinese companies ever actually conduct business activities or sign contracts. This causes wastage and duplication. The Chinese investment environment also has yet to improve. China's energy, transportation, and telecommunications infrastructure requires more balanced development. There are also gaps in relevant regulations, complex procedures for foreign investors, and low efficiency. These problems are unfavorable to promoting Korean investment in China.

From the Korean perspective, investment in China has experienced bottlenecks. First, in order to ensure a domestic industrial upgrade, many Korean investment projects in China tend to be in sunset industries or labor intensive industries. Korea has been conservative in investing in technology, and Korean investment projects in China tend to be of low technology content. Second, some Korean companies that invested in China in the early days to take advantage of the low cost of labor and raw materials have now decided to leave China because these costs have risen. Third, there are concerns within Korea about the "hollowing out" of Korean industry. While pursuing investment opportunities in China, Korean companies are also held back by fears that China would become a threat and a viable competitor.

The Future of China-Korea Economic Cooperation

Despite some issues in bilateral economic relations, China and Korea have enjoyed a positive relationship of mutual cooperation. When Chinese President Hu Jintao visited Korea in August 25–26, 2008, the historic *China-Korea Joint Declaration* was announced, affirming the long-term positive development of bilateral relations.

The joint declaration states four major areas of cooperation, namely politics, economy and trade, cultural exchange, and regional and international affairs. In terms of politics, the first high level strategic dialogue of the two countries' ministers of foreign affairs was held in 2008. This represents the launch of regular dialogue and the strengthening of communication links between the two governments. It was a precursor to subsequent visits of national security chiefs between the two countries, with the aim of resolving the question of sea boundaries.

There were 17 agreements in economy and trade, including energy, environmental protection, communication, finance, and logistics. The cultural exchange area included six agreements, including the decision to make 2010 a "Visit China" Year and 2012 a "Visit Korea" Year. In terms of regional and international affairs, the two countries agreed to support progress in the six-party talks regarding security in the Korean Peninsula. They also agreed to join efforts in combating terrorism and climate change.

The *China-Korea Joint Declaration* has been largely successful in further developing the strategic cooperative partner relationship between the two countries. We anticipate the following trends in bilateral economic relations:

Growth in trade and investment

Bilateral trade volume between China and Korea has reached USD200 billion in 2010, achieving the goal as stated in the China-Korea Joint Declaration. Since China's transitional phase after WTO accession has now ended, the Chinese economy has a higher degree of liberalization and greater clarity in its investment environment. Korean companies used to focus their investment in manufacturing industries in China. It is hoped that China's service trade, energy conservation, environmental protection, energy, information technology, and high technology sectors would become more appealing to Korean investors.

Before Lee Myung-bak was sworn into the presidency in Korea in February 2008, he proposed a "747 Plan" which pledged annual GDP growth of 7%, an increase in per capita GDP to USD40,000, and for Korea to become the seventh largest economy in the world. The Korean economy is therefore under transition and industrial upgrade in order to achieve these goals. The Chinese market offers enormous opportunity for Korea.

Economic integration of China and Korea

Efforts to set up a China-Korea Free Trade Area did not stop after several studies and conferences held in 2007 by government, industry, and academia. The *China-Korea Joint Declaration* states that the two countries will continue to study and support the progress towards establishing a free trade area.[25] If, and when, the two countries sign a bilateral free trade agreement, many existing issues can be resolved and new opportunities will surface.

Key role in advancement of East Asia regional cooperation

The concept of a free trade area in East Asia has been raised as a means to broaden regional economic integration. China and Korea have both played an active role in regional cooperation platforms, including the ASEAN 10+3 mechanism and the East Asian Summit. Both China and Korea recognize the importance of regional cooperation for East Asia, which maintains long-term stability and brings further prosperity to the countries involved.

Maintaining mutual trust between the two countries, both at a government level and in civil society, is a prerequisite to strengthening cooperation. China may need to further elaborate and implement its policy for neighborly relations. The development of China has been an opportunity for the whole world, and for Korea it is an even more important opportunity. As Korea is the country with which China has the largest trade deficit, Korea has successfully entered and utilized the China market in order to benefit its own economy. China-Korea economic cooperation has benefited not only the two countries' economies, but also supported regional stability and the core political interests of both countries. The bilateral economic relations between China and Korea will be benefited by increasing exchanges, stronger trust, and improved policies.

10

Chapter

Economic Relations between China and India

China and India were both ancient kingdoms with glorious histories. Both countries had experienced Western invasion and occupation in more recent times and struggled to liberate their people. These neighbors have at times been friendly trading partners, but they have also waged war against each other. In the 21st century, both China and India enjoyed remarkable economic achievements, and they have taken on greater power and responsibilities in the international arena. Geopolitical considerations will be central to the future of their political and economic relations.

The Historical Friendship between China and India

China and India are neighbors with more than 2,000 years of friendly relations. In the Western Han Dynasty (202 BC–AD 9), Zhang Qian was sent as an ambassador to travel to India.[1] He opened the Silk Road which paved the way for Buddhism to enter China from its Indian birthplace. Because the Central Asian states located between China and India at the time had constant battles, a maritime Silk Road was opened during the reign of Emperor Wu of Han Dynasty (141–87 BC). This was a sea route that reached the southern end of the Indian peninsula.[2]

Emperor Ming of Han (reigned AD 57–75) sent ambassadors to the Central Asian states and to India, bringing out Buddhist scripts and statues. China's first Buddhist temple, the White Horse Temple, was built as a result.[3]

In the Eastern Jin Dynasty, Buddhist monk Faxian had visited Tianzhu (today's India) in AD 399 for Buddhist scripts. He returned in AD 413 and wrote *A Record of Buddhist Kingdoms*, a masterpiece in the study of the history, geography, and religion of India.

The height of China-India historical relations was reached in the Tang Dynasty, during the reign of Emperor Taizong (626–649), when ambassadors from Tianzhu sent tulips and the bodhi tree as gifts to China. During this time, China's invention of 10-digit arithmetic spread to India.

Probably the most well-known episode of the historical ties between China and India is the story later fictionalized in literature as the *Journey to the West*. Buddhist monks Xuanzang and Yijing traveled to India, and upon their return, Xuanzang translated more than 1,300 scrolls of Buddhist texts and authored *The Great Tang Records on the Western Regions*. Yijing also brought back large numbers of Buddhist texts, and authored the *Buddhist Monk's Pilgrimage of the Tang Dynasty*. Xuanzang also translated the Daoist text *Tao Te Ching* into Sanskrit and introduced it to India. The two monks became the most important cultural ambassadors between the two countries.[4]

In Ming Dynasty, between 1405 and 1433, general Zheng He made seven exploratory trips on the sea and made several visits to India.

In ancient times, China's gold, silk, ceramics, tea, and medicinal herbs had been traded for India's spices, gemstones, and pearls. The volume of trade was very small due to the primitive transportation links. Through the process of trade, China and India had the opportunity for cultural exchange. Silk production techniques, the technology of paper making, and arithmetic from China had spread to India. Meanwhile, the method of heating sugar, block printing, and calendars of India were spread to China. In these 2,000 years of historical ties, the two cultures also shared knowledge in architecture, astronomy, and medicine. It can be said that China and India contributed to each other's cultural, trade, and technology development. These achievements form the historical basis for today's friendly ties between China and India.[5]

The Convoluted Development of China-India Economic Relations since 1949

Since the establishment of the People's Republic of China (PRC), China-India political and economic relations have gone through rollercoaster style fluctuations, with political conflicts deeply affecting trade and economic cooperation. The modern economic relationship between China and India can be understood in several stages: First steps taken in the 1950s, stagnation in the 1960s and 1970s, recovery between the mid-1970s to late 1980s, and a period of rapid growth from the late 1980s up to the present time. There were two setbacks in 1998 and 1999, when the Asian Financial Crisis hit and when India conducted tests in its nuclear weapons program.

An overview of China-India economic relations

China and India maintained friendly relations since they established diplomatic relations on April 1, 1950. That year, the bilateral trade volume was USD29.39 million, and the trade volume between 1951 and 1952 was roughly USD70 million.[6] A three-year trade agreement was signed in October 1954, and later extended twice.[7]

In April 1954, an agreement was signed regarding trade and transportation between the Tibet region of China and India. Trade at that time mainly took the form of border trade between individual merchants, and therefore limited the growth in trade volume. More importantly, China regarded the Soviet

Union as its main trading partner, while India had the United States as its main trading partner, so China and India had little interest in trading with each other. There was moderate growth in trade from 1954 onwards, but the trade volume between 1950 and 1962 was still only USD260 million.[8] During this time, China had exported rice, soybeans, raw silk, and transformers to India, while India exported cotton, jute, tobacco, and chemicals to China.

From 1959 onwards, India's support for rebellions in Tibet and its border disputes with China dampened trade between the two countries. War broke out in 1962, prompting India to sever trade ties with China. In 1962 before the war, bilateral trade reached only USD1.77 million. Trade was basically non-existent from 1962 to 1976 when relations recovered.[9]

In April 1976, China and India resumed ambassadorial diplomatic relations, signaling a recovery in political relations and creating a favorable environment for trade. After having no trade ties for 15 years, India exported 23 million rupees of goods to China in 1977.[10]

Official trade talks started in February 1978, with frequent delegations and visits since then. In March 1980, the vice minister of agriculture of China visited India. In November 1984, the deputy director-general of China's State Economic Planning Commission led a delegation to India. In May 1985, the Chinese minister of metallurgy industry visited India to expand the two countries' cooperation in metallurgy. In 1988, Indian Prime Minister Rajiv Gandhi visited China to discuss border issues and to pave the way for further cooperation with China. In March 1988, the deputy director-general of China's State Science and Technology Commission visited India to explore technological exchange and cooperation. This resulted in a technology cooperation agreement signed in December that year. In March 1989, China's minister of agriculture visited India, which led to a memorandum of understanding signed to forge closer cooperation in agricultural science.

However, as seen in Table 10.1, bilateral trade did not receive an immediate boost from these encouraging governmental exchanges. Trade relations were normalized but still in recovery. By 1987, bilateral trade still only accounted for 0.42% of the total foreign trade of India.

From 1985 to 1987, the China-India trade volume was about USD120 million per year. In 1988, the trade volume more than doubled from USD117.4 million in 1987 to USD246.3 million, an increase of 110%. From 1988 onwards, apart from the Asian Financial Crisis and the Indian nuclear weapons program testing resulting in temporary setbacks, bilateral trade enjoyed a rising trend. From 1988 to 2007, bilateral trade increased 157 times from USD246.3 million to USD38.65 billion. However, the two countries still accounted for a relatively

Table 10.1. China-India trade , 1985–2007 (USD100 million)

Year	Export	Import	Trade volume	Trade balance	China-India trade as a percentage of total China trade (%)	China-India trade as a percentage of total India trade (%)
1985	0.85	0.39	1.24	0.46	0.18	0.49
1986	0.89	0.39	1.27	0.50	0.17	0.51
1987	0.88	0.30	1.17	0.58	0.14	0.42
1988	1.49	0.98	2.46	0.51	0.24	0.76
1989	1.69	1.02	2.71	0.66	0.24	0.75
1990	1.67	0.97	2.64	0.69	0.23	0.64
1991	1.44	1.20	2.65	0.24	0.20	0.69
1992	1.58	1.80	3.39	–0.22	0.20	0.78
1993	2.59	4.17	6.76	–1.57	0.35	1.52
1994	5.73	3.22	8.95	2.51	0.38	1.72
1995	7.65	3.98	11.63	3.67	0.41	1.78
1996	6.90	7.19	14.09	–0.30	0.49	1.98
1997	9.33	8.97	18.30	0.36	0.56	2.39
1998	10.17	9.06	19.22	1.11	0.59	2.52
1999	11.62	8.26	19.88	3.36	0.55	2.41
2000	15.69	13.50	29.20	2.19	0.61	3.10
2001	18.96	17.00	35.96	1.96	0.71	3.84
2002	26.72	22.74	49.46	3.98	0.80	4.68
2003	33.44	42.51	75.95	–9.08	0.89	5.77
2004	59.27	76.77	136.04	–17.51	1.18	7.71
2005	89.34	97.66	187.01	–8.32	1.32	7.71
2006	145.81	102.77	248.59	43.04	1.41	8.40
2007	240.16	146.31	386.47	93.85	1.78	10.68

Sources: WTO Statistical Database; China customs statistics.

low percentage of each other's total foreign trade. As a percentage of the total foreign trade of China, bilateral trade accounted for 0.24% in 1988 and 1.78% in 2007. The percentage rose much more healthily from the Indian perspective, from 0.76% in 1988 to 10.68% in 2007.

The types of goods traded diversified after 1988, evolving from agricultural products and primary goods to industrial and mining products. By the late 1970s, China was exporting to India raw silk, beans, raw materials for pharmaceuticals, textiles, light industrial products, coal, food, animal products, and machinery. Indian exports to China included iron, chromium, tobacco, medicinal herbs, urea fertilizer, diamond, chemical materials, wool, and timber. In the 21st century, products traded have now changed to mainly electronics, mechanical finished products, mining resources, and related products (see Table 10.2).

Table 10.2. Main categories of goods traded between China and India, first half of 2007 (USD million)

Chinese exports to India				Indian exports to China			
HS code	Category	Value	Percentage (%)	HS code	Category	Value	Percentage (%)
85	Electric machinery, generator, audiovisual equipment and parts	2,888.5	26.5	26	Mining ore, slag and calx	2,258.2	49.7
84	Nuclear reactor, steam boiler, mechanical equipment and parts	1,862.7	17.1	52	Cotton	381.6	8.4
29	Organic chemicals	991.7	9.1	29	Organic chemicals	311.9	6.9
72	Steel and iron	709.7	6.5	74	Copper and copper products	286.7	6.3
27	Fossil fuel, oil and other product; asphalt	635.1	5.8	72	Steel	220.1	4.8
73	Steel and iron products	577.6	5.3	25	Salt, sulphur, earths and stone, plastering material and cement	146.3	3.2
39	Plastic and plastic products	289.1	2.7	39	Plastic and plastic products	144.7	3.2
89	Ships and floating structures	203	1.9	28	Organic chemicals, precious metals and other composites	129	2.8

(Cont'd)

Chinese exports to India				Indian exports to China			
HS code	Category	Value	Percentage (%)	HS code	Category	Value	Percentage (%)
50	Raw Silk	181.7	1.7	27	Fossil fuel, oil and other products; asphalt	111.4	2.5
28	Organic chemicals, precious metals and other composites	162.5	1.5	84	Nuclear reactor, steam boiler, mechanical equipment and parts	98.2	2.2
71	Jewelry, precious metal and products, fake jewelry, coins	151.9	1.4	67	Processed feather and feather products, artificial flower, artificial hair	61.2	1.4
87	Automobile and auto parts, except railway vehicles	121	1.1	85	Electric machinery, generator, audiovisual equipment and parts	40.1	0.9
90	Optics, photography, medical equipment and parts	117.1	1.1	23	Residue and waste from food industry; processed animal feed	31.4	0.7
59	Soaked, wrapped or layered knitted goods; textiles for industrial use	112.6	1.0	15	Animal and vegetable oil, fats, wax, processed cooking oil	27.5	0.6
	Citation	10,907.4	100.0		Citation	4,547.4	100.0

Source: China customs statistics.

Table 10.2 shows the strong complementarity in China-India bilateral trade. Chinese exports are typically electronics and mechanical products, while India exports are mostly mining products and semi-processed goods.

Features of China-India economic relations

The fluctuating path of bilateral trade

In theory, the size of the economies and the geographical proximity of China and India should warrant vibrant trade. Their recent history of foreign invasion should have created solidarity between them. In practice however, factors such as border disputes, the Tibet problem, and China-Pakistan relations have hindered economic relations. Moreover, both China and India are increasingly considered emerging global powers, giving rise to a competitive relationship between them which in turn eroded mutual trust.

Political and economic relations between the two countries have had a strong correlation. Trade was supported by friendship in the 1950s, and this evaporated in the 1960s with the Sino-Indian War that broke out in 1962. Economic relations stopped for 14 years as political relations remained untenably frozen. When ambassadorial diplomatic relations resumed in 1976, trade recovered and then took off in the 1980s. The 1998 and 1999 episodes of the Asian Financial Crisis and Indian nuclear weapons program testing were temporary but significant setbacks. In the 21st century, China and India managed to maintain a close friendship with regular senior governmental leaders' visits.

Momentum for rapid growth

As Fig.10.1 shows, there has been a rising trend in China-India trade since 1988, although the trend has occasionally fluctuated. Bilateral trade reached USD150 million in 1985, dropped slightly in 1987 and 1990, but kept the growing momentum rising to USD675.73 million in 1993 and to USD1.162 billion in 1995. Apart from the staggering growth rate in 1988 and 1993, in most years the rising trend maintained a steady climb which reflected the gradual stabilization of political relations through the years, especially since the 1990s. By 2007, bilateral trade had reached USD38.65 billion.

China's trade surplus with India

The bilateral trade balance has grown significantly in favor of China today. From the 1970s to 2006, China had a trade deficit with India only in the years

Fig 10.1. Growth rate of China-India bilateral trade

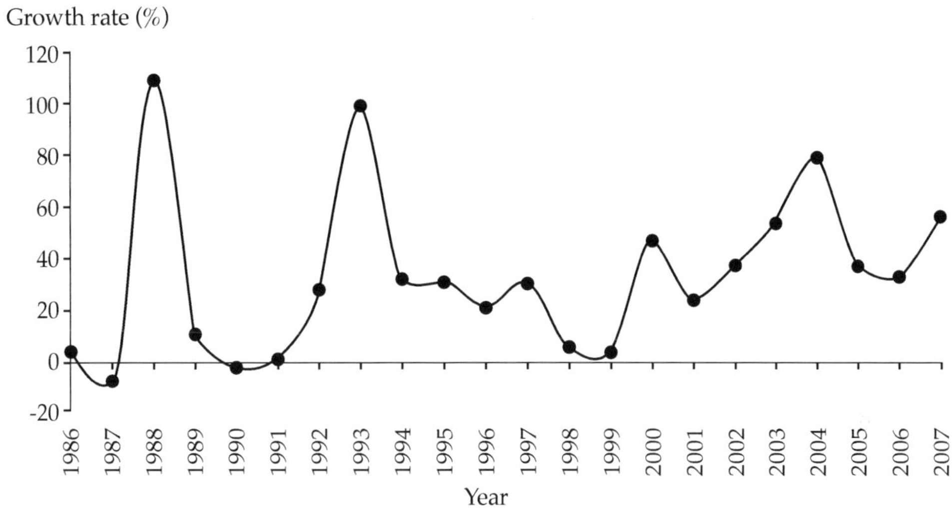

of 1992, 1993, 1996, and from 2003 to 2005. China's trade surplus with India has expanded during this time. In 1985, the surplus was USD46.4 million. It grew to USD367 million in 1995, and USD9.39 billion in 2007.

This widening trade imbalance is mainly because China and India have been in different stages of industrialization. China's industrialization and rural reforms started in the early 1980s, and later leveraged its low-cost labor to attract a large volume of foreign investment to build an export-processing manufacturing hub. In comparison, India's industrialization and urbanization started only in the late 1980s, and has proceeded slower. This means that India is in a more passive position when it comes to bilateral trade with China, thus creating the trade imbalance.

Rapid growth in trade disproportionate to the share in total foreign trade

China-India trade has accounted for an insignificant proportion of China's total foreign trade, despite the rapid growth trend since 1985. Even in the year 2007 when China-India trade reached a high point, bilateral trade only accounted for 1.78% of China's total foreign trade. On the other hand, China has become the third largest trading partner for India, ranked after the United States and Saudi Arabia. In 2007, bilateral trade accounted for 10.68% of India's total foreign trade.

Limited direct investment

The policy environment for foreign direct investment (FDI) in India has been relaxed since the 1980s and more formally liberalized in the 1990s. The reforms have significantly transformed the foreign investment landscape in India, which used to be strictly controlled back in the 1970s. However, despite the rising tide of FDI in India since 1991, Chinese investors still find it a highly bureaucratic and conservative investment environment.

As Table 10.3 shows, in the entire 1970s, India received USD454.5 million in FDI, an average of USD45.45 million per year. In the nine fiscal years between 1981 and 1990, India had USD1.13 billion in FDI, or an average of USD125.56 million per year.[11] After liberalization reforms in 1991, there was an immediate surge in foreign direct investment. From August 1991 to March 1992, FDI reached USD165 million. In the fiscal year ending 1993, FDI increased to USD383 million. It rose to USD654 million in fiscal year ending 1994 and to USD1.38 billion in 1995. Since then, FDI had risen to USD15.73 billion in 2006–2007 fiscal year, and to USD12.7 billion in the nine months between April and December 2007. As of the end of 2007, India received a cumulative FDI of USD68.9 billion.

However, Chinese direct investment in India has been very low. From April 2000 to December 2007, India received USD45.25 billion in FDI. The top eight foreign investors in India are as follows: Mauritius (USD20.104 billion, 44.3%), the United States (USD4.10 billion, 8.99%), the United Kingdom (USD3.46

Table 10.3. Foreign direct investment (FDI) in India, 1970–1999 (USD100 million)

Fiscal year	FDI	Fiscal year	FDI
1970–1980	4.55	1999–2000	24.39
1981–1990	11.30	2000–2001	29.08
1991–1992	1.65	2001–2002	42.22
1992–1993	3.93	2002–2003	31.34
1993–1994	6.54	2003–2004	26.34
1994–1995	13.74	2004–2005	37.54
1995–1996	21.41	2005–2006	55.46
1996–1997	27.70	2006–2007	157.26
1997–1998	36.82	2007–2008	126.99
1998–1999	30.83		

Sources: FDI Data Cell, Secretariat for Industrial Assistance, Department of Industrial Policy and Promotion, Ministry of Commerce & Industry of India; World Development Indicators 2003, World Bank.

billion, 7.65%), Singapore (USD2.70 billion, 5.96%), the Netherlands (USD2.54 billion, 5.6%), Japan (USD1.95 billion, 4.31%), Germany (USD1.32 billion, 2.92%) and France (USD705 million, 1.56%). In contrast to these top investors, the Chinese investment in India ranked 61st on the list, at USD3.3 million or 0.01%.

India's high tariffs, bureaucratic regulatory environment, and conservatism when it comes to allowing Chinese bidders for its government contracts have been the main factors discouraging Chinese investors. Although tariffs have been significantly reduced since India's trade liberalization reforms in 1991, they are still much higher than many other countries. Its laws and regulations are cumbersome, imposing difficulties on those who are new to the Indian investment environment. In addition, due to national security concerns India has forbidden Chinese companies to participate in international contracts in providing equipment in some sensitive sectors and in government procurement. From 2002 to 2003, India even suspended all approvals for investment from Chinese enterprises, citing a review of policy as the reason, so that the flow of Chinese investment into India was forced to zero during those years.[12]

There is also very limited Indian investment in China. According to statistics from China's Ministry of Commerce, as of the end of 2004, there were 138 Indian investment projects in China, with an actual utilization of USD98.58 million in investment. In 2003 and 2004 alone, there were 67 projects involving an investment of USD35.38 million.[13]

Main Obstacles in China-India Economic Relations

Geopolitical factors and mutual trust

India occupies an important strategic position in terms of geography. It shares a border with China in the north, and controls the western entrance to the Malacca Strait in the south. It is bounded by the Arabian Sea and the Indian Ocean, and is also neighboring the Suez Canal, the important route to the Mediterranean. Apart from China, India shares a border with six other nations. Three sets of geopolitical relations—between the U.S. and India, Russia and India, and China and Pakistan—are particularly important to China-India relations.

U.S.-India relations

India as a strong military power in Asia and its neighboring position with China has made it an attractive ally of the United States, especially in the service of America's intentions of "containing" China. Since its rapid economic growth in the 1990s, India has invested in its military power, and has become one of the eight states in the world to possess nuclear weapons. As India seeks to rise from being a regional power to becoming a global power, it lacks trust in China and views its neighbor as a competitor. The U.S. and India are therefore natural allies.

U.S. President Bill Clinton and Indian Prime Minister Atal Bihari Vajpayee signed the *India and the U.S.: A Vision for the 21st Century* document, establishing a dialogue mechanism which emphasized their goal of a "long-lasting, politically fruitful new partnership."[14] India rose in importance in American foreign relations during the George W. Bush presidency, when Secretary of State Colin Powell stated that India was crucial to maintaining the security of the Indian Ocean and neighboring areas. U.S.-Indian economic and military relations grew closer through the years. This closeness enabled India to become more influential in its political and economic engagement with the rest of the world, promoting its status towards a global power.

However, there are also some constraining factors in the U.S.-India relations. In handling any tensions with Pakistan, India may need to consider American views. In addition, China and Russia are regional powers that need to be reckoned with. Whether India decides to strengthen its relations with the U.S. or with China, India's geopolitical choices would affect China-India economic relations.

China-Pakistan relations

Pakistan is a strategically important country on the South Asia Subcontinent. China has been a traditional ally of Pakistan, while Pakistan has been in constant dispute with India over the border territory Kashmir. The friendship between China and Pakistan aroused enmity from India, which saw Pakistan as a dark shadow over China-India relations.[15]

China and Pakistan have maintained friendly relations for 60 years. In January 1950, Pakistan was the first Muslim country to recognize the People's Republic of China. It established diplomatic relations with China in May 1951, and supported China's request for re-instatement in the United Nations.[16]

In the 1990s, China changed its policy of favoring Pakistan in any conflict with India. On the question of Kashmir, China has encouraged both sides to negotiate based on the principles of peaceful co-existence, a stance that was welcomed by India and accepted by Pakistan. But there is still continued mistrust from India, which became especially apparent when China and Pakistan started a "comprehensive cooperative partnership," worked together on military technology projects, and conducted joint military exercises. India is concerned that China is assisting Pakistan in the development of anti-ballistic missiles and nuclear weapons which would affect the balance of power between India and Pakistan.

The disputed border

The border dispute between China and India has yet to be resolved and is likely to remain a destabilizing factor in China-India relations. China and India share a 1,700 km border that is generally understood as the eastern, central, and western sections. There are mainly two disputed territories, one to the west known as Aksai Chin and the other involving the northwest border of the Indian region Arunachal Pradesh. Because the border has never been officially agreed upon between the two countries, China argues that its definition of the border is based on local convention, and international law states that disputed borders should follow local conventions.[17]

In fact, the border as defined by China is based on maps from the Qing Dynasty, while the border as defined by India is based on maps printed during the British colonial rule. Talks on these disputed areas have continued today.

The Tibet issue

The Tibet issue has been a major obstacle to China-India relations. Although India has publicly stated that it recognizes Tibet as part of China, China has alleged that India has covertly supported and harbored exiled Tibetans in separatist activities. It was alleged that the March 2008 violent riots in Tibet were supported by the government-in-exile led by Dalai Lama and organized by the Tibetan Youth Congress.

From China's vantage point in geopolitics, India is using the Tibet issue for two purposes:

Tibet as a buffer between India and China

During British colonial rule, India used Tibet as a buffer region to prevent the Russian imperial invasion. Today, India may see Tibet as a buffer between China and itself, especially as China is increasingly seen as a threat to India. In 1959, India had openly allowed Dalai Lama and his exiled government to stay in India. During the Sino-Indian War in 1962, India had openly supported Tibetan independence. When India-China relations normalized, India had stated that Tibet is part of China. However, China continues to be troubled by what it alleges as covert and overt support to Tibet by India, including allowing visits or meetings with the Dalai Lama and providing funding to his causes.

Tibet as a bargaining chip when engaging China

Apart from the border dispute with China, India also wishes to gain China's support for several matters in international affairs. It hopes China would support India to become a permanent member of the United Nations Security Council, that China would support Sikkim in becoming a state in India (in the 1970s), and that China would forgo its military assistance to Pakistan. India may be using the Tibet issue as a bargaining chip with China.

The "Look East Policy" and "Look South Policy" of India

India's policies of controlling the Indian Ocean ("Look South") and forging a closer alliance with Southeast Asia ("Look East") conflict with China's political and economic interests. The Indian Ocean has vast oil resources, and possesses three of the five essential lifelines of global trade and security—namely the Suez Canal, Malacca Strait, and the Cape of Good Hope. American naval historian Alfred Thayer Mahan had said that whoever controls the seas controls the world, and this is definitely true for the Indian Ocean.[18 and 19] In terms of oil resources, the Indian Ocean, which includes the Persian Gulf region, possesses a significant amount of the world's petroleum.

The Indian Ocean is strategically important to China, partly because China is currently dependent on imports for 50% of its oil, and is projected by the International Energy Agency (IEA) to be 80% dependent on oil imports by 2030.[20]

China is the world's second largest oil consumer as of 2007, producing only 186.65 tons of oil and importing 196.8 tons in 2007. Most of China's oil is transported across the Indian Ocean through the Malacca Strait, which is also the key channel for Chinese exports to reach Europe and Africa.

China's interests in the Indian Ocean have alarmed India. As China plans to build the Gwadar Port in Pakistan, India believed that China would gain access to the Arabian Sea and the western Indian Ocean. India had responded by deploying its naval forces from the Andaman and Nicoman Islands of the Malacca Strait to the Bay of Bengal. It is also actively engaging in diplomatic exchange in South Asia and the Middle East in order to counterweigh China's growing power in the region.

The "Look East Policy" of India focuses on diplomatic relations with ASEAN, Japan, and Korea. It also serves India's interests to strengthen ties with Southeast Asian countries that have had disputes with China on the South China Sea, such as Vietnam and the Philippines. India and ASEAN signed the *Partnership Agreement for Peaceful, Progressive and Shared Prosperity* in 2004, as a milestone in its Look East Policy.[21]

India has also engaged Japan, Vietnam, and the Philppines in military cooperation, including joint military exercises, training, and military technology development. As the ASEAN region is also important to China in terms of political and economic interests, India courting ASEAN has naturally added to the mistrust between the two countries.

Competition for energy

China and India compete for energy resources because both are dependent on imports to supply their domestic oil consumption. China imports 50% of its needs, India 70%. As India is geographically close to the Middle East, it has been essential for India to continue to secure oil supplies there. From the perspective of diversifying its energy suppliers, India has also wooed Central Asia and Russia. At the same time, China obtains its oil mainly from the Middle East, Africa and Central Asia. It is inevitable, therefore, that China and India are occasionally in head-to-head competition for energy resources. Although the two countries have engaged in energy cooperation including offshore exploration, a continued competitive relationship may be inevitable as energy prices continue to rise.

The issue of trade routes

Whether in historical or modern times, there have always been three trade routes between China and India: by land, sea, or air. Currently, more than 90% of China-India trade is transported by sea through the Malacca Strait. This involves long distances, considerable time, and high costs. Such high transport cost constrains foreign trade.[22]

The land crossing Nathu La was re-opened in 2006, which is on the mountains between Tibet in China and the Sikkim region in India. At an altitude of 4,500 meters, it is the world's highest trade route in public road. The high altitude means that it is only accessible between April and October, and its opening time is restricted to four days a week between June 1 and September 30 each year. Road conditions in the area are poor, and the security check at the India border is very stringent. This land crossing is therefore another limitation to trade.

As for air cargo route, it involves areas in the north and northeast of India that are prone to civil conflicts and political instability. These economically-backward and infrastructure-deprived areas are also neighboring the sensitive regions of border disputes between India and China. So far it has been infeasible.

The Prospects of Expanding China-India Relations

China and India are the two largest developing economies with remarkable rates of growth. From 1980 to 2007, China's GDP increased at an average annual rate of 9.85%, while India's GDP grew at an average annual rate of 6.03%. Between 1997 and 2007, the GDP average annual growth rates were 9.41% and 6.77% for China and India respectively.[23]

In 2005, China's gross national product (GNP) surpassed that of France and the UK, climbing from sixth to fourth largest in the world. China maintained the fourth position in 2005 and 2006. Meanwhile, India's GNP ranked 10th in the world in 2004 and 2005, and 12th in 2006, 13th in 2007.

Against this backdrop of staggering economic growth, China has become India's second largest trading partner, behind only the U.S., while India has become China's 10th largest trading partner. However, the scale of bilateral trade between India and China is not proportional to their economic prowess.

In recent years, the mutual trust between China and India has strengthened, and both sides are willing to prioritize bilateral economic relations over immediate resolution of border disputes. The goal of reaching USD20 billion in bilateral trade in 2010 was achieved ahead of schedule in 2006. The two sides then revised the 2010 goal to USD40 billion, which was still reached early and subsequently revised again to USD60 billion. The USD60 billion goal was achieved in 2010.

China-India economic relations may be expanded and deepened in the following areas of cooperation.

Increasing proportion of trade in high technology and electrical goods

Electrical goods and high technology products feature prominently in China's exports to the rest of the world, while India's exports of software and software related services is a major strength. Leveraging these competitive strengths of each country would help promote bilateral trade.

In 2007, China exported USD701.17 billion in electrical goods and 347.83 billion in high technology products, accounting for 57.57% and 28.56% of total

Chinese exports. This means that the two categories of goods accounted for 86.13% of the total Chinese exports of USD1218.02 billion that year. Meanwhile, according to data from the National Association of Software and Service Companies (NASSCOM) of India, there were USD31 billion in exports of software and related services in the 2006–2007 fiscal year, representing 24.53% of total Indian exports of USD126.36 billion.[24] Electrical goods, however, account for a much smaller percentage of Indian exports. In 2006–2007 fiscal year, India exported USD1.96 billion in electrical goods, representing 1.55% of its total exports.

Not surprisingly, electrical goods also account for a significant proportion of Chinese exports to India. In the first 11 months of 2007, China exported USD635 million in electrical goods to India, a 74.38% increase compared to the export of electrical goods for the whole year of 2006. It represented just under 30% of the total Chinese exports of USD2.16 billion to India. However, even with the impressive growth rate, this was only a tiny fraction (2.34%) of China's total exports of electrical goods globally (USD27.13 billion in 2007).

As bilateral trade develops, China and India should expand their trade in electronic and mechanical goods and high technology products. India is in fact especially strong in software outsourcing services, genetic engineering and agricultural technology, while China maintains an advantage in computer hardware and high technology for industrial use, such as electric grid, hydro power, and transportation construction. In remarks at the China-India Economy, Trade and Investment Cooperation Summit cum CEO Forum held in November 2006 in Mumbai, Chinese President Hu Jintao also emphasized the need to diversify China-India trade and focus on trading goods with high technological content.

Progress in services trade

China has competitive strengths in international contracting and computer hardware manufacturing, while India's competitive advantage lies in computer software outsourcing. In order to resolve its weakness in infrastructure, India has planned to invest USD200 billion between 2008 and 2012 in building infrastructure in electric power, communications, ports, roads, railways, and oil.[25] China's international contracting service industry should be able to take advantage of these market opportunities in India.

While China has computer hardware manufacturers such as Lenovo, it is still lagging behind India in software development. As India is the world's largest outsourcing destination for software and the world's second largest exporter of software, second to only the U.S., China and India should be able to cooperate in the research and development of computer software and hardware.

Potential for energy cooperation

China and India currently compete for oil, but behind the competitive relationship lies the opportunity for cooperation. China imports as much as 50% of its oil for domestic consumption, while India relies on imports for roughly 70% of its oil consumption. They have competed with each other in bidding to acquire oil and natural gas fields overseas. Competition has undermined the pricing power of China and India as oil consumers, and led to Asia's oil prices being higher than in the U.S. and Europe.[26]

In face of these challenges, there may be merit in exploring cooperation instead of competition:

- As major oil consumers, China and India should align their stance in the international negotiations regarding the rising oil prices, and jointly coordinate with OPEC on issues such as oil production and pricing.
- In the acquisition of energy resources, the oil companies of China and India could join hands in bidding. This would prevent bidding wars that drive up the price of the assets, and make sure that China-India competition would not give the chance for a third-party to win the bid.
- China and India could cooperate in developing alternative energy and energy conservation technologies, which would contribute to both nations' efforts in tackling energy security and climate change.

China and India have already started to take advantage of energy cooperation opportunities. This was reinforced in the *China and India's Shared Vision in the 21st Century* document signed between Chinese Premier Wen Jiabao and Indian Prime Minister Manmohan Singh on January 14, 2008, which states that scientists from both countries will start cooperation in thermal nuclear fusion reactors. This is a significant initiative for seeking sustainable solutions for the global energy challenges. In the document, both sides also stated their belief in an international energy order and reiterated their shared interest in diversifying the global energy portfolio and developing clean and renewable energy.

Advocating for regional free trade zone

In the January 2008 *Shared Vision* document, the two countries pledged to advance regional integration, including the creation of a China-India free trade zone. They also agreed to mutually support the China-ASEAN and India-

ASEAN Free Trade Areas.

As early as 1991, India had adopted an "eastward policy" that aimed to forge closer ties with its ASEAN neighbors. After Indian Prime Minister Manmohan Singh took office in May 2004, he accelerated this policy. A free trade agreement was signed with Thailand in August 2004. In the 3rd India-ASEAN Summit in October 2004, Singh called for closer economic cooperation and the establishment of an India-ASEAN Free Trade Area. An agreement to build this free trade area was signed in November 30, 2004, known as the *Partnership Agreement for Peaceful, Progressive, and Shared Prosperity*. India and ASEAN agreed to facilitate exchange in trade, investment, tourism, culture, sports, and civil society. India would commence free trade in 2011 and 2016 with five developed countries and five developing countries of ASEAN, respectively.

Meanwhile, the China-ASEAN Free Trade Area was implemented in 2010, and was first outlined in the China-ASEAN *Comprehensive Economic Cooperation Framework Agreement* signed in November 2002.[27]

The success of their respective free trade cooperation with ASEAN provided encouraging precedents for the China-India Free Trade Area. The two sides completed a feasibility study in 2007 which pointed to concrete benefits for both countries. As the *Shared Vision* document points out, the next step is to set up a negotiation mechanism for implementing regional economic cooperation.[28]

The role of China and India in Africa

Both China and India have recognized Africa as a strategic partner in international politics and economy issues. China has used the Asia-Africa Summit, among other platforms, to forge closer ties with Africa. The first Asia-Africa Summit was held in Vientiane in 2005. This was followed by the China-Africa Cooperation Forum in November 4–5, 2006, where the participants agreed upon and issued the *Beijing Declaration and the Program for China-Africa Economic and Social Development Cooperation*.

India has also built new mechanisms for dialogue and cooperation with Africa. The first India-Africa Forum Summit was held in New Delhi on April 8–9, 2008, where an *India-Africa Cooperation Framework Agreement* and the *Delhi Declaration* were signed. The two sides pledged to strengthen bilateral economic relations in building a new partnership.

There may be grounds for cooperation between China and Africa with their African partners, despite the different motivating factors behind their wooing of Africa. India announced in 2008 that it would exempt tariffs for African exports of cotton, cocoa, mineral ore, and fruits, a policy that would cover 34 least developed countries in Africa. In addition, the India Import-Export Bank would extend USD5.4 billion in credit to support bilateral trade between India and Africa as well as trade among African nations. The credit, provided between 2009 and 2013, would support the development of railway construction, information technology, communications, energy, and biopharmaceuticals sectors. India also planned to double the scholarship granted to African students studying in India, and expand a training program for African technical personnel from 1,100 trainees to 1,600 trainees.[29]

Africa is important to India not only because of its natural resources, but also because Africa holds many votes in the United Nations that could help India gain a seat in the Standing Committee of the UN Security Council. As China already has a strong foundation in building economic cooperation and trade relations in Africa, there may be potential for China-India cooperation in their programs in Africa, such as in the areas of development aid, infrastructure, direct investment, and diplomacy.

11

Chapter

Economic Relations between China and Latin America

The History and Current Status of Economic Relations

Despite the long distances across oceans that separate China and Latin America, trade between them can be traced back to the 16th century, when a maritime route was developed from China to Mexico via the Philippines. In the early 19th century, large numbers of Chinese settlers went to Latin America, contributing to the national independence and economic development of the continent. After the establishment of the PRC, China and Latin America developed closer ties in politics, economy and trade, technology education, culture, sports, and the military. Currently, 19 of the 33 Latin American countries have established diplomatic relations and developed close economic relations with China.

Before China's WTO accession

Two trends can be gleaned from observing statistics of China-Latin America trade before WTO accession in 2001. First, China ran a trade deficit with Latin America for many years, which was eventually turned into a balance and small surplus. Second, China and Latin American countries used to import and export very similar types of goods. Both exported resource-based or agricultural

Table 11.1. Products traded between China and Latin America, 1990–2000 (%)

	China imports from Latin America			China exports to Latin America		
Product type	1990	1995	2000	1990	1995	2000
Agricultural	22.97	37.14	8.50	0.48	0.42	0.45
Automobiles	0.91	2.90	0.51	3.17	3.30	2.44
Engineering	0.48	2.75	1.22	20.10	21.40	18.50
Fashion	1.71	6.15	5.18	19.49	34.90	32.09
Finished products	65.68	75.31	46.45	70.97	98.34	98.49
High technology products	0.24	0.75	6.57	2.83	5.88	12.48
Low technology products	10.30	10.15	5.98	30.37	56.26	48.32
Medium-high technology products	23.31	10.75	5.09	27.24	30.94	28.42
Mineral	8.87	16.52	20.31	10.04	7.84	8.82
Primary products	34.32	24.69	53.55	29.03	1.66	1.51
Processed goods	21.93	5.10	3.36	3.97	6.25	7.48
Resources	31.84	53.66	28.81	10.52	8.26	9.27
Others	8.59	3.99	0.80	10.88	18.36	16.23

Source: Compiled from data from the General Administration of Customs.

products while they imported manufactured goods. By the 1990s however, the differences in products traded became more apparent. The two large economies were increasingly complementary to each other, thus creating greater potential for trade (see Table 11.1).

The vast distance and the absence of convenient transport links hindered trade development between China and Latin America prior to the 1990s. In the entire 1970s, the bilateral trade volume only reached USD1.03 billion. In the 1980s, there was an unfortunate collapse of the economies of several Latin American countries due to heavy national debt and a decade-long recession. The growth of trade relations was seriously affected, with a 2.2% average annual growth rate between 1980 and 1990. The highest trade volume was achieved in USD1.97 billion in 1990, while the lowest trade volume was USD1.44 billion in 1982. Chinese exports to Latin America were relatively low, ranging between USD390 million in 1988 to USD690 million in 1985. China experienced a trade deficit with Latin America, which grew from USD5.74 billion in the 1970s to USD6.06 billion in the 1980s.

The recovery of Latin American economies took place in the 1990s. Trade figures between China and Latin America also saw a trend of recovery and growth. In 1991, bilateral trade exceeded USD2 billion for the first time, and by 2000, it reached USD12.5 billion. China's trade deficit was also addressed by

Table 11.2. Trade balance between China and major Latin American countries, 1990–2001 (USD million)

Year	Argentina	Brazil	Chile	Colombia	Ecuador	Mexico	Panama	Peru	Venezuela
1990	229	158	–26	0.3	5.1	–174	–0.6	28.8	5.7
1991	60	143	–16	14.1	–1.7	0	–1.0	132.2	–0.9
1992	–42	405	74	–6.5	–2.2	0	–1.7	229.0	–5.3
1993	–52	591	–30	–25.1	–4.9	–344	–1.5	47.0	4.0
1994	8,312	–148	–429	–2.1	–89.4	214	–2.1	6.5	7.1
1995	–228	61	–102	–8.0	6.8	–536	–2.5	178.0	–0.4
1996	–90	–128	–141	–124.1	66.2	–798	–4.6	328.0	0.4
1997	–148	–219	–196	–170.0	112.0	–1,326	–5.0	366.0	–0.1
1998	–490	–220	–277	–257.3	–14.0	–1,894	–8.4	123.0	–27.0
1999	–485	–276	–287	–273.0	28.0	–1,987	–13.2	89.0	0.0
2000	–360	–259	–44	–142.6	–8.0	–2,964	–19.4	267.0	–164.0
2001	58	571	1	455.0	–122.0	–4,148	–21.8	281.0	–306.0

Source: Dong Yinguo, 2008.

rising exports, as exports grew over five times and imports grew 1.5 times in the 1990s. A trade balance was achieved in 1994, although there were subsequently a few more years of deficit (see Table 11.2).

After WTO accession

Economic relations between Latin America and China entered a new phase after China joined the WTO in December 2001.

Rapid increase in China-Latin America trade

China has become one of the most important trading partners with many Latin American countries. A decade ago, China had ranked 10th largest trading partner. Today, China is second or third largest trading partner for several countries in Latin America, closing the gap with the United States, which remains the top trading partner in the region.

Table 11.3 shows that bilateral trade soared since China entered the WTO. Between 2002 and 2007, bilateral trade volume rose at an average rate of 42% per year. Chinese exports to Latin America also rose 40% per year while imports from Latin America to China rose 44% per year. In 2007, China and Latin America recorded USD1.03 billion in bilateral trade, which represents a year-on-year increase of 85%.

China has enjoyed a trade surplus with Latin America in 2002, 2003, and 2007, and had a trade deficit in the years between 2004 and 2006. However, the sizes of these imbalances are relatively small and have not been a concern in economic relations. Brazil and Argentina have a longstanding trade surplus with China, but the size of the surplus has been decreasing in recent years.

Table 11.3. Trade between China and Latin America, 2002–2007 (USD million)

	Trade volume			
Year	Total	Export	Import	Trade balance
2002	178.30	94.90	83.40	11.50
2003	185.42	101.82	83.60	18.22
2004	294.59	138.13	156.46	–18.33
2005	397.44	186.82	210.62	–23.80
2006	554.60	266.88	287.72	–20.84
2007	1,026.11	515.43	510.68	4.75

Source: Ministry of Commerce website, http://english.mofcom.gov.cn.

Changes in types of products traded

Latin America exports mainly primary products to China, and imports mainly manufactured products from China. Primary products account for much higher proportion in Latin American exports to China, than Chinese exports to Latin America.

In the past decade, China's import of primary products from Latin America has increased as a proportion of total trade, while Chinese exports of manufactured goods to Latin America has decreased as a proportion of total trade.

In recent years, China has increased its export of high technology goods to Latin America, which currently accounts for over 50% of Chinese exports to the continent.

Competition between China and some Latin American countries

From 1990 to 2000, the trade surplus China had with Argentina and Brazil was reversed to a deficit, while the trade deficit China had with Mexico, Chile, and Panama became trade deficits. One of the reasons behind these changes is the fact that there is some degree of competition between China and some Latin American countries, for instance as locations for US foreign investment and as export-oriented manufacturing hubs. Therefore, China is seen by some quarters as a threat to the overall development of Latin America. However, the competition can also be seen as bringing further momentum for China and Latin America to forge other types of economic cooperation.

Growing economic relations

China has economic relations with 33 countries and 13 territories in Latin America. Diplomatic relations have been established with 13 of these countries, while 14 Latin American countries have signed trade agreements with the Chinese government. Brazil, Argentina, Panama, Chile, Peru, Mexico, Cuba, Venezuela, and Uruguay are the major trading partners of China in Latin America, accounting for 89% of total China-Latin America trade.

Features of the Economic Relations between China and Latin America

Economic relations between China and Latin America have entered a "golden age" in the new millennium, as the Chinese economy experienced stable and unprecedented growth and Latin American countries recovered from recession.

Bilateral trade concentrates in a handful of countries

Latin America comprises 48 countries or territories, but Chinese trade with the continent is focused on only a few countries. Table 11.4 shows all the countries accounting for over 1% of trade between Latin America and China.

As Table 11.4 shows, there are 12 countries that account for over 1% of trade between China and Latin America. Seven of them represent over 5%, while only three of them represent over 10%. Brazil, Mexico, and Chile account for 58% of the continent's bilateral trade with China. If we also consider Argentina, Panama, Peru, and Venezuela, seven countries would represent 83% of bilateral trade. These seven countries are China's major trading partners in Latin America.

Table 11.4. China's trade with major Latin American countries

Country	Percentage (%)
Argentina	8.13
Brazil	28.90
Chile	12.60
Colombia	2.51
Costa Rica	3.07
Cuba	2.55
Ecuador	1.14
Guatemala	1.04
Panama	5.53
Peru	5.58
Venezuela	6.18

Source: Compiled from *Statistical Yearbook of China*, 2007.

Trade in goods

Trade between China and Latin America has a simple and stable structure, with China mainly exporting electrical machinery and equipment, and apparel, while importing energy, resources, and agricultural and animal products, and food.

Traditionally, China's main exports to Latin America have been electrical products, textiles, apparel, and light industrial products. There are also exports of raw materials such as coke, semi coke, raw materials for pharmaceuticals, and dyes. Since the 1990s, electrical products have increased as a proportion of Chinese exports. Although most of these exports are still limited to mid- to low-

markets, small-sized machines, and home appliances, there is also a growing proportion of products with higher technology content. These include: tractors, machine tools, aircraft, shipping vessels, diesel engines, the production line for bearing equipment, automobiles, the assembly line for bicycles, and mid- to small-sized electric machines.

According to customs statistics from 1998, Chinese exports to Latin America were in five main categories: electrical goods (USD1.95 billion, 37%), textiles and apparel (USD1.5 billion, 28%), pharmaceuticals and cosmetics (USD330 million), light industrial products (USD290 million), and grain and vegetables (USD70 million). The top five categories of goods imported from Latin America to China were: iron sand (USD382 million, 13%), fish meal (USD185 million, 6%), copper powder (USD170 million, 6%), and crude oil, wool, electrical goods, steel, cooking oil, sugar, pulp, and leather.

Strong complementarity

China's status as the world's second largest economy means that its appetite for energy, raw materials, and agricultural products has grown and will continue to grow. China's economic development has partly been achieved at the cost of the environment, the loss of agricultural land, and depletion of domestic sources of energy and raw materials. Rising national income has also meant that there is rising demand for high-end or imported foods. Latin America has naturally become China's trading partner because of its endowment of energy and natural resources, and a large agricultural economy that produces primary goods.

After joining the WTO, China has liberalized trade and offered low cost and high quality electrical and light industrial products to the world markets, including Latin America.

In analyzing the economic recovery of Latin America in the 1990s and the continent's future growth, the United Nations Economic Commission on Latin America and the Caribbean (UNECLAC) pointed out that the economic growth in China and India would play a key role in generating demand for Latin American exports. Energy resources, primary goods, and industrial products would continue to be major exports and driving factors for economic growth in Latin America.

Low share of total foreign trade

Despite soaring growth rates of China-Latin America trade since 2001, the two trading partners still account for a small percentage of total foreign trade for each other. Table 11.5 shows that Latin America represented 2.66% of China's foreign trade in 2000, and 3.99% in 2006. During the same period of time, trade with Asia and North America decreased in proportion to the total, while trade with Europe, Australasia, Africa and Latin America had increased as a percentage of total foreign trade of China. Although Latin America's growth in percentage is highest, it is also increasing from a very low base.

Table 11.5. Trade with China, by continent (%)

Year	Asia	Africa	Europe	Latin America	North America	Australasia
2000	57.70	2.23	18.19	2.66	17.16	2.06
2006	55.73	3.15	18.76	3.99	16.25	2.12

Source: Compiled from *Statistical Yearbook of China*, 2006 and 2007.

According to China's customs statistics, Chinese exports to Latin America accounted for 2.7% of total Chinese exports in 2003, while imports from Latin America were 3.6% of the total. In the same year, according to UNECLAC data, imports from China accounted for 3.6% of total imports to Latin America, and exports to China accounted for 4%. The breakdown by country is shown in Table 11.6, and this once again demonstrates that China accounts for a relatively low proportion of foreign trade of Latin America.

Table 11.6. Trade between China and major countries in Latin America

	Export			Import		
Country	Total (USD million)	Exports to China (USD million)	Percentage of total exports to China (%)	Total (USD million)	Exports to China (USD million)	Percentage of total exports to China (%)
Argentina	293.09	27.29	9.3	127.05	4.47	3.5
Brazil	724.34	58.44	8.1	483.96	21.45	4.4
Chile	205.41	22.45	10.9	178.84	12.83	7.2
Colombia	131.39	0.60	0.5	130.95	3.98	3.0
Latin America	3,719.29	149.27	4.0	3,307.85	118.79	3.6
Mexico	1,651.03	16.77	1.0	1,703.66	32.67	1.9
Peru	86.46	7.60	8.8	81.80	3.54	4.3

Sources: Compiled from websites of United Nations Commission for Latin America and the Caribbean; and General Administration of Customs of China.

China runs trade deficit

As Chinese demand for energy resources and raw materials increase, and as the prices for energy and commodities are on a rising trend, China's trade deficit with Latin America may be expanding. Table 11.3 shows the trade balance between the trading partners going from a surplus in 2001 to a deficit in 2003 and returning to a surplus in 2007. The impending trend may be that China would return to a trade deficit, albeit a moderate one.

Issues and Prospects

The significance of China-Latin America economic cooperation

Bilateral trade and economic cooperation have benefited both China and Latin America countries, mainly in the following ways:

The Latin American market has allowed China to diversify its foreign trade markets

Latin America has seen its share of total Chinese trade rise from 2.9% in 2000 to 3.99% in 2006. This one percent change is impressive growth, and it's allowed China to reach out to previously untapped markets as part of its national strategy to reduce its dependency on its largest trading partners.

Raw materials in Latin America fuels Chinese economic growth

China's rapid economic growth and higher quality of life means that there is burgeoning demand for primary goods from vegetable oil to mining sand and crude oil. Latin America is an indispensable supplier of these resources.

Chinese demand drove up commodity prices, which may benefit Latin America. As Latin America recovered in 2002 from a five-year recession, it enjoyed rapidly increasing commodity prices because of Chinese demand. The global environment for exporting primary goods and resource-based raw materials has been significantly improved because of China. The UNECLAC has also acknowledged the contribution of China as an economic engine for Latin America.

Imports from China improve quality of life in Latin America

In its economic recovery, Latin American countries generally saw steady growth, low inflation, stable currencies, unemployment under control, as well as a reduction in poverty. The daily consumer goods imported from China are affordable and of high quality, and therefore have become popular with Latin American consumers. In addition, China's import of Latin American goods has also generated job opportunities there.

South-south cooperation is embodied in China-Latin America economic relations

As Latin America and China both belong to the developing world, their fruitful economic relations have been a successful example of "south-south cooperation," which refers to the developing world as the "global south." Both Latin America and China have become active in globalization, regional economic integration, and trade liberalization. Their rising economic voices have captured the attention of the developed world. China and Latin American countries have taken advantage of some of their shared political interests and the potential for trade development, and have created early successes in south-south cooperation. Moreover, any problems that have arisen so far, including the trade imbalance and policy uncertainties, have been manageable through bilateral dialogue.

Issues in China-Latin America economic relations

Deeper mutual understanding is required. China and Latin America are faraway regions for each other, and there are vast differences in both language and culture. This means that business practices and market operation are different, and investors and companies from both sides may need to rely on information and analysis produced in a third country. This has caused misinformation and the loss of time in seizing market opportunities.

The private sector needs to adopt a longer term mentality. The short-term profit-seeking mentality has driven both Chinese and Latin American companies to focus on traditional, low value goods and sometimes cut-throat prices and vicious competition, trying to take advantage of new market opportunities. In order to truly maximize the potential in these new markets, they should be encouraged to invest capital and manpower in order to develop the market and to open distribution and sales channels.

Inevitable competition may hamper trade and economic cooperation. China and Latin America have many similarities in their economic structures, especially in the low value-added export processing trade. Multinational companies have targeted both China and Latin America in setting up low value-added manufacturing bases for export-oriented production. This similarity makes China and Latin America competitors in global exports and reduces the potential for bilateral trade.

The scale of export credit is inadequate. The international trade of general commodities, such as electrical goods, typically involve large payments, and long product cycle. The common international practice is for the seller to provide export credit to the buyer in order to pay for these products. However, China currently provides only USD10 million, USD20 million, and USD5 million in export credit to Mexico, Argentina, and Colombia. These are inadequate and involve high interest. The provision of export credit in a larger scale would facilitate the growth in the Chinese exports of electrical goods.

Latin American economic integration may be disadvantageous to China. Latin America has been pushing forward its plans to create a common market in the region. These plans include the Andean Community, the Central American Common Market, and the Caribbean Community. If and when these initiatives successfully implement a zero-tariff free trade area in the region, it would reduce the competitiveness of Chinese products in Latin America.

The above issues may be regarded as inevitable in the process of growth in economic relations. Both sides have in fact recognized these issues, and have engaged in regular dialogue and practical measures to resolve them.

The prospects of development in China-Latin American economic relations

Expanding economic cooperation would be mutually beneficial. China needs the natural resources of Latin America, while Latin America needs the Chinese produced light industrial products. In the future, as China tries to transition to higher value-added and higher technology manufacturing, the two regions would compete less with each other and become even more compatible as trading partners.

The strong economies of both China and Latin America have created some large firms that are internationally competitive and can lead their sectors in investing in each other's markets. In order to reduce risks in investing in a new market, Chinese enterprises may explore new modes of investment in Latin America. Joining companies from a third country or forming alliances with Latin American firms may be ways to enter the market.

China may find difficulties in broadening Latin America as a market for its exports. Many Latin American countries have imposed trade barriers to limit the flow of foreign products, in particular Asian products, into their markets. A large volume of cheap goods from Asia flooded Latin America after the Asian

Financial Crisis, because the widespread currency depreciation in Asia lowered the price of those goods. As a result, various Latin American countries adopted measures to limit imports. Brazil announced five import control measures in October 1998. Colombia, Panama, Mexico, and Venezuela also adopted various measures to protect their home markets.

Argentina took a series of particularly strong actions. First, it announced a 30%–35% import tariff for textiles in October 1998, and imposed discriminatory measures specifically against non-WTO members including China. Then in January 1999, it also imposed a USD318 per kilogram import tariff on five types of Chinese toys. In July 1999, it imposed three-year quotas on five categories of goods from Brazil, China, and Pakistan, and announced plans to expedite anti-dumping investigation procedures against the large volume of cheap products entering the country. From October 1998 onwards, Argentina also set up additional obstacles against Chinese trade delegations applying for visas to visit the country, and against the temporary residence of the personnel of Chinese-invested companies in Argentina. These protectionist policies have created difficulties for Chinese exports to reach the Latin America market.

Recommended Policies and Measures

China may consider the following policies and measures in order to improve and expand its economic relations with Latin America.

Improve the trade structure

In order to address its trade deficit with Latin America, China would need to increase exports, which is unfortunately impeded by Latin American protectionism. Large Chinese industrial enterprises should be encouraged to invest in processing and assembly facilities in Latin America, in order to produce goods for the Latin American market that can circumvent the protectionist import policies of the region.

Encourage direct investment in Latin American natural resources

Resources in fish, oil, mining, and forestry are rich in Latin America and in high demand in China. There needs to be favorable policies to encourage Chinese enterprises to enter the Latin American market in order to access these resources. This may involve trade promotion events where experience sharing can take place among successful investors and relevant experts. Government officials would also participate in such events to explain the differences in investment laws and policies.

Latin America possesses 25% of the world's forests. Its redwood, sandalwood, Brazil wood, cycad sago palm, ormosia, pine, cypress, eucalyptus, and carob are valuable timber sources. Many Latin American countries have policies to encourage the development of the forestry sector, such as tax exemptions for timber processing and for importing machinery for timber processing. So far there are few Chinese companies involved in this sector, and their processed timber is typically sold within Latin America or in the international markets. Chinese enterprises should therefore be encouraged to take advantage of these business opportunities and, at the same time, contribute to addressing the shortage of natural resources in China.

Improve export finance insurance

China may consider setting up a fund to help Chinese exporters manage risks in receiving payment. Latin American importers generally use payment methods through a remitting bank, which reduces bank fees but incurs greater risks for the exporter. Many Chinese exporters have therefore demanded payment by letters of credit, but this has caused a loss in business opportunities with some Latin American importers. There is also a need to expand export credit.

Enhance mutual understanding

Latin American companies need to become more familiar with the trade system, industry policies, laws and regulations of China, so that they can trust and understand the Chinese business environment. China can set up a specialized unit within one of its government representative bodies in Latin America, in order to disseminate information about China, through channels including the media, the Internet, and by holding seminars and conferences.

The Ministry of Commerce's economic and commercial counselors' offices and the chambers of commerce in Latin American countries should promote China as a brand in various trade conventions and exhibitions. Such events can help Chinese companies reach numerous potential buyers or business partners at once, and allow Chinese businesses to gather information about industry trends in Latin America. Although some small and medium-sized enterprises from China have been exhibitors in international trade expos in recent years, they may require support and advice in their promotion efforts.

12

Chapter

Economic Relations between China and Africa

Africa has been an important political and economic arena for not only China, but also the major powers in Europe, the U.S., and Asia. They competed for influence over Africa's vast oil reserves, natural resources, large untapped consumer markets, and even African votes in the United Nations. Since the establishment of the People's Republic of China (PRC), China has generally maintained positive economic relations with the majority of African countries, especially after the Forum on China-Africa Cooperation was founded in 2000. Today, China-Africa relations are closely watched partly because of China and Africa are significant players in the developing world, and partly because the oil reserves in Africa are critical to global energy security.

Historical Overview

Indirect trade between China and Africa can be traced back to the 2nd century BC. Trade increased during the Tang and Song Dynasties (618–907 and 960–1279) when China exported ceramics, silk, and tea to Africa, while importing spices, ivory, rhinoceros horns and jewelry. China opened three sea routes to Africa during the Yuan Dynasty (1271–1368)—one went via India and the Red Sea to reach Egypt, another went via the Maldives to East Africa, and a third reached Madagascar. In the Ming Dynasty, Zheng He's naval expeditions (1405–1433) were a catalyst to stronger Sino-African relations, as four of Zheng's voyages reached the eastern coast of Africa, including what is today Somalia and Kenya.[1]

The establishment of the PRC in October 1949 served as a new starting point for Sino-African relations. The first formal diplomatic relations were established with Saudi Arabia and Egypt on May 30, 1956.

Early developments, 1949–1978

China's growing trade deficit with Africa

Sino-African trade relations enjoyed steady development in the 1950s to 1970s.[2] During this period, the predominantly civil trade developed into large-scale official trade, while imports and exports expanded from primary goods to industrial products. China's trade partners, originally limited to North Africa in the 1950s, later included Sub-Saharan Africa. The payment method shifted from payment on credit to payment in cash in foreign currency.

China consistently ran a trade deficit with Africa during this time. The deficit grew from USD5.7 million in 1950 to USD46.79 million in 1970.[3] In 1950,

China traded only with Morocco and Egypt, at a value of USD12.14 million. By 1959, China was counting 19 African countries and regions as trading partners. Trade volume grew seven times since 1950 to USD90 million, as China exported a wider range of goods beyond tea, which used to be the predominant export in 1950. Exports in the 1950s included tea and staple agricultural products (56.2%), light industrial products (16.21%), steel (11.7%), and machinery (3%).[4] By 1969, 38 countries and regions in Africa traded with China, as trade value increased to USD182 million.

Depleted foreign currency and cash flow meant that Sino-African trade returned to bartering and payment on credit. Even so, there was a widening range of products being traded. Between 1970 and 1978, Sino-African trade volume quadrupled from USD177 million to USD765 million. Both imports and exports increased fourfold.

Votes from African countries were crucial to China's restored membership in the United Nations in 1971. Since then, China actively established trade relations with 47 countries in Africa and signed trade agreements with more than 30 countries in Africa.

China had an increasingly diversified portfolio of imports from Africa during the 1970s, which included phosphates and cotton. Payment methods included both cash in foreign currency and payment on credit.

Eight Principles for Aid, 1964

As formal diplomatic relations with Africa were established, China considered the question of foreign aid to Africa. From December 1963 to February 1964, Chinese Premier Zhou Enlai made an official tour covering 10 countries in Africa, including Egypt, Algeria, Morocco, Tunisia, Ghana, Mali, Guinea-Bissau, Sudan, Ethiopia, and Somalia. In Ghana (January 18, 1964), Zhou declared the "Eight Principles for Economic Aid and Technical Assistance to Other Countries," which stipulated principles such as equality, mutual benefit, "no strings attached" and the aim to help recipient countries achieve self-reliance.

During this period, aid to Africa took the form of zero-interest or concessional loans. Industrial production, infrastructure, education, hygiene, and sports were the main areas that received assistance. The most notable project was the 1,800-km Tanzania-Zambia Railway, built between October 1970 and June 1976. It remains one of the largest foreign assistance projects in contemporary Chinese history.[5]

Between 1956 and 1977, China granted USD2.48 billion in foreign aid to 36 African countries, accounting for 58% of China's total foreign aid of USD4.28 billion during that time.

There was a drastic reduction in foreign aid to Africa in the following years, from 1976 to 1980, because of the stagnated economy at the end of the Cultural Revolution. During this time, aid to Africa stood at only USD940,000. However, among the 181 foreign aid projects China undertook between 1979 and 1983, 90% of them were in Africa.[6]

Adjustment period, 1979–1989

Fluctuating Sino-African trade relations

The economic reforms that started in 1978 prompted adjustments to China's external trade mechanisms and policies.[7] Chinese enterprises started setting up more than 150 trading company branches and representative offices, and more than 200 trading and distribution companies. These investments opened a new facet in Sino-African trade relations. The trade volume grew from USD817 million in 1979 to USD1.13 billion in 1980. Exports reached USD747 million while imports reached USD384 million. However, in 1989, the trade volume dropped to USD950 million. Overall, Sino-African trade fluctuated between USD800 million and $1.2 billion. China's trade deficit decreased due to reduced imports from Africa.

In terms of trade structure, China exported to Africa tea and animal products (17.1%), light industrial products (14.3%), textiles and garments (13.4%), machinery (5.4%) and staple agricultural products (3.7%).

Policy adjustment in foreign aid

Since the 1970s, China shifted its mode of foreign aid to Africa, moving away from granting loans and towards a wider range of engagement. In January 1982, China declared the "Four Principles on China-Africa Economic and Technical Cooperation":

1. Cooperation would follow the principle of equality and mutual benefits, respecting each other's sovereignty and non-interference.
2. Projects will be oriented towards achieving practical results.
3. The mode of cooperation is to be diversified to include the exchange of scientific and technical skills through providing technical services, training, and management personnel in areas of project contracting, infrastructure construction, industrial collaboration, and joint ventures. The Chinese experts will make no special demands and enjoy no special amenities.
4. Technical cooperation will be adjusted according to the needs and specificities of host countries.

During this time, Sino-African cooperation took the form of project contracting, the provision of labor, consulting and design, joint investment and joint operations. Project contracting and labor were provided in the fields of construction, water resources, and hydropower engineering, fishing, textiles, electronics, steel and metals, and the catering industry. Experienced professionals from China were sent to Africa, including personnel from the fields of construction and engineering, medicine, seafaring, aircraft maintenance, management, software development, and education. From the 1980s onwards, China collaborated with Africa at the firm level, through management, trusteeship, and lease management.[8]

For instance, in 1987 Chinese experts turned around an ailing sugar conglomerate in Asnières, Togo, which was built with funding from the Chinese government but suffered from a lack of technical and management expertise.[9]

Stable development, 1990–1999

Increasing trade volume with larger number of trading partners

Trade with Africa increased as a result of Chinese economic growth and the higher volume and wide diversity of goods ready for exports. China had strong capabilities to export machinery, home appliances, automobiles, motorcycles, and other electric and electronic products. At the same time, consumer demand in Africa also increased in the 1990s after economic growth and policy reforms. China also established new diplomatic relations and developed trade with some African countries. For instance, China's exports to South Africa were USD1.35 billion in 1996, which accounted for 33.4% of the total China-Africa trade that year.

The China-Africa partnership progressed against this backdrop of economic growth. In 1999, bilateral trade reached USD6.48 billion, a seven-fold increase from 1979. In terms of the geographical spread of the trading partners, China first focused on trading with North Africa and North Central Africa in the early 1990s but East and South Africa became the major trading partners later in the decade.[10] More importantly, China also imported over USD100 million per year from 14 African countries. These countries were Egypt, Nigeria, Angola, Morocco, Gabon, Sudan, Algeria, Cote d'Ivoire, South Africa, Benin, Ghana, Tunisia, Kenya, and Equatorial Guinea.[11]

In terms of the products traded, China exported mostly finished goods and imported agricultural and mining products. Chinese exports included electric machinery, textiles, and apparel, metals, petrochemicals, tea, and light consumer daily goods. Meanwhile, China imported crude oil, mining products (iron ore, manganese ore, gold, and diamonds), tropical crops (cotton, cocoa, coffee, and cashews), and timber.[12]

Increasing aid with diversified forms of assistance

China reformed its policy on development aid in late 1995, providing assistance in the form of loans with favorable terms and joint ventures with an external partner. As of the end of 1999, China had signed 39 framework agreements with 24 African countries to provide loans on favorable terms. These agreements also include providing resources and technical assistance to Africa, including the training of personnel from African countries. Between 1985 and 1999, China trained 905 technical personnel from 46 African countries, in the sectors of rice cultivation, vegetable growing, fishery, meat processing, traditional Chinese medicine, acupuncture, agricultural machinery, solar energy, and meteorological forecasting. Since the 1970s, China has encouraged Chinese enterprises to engage in cooperation projects with complete technology and management experience. As of the end of 1999, China had a cumulative total of 9,792 international contracting projects in Africa, with a total contract value of USD14.09 billion and a turnover of USD11 billion.[13]

Growth in bilateral investment

China's outbound investment developed later than its external trade, and therefore Chinese direct investment in Africa started relatively late. Before 1979, there were very few Chinese investment projects in Africa except for some enterprises implementing designated government projects. In the 1980s, China gradually set up about a dozen joint ventures or cooperatives in Africa. When China started its proactive policy to encourage outbound investment, China signed inter-governmental framework agreements between 1995 and 1999 to provide loans in support of Chinese enterprises investing in Africa. During those five years, China also set up 11 investment development service centers in Egypt, Guinea, Mali, Cote d'Ivoire, Nigeria, Cameroon, Gabon, Tanzania, Zambia, and Mozambique. These centers provided on-the-ground support and security to Chinese investors in Africa.

In 1998, the National Development and Reform Commission set out an investment plan for Africa, providing guidance on sectors, scale, and investment targets in Africa for the first time. This signified a transition in China's economic engagement with Africa, moving from exchanges based on trade to investment in production, processing, and resources development.[14] As of the end of 1999, China had a cumulative total of USD440 million investment in Africa, and had set up 351 companies in light industries, electric goods and machinery, textiles, apparel and pharmaceuticals.[15]

African investment in China also started only in the 1980s. In 1990, only Sudan, Nigeria, and Mauritius had direct investment in China, with an actual utilized investment of USD280,000.[16] As of the end of 1999, African countries had a cumulative total of USD520 million invested in China, in 622 projects covering the petrochemicals, machinery and electronics, transportation and telecommunications, light industries and home appliances, textile and apparel, biopharmaceuticals, agricultural development, entertainment and catering, and property development industries.[17] In 2000, the Forum on China-Africa Cooperation opened a new chapter in China-Africa economic relations.

Forum on China-Africa Cooperation (FOCAC)

Establishment of FOCAC

The Forum on China-Africa Cooperation (FOCAC) is a dialogue and cooperation mechanism that uses multilateral negotiations to discuss important issues for developing countries and to coordinate the stance of China and Africa on international affairs.[18] It is an important initiative of "south-south cooperation," especially since China is the largest developing country in the world and Africa is the continent with the highest concentration of developing countries. They also have common challenges and shared interests in economic development, and no historical baggage.

In October 1999, then Chinese President Jiang Zemin officially proposed the dialogue mechanism in a letter to the heads of states in the African countries with diplomatic relations with China, and to the secretary-general of the Organization of African Unit (OAU), Salim Ahmed Salim. The Ministerial Meeting of FOCAC was therefore held in Beijing on October 10–12, 2000.

Among the attendees in the Beijing 2000 ministerial meeting were 79 ministers from 44 African countries with which China has diplomatic relations, as well as the ambassador of Mali. Malawi and Libya, with which China has not yet established diplomatic relations, attended as observers. Seventeen international and regional bodies were also invited and joined. Trainees from government and the private sector who graduated from China-Africa training programs and African Young Diplomats also attended. In total, there were over 500 attendees.

The meeting resulted in the signing of the *FOCAC Beijing Declaration and the China-Africa Economic and Social Development Cooperation Outline*, which laid out a blueprint and concrete measures to engender closer cooperation. To add to the momentum of cooperation, China announced an immediate debt relief of RMB10 billion for heavily indebted countries and least developed countries in Africa. Concrete measures included: special funds to support Chinese enterprises investing in Africa, a human resources development fund, and stepping up training for African personnel. As summarized by then Chinese premier Zhu Rongji at the closing of the meeting, China-Africa cooperation would focus on increasing trade and investment, strengthening aid, broadening cooperation to multiple sectors, and the resolution of debt in Africa.

Development of FOCAC

The mechanisms and the content of cooperation of FOCAC were set out in the subsequent meetings. The *Procedures of the Follow-up Mechanism* of FOCAC was adopted at a July 2001 ministerial consultation meeting in Lusaka, Zambia. The *Procedures* stated that in the future a senior-level meeting would be held every two years, a ministerial meeting every three years, and both at locations alternating between China and Africa. As of the end of 2007, one summit, three ministerial meetings, five senior-level meetings, and one special senior-level meeting were held. The Lusaka meeting served to formalize procedures and ensure that China-Africa cooperation would not be a one-time occasion but would be a long-term process.

In the following ministerial meeting held in Addis Ababa, Ethiopia, in December 15–16, 2003, the *FOCAC Addis Ababa Action Plan, 2004–2006* was adopted. Chinese Premier Wen Jiabao announced the following measures:

- Market opening, granting zero-tariff treatment for some goods imported to China from Africa's least developed countries.
- Strengthen training and human resources cooperation, increase China's funding for training of African personnel, with the goal of training 10,000 people in three years.
- Promote mutually beneficial cooperation between Chinese and African companies, particularly supporting Chinese companies investing in Africa.
- Encourage tourism, adding eight African countries to the list of destinations where Chinese citizens could visit as individual tourists. The eight countries are: Mauritius, Zimbabwe, Tanzania, Kenya, Ethiopia, Seychelles, Tunisia, and Zambia.
- Strengthen cultural exchanges, organizing promotion campaigns and roadshows such as the "China-Africa Youth Festivals." the "See you in Beijing" arts and cultural activities, and the "Chinese Culture Tour of Africa" in 2004.

The Chinese government issued its *Africa Policy* in January 12, 2006, which was widely considered a milestone signifying the maturing of China-Africa relations.[19] The document pointed out four main areas of China-Africa cooperation:

- **Politics**
  Organize senior visits and exchanges of legislature and political parties. Set up and improve consultation mechanisms, cooperation in international affairs, and exchange of local governments.
- **Economy**
  Trade, investment, financial sector cooperation, agricultural cooperation, infrastructure construction, resources development, tourism, debt relief, economic assistance, and multilateral cooperation in trade and finance.
- **Education, science, culture, health and society**
  Cooperation in human resources development and education, technology, cultural exchange, healthcare and medicine, media, administration, consular affairs, civil society, disaster response, and humanitarian aid.
- **Peace and security**
  Military cooperation, conflict resolution, peacekeeping, judicial and police cooperation, and non-traditional security.

A summit and ministerial meeting was held in November 4–5 2006. In attendance were 35 heads of state from 48 African countries, six heads of government, one vice president and six high-level delegations, 228 ministers, and representatives from 24 international and regional bodies such as the United Nations and the African Union. The *FOCAC Beijing Summit Declaration* and the *FOCAC Beijing Action Plan 2007–2009* were adopted. The China-Africa Joint Chamber of Commerce and Industry was set up.

Chinese president Hu Jintao announced eight measures and targets to support China-Africa relations:

- Double the amount of assistance provided by China to Africa from 2006 to 2009.
- Provide USD3 billion in favorable term loans and USD2 billion in export buyers' credit.
- Set up a USD5 billion China-Africa Development Fund.
- Build a convention center for the African Union.
- Partial debt relief for heavily indebted countries in Africa.
- Move towards opening the China market to African countries.
- Set up three to five economic and trade cooperation zones in African countries between 2006 and 2009.

- Accelerate social and cultural exchange. This includes training 15,000 African personnel in three years, sending 100 Chinese agriculture experts to Africa, set up 10 agricultural technology demonstration centers, build 30 hospitals, donate RMB300 million to anti-malaria activities, and build 30 anti-malaria centers, build 100 schools in agricultural villages, send 300 Chinese youth volunteers to Africa, and increase scholarship recipients from 2,000 to 4,000 to enable more young African people to study in China.

These pledges were implemented with some success. As of the end of 2007, aid agreements were signed between China and 48 African countries. Framework agreements on loans with favorable terms were signed with 19 African countries. Debt relief agreements were signed with 32 heavily in-debt or lesser-developed countries. Construction for the African Union convention center was underway. The China-Africa Development Fund has been set up, and it has granted over USD400 million to finance four investment projects.[20] An economic and trade cooperation zone, an agricultural demonstration center, and a malaria control center were set up. Sixty malaria control experts and 37 senior agricultural technology experts were trained. A total of 239 training sessions were held for 5,931 people from 49 African countries. Anti-malaria drugs were sent to countries in need. China also sent 75 youth volunteers to three countries, and reached an agreement to build 81 village schools in 39 countries. Government scholarships for a potential 2,700 students were offered to 50 countries.[21]

Facilitator of economic relations

FOCAC has enabled China to build closer ties with Africa. So far, bilateral trade agreements have been set up with 40 African countries, joint committees for bilateral economy and trade have been set up with 36 African countries, investment promotion and protection agreements signed with 28 African countries, and agreements to avoid double taxation signed with eight African countries.[22]

China-Africa relations have developed in greater depth and breadth since FOCAC has been established. The main trends can be summarized as follows:[23]

Accelerated growth in trade

Trade increased significantly since 2000, rising six-fold from USD10.6 billion in 2000 to USD73.7 billion in 2007. In 2005, China became the third largest trading partner with Africa, ranking only after the United States and France. China was exporting home appliances, automobiles, aircraft, and satellites to Africa. Meanwhile, marble from Egypt, coffee from Cote d'Ivoire, auto parts from South Africa, electronic products from Tunisia, tobacco from Zimbabwe, peanut oil from Senegal, cotton from Mali, and cassava from Nigeria were imported into China. As of 2007, China had established trade relations with 53 African countries, and had a trade volume of over USD100 million with 38 of these countries. Trade volume with Angola and South Africa was over USD10 billion. The top five African trading partners for China were Angola, South Africa, Sudan, Egypt, and Nigeria. They accounted for 58% of China-Africa trade.[24]

From 2000 onwards, China's exports of electric goods, machinery and high technology products represented half of China's total exports to Africa.[25]

China and the South African Customs Union (SACU) have begun negotiations since June 2004 for a free trade area, but talks have progressed slowly so far.

Increased number of Chinese contracting projects in Africa

Table 12.1 shows the development of Chinese international contracting in Africa, which is an increasing trend since 2000 in the number of contracts and contract value. In 2006, China had USD28.7 billion in contracts with African countries, representing 31% of China's total international contracting industry. Africa is China's second largest market for international contracting.[26]

The international contracting projects awarded to China in Africa were initially those requiring low technical skills, such as construction of roads, railways, and bridges, or the enhancement of farmland, which required higher technical skills. Today, the projects have broadened and involve housing construction, petrochemicals, electric power, transportation, hydro-power, metallurgy, and railways. In addition, China has provided technical and management personnel to Africa to increase the African countries' own capabilities in economic construction. Since 2000, the projects where Chinese contractors were involved include over 6,000 km of roads, 3,000 km of railways, and eight large to mid-sized electric power stations.[27]

The increasing competitiveness of Chinese contractors in the African market can be seen from the rising number of projects valued over USD100 million and the rising technology content involved. From 2001 to 2006, China signed 41 large contracts valued at over USD100 million each, with the largest projects periodically reaching new records in contract value.[28]

In October 2005, seven consortiums comprising 64 of the world's top contractors had competed in the bid for the Algerian highway project.

Table 12.1. Sino-African economic cooperation, 1979–2006 (USD10,000)

Year	Contracting		Labor services cooperation		Design consulting	
	Number of contracts	Contract value	Number of contracts	Contract value	Number of contracts	Contract value
1979–1991	2,019	386,832	822	33,839	—	—
1996	411	137,154	308	13,335	71	624
1997	604	156,324	360	16,123	78	825
1998	672	187,064	547	14,414	41	434
1999	670	166,483	479	18,306	57	1,643
2000	757	208,041	545	20,063	31	1,022
2001	737	245,700	577	19,496	49	941
2002	584	278,929	372	13,012	39	971
2003	699	387,217	319	11,823	39	1,421
2004	2,721	642,970	330	23,546	65	5,605
2005	3,844	841,235	373	19,742	66	5,259
2006	5,141	2,873,567	564	13,120	86	10,224

Source: Data from 1979 to 1991 came from *Compendium of China External Economic Statistics, 1979–1991*;
1992–2004 data came *Yearbook of China External Economic Statistics;*
2005–2006 data came from *Yearbook of China External Trade Statistics.*

Competitors have included Bechtel from the U.S., Vinci Group from France, Taisei Construction from Japan, Bilfinger Berger from Germany, and Impreglio from Italy, which were ranked 1st, 5th, 7th, and 8th, respectively, in the *Engineering News-Record* world's top 225 largest international contractors that year. In April 2006, the Chinese consortium of CITIC and China Railway Construction won the bid. In May 2006, the contract for the central and western section of a highway running across Algeria was officially awarded to the Chinese consortium. The framework agreement of the contract had a value of USD6.25 billion while the final contract had a value of USD7 billion. It was then the project with the highest ever contract value.

This record was quickly broken in October in the same year, when China Railway Construction and its subsidiary China Civil Engineering Group were awarded the USD8.3 billion contract for the railway connecting Lagos and Kano in Nigeria.[29]

China has also provided labor service cooperation and design consulting to African countries, as shown in Table 12.1. However, the performance of Chinese firms in these markets have fluctuated over the years.

Strong growth in bilateral investment

Apart from the Go Global policy, China had put in place specific measures to encourage Chinese direct investment in Africa.[30] Chinese investors have set up production facilities of home appliances, construction materials, agriculture and food processing in Africa, bringing low-cost products to the African people. In fact, foreign-invested enterprises in Africa not only enjoy favorable policies instituted by the local government, but they also enjoy the favorable policies of Europe and the U.S. towards Africa. The continent is therefore a popular destination for Chinese outbound investment.

Chinese policies to encourage investment in Africa included more relaxed requirements for enterprises, export rebates for equipment, parts and raw materials for building factories. Simplified procedures and tariff reductions were put in place for Chinese companies whose investment in Africa would generate more Chinese exports, and for some new markets and products. The Chinese investors in Africa are also allowed a five-year retention of foreign currency in order to allow them to re-invest in expanding production. These policies can be considered effective in encouraging investment in Africa.

FDI from China to Africa has grown rapidly since 1996. In 2000, there were 57 Chinese-invested companies in Africa, with investment contracts of USD251 million and an actual utilized investment from the Chinese side of USD216 million. These figures were double those of 1999, and accounted for 39% of Chinese outbound investment in 2000. In 2002, there were 36 Chinese-invested companies in Africa, with investment contracts of USD73 million and the Chinese side contributing an actual utilized investment of USD63 million. Since 2002 there was faster growth in Chinese investment in Africa, as shown in Table 12.2.[31] As of 2005, Chinese investors have set up a cumulative total of 800 companies in Africa, with a cumulative investment of USD1.6 billion. Africa has become the third largest destination for outbound investment from China. However, despite the fast growth in Chinese investment in Africa, the investment accounted for only 3% of total Chinese outbound investment.[32] In 2006, there was USD370 million in Chinese FDI in Africa. Investment projects were involved in trade, production and processing, resource development, transportation, agriculture, and agricultural products.[33] As of the end of 2006, China had a cumulative total of USD6.64 billion in direct investment in Africa, an increase of more than 14 times since 1999. Cumulative FDI to Africa represents 9% of the cumulative total of Chinese outbound FDI.

Many of these enterprises are generating trade activities, and are either focused on exports or a change in country of origin. Since 2000, Chinese companies have set up over 100 overseas export processing projects, accounting for 70% of the equipment, factories, and instruments.[34] Some of the more notable projects that have generated local economic growth include: an oil refinery in Khartoum, Sudan, the China-Zambia Friendship Farm, Hisense (consumer electronics) in South Africa, Xinda Aquatic Product in Mozambique, and the Tongmei Pharmaceutical Factory in Togo.

Table 12.2. Chinese direct investment in Africa, 1996–2005 (USD million)

	1996	1997	1998	1999	2000	2001	2002	2003	2004	2005
Chinese investment	56	82	88	65	216	67	63	107	135	400

Source: Po Yingji, 2006.

Non-state investors have played a growing role in Chinese investment in Africa. According to statistics from the Import-Export Bank of China, medium-sized to large enterprises account for about 100 out of the more than 800 Chinese-invested companies in Africa. The rest are non-state investors, the most well-known of which is Huawei, an information technology and communications company which is now held up as a model investor from China's non-state sector. In 2006, Huawei recorded USD2.08 billion in sales in Africa and had products and services reaching 50 million users in 40 African countries. Chinese investors create job opportunities and enable a transfer of technical skills. For example, out of Huawei's 2,500 employees in Africa, 60% are locally hired.

Apart from the largest non-state enterprises, small and medium-sized enterprises in the non-state sector have also organized delegations to seek opportunities in Africa. In 2005 alone, Zhejiang Province, the province in China with the most advanced non-state sector, made USD5.7 million in investment in Africa. The economically advanced Jiangsu Province also held trade promotion and business matching events in Nigeria for a consecutive seven years, and has set up an economic cooperation zone in Nigeria modeled after the Suzhou Industrial Park, a product of China-Singapore cooperation.

Chinese investors also widened their involvement in a diversity of sectors. Apart from traditional energy, infrastructure, and agriculture, the sectors of communication, automobiles, machinery, and equipment, apparel, and shoes, daily goods, and tourism were new sectors of investment. In Egypt alone there were 230 wholly Chinese owned companies or joint ventures involving a Chinese stake. The Chinese investors include PetroChina, Huawei,

ZTE Telecommunications, and Sinotex, as well as automobile makers Chery, Brilliance, Geely, and Jiangnan Auto.

In contrast to the rise of Chinese direct investment in Africa, investment in the other direction is much lower. Table 12.3 shows African direct investment in China from 1995 to 2006. In terms of the number of companies, FDI from Africa first declined and then picked up again. In 1995, African investors set up 1,152 companies in China, which then shrunk to 276 companies by 999 but increased to 2,501 companies in 2006. The actual utilized FDI from Africa showed a rising trend throughout those 12 years. Apart from a small decline in 1996, there was modest growth in most years, and an accelerating trend after 2000.

China-Africa economic cooperation also included human resources development and technical experts provided by China. China provided training for African personnel since 1983, and prior to 2007 had trained 15,000 people in the sectors of economy, management, agriculture, healthcare, judiciary, education, and applied technology. These trainees would typically return to their home countries and become senior government officials or business leaders. In the FOCAC Action Plan for 2007–2009, China had pledged to train another 15,000 in personnel from Africa in three years.

China has sent over 100 experts in agricultural science to Africa, as four-fifths of African countries have not been self-sufficient in their food supplies.

Table 12.3. Direct investment from African countries to China, 1995–2006 (USD10,000)

Year	Newly registered companies	Actual utilization of investment
1995	1,152	2,055
1996	733	1,202
1997	400	8,237
1998	332	15,876
1999	276	19,606
2000	487	28,771
2001	711	32,977
2002	1,022	57,013
2003	1,428	61,776
2004	1,852	77,568
2005	2,169	107,086
2006	2,501	121,735

Source: 1992–2004 data came from *Yearbook of China External Economic Statistics;* 2005–2006 data came from *Yearbook of China External Trade Statistics.*

To address this food security issue in Africa, China has set up 10 agricultural science demonstration centers. China's rice cultivation program in Seychelles had increased the yield of rice in the country by two to three times.

Economic relations between China and Africa resulted in a healthy flow of visitors in both directions. In 2007, 379,141 African citizens had entered China, of whom 46% of them (174,186) visited for business or conventions and meeting.[35]

An increasing number of African countries have also become popular destinations for Chinese tourists. The natural scenery, the diversity of wildlife, and unique cultures in Africa have intrigued many Chinese visitors and supported the growth in the tourism industry of Africa. Although visitors from China still account for a small percentage of tourists in Africa, their numbers are growing fast. In 2007, Chinese visitors to Africa increased 36% year-on-year. The major attractions for Chinese tourists have been Egypt, South Africa, and Kenya, but visitors to Mauritius, Zimbabwe, Tanzania, Tunisia, and Gabon have also been growing in numbers.[36]

Problems and Challenges in Sino-African Economic Cooperation

Trade imbalance and increasing friction

Despite the fast growth in trade volume, China and Africa each represent only a small proportion of their total foreign trade. In 2007, the bilateral trade volume was USD73.3 billion, which was only 3.37% of China's total foreign trade. Between 1950 and 2007, China basically maintained a trade surplus with Africa. The increasing trade volume in recent years has in fact expanded the trade imbalance in favor of China. The surplus, or Africa's trade deficit, has grown from USD5.7 million in 1950 to USD1.82 billion in 2007. Since the economic reforms in China, African countries combined only had a trade surplus with China in the years of 2000, and between 2004 and 2006. The trade imbalance was for the first time in favor of Africa in year 2000, when the surplus was USD513 million. Africa's trade surplus with China was largest in 2005, at USD2.38 billion (see Table 12.4).

Many African countries are running a trade deficit with China. In 2007, China had a trade surplus with 36 out of the 53 African countries trading with China. China's surplus is over USD100 million with 22 of these countries. China's surplus is largest with Egypt, reaching USD4.12 billion that year (see Table 12.5).

Table 12.4. China-Africa trade, 1950–2007 (USD10,000)

Year	Import	Export	Trade volume	Trade balance
1950	322	892	1,214	570
1960	7,673	3,384	11,057	–4,289
1970	6,521	11,200	17,721	4,679
1980	36,411	83,477	119,888	47,066
1981	36,222	10,896	138,118	65,674
1982	35,735	11,850	155,585	84,115
1983	41,537	78,878	120,415	37,341
1984	41,567	81,846	123,413	40,279
1985	32,088	55,952	88,040	23,864
1986	25,619	75,348	100,967	49,729
1987	17,601	144,492	162,093	126,891
1988	28,897	188,384	217,281	159,487
1989	42,738	73,917	116,655	31,179
1990	36,760	129,691	166,451	92,931
1991	42,557	99,999	142,556	57,442
1992	50,438	130,194	180,632	79,756
1993	100,327	152,744	253,071	52,417
1994	89,398	174,865	264,263	85,467
1995	142,744	256,634	399,378	113,890
1996	146,448	256,634	403,082	110,186
1997	246,379	320,687	567,066	74,308
1998	147,657	405,571	553,228	257,914
1999	237,512	411,501	649,013	173,989
2000	555,507	504,201	1,059,708	–51,306
2001	479,304	600,593	1,079,897	121,289
2002	542,715	696,121	1,238,836	153,406
2003	835,999	1,018,185	1,854,184	182,186
2004	1,564,606	1381,322	2,945,928	–183,284
2005	2,106,213	1,868,160	3,974,373	–238,053
2006	2,877,174	2,668,788	5,545,962	–208,386
2007	3,628,300	3,702,800	7,331,100	74,500

Sources: Data from 1950, 1960, and 1970 came from *Yearbook of China Foreign Economy and Trade Statistics*, relevant years;

Data from 1979 to 1991 came from *Compendium of China External Economic Statistics, 1979–1991*;

1992–2004 data came from *Yearbook of China External Economic Statistics;*

2005–2006 data came from *Yearbook of China External Trade Statistics;*

Data from 2007 came from *Statistics on Trade between China and West African Countries, 2007.*

Table 12.5. China-Africa trade, 1950–2007 (USD10,000)

Country	Trade volume	Export	Import	Trade balance
Africa total	733.11	362.83	370.28	7.45
Algeria	38.29	11.40	26.89	15.49
Angola	141.20	128.89	12.31	–116.58
Benin	20.84	1.13	19.71	18.58
Botswana	1.43	0.26	1.17	0.91
Burkina Faso	1.99	1.55	0.44	–1.11
Burundi	0.137	0.007	0.13	0.123
Cameron	4.57	1.60	2.97	1.37
Cameroon	0.08	—	0.08	—
Cape Verde	0.15	—	0.15	—
Central Africa	0.15	0.07	0.08	0.01
Chad	1.43	0.84	0.59	–0.25
Chana	12.66	0.53	12.13	11.6
Cote d'Ivoire	4.54	0.41	4.13	3.72
Democratic Republic of Congo (former Zaire)	5.51	4.58	0.93	–3.65
Djibouti	1.63	0.02	1.61	1.59
Egypt	46.02	2.40	43.62	41.22
Equatorial Guinea	17.90	16.97	0.93	–16.04
Eritrea	0.22	0.03	0.19	0.16
Ethiopia	8.07	0.87	7.2	6.33
Gabon	11.97	10.95	1.02	–9.93
Gambia	1.94	0.09	1.85	1.76
Guinea	3.56	0.92	2.64	1.72
Guinea-Bissau	0.07	—	0.07	—
Kenya	9.49	0.28	9.21	8.93
Lesotho	0.58	0.01	0.57	0.56
Liberia	8.06	0.030	8.03	8.00
Libya	24.06	15.47	8.59	–6.88
Madagascar	3.58	0.30	3.28	2.89
Malawi	0.430.01	0.42	0.41	–0.01
Mali	1.61	0.36	1.25	0.89
Mauritania	7.07	5.70	1.37	–4.33
Mauritius	2.89	0.05	2.84	2.79
Morocco	25.81	4.22	21.59	17.37
Mozambique	2.84	1.24	1.60	0.36
Namibia	4.01	1.58	2.43	0.85
Niger	0.27	—	0.27	—
Nigeria	43.29	5.37	37.92	32.55

(Con't)

Country	Trade volume	Export	Import	Trade balance
Republic of Congo	32.5	28.31	4.19	–24.12
Rwanda	0.59	0.24	0.35	0.11
Sao Tome and Principe	0.02	—	0.02	—
Senegal	3.56	0.23	3.33	3.10
Seychelles	0.11	0.04	0.07	0.03
Sierra Leone	0.64	0.06	0.58	0.52
Somali	0.29	0.02	0.27	0.25
South Africa	140.41	66.13	74.28	8.15
Sudan	56.15	41.32	14.83	–26.49
Swasiland	0.32	0.19	0.13	–0.06
Tanzania	7.94	2.00	5.94	3.94
Togo	14.00	0.26	13.74	13.48
Tunisia	5.12	0.30	4.82	4.52
Uganda	2.22	0.20	2.02	1.82
Zambia	5.94	3.97	1.97	–2.00
Zimbabwe	3.38	1.42	1.96	0.54

Source: *Statistics on Trade between China and West African Countries, 2007.*

The trade imbalance is a result of the types of goods traded. China has been exporting to Africa relatively low value-added products such as textiles, raw materials for manufacturing, and metals. High technology or high value-added products have not become dominant although they have increased in importance. African exports to China are of much higher value, because they tend to be petroleum, natural gas, mining resources, and metal ores.[37]

In other words, the resource-rich countries are trading their resources in exchange for light industrial products and machinery from countries in need of resources. These two trading partners may be highly complementary for trade, but this leads to an expanding trade imbalance over time. For example, China has always had a trade surplus with Nigeria. In 2007, China imported USD537 million from Nigeria, and exported USD3.79 billion, generating a trade deficit of USD3.26 billion for Nigeria.[38] This trade imbalance has led to protectionist measures in Nigeria, where in April 2004, Nigeria had unilaterally banned the import of 41 categories of products including textiles, men's shoes, and suitcases.[39]

China's competitiveness in low-cost labor and resources has also challenged the African textiles and light industries. China's successful export of textiles to the U.S. and Europe had, to a certain extent, undermined the market share of African countries in these international markets. Cheap products of textiles, apparel, shoes, and motorcycles imported from China damaged the local competitiveness of the more backwards light industries in Africa. A series of trade frictions have arisen because of this trade imbalance. Since the establishment of the WTO, African countries initiated 48 cases of anti-dumping inquiries and protectionist measures against China. This represents 6.2% of all trade protection investigation cases in which China is involved.[40]

South Africa is the country initiating the highest number of cases against China. As of the end of 2005, South Africa has launched 36 anti-dumping investigations against Chinese exports, including light industrial goods, animal products, medical and pharmaceutical products, textiles and metals. Most of these investigations have led to high countervailing duties, forcing China to withdraw these products from the South African market. From 1996, Egypt has also initiated anti-dumping investigations against two types of electrical machinery and balled pens and colored pens.[41]

The trade imbalance has widely affected African countries. In March 2004, Mauritius initiated the *Istanbul Declaration* regarding textile quotas. African countries that participated include Madagascar, Morocco, Tunisia, Kenya, and Zambia.[42]

Irresponsible market behavior in Chinese enterprises

Many state-owned and non-state companies have entered the African market propelled by China's "Go Global" policy. However, many of them lack experience in international commerce, and are not managed by strong administrative policies from the Chinese government. This resulted in scattered operations, duplication, and vicious competition, and a general disorderly state in Chinese exports to Africa. For example, given the lucrative African market for electrical goods and machinery, some Chinese companies have tried to compete by cut-throat prices. Other Chinese companies have tried to compete through evading the import tariffs in Africa, and this has led to anti-dumping cases from African governments. In addition, some Chinese companies have tried to sell fake goods, pay bribes, or obtain illegal commissions in Africa.[43]

Chinese investors have little understanding of environmental protection, which has led to some conflicts with local communities in Africa. In Gabon, 70% of timber exports were illegally exported to China. Chinese companies also have a relatively low concept of workers' health and safety and labor relations, implement relatively low standards on working conditions, and have come under fire by Africa's strong labor unions. Chinese companies operating mines in Zambia have been criticized by workers for safety regulation infringements and low wages.[44]

Competition from Europe and the U.S.

Africa has been seen as a backyard of Europe because of its geographical location and the legacy of the colonial history.[45] Although China-Africa trade has increased rapidly, its scale is still dwarfed by the trade between Africa and its European and American partners. In 2006, 70% of exports from Africa were destined for the developed countries in the West, while 60% of imports into Africa came from those developed countries. The largest trading partners of African countries have consistently been the U.S., France, the U.K., Germany, Italy, Japan, the Netherlands, and Belgium.

As China and India have visibly strengthened their cooperation with Africa, Europe and the United States have moved to ensure their established interests in Africa.[46] A Europe-Africa Summit was first held in Egypt in 2000 and subsequently in Portugal in 2007. Energy security concerns have also driven the U.S. and Europe to strengthen their ties with Africa by stepping up economic cooperation and increasing development aid. The U.S. passed the *Africa Growth and Opportunity Act* (AGOA) in 2000, granting zero-tariff and quota-free access to textiles and apparel imports from Sub-Saharan Africa to the American market. In 2000, the EU also signed the *Cotonou Agreement* with 79 developing countries including those in Africa. The *Cotonou Agreement* lays out a cooperation framework that promotes trade liberalization and establishes the status of "regional economic partnership" among the signatories. Since 2005, almost all exports from the signatory countries have been able to enter the European market freely.

Europe and the U.S. also compete with China in the African energy sector. U.S. presidents have made frequent visits to the oil-producing countries in Africa, particularly since 9/11. The U.S. Department of Energy had budgeted USD10 billion in investments in the African oil industry in 2003. American energy companies, such as Chevron and Exxon Mobil, have also announced plans to expand their investments in Africa to gain control of more of Africa's oil resources. Oil from Africa accounts for 16% of the U.S.'s oil imports currently, and this is projected to increase to 25% by 2015, according to the U.S. Commission on National Security. Oil companies from the U.K., France, Italy, and Japan have also proactively sought to expand their energy businesses in Africa. Developed countries are projected to invest between USD40 billion to 60 billion in the African Gulf of Guinea over the next 20 years.

Political and social risk in Africa

Trade with Africa has been affected by the complex ethnic and religious tensions and conflicts on the continent. A few countries are still engaged in civil wars or military conflicts; others have unstable political regimes and have frequent changes of power. A vast income gap, social inequality, and a lack of social order may threaten the personal safety of visitors. Rampant corruption and low efficiency exist across many African countries.[47] According to the 2007 corruption perception survey by Transparency International, the Berlin-headquartered global organization against corruption, 36 countries in Africa were among those perceived as the most highly corrupt in the world and 14 others were perceived as very corrupt. Only Botswana and South Africa have cleaner records on this front.[48]

According to the World Bank's *Doing Business 2008* report on the global business and investment environment, most African countries have very poor investment environments, while only Egypt, Ghana, and Kenya were in the top 10 "improving business climates."

All these risks affect or disrupt the development of trade and investment. Civil conflict in Sudan is an example. PetroChina has cooperated with the Sudanese government on the exploration, refining, and transport of oil since September 1995, setting up a few wholly Chinese-owned or joint venture entities in Sudan. Since 2003, Sudan has been the largest supplier of foreign oil to China by country. The cooperation between Sudan and China in the oil sector has created a whole system of upstream to downstream products and distribution chains. However, civil conflicts have been constantly disruptive in Sudan since its independence in 1956. Civil conflict between the Sudanese government and a rebel group in the Southern Sudanese provinces lasted between the 1980s to 2005. Religion and the control of oil resources were major issues leading to civil conflict. An agreement regarding the distribution and control of oil resources was reached in December 2003 in Nairobi, so that the conflict was temporarily resolved. However, guerrilla conflict in Darfur quickly arose when groups in the western region of Darfur found their allocation of oil to be unfair.

Anti-government groups have launched violent attacks on oil companies and their personnel. There were incidents of Chinese oil company employees being held hostage or killed. It appears that in Africa where there is oil, there is conflict. As Africa is the source of one quarter of China's oil imports, the political situation in the region is a major risk for China's energy security strategy going forward.

The Future of Sino-African Economic Cooperation

The prospect of further cooperation

China plays an important role in the economic development of Africa, a continent that has been left behind in a globalized world.[49] Africa accounts for 20% of the world's land area and 13% of the world's population, but only less than 3% of global GDP, foreign trade, and direct investment. The United Nations Conference on Trade and Development (UNCTAD) issued the report *Asian Direct Investment in Africa* at an event in China in April 2007. At the event, UNCTAD officials pointed out that China has become one of the most important partners for Africa in trade and economic cooperation. By adopting suitable policies and measures, African countries could benefit from China's rapid economic growth and industrial upgrade by attracting direct investment from China to power growth within their economies.[50]

More importantly, China's economic involvement in Africa has been welcomed by the African elite. A survey by the Program on International Policy Attitude (PIPA) at the University of Maryland found that 62% of South Africans believe that China is making a positive influence in the world. Some African elites have perceived China as different from their Western donors and investors. Even the head of the African Development Bank has announced that, "We can learn from [the Chinese] how... to move from low to middle income status."[51]

China also recognizes its key role in Africa's development as a policy that delivers both political and economic benefits, and as a responsible contribution towards global peace and security.[52]

Potential sectors of cooperation[53]

Infrastructure

The construction and repair of roads, railways, airports, and piers and the provision of water and electric power are generally considered priorities for most African nations. Egypt launched a large-scale infrastructure construction and upgrade program in 2000, pledging to invest 20 billion Egyptian pounds per year (USD3.3 billion). Equatorial Guinea also announced in 2003 an investment of USD300 million to upgrade roads in the whole country and to rebuild facilities at its airport in the second largest city, Bata. In Algeria, the focus has been on the shortage of residential housing, where the objective is to build 175,000 units of new residential housing.

Moreover, despite ample resources in Africa for electricity generation, many countries suffer from a longstanding shortage of electricity, which severely constrains economic development. South Africa has planned to invest 50 billion South African raised USD6.16 billion to connect the different grids across the country, aiming to supply electricity to every household by 2012. Angola announced the Western Power Corridor project in March 2004. An investment of USD6 billion would be made to build 3,000 km of transmission lines in order to connect with the grids in South Africa, Botswana, Namibia, and Democratic Republic of R Congo.

Much of China's development aid for Africa has so far been focused on infrastructure building. This can be seen as the means through which China has gained the trust of African nations.

Mining and other natural resources

Africa possesses ample natural resources for mining, water supply, agriculture, and forestry. Among the world's 50 most important mining resources, it features the largest reserves of 17 of them. According to statistics from the global mining industry, Africa possesses 80% of the world's manganese, platinum, chromium, ruthenium, and iridium; over half of the world's phosphate, palladium, germanium, cobalt and vanadium; and over 30% of the world's uranium, tantalum, caesium, bauxite, zircon, and graphene. The arid Sahara desert is home to significant petroleum reserves, while the neighboring countries of Libya, Algeria, Tunisia, and Nigeria are all oil-exporting countries.[54] Developing these natural resources is a priority as commodity prices have increased in recent years. From China's perspective, Africa is an important source of the natural resources required for continued economic growth. It is no surprise that China accounts for 76% to 100% of new demand in aluminum, nickel, and copper.[55]

China's demand for oil has also increased sharply, as its expenditure on oil increases and its dependency on oil imports increases year by year. From being a net oil exporter in 1980, China became a net importer of oil in 1993, while its imported oil dependency rose from 7.6% in 1995 to 42.9% in 2005, and to 56.7% in 2011 (see Table 12.6). According to the International Energy Agency, China's imported oil dependency would increase to 67% to 72% by 2030.[56]

Africa is a key part of the solution to China's energy security concerns as it is the world's eighth largest oil-producing region and is projected to supply 30% of the new demand for oil by 2010. In recent years there has already been significant changes in the geographical regions supplying oil to China. In 1995,

Southeast Asia and the Middle East were the most important oil exporters to China. By 2000, oil exports from the Middle East increased 54% while those from Southeast Asia dropped 15%. Africa's share in China's oil imports in 1990, 1995, and 2003 were 10.8%, 24%, and 24.4%, respectively.[57] In 2005, China was importing oil from 15 African countries, including Angola, Sudan, the Republic of Congo, Equatorial Guinea, Gabon, Cameroon, Algeria, Libya, Nigeria, Chad, and Egypt. A total of 38.3 million tons were imported, representing 30% of imports. The largest amount of imports came from Angola, Sudan, and the Republic of Congo.[58]

Table 12.6. The oil production, consumption, and import statistics of China, 1980–2006 (Million ton)

Year	Production	Consumption	Import	Export	Self-sufficiency (%)
1980	106.00	87.60	0.40	13.30	113.90
1985	124.90	91.70	0.70	31.20	132.30
1990	138.30	114.90	2.80	24.90	119.00
1995	149.00	160.70	17.10	18.80	101.20
2000	162.60	230.10	70.30	10.30	73.00
2001	164.80	232.20	60.30	7.60	75.80
2002	168.90	245.70	69.40	7.20	73.10
2003	169.30	252.00	91.00	8.10	67.10
2004	175.50	292.70	122.70	5.50	60.00
2005	181.35	325.35	171.63	28.88	55.70
2006	184.77	348.76	194.53	26.26	53.00

Source: *Statistical Yearbook of China*, relevant years.

Agricultural production

Since most African countries are agricultural economies, the low level of development means that a large amount of foreign exchange is spent on importing food. This situation constrains economic development and affects political stability. Many international organizations have started agricultural projects in Africa, so the continent offers both enormous demand and enormous investment opportunity in this sector.

Some Chinese agricultural companies have successfully invested in the sector in Africa. Apart from traditional agriculture, China's high technology agriculture would also have a market in Africa. China is the earliest country in the world to engage in research and development in biotechnology for agriculture. China would possess agricultural technologies that could benefit Africa, increase its food supply, and address issues of hunger, poverty, and environmental degradation.

Manufacturing

Manufacturing in Africa is generally underdeveloped, and most industrial finished goods have to be imported. The manufacturing sector in South Africa is relatively developed, but in 2004 its manufacturing only accounted for 16% of its GDP. Nigeria has the most advanced manufacturing sector in West Africa, yet manufacturing only represented 6% of GDP. The sector is mainly comprised of small manufacturing and processing, which produces textiles, beverages, tobacco, daily cleaning products, and concrete. Kenya, the most industrialized country in East Africa, has industries contributing to 13% of its GDP. The small manufacturing facilities process flour, and produce beverages, tobacco, textiles, home electrical appliances, candies, and paper. Therefore, African companies have been interested in investing in the sectors of machinery, light industry, chemical industries, and home appliances production in China.

High technology industries

Many African countries have been trying to close the technology gap between Africa and the advanced countries. The Internet and mobile phone services have mushroomed in Africa. According to statistics from the International Telecommunication Union, the United Nations agency headquartered in Geneva, in the early 1990s Internet access in Africa was only available in South Africa, Egypt, and Tunisia. By the late 1990s, 50 countries offered Internet access. A mobile phone network was not available in half of the countries in Africa in the mid-1990s. By 2004, Africa became the first continent to see mobile phone subscribers exceed landline telephone subscribers in numbers.

China has achieved international competitiveness in several areas of technology, such as microelectronics, aerospace, biotechnology, and super conductors. In May 2004, China Great Wall Industry Corporation (CGWIC), a subsidiary of China Aerospace and Technology Corporation, participated in an international bid with the Nigerian Space Agency. The Chinese company won in spite of competition from European and American companies. The company would export a communications satellite to Nigeria, and set it into orbit using the Long March 3B rocket from the Xichang Satellite Launch Center in Sichuan Province. This was the first time China had used its homegrown rocket and satellite to provide such a service to an international customer. Chinese companies also have relatively mature products, technology, and services in telecommunication network operations, that would enter the African market.

Pharmaceuticals

African countries welcome investments in the pharmaceutical industry as diseases are rampant. AIDS and malaria are the two most serious diseases. Currently, among the 42 million HIV positive patients, 29 million of them live in Africa. Up to 15 to 20% of the population in Sub-Saharan Africa are infected, with some countries even more seriously affected. The population of Botswana is 40% HIV positive, the population of South Africa 30%, and in Zimbabwe 25%. Meanwhile, the market for anti-malaria drugs in Africa is USD20 billion a year.

Although China's pharmaceutical industry is not in an advanced stage, some traditional Chinese medicine treatments of AIDS and malaria have been increasingly recognized by other countries. For example, artemisinin extracted from the plant artemisia annua is an ingredient in anti-malaria drugs, and the plant is grown in Guangxi, Yunnan, Sichuan Provinces, and Chongqing in China, as well as in Vietnam and India. Youyang County, Chongqing is a major production area for artemisia annua. When the World Health Organization procured 30 tons of artemisinin anti-malarial drug from Youyang in 2004, it cost RMB300 million [USD47.2 million]. Beijing Holley Ketai Pharmaceuticals was the first Chinese company to export artemisinin to Africa. Millions of boxes of these anti-malarial drugs reach more than 20 African countries every year. China is also among a handful of countries in the world with the artificial cultivation technology for artemisinin. If transferred to Africa, this technology could have substantial economic and social benefits.

13

Chapter

Economic Relations between China and the Commonwealth of Independent States

The Present Status of Economic Relations between China and CIS

A *Creation Agreement* of the Commonwealth of Independent States (CIS) was signed December 8, 1991, between Russia, Ukraine, and Belarus. On December 21 the same year, eight other former Soviet states including Armenia, Azerbaijan, Kazakhstan, Kyrgyzstan, Modolva, Tajikistan, Turkmenistan, and Uzbekistan signed the Alma-Ata Protocol and joined the CIS, bringing the membership to 11 states. The CIS became a successor entity to the USSR. Georgia joined in 1993, increasing the CIS membership to 12. However, it withdrew membership in 2008 and formally left CIS in August 2009.

The CIS is the largest organization of its kind in the world, accounting for one-sixth of global land area, and featuring vast diversity in ethnicities, culture, and religion. It is a resource-rich region, responsible for 12% of the world's oil production and one-third of the world's natural gas.

China established diplomatic relations with Russia on December 27, 1991, and by June 9, 1992, had established diplomatic relations with the rest of the CIS countries. For over two decades, China has developed positive political relations with CIS countries, providing a secure environment for economic and trade relations.

The ruble economy collapsed after 1991. Political turmoil in Eastern Europe, the disintegration of the economic system based on Stalin's theory of "two parallel markets," and the disintegration of the Council of Mutual Economic Assistance brought significant uncertainty to the CIS countries. Each of them faces an enormous task before them—how to transform an originally closed or semi-closed economy into an open one that facilitates international exchange and efficient resource allocation. Based on their geographical location, these newly independent states started to build economic relations with neighbors including China. By June 1993, China had signed a series of bilateral agreements on economic cooperation with all CIS countries. To date, signed economic agreements have covered the areas of economic cooperation, investment protection, double taxation, and the quality assurance of import and export.

In these two decades, there have been both encouraging developments and complicating issues in the economic relations between China and the CIS.

Continued growth in trade between China and CIS

Because of the differences in the size and structure of economies, there is a certain degree of inconsistency and imbalance in China's economic relations with the CIS. China's trade and economic cooperation with CIS states can be better understood in three tiers.

First tier: Russia and Kazakhstan are the most important trading partners in the CIS

Russia and Kazakhstan are the two CIS states with the largest land area, sharing a 5,000 km border with China, and thus possessing a geographical advantage in conducting trade with China. Russia and Kazakhstan are China's largest and second largest trading partners, respectively, within the CIS. The two states are important to China for economic and geopolitical reasons. Russia and Kazakhstan also recognize the importance of China as an energy market, and have proactively opened cooperation in electric power, oil, and natural gas projects.

According to customs statistics, the China-Russia trade volume was USD4.63 billion in 1992.[1] There was stable development in 1993, with trade volume reaching USD7.68 billion. Since then there was a decline in trade volume, but economic cooperation expanded to a wider range of sectors and the two countries reached a higher quality of economic relations. By 2000, China and Russia had reached USD8 billion in trade volume, a year-on-year growth of 39.9%. In 2001, trade volume reached USD10.6 billion, representing a historical high and a year-on-year growth of 33.3%. In 2002, trade volume increased to USD11.93 billion, another 11.8% in growth. In 2003, it grew to USD15.76 billion, a 32.1% increase. In 2004, it grew 44% to USD21.23 billion. In 2005, it grew 37.1% to USD29.1 billion. In 2006, it grew more moderately at 15% to USD33.39 billion. Growth staggered again to 44% in 2007, when trade volume grew to USD48.17 billion.

China-Russia trade has passed the initial stage of stagnation, and entered a stage of historically rapid growth. Chinese exports to Russia have shown robust growth, but Russian exports to China have been languid. The imbalance has become apparent. From 1992 to 2007, Russia was running a trade surplus with China, but the situation then reversed, and China's trade surplus with Russia is now increasing year by year. Overall trade relations have been positive.

Kazakhstan is a close partner with China on energy projects. Trade between China and Kazakhstan had consistently increased through the years, especially after 1999. The China-Kazakhstan trade volume reached USD369.1 million in 1992, USD434.7 million in 1993, dropped slightly to USD335 million in 1994, maintained steady growth between 1995 and 1998, and reached USD636 million in 1998. Boosted by China-Kazakhstan cooperation in the oil sector, trade volume grew to USD1.14 billion in 1999, a 78.9% year-on-year increase. In 2000, it grew to USD1.56 billion. Further plans in economic and transport cooperation were reached in 2001. In 2002, trade volume reached USD1.95 billion, a 51.7% growth. In 2003, trade volume reached USD3.29 billion, a 68.7% growth. A new historic high was reached in 2004 when trade volume was USD4.5 billion, a 36.8% growth.

In December 15, 2005, the China-Kazakhstan crude oil pipeline (Atasu-Alanshakou section) was completed. This 2,770 km pipeline was China's first oil pipeline crossing international borders. It was a 50-50 joint investment between China and Kazakhstan. In the same year, China National Petroleum Corporation (CNPC) acquired PetroKazakhstan with USD4.81 billion, an acquisition that became an important driver in China-Kazakhstan energy cooperation. Bilateral trade volume jumped to USD6.81 billion in 2005, a year-on-year increase of 51.3%. It increased to USD8.36 billion in 2006, a 22.7% increase. Trade volume exceeded USD10 billion in 2007, reaching USD13.88 billion, an increase of 66%. There were also new developments in technology cooperation, as an international cooperation centre is being built in Horgas at the border of China and Kazakhstan. Kazakhstan's state nuclear company, KazAtomProm, and China Nuclear Energy Industry Corporation (CNEIC) signed a nuclear cooperation agreement, in which Kazakhstan allowed CNEIC and the Guangdong Nuclear Power Group to hold a 49% stake in the uranium fields of Kazakhstan. In return, China permitted Kazakhstan's nuclear energy companies to hold stakes in China's nuclear processing industry and nuclear power stations. This agreement was a milestone achievement for China-Kazakhstan cooperation.

Second-tier: CIS countries with close economic relations with China

Ukraine

Since January 4, 1992, Ukraine and China frequently exchanged visits of their heads of state, and signed a series of agreements on economic and technological cooperation. In 1996, the China-Ukraine trade volume reached USD840 million. However, the issue of Taiwan added strain onto Ukraine-China relations, causing the bilateral trade volume to drop to USD275 million in 1998, a decrease of 36.8% from 1997. Once Ukraine stated its "One China" policy, trade relations recovered. In 2001, trade volume increased to USD857 million, a year-on-year increase of 45.1%. In 2002, it rose to USD1.23 billion, the highest since Ukraine's independence. There was steady development since then. Trade volume increased by 76.3% to USD2.18 billion in 2003, then increased by 14.5% to USD2.49 billion in 2004. It rose again by 32% in 2005 to USD3.277 billion, and by 27% again in 2006 to USD4.16 billion. Another historic high was achieved in 2007, when trade volume reached USD6.52 billion.

Kyrgyzstan

Kyrgyzstan and China established diplomatic relations on January 5, 1992. Trade showed inconsistent growth since then, and for a long time the growth rate was low. In 1992, the China-Kyrgyzstan trade volume was USD35.48 million, which rose to USD102.2 million in 1993, USD 105 million in 1994, USD231 million in 1995, and slumped to USD105 million in 1996, maintained a similar level of USD106 million in 1997, climbed back slowly to USD198 million in 1998. Trade volume then grew slowly to USD135 million in 1999, USD177.6 million in 2000, USD201 million in 2002, USD314 million in 2003. Strong growth came after 2004, when the trade volume reached USD602 million in 2004, USD972 million in 2005, and shot up to USD2.23 billion in 2006, and reached a historical high of USD3.78 billion in 2007. Currently, a China-Kyrgyzstan-Uzbekistan highway is under construction, and China has provided USD900 million in export credit to members of the Shanghai Cooperation Organization to finance the construction of a cement factory in Batken Province.

Uzbekistan

Uzbekistan and China established diplomatic relations on January 2, 1992. Trade between China and Uzbekistan was kept at a low level, with a trade volume of around USD100 million and showed large fluctuations. The trade volume in 1992 was USD47.5 million, which rose to USD54.3 million in 1993, and then increased by nearly 130% to USD124 million in 1994. It dropped steadily at USD119 million in 1995, but rose again by 57% to USD187 million in 1996. In 1997, the trade volume grew steadily by 8% to USD202 million, but then it dropped dramatically by 55% to USD90.3 million. In 1999, it dropped again to USD40.3 million. After 2001, growth returned for China-Uzbekistan trade. In 2002, trade volume was USD130 million, a year-on-year increase of 126%. In 2003, it rose another 167% to USD347 million. In 2004, it increased by 66% to USD575 million. In 2005, it increased to USD680 million, representing a 18% increase. In 2006, it rose 43% to USD970 million. In that year, Chinese citizens were allowed to travel individually to Uzbekistan.

Belarus

Belarus declared independence on August 25, 1991, and the country established diplomatic relations with China on January 20, 1992. Trade between the two countries was very low, and has been growing slowly. According to statistics from Belarus, in 1997 the China-Belarus trade volume was USD102 million, which was more than triple the trade volume in 1992. According to statistics from China customs, the trade volume in 2000 was USD113.63 million, an increase of 337% year-on-year. In 2001, it dropped 62% to USD43.26 million. In 2002, it rose 85% to USD80.08 million. In February 2003, Huawei Corporation from China won a bid to provide telecommunication equipment to Belarus, which opened a new phase of cooperation between the two countries. In 2003, trade volume reached USD129 million, rising 61%. In 2004, it rose again by 70% to reach USD219 million. It increased in 2005 by 161% to reach USD572 million. By 2007, the trade volume had already jumped to USD839.8 million.

Tajikistan

Tajikistan and China established diplomatic relations on January 4, 1992. Due to civil unrest in the late 1980s, contact between China and Tajikistan was cut off for five years and trade was non-existent. As a result, trade grew very slowly and inconsistently thereafter. According to China customs statistics, in 1992 the bilateral trade volume was USD2.8 million. It increased in 1993 to USD12.4 million, but dropped 74.3% in 1994 to USD3.2 million. In 1995, it rose again by 6.5 times to USD23.9 million, but dropped again by 73% to 20.2 million. The trend continued in 1998 when it fell slightly by 5% to USD19.2 million, and in 1999 when it dropped 58% to USD8 million. In 2000, it rose 113.5% to USD17.17 million, but dropped in 2001 by 37.3% to USD10.8 million. From 2002 onwards the economic stability in Tajikistan became more apparent, as bilateral trade grew more steadily. In 2002, the trade volume was USD12.39 million, a year-on-year increase of 15%. In 2003 it reached 38.8 million. In 2004, after the Dushanbe-Sarykol border crossing—a previously contested border point between the two countries—was opened, trade increased further. In 2004, it rose 78% to USD68.9 million. In 2005, it again rose by 129% to USD158 million. In 2006, China and Tajikistan signed the contracts for the restoration of the Dushanbe-Chanak highway and for China to provide electricity transmission and transformer equipment, at a value of USD600 million. Trade continued to rise thereafter, growing 105% to reach USD324 million in 2006, and increased 62% to USD524 million in 2007.

Azerbaijan

Azerbaijan declared independence on August 30, 1991, and established diplomatic relations with China on April 2, 1992. Economic cooperation between the two countries was constrained because of the remote location and the low economic development of Azerbaijan. According to China customs statistics, trade was USD15.7 million in 1997, USD1.3 million in 1998. The main exports from China were knitted products, shoes, toys, and mechanical and electrical equipment, while the main import to China was raw cotton. In 1999, the trade volume increased slightly to USD1.14 million. It rose to USD6.17 million in 2000, and by nearly 150% to USD15 million in 2001. Trade volume reached USD184 million in 2004, as economic cooperation continued to expand. Chinese petroleum companies stepped up investment in Azerbaijan, launching several energy projects. Cooperation in telecommunications and electric power also expanded. Trade volume increased to USD258 million in 2005, USD369 million in 2006, and USD477 million in 2007.

Turkmenistan

Trade with Turkmenistan grew slowly after Turkmenistan and China established diplomatic relations in January 6, 1992. Trade volume was at USD4.5 million in 1992, USD4.7 million in 1993, USD11.3 million in 1994 (+142%), USD17.6 million in 1995 (+56%), USD11.5 million in 1996 (–35%), USD15.2 million in 1997 (+33%), USD 12.5 million in 1998, and USD9.49 million in 1999 (–24%). The two countries started discussions on oil and gas cooperation in 2000. Trade volume increased to USD16.2 million in 2000 (+70%), USD87.5 million in 2002 (+168%), USD113 million in 2003 (+29%), USD98.7 million in 2004 (-13%), USD 110 million in 2005 (+11%), USD179 million in 2006 (63%), and USD353 million in 2007 (+97%).

Georgia

Georgia, which left the CIS in 2009, had established diplomatic relations with China in June 9, 1992. The remote location, inconvenient transportation and slow economic reconstruction in Georgia meant that its economic cooperation with China had been limited. According to statistics from China customs, the trade volume was USD4 million in 1997, USD7.7 million in 1998, USD12.5 million in 1999, USD3.9 million in 2000, USD7 million in 2001, USD11.5 million in 2002, USD28.1 million in 2003, USD57 million in 2004, USD43.4 million in 2005, USD85.3 million in 2006, and was at a new high at USD192 million in 2007.

Third tier: Armenia and Moldova have small economies and limited economic ties with China

Economic cooperation between China and Armenia has been limited in scale. The two countries established diplomatic ties on April 6, 1992. The bilateral trade volume was USD370,000 in 1997, USD840,000 in 1998, USD11.6 million in 1999, and USD5.3 million in 2000. In 2001, the trade volume was USD3.4 million, of which USD2.3 million was Chinese exports and USD1.2 million was imports from Armenia. The trade volume grew to USD8.6 million in 2002 (+150%), and dropped to USD6.5 million in 2003 (–25%). In 2004, the largest economic cooperation project to date—the Shanxi-Nairit Synthetic Rubber Company was set up. In 2004, the trade volume increased to USD13.9 million. Further economic cooperation agreements were signed in September 2005 in Beijing, at the fourth meeting of the economic cooperation committee between the Chinese and Armenian government. The synthetic rubber company has proven a success, boosting overall bilateral trade to USD23.4 million (+69%). The trade volume further increased to USD41.5 million in 2006 (78%), and to USD89.2 million in 2007.

Modolva and China held three rounds of economic cooperation committee meetings between 1996 and 2006, strengthening economic ties since the establishment of diplomatic relations on January 30, 1992. Chinese exports to Moldova typically included frozen chicken, textiles, metal processing machine tools, light industrial products, and shoes. Modolvan exports to China were typically steel billets and crude forgings, and military instrument and meters. According to statistics from Chinese customs, bilateral trade volume was USD8.1 million in 2000, and increased to USD14.7 million in 2001. It dropped in 2002 to USD5.9 million, and recovered in 2003 to USD14.7 million. From 2004 to 2007, the bilateral trade volume was USD24.1 million, US51.6 million, USD32.2 million, and 51.4 million respectively.

Cooperation and competition in China-CIS economic relations

The CIS has been a loose organization with endless internal restructuring since its inception. The Council of Heads of State and the Council of Heads of Government of CIS had signed several thousands of documents and agreements over the years, setting up organizations such as a payment union, customs union, inter-state economic committee, inter-state bank and inter-state economic judiciary. However, despite the initially good intentions, these agreements mostly turn out to be empty and ceremonial, and failed to deliver real benefits. Many CIS government leaders even do not remember the agreements they have signed. "From the very beginning, the policies of each CIS country were against these objectives," wrote Igor Ivanov, the former Foreign Minister of Russia (1998–2004). There has been a centrifugal tendency in politics, economy and trade, culture and other sectors, making it difficult to tread the original path of mutually beneficial cooperation."[2]

Although the loose organization of CIS had aspired to model itself after the more close-knit European Union, conflicting political and economic interests among the CIS countries has blocked such efforts. The economies within CIS tend to be based on raw materials, natural resources, and low value-adding industries, heightening competition between states. There is low complementarity between Russia and the rest of the CIS states, so there is little momentum for trade within CIS.

Efforts have been made to cope with these problems. Various regional organizations were set up between 1994 and 1999, including the Central Asia Economic Union whose membership includes Kazakhstan, Kyrgyzstan, Uzbekistan, and Tajikistan (the lattermost joined in 1998); the Customs Union set up by Russia, Belarus, Kazakhstan, Kyrgyzstan, and Tajikistan, which was renamed the Eurasian Union in October 2000); the Union State that includes Russia and Belarus; and the GUAM alliance formed by Georgia, Ukraine, Uzbekistan, Azerbaijan, and Moldova.[3]

In 2003, Russia led the effort to build a Common Economic Space with Ukraine, Kazakhstan, and Belarus, aspiring to create an economic core to the CIS. These efforts have been met with many obstacles so far, and it would remain to be seen whether Russia's strategy of "energy in return for security" would yield results for regional economic growth.

The incessant changes and restructuring within the CIS might have been an essential process for economic development of that region. However, these changes have exposed the weaknesses and lack of power of the CIS organization itself, and have created confusion for the trading partners of CIS countries. To a certain extent, the creation of regional free trade unions creates exclusion effect that is disadvantageous to countries external to the organization. We would expect that these unions within CIS could create a challenge or competition with China, and could have a negative impact on China-CIS economic relations.

There is also a particularly strong competitive relationship between China and Russia. On one hand, China and Russia have different strengths and strong complementarity in the areas of natural resources, energy, electric power, infrastructure, aviation and aerospace, agriculture, light industry and labor services. These different strengths mean that there is room for opening cooperation between the two countries.

On the other hand, the countries are in different stages of economic development, possess different factors of endowment and have varying labor productivity, which have led to low momentum for developing trade and investment. The proportion of processing trade and intermediary trade is relatively low, constraining further Sino-Russian trade development. At the same time, both China and Russia are in the stage of attracting foreign direct investment, and can be seen as competitors for FDI. As a result, the current trade and economic cooperation between China and Russia are disproportionately small compared to the size and economic potential of the two countries. Moreover, as both are transitional economies, each country's market economy have features that are incoherent with international practice, and their legislation and administrative systems for promoting trade may not be most suitable for the needs of developing economic cooperation between the two nations.

Features of the Economic Relations between China and CIS

China-CIS trade kept low relative to total Chinese foreign trade

CIS accounts for a very small proportion of Chinese foreign trade. According to China customs statistics in 2007, China's foreign trade reached USD2.17 trillion. China-Europe trade was at USD447.93 billion, or 20% of the total. CIS accounted for a mere USD76 billion, or less than 3.5%, in China's foreign trade that year.

China and its largest trading partner in CIS, Russia, are both populous nations with large land areas, and share a 4,300 km border, but bilateral trade has accounted for a low and inconsistent percentage of China's total foreign trade. The highest percentage was achieved in 1993 (3.9%), and the lowest percentage was in 1999 (1.6%). In recent years, Russia has accounted for between 1.9% to 2% of China's total foreign trade. Even as Sino-Russian trade has grown in absolute number up to the year 2007, its percentage of China's foreign trade was still 2.2%.

At the same time, there is a vast trade imbalance between China and the CIS countries. Russia and Kazakhstan account for roughly 80% of China's trade with the CIS. In 2007, China and the CIS had a total of USD76 billion in bilateral trade. Russia accounted for 48.17 billion, or 64%, while Kazakhstan accounted for USD13.88 billion, or 18%.

Trade focuses on low value goods

Goods with low technology content and low value-added tend to dominate trade between China and CIS countries. Other types of economic cooperation such as trade of technology and services are almost non-existent. Food and light textiles account for over 50% of Chinese exports to CIS countries, while petrochemical products, metals, fossil fuel, paper pulp, and sea products account for over 80% of imports from CIS to China.

For example, among Chinese exports to Russia in 2004, textiles and raw materials for textiles accounted for 26%, leather and fur products 25%, electrical equipment and parts 15%, shoes and boots 37%, toys, furniture, and other miscellaneous products 4%, and others 21%. Among Russian exports to China, mining products accounted for 37%, steel and base metal 17%, petrochemical products 14%, timber and related products 12%, animal products 6%, and others 14%.

In the trade between China and Kazakhstan, more than 80% of Kazakh exports to China were energy (58%) and natural resources such as ferrous and non-ferrous metals (24%). Chinese exports to Kazakhstan included machine manufacturing products and metal processing products (69%), food (9%), and other goods.

Kyrgyzstan's exports to China are 23% raw materials for textiles and apparel, and 60% ferrous and non-ferrous metals. Uzbekistan's exports to China are mainly labor services (48%), machine and equipment (19%), cotton (4%), food (4.6%), and non-ferrous metals (1.5%). Chinese exports to Uzbekistan include 48% machinery manufacturing products, 19% petrochemical products, and 9% food. Turkmenistan's exports to China were mainly energy (83%), cotton and other raw materials for textiles (5%), while Chinese exports to Turkmenistan were mainly machinery manufacturing and metal processing products (60%).

Lack of diversification in economic cooperation

Apart from trading, economic cooperation has been limited. Investment projects tend to be few in number, small in scale and typically fail to create momentum for further investment. For instance, there were 549 Chinese investment projects in Russia approved by the Chinese Ministry of Commerce in 2004, with investment contracts worth USD582 million, accounting for only under 5% of Chinese outbound investment. By June 2006, the number of Chinese investment projects in Russia increased to 700, and the contract value had risen to USD1.34 billion.

In the same year, there were 1,912 Russian-invested enterprises in China, with investment contracts worth USD1.52 billion and an actual utilization of investment of USD570 million. These figures lag far behind the goal for Russian outbound investment in China to reach USD15.5 billion by 2010. As for other Central Asian nations such as Kazakhstan, many economic agreements and letters of intent were signed but many were not implemented and those that have been executed have yet to reach a state of effective cooperation.

Lack of a trade service system at an international level

Currently, bank settlement, trade arbitration, and export credit and insurance services have not been able to meet the needs for trade and economic cooperation. There are issues such as low efficiency of customs and trading activities that take place against the rules, leading to the loss of customs tariffs and the understatement of value of goods in customs declaration. Departments such as customs, border security, transportation, tax, environmental protection, and public security have been acting without coordination, sometimes following conflicting laws and regulations. All these issues have undermined the healthy, stable, and orderly development of bilateral economic relations.

Constraining Factors in the Development of China-CIS Economic Relations

There are some constraining factors that have obstructed the development of further economic relations between China and CIS.

First, economic development is the key. We expect that China would benefit from, and also contribute to, the economic growth of CIS countries, especially those that share a border with China. After the disintegration of the USSR, many CIS countries suffered from years of recession and economic crises, hampering foreign trade. However, from 1999 onwards, Russia has enjoyed about a decade of economic growth, as can be seen from its fiscal improvements, increased gold and foreign exchange reserves, consecutive years of fiscal surplus, reduction in foreign debt, and stability of government funds. The five countries in Central Asia also experienced positive economic growth, with Kazakhstan being the prime example. Leveraging its oil exports, the GDP of Kazakhstan grew 9% or above for eight consecutive years, reaching USD80.4 billion in 2006. Its GDP per capita rose to nearly USD7,000, and its annual income per capita was USD3,700. Based on these statistics, Kazakhstan is not far from a mid-sized developed country. The potential for growth can also be seen in Turkmenistan, Uzbekistan, and Tajikistan.

Second, more comprehensive systems would help protect trade and economic cooperation. China and CIS countries are all transitional economies. They are in the process of changing the ways of a planned economy, and reforming their trade systems, legislation, and administrative methods to align with international practice and to adapt to a market economy. These reforms are important because the trade and economic activities of both China and CIS are often government-led. The growth in trade between China and CIS would therefore also be government-led, especially as China and CIS are in slightly different stages of creating a market economy, and they have yet to build mutual trust in each other's markets. Because bilateral trade is not entirely based on market needs, and instead often relies on inter-governmental orders, inconsistency, and uncertainties may be created. It has become apparent that bilateral economic relations cannot rely only on government activities. Therefore, both China and CIS would need to focus on cultivating their domestic markets, support the economic environment with a suitable regulatory framework.

Third, bilateral investment needs to be supported by economic power of the countries involved. Thus far, there has been a lack of concrete cases of success in economic cooperation between China and CIS. However, as CIS economies are growing rapidly, coupled with Chinese economic growth, previous problems of inadequate investment capital would be gradually eliminated. As global energy prices continue to rise, there are increasingly lucrative opportunities in developing the energy and resources sectors. It is projected that China-Russia and China-Kazakhstan direct investment would increase and generate stronger interest in trade development. Energy projects alone are expected to contribute USD8–10 billion towards bilateral trade each year.

Fourth, there needs to be a new and more realistic understanding of the potential for trade and economic cooperation between China and Russia. If we look at the competitiveness of various industries and sectors in the two countries, we would not see significant changes in the types of goods traded in the next five to six years. Energy, natural resources, light textiles, and daily consumer goods would still dominate trade, but may decrease as a proportion of total bilateral trade. Machinery and electrical products, as well as high technology products are likely to increase in importance and become bright spots for growth. Energy and resources would still be the main areas for Sino-Russian cooperation, but there would also be growth in service trade.

In order to boost bilateral investment, there needs to be new policies in utilizing foreign investment, increasing the quality of FDI, and the effectiveness in using foreign investment to generate a positive economic impact. There may also need to be stronger financial supervision of Chinese- and Russian-invested companies in the two countries.

In conclusion, both China and its CIS trading partners would need to evaluate the needs of their domestic economies, and explore new ways of economic cooperation. This could include devising new sectors of common interests, strengthening energy cooperation projects, and improving the investment environment. As long as there are practical steps taken to resolve some of the constraining factors and to create a more proactive long-term strategy of cooperation, we are optimistic about China's economic relations with the CIS, and, in particular, with Russia and Kazakhstan.

14

Chapter

China's Cooperation with Major International Economic Organizations

China and the World Bank

An overview of the World Bank

The World Bank comprises two institutions, the International Bank for Reconstruction and Development (IBRD) and the International Development Association (IDA).[1]

The World Bank Group is formed by the above institutions together with the International Finance Corporation (IFC), the International Center for Settlement of Investment Dispute (ICSID), and the Multilateral Investment Guarantee Agency (MIGA).

The World Bank was formed at the Bretton Woods conference in July 1944 (formally known as the United Nations Monetary and Financial Conference). The IBRD was officially established in an agreement signed by representatives of 28 countries on December 27, 1945.[2]

The IBRD started operations in June 1945, and became a special organization of the United Nations in November 1947. The IBRD is headquartered in Washington D.C., and has 185 member countries as of June 2008.[3]

The IBRD mainly provides loans and development aid to middle-income countries and low-income countries with good credit. Its objective is to support sustainable development and reduce poverty.

The International Development Association (IDA) was set up on September 24, 1960 to help the poorest countries in the world with interest-free loans and grants.[4]

There are 166 member countries as of June 2008.[5] Its objectives are to support development in underdeveloped parts of the world, improve quality of life, and address the inequality between developed and developing countries. The IBRD and IDA staff share staff and headquarters, and use the same standards to evaluate projects.[6]

China joins the World Bank

China joined the IBRD in December 1945 and the IDA in September 1960.7 After the establishment of the People's Republic of China (PRC), China's legal membership in the World Bank was occupied by Taiwan. It was only in April 1980 that China's membership in IBRD, IDA, and IFC were reinstated. Since then, China attended the annual meeting of the World Bank. Currently (as of June 2008), Chinese Finance Minister Xie Xuren has been representing China at the World Bank. Since its reinstatement, China itself is a voting entity and can appoint its own executive director.

As of the end of 2007, China has USD4.48 billion in subscription to capital stock, or 2.85% of total subscriptions, at the IBRD. It has 45,049 votes, or 2.78% of total votes, ranking sixth among World Bank member countries.[8]

As of April 28, 2008, China had 332,400 votes in the IDA, or 1.95% of total votes, ranking 13th among member countries.[9]

Cooperation between China and the World Bank

Robert Zoellick, president of the World Bank, visited China in December 2007 and stated that China was no longer a country aided by the World Bank, and instead was an important partner of the World Bank.[10]

Regular meetings

Cooperation with the World Bank is a high priority for China. China participates in the autumn and spring meetings of the World Bank every year, plays a key role on the board of directors, and is involved in the policy making and the granting of external loans by the World Bank. Senior Chinese government officials also frequently meet with World Bank officials.

The World Bank China Office manages the institution's activities in China. The Chinese Ministry of Finance is the main government ministry interacting with the World Bank and implementing related activities, while the National Development and Reform Commission (NDRC) also participates in the cooperation. There are annual reviews held in relation to the World Bank's three-year rolling loan program for China. All loan items go through a technical, economic, financial, environmental, and social evaluation before they reach the final approval stage with the creditor and borrower. The loan projects are regularly monitored or inspected.

The World Bank has also provided advice on important issues in China's economic construction, such as the mode of economic development, macro economy administration, inflation, and economic cycles. It could be said that the World Bank played a role in ensuring the success of China's economic reforms.

In February 4, 2008, Chinese academic Justin Yifu Lin was appointed as senior vice president and chief economist of the World Bank. Lin has become the first person from a developing country to be appointed to his position. This shows the changes in the World Bank and the changing role of China in the world economy.[11]

World Bank aid to China

In the 20 years after the reinstatement of China in the World Bank, relations between China and the World Bank have matured to one of the largest cooperative partnerships in the world.

When China was first reinstated, the aid provided by the World Bank aimed to support economic reforms. The focus was on increasing productivity of agricultural labor, strengthening the financial industry, developing exports, elevating the market position, and accelerating economic integration. The early World Bank loans tended to emphasize advanced project evaluation, management, and experience of constructing an economy. These objectives and focus changed as the Chinese economy grew.

It was also affected by the reforms of the World Bank. In 1997, then World Bank president James Wolfensohn launched a reform plan for the World Bank, which aimed at more effective poverty reduction. There were the following changes in the World Bank's policy towards China:

- Support China in obtaining direct financing. This is mainly achieved through promoting foreign direct investment in China by encouraging foreign investors to participate in projects or project design.
- Support the corporate restructuring of Chinese state-owned companies, including re-structuring, commercialization, and privatization.
- Encouraging a diversified economy and the construction of infrastructure and public utilities.[12]

A Country Partnership Strategy (2006–2010) for China was tabled and approved in the board of directors meeting of the World Bank in May 2006. The new objectives for the strategy were to help China better integrate into the world economy, to reduction poverty and inequality, to cope with shortage of resources and environmental challenges, strengthen financial departments, and improve governance and market systems. China received the following aid support in accordance with this strategy:

- Accelerate China's integration into the world economy. Encourage China to participate in multilateral economic organizations, reduce domestic and external trade barriers, and support the development of Chinese trade and investment overseas.
- Reduce poverty, inequality, and social exclusion. Promote balanced development of urban and rural areas, support local economies in agricultural villages, expand basic social services, and infrastructure, particularly in rural agricultural communities.
- Face the shortage of resources and environmental challenges. Reduce

ozone pollution, conserve water, improve the efficiency of energy utilization (partially through price reforms), improve the administration and management of land, and execute international agreements.

- Support the strengthening of financial intermediaries. Expand financial services, especially in small- to medium-sized enterprises, develop a capital market, cope with systemic risk, and maintain stability in the financial system.
- Strengthening governance and market systems. Increase competitiveness of enterprises, reform government departments, and improve the financial accountability between government departments.

World Bank loans to China

The size of loans

World Bank loans to China initially had an increasing trend in the 1980s and 1990s, until China's rapid economic development meant that the amount of loans received was reduced towards the late 1990s.

World Bank loans to China started with USD200 million in 1981, and increased to USD1.5 billion by the end of the 1980s. In 1993–1995, the annual loan amount peaked at roughly USD3 billion. From 1996 onwards, the size of loans was reduced. China "graduated" from the IDA in June 1999, which meant that the World Bank institution that is responsible for providing zero-interest loans to the world's poorest developing countries will no longer provide loans to China. From then on, China only received loans from IBRD.[13]

In 2000, World Bank loans to China were reduced to USD1.5 billion, and to USD563 million in 2002. The loan amount was increased again in 2003, but it was still lower than the peak in the mid-1990s (see Table 14.1). At the same time, the loan process became more selective, and loans focused on the lesser developed sectors or geographical regions of China, in order to achieve more effectively the objective in poverty reduction.[14]

Distribution of loans by sector

World Bank loans were distributed across several sectors that are important to the national economy, including transportation, urban development, rural development, energy, and human development (see Table 14.2).

In recent years, loans have focused on resolving the social and environmental impact of rapid development in China. Over 60% of World Bank loans are in environmental protection. Urban projects have emphasized services that

Table 14.1. World Bank loans to China (USD million)

Financial year	Number of projects	Hard loans*	Soft loans†	Total loan amount
1981	1	100.00	100.00	200.00
1982	1	0.00	60.00	60.00
1983	6	463.10	150.40	613.50
1984	10	616.00	423.50	1,039.50
1985	12	659.60	442.30	1,101.90
1986	11	687.00	450.00	1,137.00
1987	11	867.40	556.20	1,423.60
1988	14	1053.70	639.90	1,693.60
1989	12	833.40	515.00	1,348.40
1990	5	0.00	590.00	590.00
1991	10	601.50	977.80	1,579.30
1992	16	1,577.70	948.60	2,526.30
1993	18	2,145.00	925.00	3,070.00
1994	14	2,145.00	925.00	3,070.00
1995	16	2,369.50	630.00	2,999.50
1996	15	2,100.00	480.00	2,580.00
1997	11	2,490.00	325.00	2,851.00
1998	16	2,323.00	293.40	2,616.40
1999	19	1,674.40	422.61	2,097.01
2000	8	1,672.50	0.00	1,672.50
2001	8	787.50	0.00	787.50
2002	5	562.90	0.00	562.90
2003	6	1,145.00	0.00	1,145.00
2004	9	1,218.27	0.00	1,218.27
2005	9	1,030.30	0.00	1,030.30
2006	11	1,454.33	0.00	1,454.33
2007	10	1,641.00	0.00	1,641.00
2008	12	1,513.40	0.00	1,513.40
Total	296	33,741.50	9,946.71	43,688.21

Notes: (1) The financial year ends in June 30, 2008.
(2) Due to incomplete data sets, the grand total may not equal to the sum of the data from each year.
* International Bank of Reconstruction and Development loans imposes stricter conditions, and these are known as hard loans.
† The International Development Association loans offer more advantageous conditions and are zero-interest. They are known as soft loans or IDA credit.

Source: "Loans of The World Bank to China by Financial Year," The World Bank, http://www.worldbank.org.cn/Chinese/Projects/projects_all.asp.

Table 14.2 Recipient of World Bank loans to China (USD million)

Sector	Number of projects	Hard loan	Soft loan	Total
Agriculture	71	5,305.87	5,288.60	10,594.47
Education	19	285.30	1,442.10	1,727.40
Energy	37	7,110.23	37.00	7,147.23
Environmental protection	21	2,507.50	317.00	2,824.50
Health	12	186.00	786.60	972.60
Industrial sector	20	2,773.40	239.30	3,012.70
Provision of water and environmental hygiene	9	468.00	510.00	996.00
Social security	1	50.00	0.00	50.00
Technical assistance	14	190.40	246.31	436.71
Transport	62	11,173.00	569.60	11,742.60
Urban construction	27	3,633.80	411.80	4,045.60
Others*	3	40.00	98.40	138.40
Grand total	296	33,741.50	9,946.71	43,688.21

Notes: Data by sector from January 1981 to June 2008.

* Includes a 1990 reconstruction project after an earthquake in northern China, a 1998 recovery project after the Hebei Province earthquake, and a 1999 emergency recovery project after floods in the Yangtze River.

Source: "World Bank Loans to China, by Sector," The World Bank, http://www.worldbank.org.cn/Chinese/Projects/projects_all_dept.asp.

improve the city environment, such as provision of water, treatment of sewage and solid waste, environmental hygiene, and city transportation. Transportation projects have focused on building roads in rural areas and improving urban transportation. Education, health, and poverty reduction in rural areas have been supported by both IBRD loans and grants from United Kingdom's Department of International Development. China has one of the best track records in executing loans from the World Bank.[15]

Geographical distribution of World Bank loans

The inland and western regions of China have lagged behind in economic development. The Chinese government has already tried to use policies to encourage investment in western China. Loans from the World Bank are therefore aligned with Chinese government policy, and have been focused on poorer areas and regions with weaker economies (see Table 14.3).

Table 14.3 Chinese provinces receiving World Bank loans

Province/ Municipality	Number of projects	Hard loan (USD million)	Soft loan (USD million)	Mixed loan (USD million)	Percentage of total loan amount (%)
Anhui	31	1033.67	267.08	35.78	3.06
Beijing	21	590.41	263.98	33.50	2.03
Chongqing	13	580.00	82.30	0.00	1.52
Fujian	29	1181.58	196.98	25.43	3.21
Gansu	16	312.07	389.96	0.40	1.61
Guangdong	31	1187.04	364.20	40.33	3.64
Guangxi	28	769.63	281.60	40.92	2.50
Guizhou	14	162.40	156.33	19.00	0.77
Hainan	7	37.48	110.41	0.00	0.34
Hebei	30	633.59	290.13	47.42	2.22
Heilongjiang	21	505.83	179.17	1.54	1.57
Henan	32	2077.89	375.57	23.09	5.67
Hubei	41	1790.98	300.66	40.43	4.88
Hunan	30	1175.95	271.45	55.86	3.44
Inner Mongolia	26	812.10	287.37	28.64	2.58
Jiangsu	34	1727.71	278.18	169.89	4.98
Jiangxi	24	510.65	275.42	80.44	1.98
Jilin	16	21.42	268.72	65.20	0.81
Liaoning	35	1444.29	331.67	69.13	4.22
Ningxia	9	53.00	59.90	0.08	0.26
Qinghai	6	0.00	14.60	0.23	0.03
Shaanxi	22	530.00	326.61	30.51	2.03
Shandong	30	1032.26	312.20	20.94	3.13
Shanghai	32	2005.21	204.34	54.56	5.18
Shanxi	21	545.93	245.99	28.01	1.88
Sichuan	36	1962.40	503.30	19.80	5.69
Tianjin	21	667.53	184.74	55.13	2.08
Xinjiang	17	1009.51	299.00	0.00	3.00
Yunnan	25	353.89	239.52	22.84	1.41
Zhejiang	35	2296.27	276.46	16.51	5.93

Note: Some projects involve more than one province or municipality. They are counted into all locations involved. Data are from January 1981 to June 30, 2008.

Source: "World Bank Loans to China, by Sector," The World Bank, http://www.worldbank.org.cn/Chinese/Projects/projects_all_area.asp.

Knowledge cooperation and technical assistance

Knowledge sharing and knowledge transfer are important areas of the cooperation between the World Bank and China. The World Bank undertakes advisory and consultancy work based on international experience on issues faced by China, and engenders policy debates at an international level. Analysis from the World Bank has supported China's management of the macro economy, reduced systemic risk in the finance sector, improved the environment for the private sector, and effectively resolved constraints in regional economic growth and service provision in western and northeastern China. China has also benefited from World Bank research in relation to utilization of natural resources and sustainability.

The World Bank has completed dozens of reports and publications on the Chinese economy since China's reinstatement in the 1980s. In 1981 and 1984, the World Bank made two thorough, large-scale studies of the Chinese economy. From 1982 to June 2008, there were 176 research reports completed on Chinese economy and sectors. Between 2005 and June 2008, there were eight research papers completed on China. These reports and publications focused on macro economy, rural development, and the fiscal and financial sectors, effectively supporting China's economic reforms.[16]

Knowledge sharing between China and the World Bank has become bilateral instead of unilateral. China's experience of economic growth and poverty reduction has been disseminated to other countries. A poverty reduction conference was held in Shanghai in May 2004, which became a milestone in the knowledge sharing cooperation between China and the World Bank. In sharing its experience of poverty reduction, China encouraged a re-think of the Washington Consensus[17] and emphasized practicality.

The World Bank has also provided vast and wide-ranging technical assistance to China, helping China to set up a competitive bidding procurement system, and accounting and auditing system aligned with international practice, management of water resources. This has supported improvements in governance, and development in rural economies, social security, and poverty reduction, as well as energy and rescue management, and reforms in public administration and public services.[18]

China has also been the largest and most important customer of the World Bank Institute, the training arm of the World Bank. China spends over USD1 million a year and arranges for over 7,000 personnel participate in World Bank training.[19]

After the Sichuan earthquake in May 12, 2008, the World Bank provided technical assistance in addition to a USD1.5 million grant. It authored a short term action plan in relation to disaster recovery, making recommendations for the Chinese government, and organized a group of international experts to hold seminars to share experience from other countries with government departments responsible for reconstruction.[20]

World Bank assistance to Chinese civil organizations

Since 1995, the World Bank has maintained regular contact with civil organizations in China, providing the following support.

Create a favorable environment

In 2001, the World Bank and the China Ministry of Civil Affairs (MCA) started a capacity building project for the department responsible for the registration of civil organizations. This indirectly created a better environment for the activities of civil organizations in China.

A study on taxation of non-profit organizations in China was launched by the World Bank in 2004, upon the request of the MCA. The study analyzes and evaluates the existing laws, regulations, and policies related to non-profit organizations, introduces international experiences, and provides recommendations for reforms in China. In the same year, the World Bank and the Research Center of Non-Profit Organization Laws at the Peking University started a translation project of foreign non-profit sector laws, in order to provide reference to Chinese legislators, policymakers, and academic personnel.

Direct funding

The World Bank Small Grants Program directly funds civil organizations. The World Bank China Office launched the program in China in 1999, funding between six to ten projects every year. By the end of 2006, a total of 53 civil organization projects have received funding under this scheme.[21]

Direct cooperation and engagement

In formulating the Country Partnership Strategy (2006–2010) for China, the World Bank invited civil organizations in China to contribute their views. In granting loans, the World Bank has also invited civil organizations in project design, preparation, evaluation, and implementation.[22]

Other important cooperation

Grants from China to the World Bank

China first announced its decision to make grants to the International Development Association at the IDA closing session in December 2007. Since grants to the IDA have been typically provided by developed countries, China's offer to provide grants can be seen as a show of its willingness to take responsibility as a country of high economic growth.

China's active participation in World Bank policymaking

As the World Bank was reviewing the role of its loans in infrastructure building in early 2003, China and India issued a joint statement to emphasize the importance of infrastructure projects in pushing forward economic growth and reducing poverty in developing countries. This move had a strong impact on the World Bank. In order to achieve the best interests of borrowing countries, China also actively participated in the July 2003 discussions regarding country aid strategies and simplifying the policy and procedures for loans.[23]

China and the International Monetary Fund

Overview of the International Monetary Fund

The International Monetary Fund (IMF) is an inter-governmental international financial institution. It was formed in the Bretton Woods Conference in July 1944, officially established in December 27, 1945, and entered into operation in March 1947. It became a United Nations organization in November 1947. It is headquartered in Washington D.C., and has 185 member countries as of June 2008.[24]

The quotas and voice of China in the IMF

China was a founding member of the IMF, and obtained 7.2% of the quotas at the time (550 million in special drawing rights, SDR).[25] It ranked third among the membership just after the United States and the United Kingdom, and was one of the countries with the right to appoint an executive director of its choice.[26]

After the establishment of the PRC, China requested reinstatement in the IMF. However, the international political environment was such that Taiwan occupied the seat of China in the IMF. When China was finally reinstated in

April 17, 1980, its position in the IMF fell to 16th, because Taiwan had declined to increase its quotas over the years.

China's quotas were increased to 1.2 billion Special Drawing Rights (SDRs) from 550 million SDRs in September 1980. In November that year, an ad hoc increase of quotas was approved and China increased to 1.8 billion SDRs, climbing to the eighth position. China became a voting entity on its own, and obtained the right to elect an executive director of its choice.[27]

In 1983, in the following round of quota review, China again increased its quota to 2.39 billion SDRs.[28] It was increased again to 3.39 billion SDRs in 1992, reaching 2.35%, and ranking eleventh.[29]

By the end of 2000, China's quotas reached 4.69 billion SDRs, but the percentage dropped to 2.21%. China kept the 11th position.[30]

China made repeated requests to increase its quotas, in order to suit its economic needs. An increase was made in February 2001, when China's quota increased to 6.37 billion in special drawing rights (SDR)[31] or 2.98% of total quotas.[32] China then ranked eighth.[33]

Despite the rising economies of developing countries, the developing world still has limited quotas and voices in the IMF. In September 10, 2006, an ad hoc increase in quotas for four countries including China was approved.[34] After the increase, China would have 8.09 billion in SDR, or 3.72% of all member countries. China would rank sixth in the IMF membership.[35]

IMF support and assistance to China

China received support from the IMF in the following ways:

Regular Meetings and discussions

According to Article 4 of the *IMF Agreement*, the IMF would regularly discuss economic and financial policies with member countries, and monitor international economic changes in order to alert members to hidden risks.

An IMF delegation visits China every October to hold regular meetings with government departments involved in fiscal budgets, tax, finance, and macro-economy. In November 2004, China first agreed to the publication of an IMF report on China. The report was also published in 2005 and 2006.[36]

Apart from giving positive reviews on China's economic growth, macroeconomic controls, and structural reforms, the IMF also made recommendations on resolving China's regional inequality, improving corporate governance of state-owned enterprises, reducing bad debt in the financial sector, and gradually opening the financial market.[37] These have been welcomed by China as constructive suggestions.

Loans to China

As an IMF member country, China has the right to request loans to compensate for its current account deficit, if any, in order to ensure a sound economic structure. In the early years of China's economic reforms, continued growth led to inflation, and a broadening current account. The IMF therefore provided 759 million SDR (or USD880 million) and 598 million in SDRs (USD730 million) to China.[38]

These loans addressed the current account deficit and supported China's economic reforms. Both loans were repaid in the early 1990s. Since then, China did not make any further requests for IMF loans for this purpose. This is partly because of a stronger economy and better macroeconomic controls in China. But it is also because the IMF added harsh loan conditions that would involve changes in the domestic macroeconomic policies. China therefore adopts a very cautious attitude towards this kind of loan from the IMF.

Policy consultation and technical assistance

The IMF provided helpful advice for a series of reforms in China. This included the central bank reforms in the 1980s, the currency exchange reforms in 1994, the *People's Bank of China Law* in 1995, the current account convertibility of currency in 1996, and the fiscal and taxation system reforms in the 1990s.

In addition, the IMF has also provided technical assistance to China. Numerous delegations, visits, seminars and training activities were organized through the IMF as technical assistance to China. They involve areas such as fiscal policy, taxation, legislation for commerce and central bank, currency tools, and the creation of an interbank market, and current account convertibility of currency, as well as economic and financial statistics (see Table 14.4).

China made a self-evaluation in July 2003 based on the Financial Sector Assessment Program (FSAP) devised by the IMF and the World Bank. A working group led by the People's Bank of China and eight ministry-level departments were formed to assess the stability of the Chinese financial system. The IMF provided technical assistance through this process.[40 and 41]

The IMF has also provided training to personnel from Chinese government departments. The training content included monetary policy, revenue and tax policy, banking regulation, foreign exchange management, current account management, and macroeconomic statistics. Each year, China sends several dozens of personnel to the IMF in Washington, D.C., Vienna, and Singapore for training in macro-economy and finance sector policies. In May 2004, the IMF's fourth training base in the world opened in Dalian.

Table 14.4 IMF technical assistance to China

Tax system reform

Department	Form of assistance	Date
Fiscal Affairs Department (FAD)	Delegation on value-added tax and inheritance tax	April 2001
	Delegation on preferential tax rates	September 2001
	Delegation on tax for finance department August	September 2002
	Delegation on personal income tax	November 2003
	Delegation on handling value-added tax in financial services	April 2006
	Five delegations on computerization	June 2000–October 2002
	Two delegations on strategic planning	November 2001–August 2002
	Seminar on strategic planning (in Washington, D.C.)	October 2002
	Delegation on income management	November 2003
	Evaluation of computerization project	September 2004
	Delegation on pilot projects on business process improvement	November 2005
	Delegation on IT modernization	June 2006

Public finance administration (Cont'd)

Department	Form of assistance	Date
Fiscal Affairs Department (FAD)	Training on government fiscal administration information system	February 2001
	Delegation on treasury / accounting reform, macro fiscal coordination	November 2001
	Delegation on budgeting, categories in budgets, and treasury reform	June 2002
	Delegation on categories in budgets	March 2002
	Training on budgeting and treasury modernization (in Washington, D.C.)	October 2003
	Delegation on treasury and accounting reform	November 2003
	Delegation on budgeting methods	March 2004
	Delegation on cash management	April 2006

Inter-governmental fiscal relation

Department	Form of assistance	Date
Fiscal Affairs Department (FAD)	Delegation on inter-governmental fiscal relations	November 2002
	Delegation on provincial level fiscal risk	November 2003

Statistics (Cont'd)

Department	Form of assistance	Date
Statistics Department (STA)	Seminar on General Data Dissemination System (GDDS)	April 2001
	Seminar on currency and bank statistics	April 2001
	Delegation on trade statistics	June 2001–January 2002
	Delegation on General Data Dissemination System[39]	February-March 2002
	Seminar on international income and expenditure	August 2002
	Delegation on government fiscal statistics	September 2002
	Seminar on GDDS and special standards (in Washington, D.C.)	September 2002
	Evaluation of GDDS	December 2003
	Delegation on government fiscal statistics	January 2005
	High-level seminar on macroeconomic statistics	January 2005
	Delegation on currency and finance statistics	February–March 2005
	Seminar on international investment positions	April 2005

Currency policy and banking regulation (Cont'd)

Department	Form of assistance	Date
Monetary and Financial Systems Department (MFD)	Delegation on banking regulation	October 2003
	Bank restructuring	April 2004
	Anti-money laundering/ anti-terrorism financing issues	September 2003
	Seminar on anti-money laundering and anti-terrorism financing issues	April 2004
	Delegation on anti-money laundering and anti-terrorism financing issues	January 2005

Inspection activities for technical assistance

Department	Form of assistance	Date
Fiscal Affairs Department (FAD)	Visit to approve United Nations Development Program/IMF/China fiscal reform technical assistance	February 2001
Fiscal Affairs Department (FAD)/ Technical Assistance Secretariat (TAS)	Tripartite approvals and evaluation of technical assistance for fiscal reforms, by UNDP, IMF and Chinese government.	anuary 2002, February 2003
Monetary and Financial Systems Department (MFD)	Delegation for technical assistance to support banking department reforms	July 2002
Monetary and Financial Systems Department (MFD)	Delegation for technical assistance to support finance department reforms	October 2003
Fiscal Affairs Department (FAD)	Participation in training on fiscal reforms by UNDP and International Development Association (IDA)	February 2004
Fiscal Affairs Department (FAD)	Visit to discuss technical assistance for UNDP/IDA fiscal reform projects	December 2004

Training (Cont'd)

Department	Form of assistance	Date
IMF Institute (INS)	Financial planning and policy training (3 programs)	July 2000–June 2002
IMF Institute (INS)	High-level seminar on banking reforms	March 2001
Monetary and Financial Systems Department (MFD)	Convertibility of capital accounts	April 2001
Monetary and Financial Systems Department (MFD)	Training on currency policy and operation	May 2001–June 2002
Monetary and Financial Systems Department (MFD)	Banking risk management	July 2001
Fiscal Affairs Department (FAD)	Training on administration of public expenditure	June-July 2002
Monetary and Financial Systems Department (MFD)	Central bank accounting	November 2002
IMF Institute (INS)/ Monetary and Financial Systems Department (MFD)	High-level seminar on conducting currency policy	April 2004
IMF Institute (INS) / Monetary and Financial Systems Department (MFD)	High-level seminar on currency issues	May 2004
Statistics Department (STA)	Seminar on coordination securities investment survey	April 2004
Statistics Department (STA)	Seminar on quarterly national product accounts	September 2004
Monetary and Financial Systems Department (MFD)	Training on currency strategy and operation	May 2005

Sources: IMF, 2006, "China—Summary of Technical Assistance, 2001–2006," People's Republic of China 2006 Article IV Consultation—Staff Report; Staff Statement; and Public Information Notice on the Executive Board Discussion, October, 46–47.

Through the IMF, Asian countries including China can send its young, high-potential government officials to complete a master's degree in economics in Japan or Australia. This is a scholarship program that started in 1996 in Japan and 1997 in Australia. It is funded by the Japanese and Australian governments. Many of the Chinese government officials trained in these programs have risen through the ranks.[42]

International conferences and senior level visits

China sees the IMF as an important platform where China would assert its stance on the global economic and financial systems and other important international affairs. The IMF is also a key window for China and the rest of the world to engage in policy dialogue.

Since 1980, IMF managing directors and deputy managing directors have made regular visits to China, and exchanged views with the heads of the Chinese government and other senior officials. Every year, China sends a delegation led by the People's Bank and the Ministry of Finance to participate in the joint annual meeting and spring meeting of the IMF and the World Bank. In September 1997, the IMF and the World Bank held its annual meeting in Hong Kong, which had at the time just returned to Chinese sovereignty.

The contribution of China to the IMF

Former IMF managing director Michel Camdessus had once said, "China is not only a beneficiary of the *IMF Agreement*, but is also a model member country of the IMF." The following discussion outlines China carrying out its responsibilities as an IMF member.[43]

Provision of funds

As China improved its current account and foreign exchange reserves through the 1980s, it became increasingly capable to contribute part of its funds towards IMF's various initiatives.

The IMF set up the structural adjustment facility (SAF) in 1986 and the extended structural adjustment facility (ESAF) in 1987 aimed to help developing countries in economic restructuring. In order to allow the funding to go to the poorer nations in need, China opted not to participate even though it was qualified as a developing country.[44]

Upon the request of IMF, China contributed 100 million SDRs in loans to the ESAF trust loan account, intended for assisting heavily indebted poor countries in loan restructuring. To provide additional support, China also donated 12 million SDRs to the ESAF loan subsidy account.

After the Asian Financial Crisis in July 1997, China provided USD2.5 billion to the IMF for lending to countries in crises. China also provided roughly USD1 billion bilateral loans to Thailand, as part of an IMF aid package granted to Thailand. China also pledged USD300 million in funding as a second line of defense for the rapidly devalued Indonesian currency.[45]

In 1999, China supported the IMF Heavily Indebted Poor Countries (HIPC) Initiative by providing 13.13 million SDRs towards the program for global poverty reduction.

In June 2001, China contributed 100 million SDRs to the IMF poverty reduction and growth facility loans.

In May 2005, China made another donation of USD2 million to the IMF Post-Conflict and Natural Disaster Emergency Assistance Subsidy Account.[46 and 47]

Impact on IMF policy and decision-making

China has played an active role in the IMF in representing the voice of developing countries especially after the 1997 Asian Financial Crisis. Apart from recognizing the contribution of the IMF in assisting countries in crises, China has also criticized the IMF for overlooking the actual situation in the developing world. China has objected to having developed countries dominate the IMF's decisions on global financial affairs. In particular, advanced countries should strengthen their supervision of the highly leveraged investment funds and offshore financial centers, China argues, instead of insisting on financial regulation reforms in developing countries.

China has also defended its financial system and monetary policy against IMF criticism, mostly reiterating the principle that the IMF should respect the varying needs and individual conditions particularly in developing countries. When urged to follow either a fixed exchange rate or a free floating exchange rate system, China has argued that neither system is a formula to success, that each currency exchange system should be in accordance with the needs of the country. China has also responded to IMF requests for higher transparency in the financial system by reiterating the principles of respecting the needs in individual countries. There is continued tension between the developed countries and developing countries in the IMF, but China's assertions on behalf of its own interests and the general interests of developing countries have made a visible impact on IMF decision-making.[48]

China and the World Trade Organization

The World Trade Organization

The World Trade Organization (WTO) is an international organization that supervises and liberalizes global trade, and coordinates multilateral, inter-governmental trade relations. It was set up under the *Marrakech Agreement*, which replaced the *General Agreement on Tariffs and Trade* (GATT) with the new WTO. It started operation in January 1995. Headquartered in Geneva, there were 152 member countries or regions as of May 2008.[49]

Re-admission to GATT and accession to WTO

China was a founding member of GATT. A *Protocol of Provisional Application* was signed by the Kuomintang government in April 21, 1948, so that China became a contracting party in May 1948. However, in 1950 the Taiwanese government wrote to the General Secretary of the United Nations to withdraw from GATT. Protests from Beijing were ignored at the time. After the early fruits of the economic reforms which started in 1978 became apparent, China submitted an application in July 1986 for reinstating its contracting party status in GATT.

China's reinstatement appeared likely up to May 1989. However, after June 1989, the West imposed trade sanctions on China and the reinstatement talks were suspended.

In April 1994, China attended the Uruguay Round in full participating partner status. China signed the final agreements from that round, which means that if China were to become a member of the GATT or WTO, the Uruguay Round agreements would be binding on China.

Negotiations for China's reinstatement into GATT started in late 1992. However, the conditions demanded by some of the Western countries were found by China to be unacceptably harsh. China therefore did not become a founding member of WTO in 1995. The GATT reinstatement talks then become WTO accession talks.

In the WTO accession talks, 37 WTO member countries initiated bilateral talks with China. This included 15 European Union member countries, which means that the actual number of countries was 51. The bilateral negotiations were completed by September 13, 2002.

China and the WTO officially signed the accession agreement in November 2001. China officially became a WTO member in December 11, 2001.[50]

The implementation of WTO accession commitments

China had carried out its WTO commitments in terms of lowering tariffs, opening the domestic market, improving the protection of intellectual property rights, and increasing the transparency of trade policies.

Trade in goods

Eliminated import quotas for general goods

The right to conduct foreign trade in China was liberalized in 2004. Companies participating in foreign trade simply need to register with the Ministry of Commerce instead of obtaining approvals. These actions were taken based on the *Foreign Trade Law* passed by the Chinese legislature in April 2004, and subsequently the Registration Measures for Foreign Trade Operations issued by the Ministry of Commerce in July 2004. These changes abolished the approval process that had been in operation for 50 years, implementing half a year earlier than scheduled the WTO commitment of liberalizing the trade of goods.

In January 2005, in accordance with the WTO commitment implementation schedule, China abolished its import quota system.

Lowering of tariffs

General tariffs have been reduced from 15.3%[51] at the time of accession to 9.8%.[52] Tariffs of agricultural goods have been reduced from 23.2%[53] to 15.2%,[54] while industrial goods have seen tariffs cut from 14.7%[55] to 8.9%.[56]

Trade in services

China has liberalized trade in 104 service sub-sectors, out of a total of 160 sub-sectors as defined by the WTO. This is close to the average of 108 liberalized service sub-sectors among WTO members.[57] This shows that China has already implemented its WTO accession commitments, providing opportunities for market access.

Banking

Banking Restrictions were liberalized for foreign-invested banks that operated foreign exchange services in China. Once restrictions on the type of customers were lifted, foreign banks were allowed to provide their services to Chinese enterprises and Chinese citizens. These banks were also able to set up Renminbi business in Shanghai, Shenzhen, Tianjin, and Dalian, and since then have been permitted to enter many other Chinese cities.

By December 2006, other restrictions on foreign-invested banks were lifted, including ownership and the setting up of operations. Geographical and customer type restrictions were fully eliminated. In short, foreign banks were given national treatment.[58]

A series of legislations on the banking sector were developed, ensuring a smooth transition into a liberalized banking sector. These new laws issued between 2001 and 2003 covered administration of foreign-invested financial institutions, the *Commercial Banking Law*, the *Law for Supervision and Administration of the Banking Sector*, the administration of foreign-invested financial institutions obtaining shareholding in Chinese financial institutions. Further laws were issued or revised in 2006, concerning the banking sector regulation and the supervision of foreign-invested banks.

In addition, the China Banking Regulatory Commission (CBRC) also issued new or revised regulations on foreign-invested financial institutions obtaining shareholding in Chinese financial institutions; and on the supervision of auto finance companies[59] and lease financing companies. Four foreign-invested financial services companies[60] and nine auto finance companies[61] have been approved by the CBRC, as of 2007.

Insurance

Foreign non-life insurance companies were allowed to be set up in China in all forms of ownership structures from 2003 onwards. Foreign property insurance companies were allowed from May 2004 onwards to be set up as wholly-owned foreign enterprises, while other forms of ownership structure were also unrestricted.[62]

Restrictions on foreign insurance agent firms were also lifted in December 2006. Restrictions on geographical regions where foreign insurance companies operate were also eliminated at the end of 2004. In terms of restrictions on business activities, foreign non-life insurance companies could be involved in all types of insurance activities from the end of 2003. From 2004 onwards, apart from insurance mandated by law, foreign-invested life insurance companies and foreign-invested insurance agent firms were unrestricted in their activities.[63]

As of the end of 2006, the insurance sector can be considered fully liberalized. The only exceptions are the rule that foreign-invested property insurance companies cannot offer third-party liability insurance, and that foreign-invested life insurance companies must be set up as joint ventures with foreign ownership at 50% or less.

Securities

Four joint-venture securities firms and 31 joint-venture fund management companies have been approved to operate in China, in accordance with WTO accession commitments. In addition, the China representative offices of four overseas securities institutions have become special members in the Shenzhen and Shanghai stock exchanges. There are also overseas securities institutions—41 in Shanghai and 19 in Shenzhen—that have been permitted to directly trade in B stocks (i.e. stocks traded in foreign currencies).

Beyond the commitments for WTO accession, China also initiated the Qualified Foreign Institutional Investors (QFII), Qualified Domestic Institutional Investors (QDII) schemes that further liberalize the securities sector.[64]

Circulation of commerce

There were 11,085 approved foreign-invested companies in retail, accommodation, food and beverages, and resident services, as of the end of 2007. This involved the utilization of USD8.46 billion in foreign capital.[65]

Telecommunication

China has been an attractive new market for foreign telecommunication service providers. As of September 2006, the Ministry of Industry and Information Technology (MIIT) has received 29 applications from foreign-invested telecommunication service providers. All were applying to operate value-added services instead of analog or digital communications services. At that point, there were 14 applications reviewed and five were awarded telecommunication operation licenses.[66]

In implementing the WTO accession commitments, China has permitted foreign investors to enter the basic telecommunication market in any geographical region from December 11, 2007 onwards, with the only restriction being that the enterprises would have no more than a 49% foreign shareholding. So far, no foreign investor has taken advantage of these opportunities. However, foreign investors have participated in the market by forging cooperation with Chinese telecommunication firms through share acquisition in overseas stock exchanges. Vodafone Group from the UK has acquired a 3.27% stake in China Mobile; Telefonica from Spain has acquired a 5% stake in China Netcom; while SK Telecommunication from South Korea has become the second largest shareholder in China Unicom.[67]

Law, accounting, medicine, and education

As of December 11, 2006, there were 195 foreign law firms operating in China; seven foreign accounting firms, and 18 branch offices; 52 healthcare projects involving Sino-foreign joint ventures or cooperatives; and 851 education institutions and projects involving Sino-foreign cooperation.[68]

Tourism

The tourism sector had typically achieved WTO accession commitments earlier than scheduled. Foreign investors were allowed to set up shareholding or wholly-owned travel agencies from July 2003 onwards, based on the regulations issued by China National Tourism Administration and the Ministry of Commerce. As of the end of 2006, there were 25 Sino-foreign joint ventures or wholly-owned travel agencies. Restrictions were also lifted on the setting up of branches of foreign-invested travel agencies from July 2007 onwards, which was four months ahead of schedule.[69] These agencies were also given national treatment in terms of registered capital requirements.

In the hotel and restaurant industries, WTO commitments were implemented four years ahead of schedule.

Intellectual property rights

The *Patent Law, Trademark Law,* and *Copyright Law* and the respective detailed guidelines for implementation have formed a strong foundation of legislation in protecting intellectual property rights (IPR) in accordance with WTO accession commitments. A national IPR protection working group was set up in 2004, which was a task force coordinated between judicial and administrative departments. The working group monitored the most important cases of IPR violation and oversaw IPR protection activities nationwide. At the provincial and local levels, efforts have been made to draft detailed legislation and to adopt various measures to combat the prevalence of fake goods.

China has made it a priority to educate the public about the protection of intellectual property rights. A week of education programs was held in April 2004 to promote intellectual property rights as a way of respecting labor, knowledge, and human capital.[70]

Transparency in trade policy

Prior to WTO accession, foreign investors in China have complained about the duplication, self-contradiction, incompleteness, opaqueness, and varying implementation of the body of laws and regulations related to trade policy. There has also been the belief that the lack of transparency may lead to corruption.

As part of its accession commitment to enhance transparency in its trade and investment policy, China reviewed and re-organized these laws and regulations at the national and provincial levels. Between 1999 and 2005, the body of trade and investment laws were reviewed, including 20 pieces of newly enacted or revised legislation from the National People's Congress and 47 pieces of administrative regulations from the State Council. A total of 756 rules and regulations issued before year 2000 were also reviewed, and the results were published in 2001.

At the same time, the State Council also requested that local regulations and other policies are also reviewed and re-organized. Within four years, 3,948 programs requiring administrative approvals from one or more of 65 government departments were evaluated, of which 1,195 programs were abolished and 82 of the processes were revised. A new *Administrative Licensing Law* also made clearer definitions to the administrative powers and procedures of government departments.[71]

Moreover, apart from conducting public consultations when drafting laws and policies, efforts were made to ensure that policy implementation is uniform across the country. If anyone or any company encounters a gap in implementation of laws, regulations, and other policies, they can report it to the relevant authorities.

China also set up a WTO notification and inquiry center, which provides information on Chinese trade policy, and makes regular public reports about changes in the body of laws and regulations relevant to trade. In addition, the general public can access the *China Foreign Trade Documents* for a compilation of trade-related laws and policies.

Accepting the WTO review of China trade policy

Based on the Trade Policy Review Mechanism (TPRM), four member countries with the largest share in the global trade market would have their trade policy reviewed once every two years, while the countries ranking 5th to 20th in market share would have a review every four years. In April 2006, the WTO made its first Trade Policy Review on China.

As a new WTO member, China sees the review process as a platform for policy dialogue and information exchange with other member countries. The Trade Policy Review focuses on the member's trade policy and practice, as well as issues related to macro-economy and development.

China's first Trade Policy Review meeting was chaired by Colombia's Ambassador to the WTO, with Singapore, India, Chile, the U.S., the EU, Canada, Australia, Japan, and Switzerland also participating as members of the review body. China was represented by a delegation from the Ministry of Commerce. The review body has generally provided positive feedback on Chinese economic development, recognizing that China's accession has brought opportunities to the world markets. They also affirmed the contribution made by China in the Doha Round (started 2001, failed 2008), at which China and India asserted the stance of the developing world. A 303-page *China Trade Policy Review Report* was published after the review, acknowledging the successes while also raising some concerns about China's macroeconomic and trade policies.

Between 2004 and 2006, China's share in global trade became the third largest in the world, and therefore a trade policy review would take place every two years. The next review was in May 2008. The WTO review body made a comprehensive review of Chinese trade policy and its implications on global multilateral trade. Nineteen WTO members submitted over 900 questions to China on many facets of Chinese economic and trade developments. Before the meeting, China made written responses to 524 of the questions. Other responses were provided to the WTO secretariat within one month after the review meeting, which was within the timeline stipulated by WTO rules.[72] Many members of the review body recognized the significant efforts of market liberalization in China.

China and the WTO dispute settlement mechanism

The dispute settlement mechanism plays an essential function within the WTO in promoting the reliability and predictability of the international multilateral trade system. Using the dispute settlement mechanism to resolve trade frictions is an important tool in safeguarding the normal operation of global trade.

China as complainant and respondent

Since China became a member of the WTO, it has mostly been a respondent instead of the complainant to trade disputes, apart from cases in which China participated as a third party.[73] In the early years of WTO membership, trade conflict between China and its trading partners was usually resolved through diplomacy. Since then, China has learned to use the WTO dispute settlement mechanism to resolve conflict instead.

China raised two cases as a complainant in the WTO. The first was in 2002, when China, together with the EU, South Korea, Japan, and four other countries raised a case against the U.S. for the protectionism in its steel industry. At the end of 2003, the protectionist measures of the U.S. were corrected. The second case launched in September 2007, when China imposed anti-dumping duties on coated paper imported from the U.S. China took the case to WTO dispute settlement. The case was dismissed because China would need to prove that apart from dumping caused by lower prices sold in China compared to the home market, there is also damage made to the Chinese market. The damage was not proven in this case. This coated paper case was the first time China launched a case as a complainant. Because of the weaknesses in the case, this was also seen as a sign that China was immature in its use of WTO dispute settlement.

In the first five years of its WTO membership, China was very cautious about risks involved in losing a case in the WTO, and therefore preferred to use diplomatic channels to settle disputes or complaints. In the five cases raised against China between March 2004 and February 2006, China reached a settlement with the complainant through diplomatic negotiations. However, over time China realized that the cases raised as disputes can reflect the inadequacies of some of the policies and reforms in China. The decision reached in the WTO dispute settlement mechanism can in fact promote positive change in China's trade policy. China gradually warmed up to using the WTO dispute settlement system instead.

China lost its first case in the WTO dispute settlement system in 2008, in a case first launched by the U.S., the EU and Canada in March 2006. The US alleged that it was against WTO regulations that China imposes the same tariffs for imported auto parts and vehicles. This was the first case in which China took the initiative to refer to WTO dispute settlement. The investigation was prolonged as China produced a large volume of data and evidence in defense of its policy. In the end, however, the WTO expert panel decided that China was in violation of relevant trade rules.

Three more cases involving China that arose in 2007 were referred to WTO dispute settlement. The U.S. and Mexico alleged that some of China's policies created a prohibitive subsidy. (In this case, Canada participated as a third party.)[74] The U.S. also raised two issues on market entry in relation to the intellectual property rights protection and copyright as complaints to the WTO dispute settlement system. (The EU, Japan, and South Korea participated as third parties.)

A Chinese expert in the WTO Dispute Settlement Body

WTO disputes are typically adjudicated by an expert panel of three. The experts would be chosen from a representative list of experts nominated by member countries. Nominating experts is an important right for WTO members.

China has thus far nominated five experts to enter the list. They are Zhang Yuqing, Zeng Lingliang, and Zhu Lanye, who were nominated in 2004, and Dong Shizhong and Zhang Yuejiao, who were nominated in 2006. These five experts play a key role in representing China's participation in WTO affairs.

Zhang Yuejiao was then appointed to the appellate body[75] of the WTO dispute settlement mechanism in November 2007. She is the first appellate body member of Chinese nationality.

Research center on WTO dispute settlement

The International Dispute Resolution Research Center was set up in Shanghai on May 11, 2008, by the Shanghai Institute of Foreign Trade and the Shanghai WTO Affairs Inquiry Center. Appellate body member Zhang Yuejiao and the other four China-nominated legal experts in the WTO dispute settlement body are all on the research institute's academic committee. The research institute helps relevant Chinese government departments become more familiar with the dispute settlement mechanism of the WTO.

China's participation in other WTO matters

China has fully supported the WTO review process of its trade policy. This includes providing reports and information that comprehensively reflect the trade policy of China. At the same time, China plays a constructive role when it participates in the review of trade policy for other WTO member countries.[76]

In 2002, China participated in the trade policy reviews for its major trading partners, including the EU, Japan, Australia, Mexico, and India, providing recommendations for some practices that may infringe WTO regulations.

The Chinese delegation has also attended many WTO ministerial meetings, as well as the first Global Aid for Trade Review meeting held in Geneva in 2007.

China has applied in December 2007 to join the WTO *Government Procurement Agreement* (GPA). A preliminary bid list has been submitted to the WTO and negotiations on joining the GPA are underway.

China and the Asian Development Bank

Overview of the Asian Development Bank

Asian Development Bank (ADB) is a regional development bank that was set up in August 22, 1966, with the sponsorship of the United Nations Economic and Social Commission for Asia and the Pacific (UNESCAP). Headquartered in Manila in the Philippines, the ADB was established based on the ABD Charter that was approved in the Second APEC Ministerial Meeting held in Manila in 1965. There were 31 founding members of the ADB in 1966. As of June 30, 2008, ADB had 67 members, 48 of which are from Asia Pacific, and 19 from outside of Asia.[77]

The objectives of the ADB are: to provide loans and technical assistance to members; to support and coordinate members in policymaking in the economy, trade, and development areas; to facilitate cooperation with the United Nations and related bodies; and to accelerate economic development in the Asian Pacific region.

China joins the ADB

When the ADB was established, Taiwan had used the title of "China" to join as a member. In February 1986, the ADB officially accepted the People's Republic of China to join the ADB. China officially became the 48th ADB member on March 10, 1986. Taiwan was then renamed "Chinese Taipei" on the ABD member register.[78]

As of February 2007, China has 228,000 stocks in the ADB, which represents a 6.43% stake. It has 241,232 votes, which represents 5.44% of member votes, the third largest voice in the membership.[79]

The board of directors, which is elected by member countries, is the highest decision-making body in the ADB. In the 20th board of directors' annual meeting in 1987, it was approved that China had a seat on the board of directors. A director's office was set up in China in July 1987. The People's Bank of China is the official point of liaison for the ADB, as well as the custodian bank for ADB in China, responsible for maintaining the renminbi held by ADB and other ADB assets in China. In June 2000, an ADB China Office opened in Beijing.

The cooperation between China and the ADB

ADB's China strategy and its discussions with China

The ADB's China strategy is mainly focused on elevating economic efficiency, reducing poverty in the inland provinces of China, and environmental protection and management of natural resources. Using loans and technical assistance, ADB activities support the growth of essential sectors in the economy, and this ultimately strengthens the macroeconomic policies of the Chinese government.

ADB and China devise a Country Partnership Strategy once every three years. In order to use market mechanisms most effectively, the strategy may be revised or updated every year to support a strong and regionally balanced economic growth. The ADB also holds regular policy discussions with China, exploring innovation policies in social services such as education and health.

The *Poverty Reduction Partnership Agreement* signed between China and the ADB in September 2003 delivers high praise for the achievements in poverty reduction in China over the past decades. It also objectively discusses the challenges of further poverty reduction in China, and makes recommendations for how ADB can support China's policies in this regard. The ADB is the first international multilateral development bank to sign such a poverty reduction agreement with China.[80]

Bank loans and technical assistance

Since China joined the ADB in 1986, there has been an increase in the loans and technical assistance provided to China. ADB's support has also been distributed across industry sectors and geographical regions.

Loans and technical assistance from ADB to China started in March 1986 (see Table 14.5 and 14.6). As of the end of 2007, China had a cumulative total of 139 projects supported by the ADB, with a total of USD13.9 billion in loan commitments. China is the second largest borrower from the ADB, representing 14.4% of loan commitments. China is also the largest recipient of ADB technical assistance, receiving a total of USD290 million in assistance in 558 projects.[81]

In terms of the industry sectors receiving technical assistance, initially two-thirds of ADB loans were used to develop the industrial and financial sectors between 1987 and 1990. From 1991 onwards, transportation became the largest sector utilizing ADB loans, followed by energy, the environment, provision of water and sewage treatment, agriculture and natural resources, and industrial and financial sectors (see Table 14.7).

Table 14.5. Asian Development Bank loans to China, 1987–2006

Year of approval	Number of projects	Loan amount (USD million)
1987	2	133.3
1988	3	236.4
1989	1	39.7
1990	1	50.0
1991	6	496.3
1992	8	853.0
1993	8	1,050.0
1994	8	1,167.0
1995	10	1,201.0
1996	10	1,032.0
1997	5	656.0
1998	7	1,162.0
1999	7	1,232.0
2000	5	814.3
2001	6	997.0
2002	6	833.5
2003	7	1,488.0
2004	7	1,259.9
2005	7	1,478.8
2006	10	1,522.0
Total	124	17,702.2

Source: Collated from "Asian Development Bank loans to China by Year (as of end of 2006)." Asian Development Bank, http://www.adb.org/Documents/Translations/Chinese/loans-end-2006-year-CN.pdf.

Table 14.6. Asian Development Bank technical assistance to China, 1987–2006

Year	Number of projects	ABD funding (USD million)	Japan Special Fund (USD million)	Other funding (USD million)	Total (USD million)
1986	1	7.50	0.00	0.00	7.50
1987	5	65.20	0.00	75.00	140.20
1988	10	111.00	183.10	41.80	335.90
1989	6	28.50	330.00	0.00	358.50
1990	4	177.70	0.00	0.00	177.70
1991	30	1,021.70	360.90	60.00	1,442.60
1992	32	963.20	413.48	0.00	1,376.68
1993	38	715.90	913.93	0.00	1,629.83
1994	41	364.60	1,307.60	71.50	1,743.70
1995	45	490.25	1,246.94	103.70	1,840.89
1996	25	441.70	867.70	0.00	1,309.40
1997	36	644.80	1,143.57	149.80	1,938.17
1998	31	1,110.30	1,130.70	110.00	2,351.00
1999	25	465.80	1,459.20	68.00	1,993.00
2000	25	566.50	1,105.04	0.00	671.54
2001	17	866.80	263.00	115.00	1,244.80
2002	24	757.30	270.00	292.40	1,319.70
2003	25	915.00	45.00	336.00	1,296.00
2004	31	1,115.40	80.00	475.00	1,670.40
2005	33	1,484.00	0.00	349.46	1,833.46
2006	25	1,265.50	0.00	92.50	1,358.00
Total	509	13,578.65	11,120.16	2,340.16	27,038.97

Note: (1) Asian Development Bank funding comes from ordinary capital resources, Asian Development Fund, Technical Assistance Special Fund, Japan Special Fund and joint financing.
(2) Other funding sources: Poverty Reduction Cooperation Fund, Norway, World Environment Fund, Spain, United Nations Development Program, France, Canada, Denmark, and Italy.

Source: Collated from "Asian Development Bank Technical Assistance to China by Year (as of end of 2006)," Asian Development Bank website, http://www.adb.org/Documents/Translations/Chinese/tas-end-2006-year-cn.pdf.

Table 14.7. Asian Development Bank loans to China, 1987–2006

Department	Number of projects	Loan amount (USD million)
Agriculture and natural resources	16	1,322.0
Energy	21	2,326.7
Industry and finance	11	1,216.8
Provision of water, public hygiene and waste treatment	16	1,721.2
Transport	54	1,0262.5
Others *	6	853.0
Total	124	1,7702.2

Note: * Includes inter-departmental projects and other projects not assigned to particular sectors.

Source: Collated from "Asian Development Bank Loans to China by Sector (as of end of 2006)," Asian Development Bank website, http://www.adb.org/Documents/Translations/Chinese/loans-end-2006-sector-cn.pdf.

In recent years, the focus of ADB loans and technical assistance to China has shifted to the following:

Development of inland and western regions

- Provide loans to infrastructure building for the inland and western provinces, especially supporting projects of high social and economic impact, such as electric and hydro power. Focus is also placed on railway and natural gas projects. Support national bond issuing to finance projects in the western regions.
- Expand agricultural credit and support the growth of agriculture.
- Leverage trust loans in order to encourage economic restructuring in the western provinces. Select a group of small towns and cities with a certain scale, and invest in the provision of water and electric power. Also support small and medium-sized enterprises with market potential, efficiency, and good credit.
- Improve the operation of commercial banks and the level of financial services in the western provinces. Support state-owned banks in reforms, raising the competitiveness of their branches in the western provinces. Accelerate the approval of joint-stock banks setting up branches in the western provinces, and assist the development of joint-stock banks and small and medium-sized

enterprises in their development in inland China.

Reform of state-owned enterprises

Assist China to reform SOEs, especially in improving their financial management and governance structure.

Legal and judiciary reforms

ADB grants have supported China's legislative and judiciary reforms in relation to its transition to a market economy(see Table 14.8).

Other cooperation

ADB grants to China

A USD2 million loan from the ADB supported the relevant Chinese government departments to combat SARS at the provincial and municipal level. China also received USD1 million in emergency technical assistance funding from the ADB in May 2008, to help the post-disaster reconstruction after the Sichuan earthquake.[82]

Chinese donations to ADB

China donated USD30 million to the ADB Asia Development Fund and another USD20 million to set up a special fund for poverty reduction and regional cooperation. This donation was announced by Chinese Premier Wen Jiabao at the Poverty Reduction Conference in Shanghai in May 2004.[83]

ADB RMB-denominated bonds issued in China

In October 2005, the ADB issued RMB1 billion bonds in the inter-bank market in China. This allowed China to gain hands-on knowledge about international bond issuing, as the ADB was the first foreign entity to enter Chinese bond market. Instead of simply attracting foreign investment, the ADB bond issuing process highlighted to China the importance of using technical skills and financial instruments, and of cultivating professionals. In this way, ADB helped the internationalization of the Chinese bond market.[84]

Table 14.8. Asian Development Bank technical assistance by sector, 1987–2006 (USD10,000)

Sector	Number of projects	ABD funding (USD10,000)	Japan Special Fund (USD10,000)	Other funding (USD10,000)	Total (USD10,000)
Agriculture and natural resources	84	2,260.15	2424.02	463.96	5,148.13
Banking system	16	156.30	800.70	230.00	1,187.00
Cross department	28	814.40	751.80	202.50	1,768.70
Education	9	270.00	150.00	50.00	470.00
Health, nutrition and social security	4	250.00	40.00	81.00	370.00
Industrial and trade projects	50	1,218.70	1,167.60	135.50	2,521.80
Law, economic administration, public policy	79	2,806.60	656.84	182.00	645.44
Provision of water, hygiene facilities and waste treatment	29	764.60	736.30	269.70	1,770.60
Transport and telecommunications	103	2,325.10	2,424.60	359.00	5,108.70
Total	509	10,969.65	11,120.16	2,340.16	24,429.97

Notes: (1) Asian Development Bank funding comes from ordinary capital resources, Asian Development Fund, Technical Assistance Special Fund, Japan Special Fund, and joint financing.

(2) Other funding sources: Poverty Reduction Cooperation Fund, Norway, World Environment Fund, Spain, United Nations Development Program, France, Canada, Denmark, and Italy.

Source: "Asian Development Bank Technical Assistance by Sector," Asian Development Bank, http://www.adb.org/Documents/Translations/Chinese/tas-end-2006-sector-cn.pdf.

Notes

Chapter 1

1. *Deng Xiaoping wen xuan*, 1993, p.64, 90, 202.
2. "Opening to the world markets makes a country's production and consumption international. The state of self-sufficient, closed isolation of some countries and some peoples in the past would be replaced by exchanges and inter-dependency of various countries and peoples," in *Communist Manifesto* in *Makesi En'gesi xuan ji*, 1995.
3. Deng Xiaoping, 1997, p.55.
4. "Zhongguo Gongchandang dishiyi jie zhongyan weiyuanhui disan ciquanti huiyi gongbao," 1992, p.99.
5. Jiang Zemin, 1997, p.22, 25.
6. The Protocol for Accession to the WTO was signed between China and the WTO on November 11, 2001. China officially became a WTO member on December 11 the same year. See WTO website, "China and the WTO," July 20, 2008, http://www.wto.org/english/thewto_e/countries_e/china_e.htm.
7. The central regions of China generally refers to the six provinces of Shanxi, Henan, Anhui, Jiangxi, Hubei, and Hunan, covering 1.03 million square km in land area, or 10.7% of China's land mass. Among its 360 million people, there are 244 million living in rural areas. This accounts for 28% of the country's population and 20% of the national economy, and acts as a center for commercial food crops, energy raw materials, and manufacturing. It is also a hub for the distribution of resources and products across the country, and therefore plays an important role in the economic and social landscape of China.
8. Wu Bangguo, 2004.
9. Jia Qinglin, 2008.
10. International Monetary Fund (IMF), World Economic Outlook Database, April 2008.
11. World Trade Organization secretariat, August 26, 2008, http://www.wto.org/english/news_e/pres08_e/pr520_e.htm.
12. Ministry of Finance, 2007.
13. Department of Foreign Investment Affairs, Ministry of Commerce.
14. Department of Outward Investment and Economic Cooperation, Ministry of Commerce.
15. Zhou Yingfeng and Wang Youling, 2008.
16. Wang Jiarui, 2007.
17. Mao Lei, 2008.
18. "Work Report of Jia Qinglin at the 11th Chinese People's Political Consultative Conference Standing Committee", 2008.
19. The Chinese People's Association for Friendship with Foreign Countries website, July 29, 2008.
20. China International Friendship Cities Association website, July 29, 2008 .
21. Ministry of Commerce data.

22. National Bureau of Statistics data.
23. Ministry of Commerce, 2007.
24. The agriculture, rural areas, and farmers form the three issues in "*sannong*" (the Three Rural Issues) that are in need of deep reform in China. These three interconnected aspects of rural society have been credited with supporting the industrialization and modernization of China, but have not yet enjoyed the benefits of rapid economic growth. Instead, the growth rate of rural income has decreased in recent years.
25. Hu Jintao, 2005.
26. *South China Morning Post*, February 21, 2005, cited in *Cankao xiaoxi* 參考消息(Reference News), February 24, 2005.
27. International Monetary Fund, World Economic Outlook, http://www.imf.org/external/pubs/ft/weo/2007/02/pdf/text.pdf/.
28. Wang Yi, 2007.
29. Li Shijia and Bai Jie, 2008.
30. "Zuolike chengzan Zhongguo dui Fei huanzhu touzi" 佐利克稱讚中國對非援助投資 (Zoellick Praises China's Aid and Investment in Africa), Voice of America report on October 22, 2007, cited in *Cankao xiaoxi* 參考消息 (Reference News).
31. "Zhonghua Renmin Gongheguo 2007 nian guomin jingji he shehui fazhan baogao" 中華人民共和國 2007 年國民經濟和社會發展報告 (China National Economy and Social Development Report 2007), *Renmin ribao* 人民日報 (People's Daily), February 29, 2008.
32. Luo Chunhua, 2007.

Chapter 2

1. General Administration of Customs, http://www.xagsjcj.gov.cn/ReadNews.asp?NewsID=5853.
2. Ibid.
3. Sun Tingting, 2008.
4. Hong Lei, 2005.
5. Wang Shouchun, 1988.
6. "2007 nian Zhongguo maoyi shuncha zaichuang xingao" 2007 年中國貿易順差再創新高 (China 2007 Trade Surplus Reaches Historical High), *Caijing* 財經 (Caijing Magazine), January 11, 2008, http://www.caijing.com.cn/20080111/45032.shtml.
7. WTO Secretariat, http://www.wto.org/english/news_e/pres08_e/pr520_e.htm.
8. *Zhongguo tongji zhaiyao 1998* 中國統計摘要 1998 (Selected China Statistics 1998) (Beijing, China Statistics Publishing, 1998).
9. "Zhongguo waimao zai jiegou tiaozheng zhong jiasu fazhan" 中國外貿在結構調整中加速發展 (China Foreign Trade Growth Accelerates as Structure Changes), in *Guoji Shangbao* 國際商報 (International Trade News), February 21, 2008.
10. Sun Tingting, 2008.
11. Cheng Yijun, 2007.

Chapter 3

1. United Nations Committee on Trade and Development report 1999, in Wei Houkai 魏後凱, and Liu Changquan 劉長全, "Zhongguo liyong waizi de fumian xiaoying ji zhanlüe tiaozheng silu" 中國利用外資的負面效應及戰略調整思路 (China's Adjustment Based on the Negative Effect and Strategies of Foreign Funds), *Henan shehui kexue* 河南社會科學 (Henan Social Sciences), 1999, no. 5.
2. Liu Jinben 劉金鉢, and Ren Rongming 任榮明, "Waishang zhijie touzi dui Shanghai guonei touzi de zaichu xiaoying yanjiu" 外商直接投資對上海國內投資的擠出效應研究 (A Study on the Crowding-Out Effect on Domestic Investment in Chanhai by Foreign Direct Invesment), *Gongye gongcheng yu guanli* 工業工程與管理 (Industrial Engineering and Management), 2003, no.3.
3. Yang Liuyong 楊柳勇, and Shen Guoliang 沈國良, "Waishang zhijie touzi dui Shanghai guonei touzi de zaichu xiaoying yanjiu" 外商直接投資對上海國內投資的擠出效應研究 (A Study on the Crowding-Out Effect on domestic Investment in Chanhai by Foreign Direct Invesment), *Tongji yanjiu* 統計研究 (Statistical Research), 2002, no. 3.
4. Wang Haoyong and Kong Xian, 2003.
5. Zhu Caihua, 2008.
6. "Zhongguo qifei" 中國起飛 (China Takes Off), in *Waijiao zhengce* 外交政策 (Foreign Policy), cited in Hu Xinghua 胡興華, and Wang Xiaoxian 王孝仙, "FDI moshi guoji bijiao yu Zhongguo de xuanze—Dui woguo FDI moshi cunzai wenti de xikao" FDI 模式國際比較與中國的選擇—對我國FDI模式存在問題的思考 (International Comparison of FDI modes and China's Choice: Thoughts on Issues of China's FDI), *Caimao jingji* 財貿經濟 (Finance & Trade Economics), 2004, no. 11.
7. Aitken, B., A. Harrison, and R. E. Lipsey, 1995. "Wages and Foreign Ownership: A Comparative Study of Mexico, Venezuela, and the United States," papers 95–21, Graduate School of Business, Columbia University.
8. Lu Di, "Waishang yu Zhongguo jingji fazhan—Quyu he chanye fenxi zhengju" 外商投資與中國經濟發展—區域和產業分析證據 (Foreign Investment and China's Economic Development: An Analysis of the Evidence from Various Regions and Industries), *Jingji yanjiu* 經濟研究 (Economic Research Journal), 2003, no. 9.
9. Hu Xinghua and Wang Xiaoxian, 2004.
10. Lun Jinyong, 2001.

Chapter 4

1. Xu Wenkai, 2003.
2. Department of Outward Investment and Economic Cooperation, Ministry of Commerce, 2008.
3. Every August, *Engineering News-Record* publishes an annual ranking of the world's Top, 225 International Contractors, along with statistics on their operating performance. The ranking reflects the general landscape in the international contracting industry.
4. Xing Houhuan, 2008.
5. "Qiantan Zhongguo weilai gongcheng chengbao gongying shichang de xin geju" 淺談中國未來工程總承包供應市場的新格局 (A Discussion of the New Order of the Supply Market for China's International Contracts), International contracts section, Ministry of Commerce, http://chinca.mofcom.gov.cn/aarticle/tongjiziliao/200805/20080505525205.html.

6. "2007 nian Zhongguo duiwai chengbao gongcheng, laowu hezuo he sheji zixun yewu tongji" 2007 年中國對外承包工程、勞務合作和設計諮詢業務統計 (Statistics on China's International Contracting, Labor Service Cooperation and Design Consulting, 2007), Department of Outward Investment and Economic Cooperation, Ministry of Commerce, August 20, 2008, http://hzs.mofcom.gov.cn/aarticle/date/200801/20080105354377.html.
7. Ministry of Commerce research and statistics.
8. Du Hongmei et al., 2008.
9. Davis Langdon & Seah International.
10. Construction, Building & Engineering News, "Engineering News-Record," http://enr.construction.com/.
11. "2008 niandu shangbannian woguo duiwai chengbao gongcheng, laowu hezuo he sheji zixun yewu tongji" 2008 年上半年度我國對外承包工程、勞務合作和設計諮詢業務統計 (Statistics on China's International Contracting, Labor Service Cooperation and Design Consulting, as of First Half of 2008), Department of Outward Investment and Economic Cooperation, Ministry of Commerce, July 11, 2008, http://hzs.mofcom.gov.cn/aarticle/date/200807/20080705659906.html.
12. China International Contractors Association 中國對外承包工程商會, *Zhongguoduiwai laowu hezuo fazhan baogao 2006–2007* 中國對外勞務合作發展報告 2006–2007 (China External Labor Cooperation Development Report, 2006–2007).
13. China International Contractors Association 中國對外承包工程商會, *Zhongguo duiwai laowu hezuo niandu baogao 2004* 中國對外勞務合作年度報告 2004 (Annual Report of China Foreign Labor Service Cooperation 2004).
14. International Labor Organization, "Towards a fair deal for migrant workers in the global economy" (report presented at the International Labor Conference, 92nd session, 2004).
15. Li Li and Chen Xun, 2008.

Chapter 5

1. Wang Shouchun and Xu Yu, 1988, p.292.
2. Ibid.
3. The Economic and Commercial Counselor's Office of the Embassy of the People's Republic of China in the United States of America, "An Overview of U.S. External Trade and Sino-U.S. Trade, 2007."
4. "Introduction to Sino-U.S. Economic and Trade Relations," The Economic and Commercial Counselor's Office of the Embassy of the People's Republic of China in the United States of America, April 18, 2007, http://us.mofcom.gov.cn/aarticle/zxhz/hzjj/200704/20070404584987.html.
5. Ibid.
6. Ibid.
7. "Meiguo dui hua touzi qingkuang: Xinzeng qiye shu/lingyu ji diqu fenbu/linian bianhua" 美國對華投資情況: 新增企業數/領域及地區分佈/歷年變化 (American Investment in China: New Firms, Sectors, Geographical Spread and Trends), Zhongguo fazhan menhu wang 中國發展門戶網 (China Development Gateway), April 9, 2008, http://cn.chinagate.cn/reports/2008-04/09/content_14646490.htm.

8. Speech by Mr Xu Xu, Special Commissioner in Shanghai for the Ministry of Commerce at U.S.-China Business Matchmaking Conference 2008, http://www.usachina.org/exchange/news.asp?filename=/develop/vhosts/vhosts2/usachina.org/web/exchange/news/20080606040.txt.
9. Huang Wei, 2005.
10. See note 8 above.
11. "Overview of U.S.-China Business Matching Conference 2008," http://www.usachina.org/exchange/news.asp?filename=/develop/vhosts/vhosts2/usachina.org/web/exchange/news/20080606040.txt.
12. State Council Information Office 國務院新聞辦公室, "Guanyu Zhong Mei maoyi pingheng wenti" 關於中美貿易平衡問題 (On the Issue of China-U.S. Trade Imbalance), *Renmin ribao* 人民日報 (People's Daily), March 22, 1997.
13. Lin Yu, 2006.
14. "Zhong Mei dier ci zhanlüe jiongji duihua pingshu" 中美第二次戰略經濟對話述評 (Commentary on the Second U.S.-China Strategic and Economic Dialogue), Guoji zhanwang 國際展望 (International Outlook), Shanghai, June 2007, http://news.163.com/07/0611/16/3GNH9IUG00011232_2.html
15. Years guesstimated—since the argument seems to have been made in 2007.—Ed.
16. The Economic and Commercial Counselor's Office of the Embassy of the People's Republic of China in the United States, "Introduction to Sino-U.S. Economic and Trade Relations," April 18, 2007. http://us.mofcom.gov.cn/aarticle/zxhz/hzjj/200704/20070404584987.html
17. Bergsten et al., 2006.
18. On April 10, 2007, the U.S. raised the issue of intellectual property rights and market entry for publications in China to be resolved by the WTO dispute settlement panel. The alliance was set up in 1984, representing a membership of 1,900 companies related to intellectual property rights protection and includes seven industry associations.
19. Xu Chaoqing and Wu Guo, 1998, p.167.
20. Wu Yi 吳儀, "Zhengcheng duihua gongmou fazhan" 真誠對話共謀發展 (Sincere Dialogue, Joint Development), (speech at the Welcoming Banquet of Eight U.S. Organizations, Washington DC, May 24, 2007), http://www.china-embassy.org/chn/zmgx/t339322.htm.
21. Ibid.
22. "Mei gongbu maoyi 'hei mingdan' maodou zhizhi Zhonguo Oumeng" 美公佈貿易"黑名單"矛頭直指中國歐盟 (U.S. Has China and EU on Trade Black List), *Shanghai zhengjuan bao* 上海證券報 (Shanghai Securities News), April 4, 2007.
23. "Zhongguo jingji zengzhang dui shijie GDP zengzhang de gongxian paiming dier" 中國經濟增長對世界GDP 增長的貢獻率排名第二 (Chinese Economic Growth Takes Second Place in World GDP Growth), http://www.jinlanmeng.cn/
24. Speech by Timothy D. Adams, Undersecretary for International Affairs, U.S. Treasury, to the U.S.-China Business Council, September 15, 2005. See "U.S. Commerce Undersecretary: U.S.-China Relations Will Affect Global Economic Landscape," China News Service, September 18, 2005.
25. Wu Yi 吳儀, "Tuijin Zhong Mei maoyi huli gongying" 推進中美貿易互利共贏 (It's Win-Win on China's Trade), *Zhongguo zhengjuan bao* 中國證券報 (China Securities News), May 18, 2007.

26. Wu Yi 吳儀, " Meiguo yijing chengwei Zhongguo fuwuye kaifang de zuida shouyizhe" 美國已經成為中國服務業開放的最大受益者 (U.S. Has Become Largest Beneficiary of Chinese Service Sector Liberalization) (speech at U.S.-China Business Council, May 25, 2007), http://www.ce.cn/cysc/cysczh/200705/25/t20070525_11491330.shtml.
27. "Zhongguo shi quanqiu touzi huibao lü zuigao diqu, Meiguo bacheng qiye yingli" 中國是全球投資回報率最高地區，美國八成企業盈利 (China Offers Highest Rate of Return, 80% U.S. Companies Make Profit), http://www.e23.cn/jinan/end.jpg?ArticleID=200622800071.

Chapter 6

1. Ministry of Commerce data, China.
2. According to a report published March 16, 2004 by the WTO Information Inquiry Center, China Institute for Reform and Development (CIRD).
3. Ibid.
4. Arthur Kroeber, chief editor of *China Economic Quarterly*.
5. Marte Fischer, "The End of Price Stability?—Protectionism Against China would Undermine Prosperity," in *WirtschaftsWoche* 26 (2007).
6. *Financial Times*, September 28, 2007.
7. "A Convenient Excuse," in *WirtschaftsWoche*, February 16, 2006.
8. See Article 15 of the *Protocol on the Accession of the People's Republic of China*, World Trade Organization.
9. Council Regulation No. 905/98 of 27 April 1998 amending Regulation No. 384/96 on protection against dumped imports from countries not members of the European Community.O.J.1998 L 128/18.
10. Council Regulation 1972/2002 of November 5, 2002 amending Regulation No. 384/96 on protection against dumped imports from countries not members of the European Community, (2002) O.J.L305/1.
11. Yang Liming, 2004.
12. Li Lian, 1999, p.136.
13. Strange, 1990, p.128.

Chapter 7

1. For details, see Chen Wen 陳文, "Dongmeng ziyou mouyiqu he Zhongguo—Dongmeng ziyou mouyiqu" 東盟自由貿易區和中國—東盟自由貿易區 (The ASEAN Free Trade Area and the China-ASEAN Free Trade Area) in *Dongnanya zongheng* 東南亞縱橫 (Understanding Southeast Asia), 2003.

Chapter 8

1. Unless otherwise noted, data in this chapter has come from the Ministry of Commerce of China (or the former Ministry of Foreign Trade and Economy) and the Cabinet Office of the Government of Japan.

2. Website of Ministry of Foreign Affairs of Japan, http://www.mofa.go.jp/mofaj/gaiko/oda/index.html.
3. International Monetary Fund, *World Economic Outlook*, April 2004, p.165, 171.
4. Japan External Trade Organization, *Japan-China Trade 2003*, February 18, 2004.
5. See the official website of the Cabinet Office, Government of Japan, http://www.esri.cao.go.jp/jp/sna/.
6. Japan External Trade Organization, http://www.jetro.go.jp/ec/j/trade/gaikyo200402.html.
7. Kwan C. H., "The Complementary Relationship between China and Japan: Changes After 2000," September 12, 2003.
8. Ibid.
9. Bank of Japan, National Survey on Business Sentiment, April 1, 2004.
10. See note 4 above.
11. Ibid.
12. "Shangwu tongji" 商務統計 (Commerce Statistics), Ministry of Commerce, http://zhs.mofcom.gov.cn/tongji.shtml.
13. Japan External Trade Organization, *Japan-China Trade 2006*, March 8, 2007.
14. Japan External Trade Organization, http://www.jetro.go.jp/jpn/stats/fdi/data/outstate0401.pdf; *Zhongguo touzi zhinan* 中國投資指南 (China Investment Guide), http://fdi.gov.cn.
15. Ministry of Foreign Affairs, http://www.mofa.go.jp/mofaj/gaiko/oda/index.html.
16. International Monetary Fund, *World Economic Outlook*, September 2005; Japan External Trade Organization, http://www.jetro.go.jp/jpn/stats/fdi/data/instate0402.pdf.
17. Cabinet Office, Government of Japan, *Annual Report on the Japanese Economy and Public Finance, 2005*, p.47.
18. http://rank.nikkei.co.jp/keiki/bukka1/2.cfm.
19. Bank of Japan 日本銀行, "Zhuyao jinrong jingji zhibiao·Shiti jingji" 主要金融經濟指標・實體經濟 (Main Indicators of Finance and Economy: Tangible Economy), November 1, 2005, p.59
20. See note 16 above.
21. "Zhou Xiaochuan jiemi huilü xinjizhi cankao de 'yi lanzi' zucheng yuanze" 周小川揭秘匯率新機制參考的"一籃子"組成原則 (Zhou Xiaochuan Reveals Secret of Principles behind Basket of Currencies for Reference in New Currency Exchange Mechanism), *Renmin wang* 人民網 (People's Daily), August 11, 2005.
22. "Wen Jiaobao he An Pei chuxi Zhong Ri jingji gaoceng duihua jizhi huiyi" 溫家寶和安倍出席中日經濟高層對話機制會議 (Wen Jiabao and Abe Shinzo Attend China-Japan Economic High Level Dialogue Mechanism Meeting), *Xinhua wang* 新華網 (Xinhua News Net), January 13, 2007
23. "Wen Jiabao: Zhong Ri liangguo ying jixu jiaqiang huanbao, nengyuan hezuo" 溫家寶：中日兩國應繼續加強環保、能源領域合作 (Wen Jiabao: China and Japan Should Continue to Strengthen Cooperation in Environmental Protection and Energy), *Xinhua wang* 新華網 (Xinhua News Net), April 12, 2007.
24. Ministry of Economy and Industry of Japan, *White Paper on Small and Medium Enterprises*, 2006.
25. "Wen Jiabao: Zhong Ri liangguo ying tuokuan jinrong hezuo lingyu" 溫家寶：中日兩國應繼續拓寬金融合作領域 (China and Japan Should Continue to Broaden Cooperation in Financial Sector), *Xinhua wang* 新華網 (Xinhua News Net), April 12, 2007.

Notes

Chapter 9

1. Korea Economic Planning Board. From *Korea Herald*, August 15, 1994.
2. The Ministry of Finance is now known as the Ministry of Strategy and Finance.
3. Data from Korean International Trade Association, http://www.kita.net.
4. Liu Saili, 1999, p.259.
5. Ministry of Commerce website.
6. Ministry of Commerce website.
7. Information originally from the Korean Ministry of Foreign Affairs, quoted in Ministry of Commerce website, http://kr.mofcom.gov.cn/aarticle/jmxw/200802/20080205391165.html.
8. *Zhong Han maoyi* 韓中貿易 (Korea-China Trade), 2007, no. 3.
9. *Zhonghua gongshang shibao* 中華工商時報 (China Business Times) September 3, 2008.
10. Ministry of Foreign Affairs website, March 31, 2004.
11. Samsung website, August 6, 2008, http://china.samsung.com.cn/enterprise/samsung_china_current.asp.
12. Information from Beijing Hyundai Motor Co. Ltd., in Ministry of Commerce website, http://kr.mofcom.gov.cn/aarticle/jmxw/200802/20080205392357.html.
13. Liu Saili, 1995.
14. Ministry of Commerce website.
15. Ministry of Commerce website.
16. Data from Korea Tourism Organization, cited in China Ministry of Commerce website, http://kr.mofcom.gov.cn/aarticle/jmxw/200802/20080205391159.html.
17. Xu Baokang, 2008.
18. "Zhong Han lianhe shengming 中韓聯合聲明 (China–South Korea Joint Declaration), *Renmin ribao* 人民日報 (People's Daily), May 29, 2008.
19. China International Friendship City Association website, September 21, 2007.
20. *Donggan Hanguo tekan* 動感韓國特刊 (Dynamic Korea), a magazine published as part of the "2007 China-Korea Year" activities, August 22, 2007.
21. Data from Ministry of Commerce website, August 6, 2008, http://countryreport.mofcom.gov.cn/economy/view.asp?news_id=6849.
22. Ministry of Commerce website.
23. Ministry of Commerce website.
24. Deutsche Welle radio program, July 26, 2007, "The U.S. and China Led the Survey 'Who's Our Friend, Who's Our Enemy,'" reported in "Foreign Views on China," *Cankao Xiaoxi* 參考消息 (Reference News), July 28, 2007.
25. "Zhong Han lianhe gongbao" 中韓聯合公報 (China-Korea Joint Declaration), *Renmin ribao* 人民日報 (People's Daily), August 26, 2008.

Chapter 10

1. At that time, India was known as "*Shendu*" to the Chinese.
2. The Maritime Silk Road starts from Guangzhou or Quanzhou across the South China Sea. It was an important route for trade and cultural exchange between China and other countries.

3. "Baima Si" 白馬寺 (White Horse Temple), *Baidu baike* 百度百科 (Baidu Encyclopedia), http://baike.baidu.com/view/4032.htm.
4. Liu Shuxia, 2007.
5. Wu Hongfei, 2002.
6. Zhao Bole 2003, p.319.
7. In 1957, the China-India Trade Agreement was extended to the end of 1958, and then in May 1959 it was extended again to the end of 1959.
8. Sun Peijun, 1991, p.299.
9. Except for the 1994 trade volume of USD270,000; Ibid.
10. Wu Hongyang, 1995.
11. Table 10.3 shows 10 fiscal years during 1970–1980.
12. Liu Saili, 2005.
13. Cao Yuxi, 2006.
14. Ren Yujun, 2001.
15. Zhang Chunyan, 2006.
16. Zhang Minqiu, 2002.
17. "Zhong Yin lingtu zhengduan 'san tiao xian" "中印領土爭端" 三條線 (The "Three Lines" in the Border Conflict of China and India), *Zhongguo xinwen wang* 中國新聞網 (China News Service), May 31, 2006.
18. Hu Xin, 1982, p.2.
19. Zhang Chunyan, 2006.
20. "07 nian shiyou jinkou liang jin 2 yi dun, jinkou bufa chengxian chao sudu" 07 年石油進口量近2億噸，進口步伐呈現超速度 (Imported Nearly 200 million tons in Oil in 2007, Super Speed in Import), *Xinhua wang* 新華網 (Xinhua News Net), March 3, 2008.
21. Zhang Chunyan, 2006.
22. Yang Wenwu and Ni Chunqin, 2007.
23. International Monetary Fund, World Economic Outlook Database, April 2008.
24. "Yindu 2005–2006 cainian ruanti chukou zeng 33%, 4 nian nei chao 600 yi meiyuan" 印度2005—2006 財年軟體出口增33%，4年內超600億美元 (Indian Software Export Grew 33% in 2005–2006 Fiscal Year, to Exceed USD60 million in Four Years," National Development and Reform Commission, July 21, 2006, http://www.sdpc.gov.cn/gjscy/xxcu2/t20060721_77255.htm.
25. Zhang Yanhua, 2007.
26. India and the East Asian countries of China, Japan, and South Korea have burgeoning demand for oil. East Asia alone accounts for a quarter of the world's oil consumption, but these countries are not gaining the status and power proportionate to their oil consumption. Their influence on the price of oil is weaker than Europe and the U.S., which in fact use less oil. Since 1992, the average barrel of oil in Asia costs USD1 to USD1.50 more than in Europe and the U.S.
27. A cooperation framework agreement on trade in goods was signed between China and ASEAN in November 2004. From July 2005 onwards, both sides will impose zero tariffs on roughly 7,000 categories of goods.

28. "Zhonghua renmin gongheguo he Yindu gongheguo guanyu ershiyi shiji de gongtong zhanwang" 中華人民共和國和印度共和國關於二十一世紀的共同展望 (China and India's Shared Vision in the 21st Century), Ministry of Foreign Affairs website.
29. Ren Yan, 2008.

Chapter 12

1. Shu Yunguo, 2001.
2. Yu Peiwei, 2006.
3. For further reference, see *Zhongguo duiwai jingji maoyi nianjian* 中國對外經濟貿易年鑒 (China Trade and External Economic Statistical Yearbook) of relevant years.
4. Data from *Zhongguo duiwai jingji maoyi nianjian* 中國對外經濟貿易年鑒 (China Trade and External Economic Statistical Yearbook), relevant years.
5. Chen Miaogeng, 2006.
6. Li Anshan, 2006.
7. Yu Peiwei, 2006. Also see *Zhongguo duiwai jingji maoyi nianjian* 中國對外經濟貿易年鑒 (China Trade and External Economic Statistical Yearbook) of relevant years.
8. Shu Yunguo, 2007.
9. Li Anshan, 2006.
10. Liu Saili, 1999, p.278–80.
11. Compiled from data in *Zhongguo duiwai jingji maoyi nianjian* 中國對外經濟貿易年鑒 (Yearbook of China Foreign Economy and Trade Statistics).
12. Liu Saili, 1999, p.279.
13. *Zhong Fei jingmao fazhan wushi nian* 中非經貿發展五十年 (Fifty Years of China-Africa Economic and Trade Relations), Forum of China-Africa Cooperation, July 2008, http://www.focac.org/chn/zfjmhz/t155757.htm.
14. Po Yingji, 2006.
15. See note 13 above.
16. Liu Saili, 1999, p.282.
17. See note 13 above.
18. "Zhong Fei guanxi chengshang xin shiji de hangchuan—Zhong Fei hezuo luntan 6 zhounian lichen huigu" 中非關係乘上新世紀的航船—中非合作論壇6周年歷程回顧 (New Journey for China-Africa Relations in the 21st Century—A Review of Five Years of FOCAC), Forum of China-Africa Cooperation Beijing Summit, September 2006, http://www.focacsummit.org/zfhzlt/2006-09/15/content_175.htm.
19. Li Anshan, 2006.
20. The China-Africa Development Fund aims to encourage and expand the investment of Chinese enterprises in Africa. It supports infrastructure investments in energy, transportation, electric power, and telecommunications. It was approved by the Chinese government in March 2007. Initially funded by the China Development Bank, it was set up as a limited company in Beijing in June 26, 2007 to serve Chinese enterprises interested in opening business and investment activities in Africa.

21. Department of Western Asian and African Affairs, Ministry of Commerce 商務部西亞非洲司, 2008, "Gaige kaifang 30 nian lai, Zhong Fei jingmao guanxi quan fangwei kuayueshi fazhan" 改革開放30年來，中非經貿關係全方位跨越式發展 (Thirty Years of Economic Reform: China-Africa Relations Developed in Leaps and Bounds).
22. "Zhong Fei jingmao hezuo 50 nian" 中非經貿合作50年 (Fifty Years of China-Africa Economic Cooperation).
23. Director-General of the Department of Western Asian and African Affairs, Ministry of Commerce, "Zhong Fei jingmao hezuo qianli juda 中非經貿合作潛力巨大—訪西亞非洲司司長周亞濱 (Vast Potential in China-Africa Economic Cooperation—An Interview with Zhou Yabin).
24. Data compiled from "2007 nian woguo yu Xiya Feizhou guojia maoyi tongji" 2007年我國與西亞非洲國家貿易統計 (Statistics on China-Africa Trade), Department of Western Asian and African Affairs, Ministry of Commerce 商務部西亞非洲司, 2007," http://xyf.mofcom.gov.cn/aarticle/date/200802/20080205397352.html.
25. See note 22 above.
26. "Zhong Fei jingmao he zuo" 中非經貿合作 (China-Africa Economic Cooperation), *Jingji ribao* 經濟日報 (China Economic News).
27. Ibid.
28. See note 23 above.
29. An Dong 安東, "Duiwai chengbao gongcheng, quanqiu guaqi 'Zhongguo feng'" 對外工程承包，全球刮起"中國風" (The Global China Trend of International Contracting), 25 July 2008.
30. Unless otherwise noted, information from this section comes from "Zhongguo dui Feizhou de touzi zhengzai you zhengfu zhudao zouxiang qiye zhudao 中國對非洲的投資正在由政府主導走向企業主導 (Chinese Investment in Africa Changes from Government-Led to Enterprise-Led), May 2007, http://www.gov.cn/jrzg/200705/15/content_615583.htm.
31. Po Yingji, 2006.
32. "Lianheguo baogao cheng Zhongguo dui Feizhou zhijie touzi yi jinru xin shidai" 聯合國報告稱中國對非洲直接投資已進入新時代 (United Nations Reports Says Chinese Investment in Africa Enters New Era," Ministry of Commerce, April 16, 2007, http://zsj.xjbz.gov.cn/ReadNews.asp?NewsID=1621.
33. Wei Qin, 2007.
34. "Shangwu bu zhuanjia: Zhongguo dui Feizhou zhijie touzi 7 nian zengchang 14 bei" 商務部專家：中國對非洲直接投資7年增長14倍 (Chinese Investment in Africa Increased 14 Times in Seven Years, Say Mofcom Experts," http://www.ceceo.cn/Detail.asp?II_ID=20854&CLS=031.
35. According to "2007 nian rujing waiguoren renshu" 2007年入境外國人人數 (Foreign visitors entering China, 2007), China National Tourism Administration 國家旅遊局, June 2008, http://www.cnta.gov.cn/html/20086/20086221293317.html.
36. "Zhongguo chujingyou shichang huoyue, chujingyou mudidi yi da 134 ge" 中國出境遊市場活躍，出境旅遊目的地已達134個 (The Active Market for Chinese Visitors Traveling Overseas, Destinations Increases to 134), China National Tourism Administration 國家旅遊局, June 2008, http://www.cnta.gov.cn/html/20086/20086214465318452.html.
37. Fu Yue, 2007.
38. See note 24.

39. Shu Yunguo, 2008.
40. He Wenping, 2006.
41. Shu Yunguo, 2008.
42. Song Zhiyong, 2006.
43. Shu Yunguo, 2008.
44. Kurlantzick, 2006.
45. Shu Yunguo, 2008.
46. "An Awkward Meeting," *The Economist*, December 8, 2007.
47. Liu Saili, 1999, p.289.
48. Transparency International, "2007 Corruption Perception Index Regional Highlights: Africa," http://www.transparency.org/publications.
49. Liu Guijin 劉貴今, "Jin Zhongguo yuanyi yu gengduo guojia yidao wei Feizhou fazhan zuo gongxian" 今中國願意與更多國家一道為非洲發展作貢獻 (China is Willing to Work with Other Countries to Contribute to Development in Africa), http://www.gov.cn/jrzg/200805/28/content_996986.htm.
50. See note 33 above.
51. Kurlantzick, 2006.
52. See note 26 above.
53. Po Yingji, 2006.
54. Zhang Chengnan, 2006.
55. Tull, 2006.
56. Yao Guimei, 2006.
57. Lai Hongyi, 2007.
58. Yao Guimei, 2006.

Chapter 13

1. From *Zhongguo haiguan tongji (1990–2000)* 中國海關統計 (1990–2000) (China Customs Statistics Yearbook (1990–2000)), and the websites of the Ministry of Commerce of China and the Ministry of Foreign Affairs of China.
2. Ivanov 2002, p.67–68.
3. On October 10, 1998, Georgia, Ukraine, Azerbaijan, and Moldova reached the agreement to form an informal alliance called GUAM. Uzbekistan joined in April 1999.

Chapter 14

1. "About Us," http://web.worldbank.org/WBSITE/EXTERNAL/EXTABOUTUS/0,,pagePK:50004410~piPK:36602~theSitePK:29708,00.html.
2. The IBRD was the first institution of the World Bank to be set up. At the beginning, the name World Bank referred to the IBRD.
3. "Total member countries in each institution," The World Bank, http://web.worldbank.org/WBSITE/EXTERNAL/EXTABOUTUS/0,,contentMDK:20625941~pagePK:51123644~piPK:329829~theSitePK:29708,00.html.

4. Supplementary terms for the IDA were signed on March 24, 1981.
5. "Total member countries in each institution," The World Bank, http://web.worldbank.org/WBSITE/EXTERNAL/EXTABOUTUS/0,,contentMDK:20625941~pagePK:51123644~piPK:329829~theSitePK:29708,00.html.
6. "What is IDA?" The World Bank, http://web.worldbank.org/WBSITE/EXTERNAL/EXTABOUTUS/IDA/0,,contentMDK:21206704~menuPK:83991~pagePK:51236175~piPK:437394~theSitePK:73154,00.html.
7. "IDA Members," The World Bank, http://web.worldbank.org/WBSITE/EXTERNAL/EXTABOUTUS/0,,contentMDK:20122864~menuPK:329835~pagePK:51123644~piPK:329829~theSitePK:29708,00.html.
8. "IBRD: Votes and Subscriptions," The World Bank.
9. "IDA: Votes and Subscriptions," The World Bank, http://web.worldbank.org/WBSITE/EXTERNAL/EXTABOUTUS/ORGANIZATION/BODEXT/0,contentMDK:20124822~isCURL:Y~menuPK:64020035~pagePK:64020054~piPK:64020408~theSitePK:278036,00.html.
10. Xu Yisheng, 2008.
11. Ibid.
12. He Zhongshun, 2007, p.325.
13. "IDA Graduates," The World Bank, http://web.worldbank.org/WBSITE/EXTERNAL/EXTABOUTUS/IDA/0,,contentMDK:20054573~pagePK:83988~piPK:84004~theSitePK:73154,00.html.
14. "MOU of The World Bank's Provision of Aid to China," The World Bank, January 22, 2003.
15. "World Bank Aid to China," The World Bank.
16. "Research Reports and Publications," The World Bank.
17. The Washington Consensus refers to the belief that whole reform packages by Washington DC-based organizations including the World Bank, IMF, and the US Treasury would be effective in guiding the economies of Latin America, Eastern Europe, and Southeast Asia out of crises. Once implemented, many of these countries encountered a series of economic and financial crises, and a lowering of the quality of life. It is believed that the Washington Consensus mainly served the interests of the international capital.
18. Jiang Guocheng 江國成, "Shijie yinhang yu caizheng bu qianchu jingji gaige jishu yuanzhu" 世界銀行與財政部簽署經濟改革技術援助協議 (World Bank and Ministry of Finance Signs Agreement of Technical Assistance for Economic Reforms," *Zhongguo jingji wang* 中國經濟網 (China Economic Net), June 21, 2006, http://www.ce.cn/xwzx/gnsz/gdxw/200606/21/t20060621_7461690.shtml.
19. De Nevers, Michele E, "World Bank Institute: Global Strategy and Projects in China," March 17, 2005.
20. Lu Zheng 盧錚, "Shijie yinhang 2008 cainian dui hua daikuan 15.13 yi meiyuan" 世行2008財年對華貸款15.13億美元 (World Bank Loans China USD1.53 Billion in 2008 Fiscal Year), *Zhongguo zhengjuan bao* 中國證券報 (China Securities News), June 26, 2008, http://www.cs.com.cn/xwzx/03/200806/t20080626_1505568.htm.
21. "China Development Marketplace selects 100 projects," The World Bank China Development Marketplace, March 25, 2008, http://www.developmentmarketplace.org.cn/News/newsdetail.asp?expand=news&id=41.

22. "The World Bank and Civil Organizations in China," The World Bank, http://www.worldbank.org.cn/Chinese/Resources/Resources.htm.
23. Institute for International Studies, Tsinghua University 清華大學國際問題研究所, and Research Center of Economy and Diplomacy, Tsinghua University 清華大學經濟外交研究中心, *Zhongguo jingji waijiao 2006* 中國經濟外交2006 (China's Economic Diplomacy 2006), (Beijing: Renmin University Press, 2007), p.107.
24. International Monetary Fund, http://www.imf.org/external/about.htm.
25. Wang Dexun and Zhang Jinjie, 2004, p.200.
26. Li Hongmei, 2007, p.78.
27. Dai Xianglong, 2001.
28. Wang Dexun and Zhang Jinjie, 2004, p.201.
29. Ibid.
30. Dai Xianglong, 2001.
31. "Zhongguo renmin yinghang guanyu wo guo zai guoji huobi jijin zuzhi tebie zengzi fenge renjiao de qingshi" 中國人民銀行關於我國在國際貨幣基金組織特別增資份額認繳的請示 (The People's Bank of China Report on the Subscription of Special Drawing Rights by China in the International Monetary Fund), People's Bank of China 中國人民銀行, February14, 2001.
32. "Zhongguo zhengfu daibiaotuan chuxi 2006 nian guoji huobi jijin zuzhi he shijie yinhang lianhe nianhui" 中國政府代表團出席2006年國際貨幣基金組織和世界銀行聯合年會 (The Chinese Government Delegation Attends the 2006 Joint Annual Meeting of the IMF and World Bank), People's Bank of China 中國人民銀行, September 19, 2006, http://www.pbc.gov.cn/detail.asp?col=100&ID=1937.
33. See note 31 above.
34. The other three countries were South Korea, Turkey, and Mexico.
35. "IMF Members: Quotas and Voting Power, and IMF Board of Governors," International Monetary Authority, June 20, 2008, http://www.imf.org/external/np/sec/memdir/members.htm.
36. The Article IV *Consultation Staff Reports* for the years 2004, 2005, and 2006 are available on the IMF website, www.imf.org. The 2007 report was not available at the time of print.
37. Fan Haitao, 2005.
38. Dai Xianglong, 2001.
39. China officially joined the IMF General Data Dissemination System (GDDS) on April 20, 2002, a significant development for China's own development in statistics and for China-IMF cooperation.
40. See note 23, p.116.
41. Chinese Premier Web Jiabao announced on February 14, 2008, in a meeting with IMF Managing Director Dominique Strauss-Kahn that China will participate in the IMF's FSAP from 2008 onwards.
42. Li Hongmei, 2007, p.84.
43. Wang Dexun and Zhang Jinjie, 2004, p.203.
44. China and India are the two countries with the largest quotas that are also qualified for the SAF and ESAF loans. The SAF and ESAF are intended to provide financial assistance with favorable conditions to support countries in adjusting their fiscal income and expenditure. Within the IMF, these loan facilities are allocated according to quotas.

45. See note 43.
46. "Woguo jueding xiang guoji huobi jijinzuzhi 'jinji yuanzhu tieshi zhanghu' juankuan" 我國決定向國際貨幣基金組織"緊急援助貼息帳戶"捐款 (China Decides to Donate to IMF Emergency Assistance Subsidy Account), People's Bank of China 中國人民銀行, May 20, 2005, http://www.pbc.gov.cn/detail.asp?col=100&ID=1494.
47. Most recently in June 2012, China agreed to provide US$43 billion to the IMF to be distributed to the failing financial systems in Europe.—Ed.
48. Dai Xianglong, 2001.
49. "Members and Observers," World Trade Organization, http://www.wto.org/english/thewto_e/whatis_e/tif_e/org6_e.htm.
50. "China and the WTO," World Trade Organization, http://www.wto.org/english/thewto_e/countries_e/china_e.htm.
51. "Huli gongying gouzhu hexie woguo duiwai kaifang shuiping xianzhu tigao—Jingji shehui fazhan xilie pingshu zhi si" 互利共贏構築和諧我國對外開放水準顯著提高—經濟社會發展系列評述之四 (Mutual Benefit, Building Harmony, Opening the Chinese Economy: Economic and Social Development Series, Fourth Commentary), *Zhongguo jingji wang* 中國經濟網 (China Economic Net), 2006, http://finance.ce.cn/dissertation/macro/dwkf/.
52. Ministry of Finance, 2008b.
53. Ministry of Finance, 2008a.
54. Ministry of Finance, 2008b.
55. " CEPA zhishi duben" CEPA 知識讀本 (Readings on CEPA), General Administration of Customs 中國海關總署, Nov 25, 2005, http://www.customs.gov.cn/publish/portal0/tab5298/info14450.htm.
56. Ministry of Finance, 2008b.
57. "2007 nian toushi Zhongguo wen yu da" 2007年透視中國問與答 (Q&A About China, 2007), Sep 29, 2007, http://www.china.com.cn/aboutchina/zhuanti/200709/29/content_8984676.htm
58. "Zhongguo yinhang ye duiwai kaifang baogao" 中國銀行業對外開放報告 (Report on the Liberalization of the Chinese Banking Industry), China Banking Regulatory Commission 中國銀行業監督管理委員會, Mar 22, 2007.
59. The *Administrative Measures for Auto Finance Companies* was a document issued by the China Banking Regulatory Commission on January 24, 2008 by decree no.1. The document replaced the administrative measures and the implementation detailed guidelines issued in October and November 2003.
60. "Guo kaotou ni chengli caiwu gongsi" 國開投擬成立財務公司 (State Development Investment Corporation Intends to Set Up Financial Services Firm), Jan 10, 2008, http://finance.sina.com.cn/chanjing/b/20080110/11264389709.shtml.
61. "Yinjianhui fabu shishi xin de 'qiche jinrong gongsi guanli banfa'" 銀監會發佈實施新的"汽車金融公司管理辦法" (CBRC Issues and Implements New "Administrative Measures for Auto Finance Companies"), China Banking Regulatory Commission 中國銀行業監督管理委員會, Jan 30, 2008, http://www.cbrc.gov.cn/chinese/home/jsp/docView.jsp?docID=20080130B0944DC5CC5EC023FF02FC0B0D2A4100.

62. "Guanyu waiguo caichan baoxian fengongsi gaijian wei duzi caichan baoxian gongsi youguan wenti de tongzhi" 關於外國財產保險分公司改建為獨資財產保險公司有關問題的通知 (Notice Regarding Issues Related to Foreign Property Insurance Companies Restructuring into Wholly Owned Entities), China Insurance Regulatory Commission 中國保險監督管理委員會, May 10, 2004, http://www.circ.gov.cn/tabid/434/InfoID/18719/Default.aspx?SkinSrc=%5bL%5dSkins%7cindexej%7cindexer.
63. "Guanyu yunxu waiguo baoxian jingji gongsi sheli waishang duzi baoxian jingjigongsi de tonggao" 關於允許外國保險經紀公司設立外商獨資保險經紀公司的公告 (Public Announcement Regarding Allowing Foreign Insurance Agent Firms to Set Up Wholly-Owned Foreign Entities), China Insurance Regulatory Commission 中國保險監督管理委員會, Dec 11, 2006, http://www.circ.gov.cn/tabid/434/InfoID/39799/Default.aspx?SkinSrc=%5bL%5dSkins%7cindexej%7cindexer.
64. "Zhangjianhui jiang quanmian kaizhan zhengjuan ye he ziben shichang duiwai kaifang pinggu" 證監會將全面開展證券業和資本市場對外開放評估 (CSRC to Conduct a Comprehensive Review of the Liberalization of the Securities and Capital Markets), China Securities Regulatory Commission 中國證券監督管理委員會, Jun 23, 2008, http://www.csrc.gov.cn/n575458/n818828/n8412307/10624907.html.
65. Wan Dianwu and Li Xihua, 2008.
66. "2007 nian Zhongguo tongxun ye de fuwu maoyi" 2007年中國通訊行業的服務貿易 (Service trade in the China telecommunications industry, 2007), Institute on International Trade and Economic Cooperation, Ministry of Commerce 國商務部國際貿易經濟國際合作研究院, Jun 26, 2008, http://tradeinservices.mofcom.gov.cn/g/20080626/49030.shtml.
67. Ibid.
68. "Zhongguo ru shi wu zhounian" 中國入世五周年 (Five Years Since China's WTO Accession), http://focus.jrj.com.cn/special/home/rswzn.htm.
69. Shao Qiwei, 2007.
70. "Shimao si Zhang Xiangchen sizhang tan Zhongguo canyu WTO de youguan qingkuang" 世貿司張向晨司長談中國參與WTO的有關情況 (Director General Zhang Xiangchen, Department of WTO Affairs, Discusses China's Participation in the WTO) .
71. See note 68 above.
72. "WTO dui hua dier ci maoyi zhengce shenyi jiesu gefang jiji pingjia Zhongguo gaige kaifang qude de juda chengjiu" WTO 對華第二次貿易政策審議結束各方積極評價中國改革開放取得的巨大成就 (Second WTO China Trade Policy Review Completed, Achievements in China's Economic Reforms Receive Positive Evaluation), Ministry of Commerce, May 27, 2008, http://www.mofcom.gov.cn/aarticle/ae/ai/200805/20080505559447.html.
73. As of May 2008, China participated in 56 cases as a third party in the WTO conflict resolution mechanism.
74. An expert panel was set up on August 31, 2007, to launch an investigation, but the matter was settled through discussions between the parties. On November 29 that year, China's Ambassador to the WTO Sun Zhenning and the respective ambassadors from Mexico and the U.S. signed a memorandum of understanding (MoU) in relation to the settlement to the dispute. According to the rules of WTO dispute settlement, the solutions agreed upon in the MoU would be reported

back to the WTO. This signifies that the complainant and respondent will resolve the conflict by engaging each other in discussion, and would no longer need a decision from the expert panel.

75. The appellate body of the WTO dispute settlement mechanism is the highest body to adjudicate on trade disputes. Its seven members would need to be broadly representative of the interests of WTO members, and should possess expertise in international trade laws.
76. See note 40, p.236.
77. "Membership," Asian Development Bank, http://www.adb.org/about/members.
78. "Partnership and Cooperation to Support Development," Asian Development Bank, July 2005.
79. Ibid.
80. Institute for International Studies 清華大學國際問題研究所, Tsinghua University, and Research Center of Economy and Diplomacy, Tsinghua University 清華大學經濟外交研究中心, *Zhongguo jingji waijiao 2006* 中國經濟外交2006 (China's Economic Diplomacy 2006), (Beijing: Renmin University Press, 2007), p.108.
81. "Xie Xuren buzhang chuxi di sishiyi jie hang nianhui" 謝旭人部長出席第41屆亞行年會 (Minister of Finance Xie Xuren Attends the 41st ADB Annual Meeting), Ministry of Finance, May 16, 2008, http://www.mof.gov.cn/news/20080516_1680_32757.htm.
82. Asian Development Bank, "ADB Grants China USD1 Million in Emergency Aid Grant to Support Post-Earthquake Disaster Recovery," May 27, 2008.
83. "Guanyu yinfa Wen Jiabao zongli, Hui Liangyu fuzongli zai Shanghai quanqiu fupin dahui shang de jianghua deng dang de tongzhi" 關於印發溫家寶總理、回良玉副總理在上海全球扶貧大會上的講話等檔的通知 (Regarding the Dissemination of the Speech of Premier Wen Jiabao and Vice Premier Hui Liangyu at the Shanghai World Poverty Reduction Conference and Other Documents), State Council Leading Group of Poverty Alleviation and Development 國務院扶貧開發領導小組辦公室, May 31, 2004, http://220.171.0.115/FPApp/xxcj/Fp_Xxcj_Demo?dh=200512100018&placement=0501.
84. "Zhongguo renmin yinhang pizhun guoji jinrong gongsi he Yazhou kaifa yinhang zai quanguo yinhang jian zhaijuan shichang faxing Renminbi zhaijuan" 中國人民銀行批准國際金融公司和亞洲開發銀行在全國銀行間債券市場發行人民幣債券 (The People's Bank of China Approved IFC and ADB to Issue RMB-Denominated Bonds in the China Inter-Bank Bond Market), People's Bank of China 中國人民銀行, October 9, 2005, http://www.pbc.gov.cn/publish/bangongting/82/1705/17054/17054_.html.

References

Chinese materials:

Cao Yuxi 曹譽曦. 2006. "Yindu ren yanzhong de Zhongguo jingji" 印度人眼中的中國經濟 (The Chinese Economy in the Eyes of the Indian People), December 1.

Chen Li 陳力. 2007. *Guoji maoyi jiuji falü zhidu zhong de fei shichang jingji guize: Yi Meiguo oumeng wei shijiao* 國際貿易救濟法律制度中的非市場經濟規則：以美國歐盟為視角 (The Non-Market Rules of the Legal System of International Trade and Aid: With the United States and European Union as a Vantage Point). Shanghai: Shanghai People's Publishing.

Chen Miaogeng 陳苗耕. 2006. "Zhong Fei youhao guanxi de huiwang lichen" 中非友好關係的輝煌歷程 (The development of friendly relations between China and Africa). *Guoji wenti yanjiu* 國際問題研究 (Journal of International Studies), no. 6.

Chen Wenjing 陳文敬. 2008. "Zhongguo duiwai kaifang sanshi nian huigu yu zhanwang (1)" 中國對外開放三十年回顧與展望（一）(Review and outlook for 30 years of economic reforms in China, part 1). *Guoji maoji* 國際貿易 (International Trade), no 2.

Chen Ye 陳葉. 2007. "Zhongguo-Dongmeng ziyou maoyi qu de qianjing fenxi" 中國—東盟自由貿易區的前景分析 (Analysis of the prospects of the China-ASEAN free trade area). *Jingji yanjiu daokan* 經濟研究導刊 (Journal of Economic Research), no. 11.

Cheng Siwei 成思危. 2006. "Cong sige fangmian tantao woguo yu Lamei guanxi de fazhan" 從四個方面探討我國與拉美關係的發展 (Exploring China-Latin American relations in four aspects). *Lading meizhou yanjiu* 拉丁美洲研究 (Journal of Latin American Studies), no. 2.

Cheng Yijun 程亦軍. 2007. "Zhong E maoyi mianlin de wenti yu nuli fangxiang" 中俄貿易面臨的問題與努力方向 (Issues and future direction for China-Russia trade). *Zhong E meng zixun wang* 中俄蒙資訊網 (China-Russia Economic and Trade Cooperation Network), July 12. http://www.nmg.xinhua.org/nmgwq/2007-04/12/content_9765971.htm.

China Institute of International Studies 中國國際問題研究, ed. 2008. *Guoji fengyun lu 2007/2008* 國際風雲錄 2007/2008 (Important Global Events, 2007–2008). Beijing: World Affairs Publishing.

Chinese Communist Party 中國共產黨. 1992. *Zhonggong zhongyang wenjian xuanbian* 中共中央檔選編 (Selected Documents of the Chinese Communist Party). Beijing: CPC Central Committee Party School Publishing.

Dai Xianglong 戴相龍. 2001."Quzhe de lichen youxiao de hezuo—Zhongguo chongfan guoji huobi jijin zuzhi 21 nian huigu yu zhanwang" 曲折的歷程有效的合作—中國重返國際貨幣基金組織21年回顧與展望 (Convoluted Journey, Effective Cooperation: Review and Outlook for China 21 Years After Its Return to the IMF). *Renmin ribao* 人民日報 (People's Daily), April 19.

Deng Xiaoping 鄧小平. 1997. *Jianshe you Zhongguo tese de shehuizhuyi* 建設有中國特色的社會主義 (Building Socialism with Chinese Characteristics) (reprint), Beijing: People's Publishing House.

Deng Xiaoping wen xuan 鄧小平文選 (Selected Writings of Deng Xiaoping). 1993. Beijing: People'Publishing House, vol. 3.

Department of Outward Investment and Economic Cooperation, Ministry of Commerce 商務部對外經濟合作司. 2008. "2007 nian quanguo duiwai chengbao gongcheng qiye 30 qiang" 2007年全國對外承包工程企業30強 (Top 30 International Contractors in China, 2007). *Guoji jingji hezuo* 國際經濟合作 (International Economic Cooperation), no. 3.

Department of Trade and External Economy Statistics, National Bureau of Statistics 統計局貿易外經統計司, ed. *Zhongguo duiwai maoyi tongji nianjian* 中國對外貿易統計年鑒 (Yearbook of China External Trade Statistics).

——, ed. *Zhongguo duiwai jingji tongji nianjian* 中國對外經濟統計年鑒 (Yearbook of China External Economic Statistics).

Department of Trade and Resources, National Bureau of Statistics 統計局貿易外經統計司, China Statistics Information Advisory Service Center 統計信息服務中心, ed. 1992. *1979–1991 nian Zhongguo duiwai jingji tongji daquan* 1979–1991年中國對外經濟統計大全 (Compendium of China External Economic Statistics, 1979–1991).

Department of West African Affairs, Ministry of Commerce 商務部西亞非洲司. *2007 nian woguo yu Xiya Feizhou guojia maoyi tongji* 2007年我國與西亞非洲國家貿易統計 (Statistics on Trade between China and West African Countries, 2007).

Devuyst, Y., and Men Jing 門鏡. 2007. *Ouzhou yitihua jincheng—Oumeng de juece yu duiwai guanxi* 歐洲一體化進程—歐盟的決策與對外關係 (The European Union Transformed: Community Method and Institutional Evolution from the Schuman Plan to the Constitution for Europe). Beijing: China Renmin University Press.

Dong Yinguo 董銀國. 2008. "Zhongguo yu Lading Meizhou maoyi huigu yu zhanwang" 中國與拉丁美洲貿易回顧與展望 (Review and prospects of China-Latin American trade). *Guoji shangwu yanjiu* 國際商務研究 (International Business Research), no. 2.

Du Hongmei 杜紅梅 et al. 2008. "Zhongguo guoji gongcheng chengbao yewu fazhan de kunjing yu duice" 中國國際工程承包業務發展的困境與對策 (Problems and solutions for the international contracting industry of China). *Duiwai jingmao wushi* 對外經貿務實 (Practice in Foreign Economic Relations and Trade), no. 2.

Du Xinquan 屠新泉. 2005. *Zhongguo zai WTO zhong de diwei, zuoyong he celue* 中國在WTO中的定位、作用和策略 (China's Positioning, Function and Strategy in the WTO). Beijing: Publishing House of the University of International Business and Economics.

Economic and Commercial Counselor's Office of the Mission of China to the EU, Department of European Affairs, Ministry of Commerce 商務部歐洲司辦公室. 2006. *Oumeng shangwu zhengce zhinan* 歐盟商務政策指南 (Guide to the Business and Investment Policy of the European Union). Beijing: Tsinghua University Press.

Eluosi he Dong'ou Zhongya guojia nianjian 俄羅斯和東歐中亞國家年鑒 (Yearbook of Russia, Eastern Europe and Central Asian Countries). 2004. Beijing: World Affairs Publishing.

Fan Haitao 范海濤. 2005. "Guoji huobi jijin zuzhi zhuxi 12 zai jianzheng Zhongguo jingjiqiji" 國際貨幣基金組織主席12載見證中國經濟奇跡 (IMF Managing Director Witnessed China's Economic Miracle for 12 Years). *Beijing qingnian bao* 北京青年報 (Beijing Youth Daily), October 26.

Fan Ying 樊瑩. 2008. "Zhongguo yu Oumeng shuangbian maoyi shiheng de yuanyin ji yingxiang tanjiu" 中國與歐盟雙邊貿易失衡的原因及影響探究 (Exploring the causes and effects of the bilateral trade imbalance between China and the European Union). *Guoji jingji hezuo* 國際經濟合作 (International Economic Cooperation), no. 2.

Fu Yue 傅悦. 2007. "Zhong Fei maoyi de xinshiqi fazhan" 中非貿易的新時期發展 (A new era of development in China-Africa trade). *Zhongguo jingmao* 中國經貿 (China Economy and Trade), no. 7.

Gu Lieming 顧列銘. 2005. "Zhongguo Lamei jingmao guanxi xunsu fazhan" 中國拉美經貿關係迅速發展 (China-Latin American economic and trade relations develops rapidly). *Dangdai shijie* 當代世界 (Contemporary World), no. 4.

Gu Qingzhi 辜慶志. 2008. "Zhongguo yu dongmeng de jingji hezuo" 中國與東盟的經濟合作 (Economic cooperation between China and ASEAN). *Jingji shi* 經濟師 (China Economist), no. 1.

Guo Delin 郭德琳. 2007. "Yi Zhili wei pingtai fazhan yu Lamei diqu jingmao guanxi" 以智利為平臺發展與拉美地區經貿關係 (Developing economic and trade relations with Latin America using Chile as a platform). *Guoji jingji hezuo* 國際經濟合作 (International Economic Cooperation), no. 6.

He Wenping 賀文萍. 2006. "Guanyu jiaqiang Zhong Fei quanfangwei hezuo de ruogan xikao" 關於加強中非全方位合作的若干思考 (Some thoughts on strengthening the full economic cooperation between China and Africa). *Xiya Feizhou* 西亞非洲 (West Asia and Africa), no. 8.

He Zhongshun 何中順. *2007 xin shiqi Zhongguo jingji waijiao lilun yu shijian* 2007 新時期中國經濟外交理論與實踐 (Theory and Practice of China's Economic Diplomacy in a New Era). Beijing: Current Affairs Publishing House.

Hong Lei 洪雷. 2005. "Jiedu xin xiuding de'jinchukou shangpin jianyanfa shishi tiaoli'" 解讀新修訂的《進出口商品檢驗法實施條例》 (Interpreting the new"Regulations for the Implementation of Import and Export Inspection Law"). *Guoji shichang* 國際市場 (International Markets), no. 11.

Hu Jianbo 胡劍波. 2008. "Zhongguo xishou FDI: Xianzhuang, tezheng ji duice" 中國吸收FDI：現狀、特徵及對策 (China FDI inflow: Current status, features, and strategies). *Guoji jingji hezuo* 國際經濟合作 (International Economic Cooperation), no. 6.

Hu Jintao 胡錦濤. 2005. "Nuli jianshe chijiu heping, gongtongfanrong de hexie shijie—Zai lianheguo chengli 60 zhounian shounao huiyishang de jianghua" 努力建設持久和平、共同繁榮的和諧世界—在聯合國成立60周年首腦會議上的講話 (Making Great Efforts to Build a Harmonious World with Long-lasting Peace and Common Prosperity—Speech at the United Nations 60th anniversary Summit). *Renmin ribao* 人民日報 (People's Daily), September 16.

——. 2007. *Gaoju zhongguo tese shehui zhuyi weida qizhi, wei duoqu quanmian jianshe xiaokang shehui xin shengli er fendou—Zai zhongguo gongchandang di shiqi ci quanguo daibiao dahui shang de baogao* 高舉中國特色社會主義偉大旗幟，為奪取全面建設小康社會新勝利而奮鬥—在中國共產黨第十七次全國代表大會上的報告 (Report at the 17th National Congress of the Communist Party of China: Hold High the Great Banner of Socialism with Chinese Characteristics and Strive for New Victories in Building a Moderately Prosperous Society In All Respects). Beijing: People's Publishing House.

Hu Xin 胡欣. 1982. *Yindu yang zongheng tan* 印度洋縱橫談 (Perspectives on the Indian Ocean). Fuzhou: Fujian People's Press.

Hu Xinghua 胡興華, and Wang Xiaoxian 王孝仙. 2004. "FDI moshi guoji bijiao yu Zhongguo de xuanze—Dui woguo FDI moshi cunzai wenti de sikao" FDI模式國際比較與中國的選擇—對我國FDI模式存在問題的思考 (International comparison of FDI modes and China's choice: Thoughts on China's FDI mode problems). *Caimao jingji* 財貿經濟 (Finance and Trade Economics), no. 11.

Huang Hanmin 黃漢民. 2007. *Guoji jingji hezuo* 國際經濟合作 (International Economic Cooperation). Shanghai: Shanghai University of Finance and Economics Press.

Huang Hui 黃輝. 2005. *Zhongou maoyi mocha* 中歐貿易摩擦 (China-European Trade Friction). Beijing: Social Sciences Academic Press.

Huang Wei 黃蔚. 2005. *Meiguo duihua zhijie touzi fazhan de shizheng yanjiu ji qushi fenxi* 美國對華直接投資發展的實證研究及趨勢分析 (An analysis of empirical evidence and trends in U.S. direct investment in China). *Guoji maoyi wenti* 國際貿易問題 (International Trade Issues) no. 12, 98–103.

Institute of Eastern Europe and Central Asia, China Academy of Social Sciences 中國社會科學院東歐中亞研究所, ed. 1999. *Eluosi he Dongou Zhongya guojia nianjian* 俄羅斯和東歐中亞國家年鑒 (Yearbook of Russia, Eastern Europe and Central Asian Countries). Beijing: Contemporary World Publishing.

——, ed. 2000. *Eluosi he Dong'ou Zhongya guojia nianjian* 俄羅斯和東歐中亞國家年鑒 (Yearbook of Russia, Eastern Europe and Central Asian Countries). Beijing: Contemporary World Publishing.

Institute for Economy and Resource Management, Beijing Normal University 北京師範大學經濟與資源管理研究所. 2003. *Zhongguo shichang jingji diwei fazhan baogao* 中國市場經濟地位發展報告 (Report on the Development of Market Economy Status in China). Beijing: Publishing House of the University of International Business and Economics.

Institute for International Studies, Tsinghua University 清華大學國際問題研究所, and Research Center of Economy and Diplomacy, Tsinghua University 清華大學經濟外交研究中心. 2007. *Zhongguo jingji waijiao 2006* 中國經濟外交2006 (China's Economic Diplomacy, 2006). Beijing: Renmin University Press.

Jia Qinglin 賈慶林. 2008. "Jiwangkailai kaichuang youyi yu hezuo de meihao mingtian" 繼往開來開創友誼與合作的美好明天 (Linking Past and Future, Start a Bright Tomorrow of Friendship and Cooperation). *Renmin ribao* 人民日報 (People's Daily), May 7.

"Jia Qinglin zai quanguo zhengshe shiyi jie yi ci huiyi shang zuo de changwei gongzuo baogao" 賈慶林在全國政協十一屆一次會議上做的常委會工作報告 (Work Report of Jia Qinglin at the 11th Chinese People's Political

Consultative Conference Standing Committee). 2008. *Renmin ribao* 人民日報 (People's Daily), March 4,.

Jiang Ruiping 江瑞平. 2004. "Lun xin jieduan zhongri maoyi wu da tedian" 論新階段中日貿易五大特點 (Five main features of Sino-Japanese trade in a new era). *Riben xuekan* 日本學刊 (Japanese Studies), no. 4.

——. 2005. "Jibian zhong de Zhong Ri jingji guanxi" 激變中的中日經濟關係 (Cataclysmic Sino-Japanese economic relations). *Zhongguo jingji* 中國經濟 (China Economy), no. 2–3.

——. 2006. "Zhong Ri jingji guanxi de kunjing yu chulu" 中日經濟關係的困境與出路 (The difficult position and way out in Sino-Japanese economic relations). *Riben xuekan* 日本學刊 (Japanese Studies), no. 1.

——. 2007. "Lun zhongri zhanlüe huhui guanxi de jingji hanyi" 論中日戰略互惠關係的經濟含義 (The economic significance of a mutually beneficial Sino-Japanese strategy). *Riben xuekan* 日本學刊 (Japanese Studies), no. 4.

Jiang Shixue 江時學. 2007. "Zhong La jingmao guanxi de fazhan youli yu tuidong nannan hezuo" 中拉經貿關係的發展有利於推動南南合作 (Developing China-Latin American relations supports the growth of South-South cooperation). *Dangdai shijie* 當代世界 (Contemporary World), no. 6.

Jiang Zemin 江澤民. 1997. "Gaoju Deng Xiaoping lilun weida qizhi, ba jianshe you Zhongguo tese shehui zhuyi shiye quanmian tuixiang 21 shiji—Zai Zhongguo gongchandang dishiwu ci quanguo daibiao dahui shang de baogao" 高舉鄧小平理論偉大旗幟，把建設有中國特色社會主義事業全面推向21世紀—在中國共產黨第十五次全國代表大會上的報告 (Hold High the Great Banner of Deng Xiaoping Theory for an All-round Advancement of the Cause of Building Socialism with Chinese Characteristics to the 21st Century—Report at the 15th National Congress of the Communist Party of China. *Zhongguo gongchandang dishiwu ciquanguo daibiao dahui wenjian huibian* 中國共產黨第十五次全國代表大會文件彙編 (Documents from the 15th National Congress of the Communist Party of China) Beijing: People's Publishing House.

Kang Sheng 亢升. 2007. Dongdang Feizhou de Zhongguo shiyou anquan 動蕩非洲的中國石油安全 (China oil security in a turbulent Africa). *Xiya Feizhou* 西亞非洲 (West Asia and Africa), no. 2.

Lan Qingxin 藍慶新, and Xia Zhanyou 夏佔友. 2007. *Zhongguo qiye "zouchuq"* 中國企業"走出去" (Chinese Enterprises "Go Global"). Beijing: University of International Business and Economics Press.

Li Aijun 李愛軍, and Zhang Aizhen 張愛真. 2007. "Zhongguo yu Baxi de maoyi hubuxing fenxi" 中國與巴西的貿易互補性分析 (An analysis of the complementarity of trade between China and Brazil). *Guangxi caijing xueyuan xuebao* 廣西財經學院學報 (Journal of Guangxi University of Finance and Economics), no. 10.

Li Anshan 李安山. 2006. "Lun Zhong guo dui Feizhou zhengce de tiaoshi yu zhuanbian" 論中國對非洲政策的調適與轉變 (Adjustments and shifts in Chinese policy towards Africa). *Xiya feizhou* 西亞非洲 (West Asia and Africa), no. 8.

Li Hongmei 李紅梅. 2007. *Guoji jingji zuzhi* 國際經濟組織 (International Economic Organizations). Beijing: Machinery Industry Press.

Li Shijia 李詩佳, and Bai Jie 白潔. 2008. "Zhongguo waijiao jianxing 'hexie' linian" 中國外交餞行"和諧"理念 (China's Diplomacy Implements the "Harmony" Concept). *Renmin ribao* 人民日報 (People's Daily), February 29.

Li Li 李麗, and Chen Xun 陳迅. 2008. "Zhongguo duiwai laowu hezuo xianzhuang" 中國對外勞務合作現狀 (The present landscape of foreign labor services cooperation of China). Guoji jingji hezuo 國際經濟合作 (International Economic Cooperation), no. 1.

Li Lian 李練. 1999. Fan qingxiao falü yu shiwu 反傾銷法律與實務 (Anti-Dumping Law and Practice). Beijing: China Development Publishing.

Li Mingde 李明德. 2001. "Zhong La guanxi de xin fazhan" 中拉關係的新發展 (New development in China-Latin America relations). *Qiushi* 求是 (Seeking Truth), no. 12.

Li Shenming 李慎明. 2007. *Zhongguo heping fazhan yu guoji zhanlüe* 中國和平發展與國際戰略 (The Peaceful Development and Global Strategy of China). Beijing: China Social Science Publishing.

Li Yanchang 李延長. 2003. "Zhong Fei jingmao guanxi fazhan de xianzhuang yu qianjing" 中非經貿關係發展的現狀與前景 (The present and future development of China-Africa economic and trade relations). *Shaanxi shengxingzheng xueyuan Shaanxi sheng ganbu guanli xueyuan xuebao* 陝西省行政學院陝西省幹部管理學院學報 (Journal of Shaanxi Province Management Institute, Shaanxi Province Academy of Governance), no. 4.

Liang Xiaodan 梁曉丹. 2007. "Shi lun zhidu bianqian dui Dongya jingji yitihua de yingxiang" 試論制度變遷對東亞經濟一體化的影響 (Comments on the effect of institutional changes on the unification of Southeast Asia economies). *Jingji yanjiu daokan* 經濟研究導刊 (Journal of Economic Research), no. 9.

Lin Yu 林鈺, ed. 2006. *Shewai jingji guanxi—Zhongguo yu zhuyao maoyi huoban* 涉外經貿關係—中國與主要貿易夥伴 (External Economic Relations: China and Its Major Trading Partners). Shanghai: Publishing House of

Shanghai University of Finance and Economics.

Liu Houjun 劉厚俊. 1994. *Zhongxifang maoyi* 中西方貿易 (Trade Between the East and the West). Nanjing: Nanjing University Press.

Liu Ronggen 劉榮根. 2002. "Dui Zhongguo yu Lading Meizhou guanxi de kanfa" 對中國與拉丁美洲關係的看法 (Views on China-Latin American relations). *Lading meizhou yanjiu* 拉丁美洲研究 (Journal of Latin American Studies), no. 5.

Liu Saili 劉賽力. 1995. "Zhonghan jingmao guanxi de huigu yu zhanwang" 中韓經貿關係的回顧與展望 (Review and prospects of China-Korea economic and trade relations). *Waijiao xueyuan xuebao* 外交學院學報 (Journal of China Foreign Affairs University), no. 2.

——, ed. 1999. Zhongguo duiwai jingji guanxi 中國對外經濟關係 (China External Economic Relations). Beijing: China Economy Publishing.

——. 2005. "Zhong Yin jingmao guanxi de zoushi yu qianjing" 中印經貿關係的走勢與前景 (The trajectory and prospects of China-India economic and trade relations). *Ye Fei zongheng* 亞非縱橫 (Asia and Africa Issues), no. 3.

——. 2006. "Hezuo gongying de Zhong Han jingji guanxi" 合作共贏的中韓經濟關係 (Cooperative and mutually beneficial China-Korea economic relations). *Guoji wenti yanjiu* 際問題研究 (Journal of International Studies), no. 3.

——. 2007. "Hanguo duihua zhijie touzi qianxi" 韓國對華直接投資淺析 (An analysis of Korean FDI in China). In *Hanguo xuelun wenji* 韓國學論文集 (Anthology of the Discourse on Korean Studies). Shenyang: Liaoning Nationality Publishing House.

——. 2008. "Yunyu zhong de zhonghan ziyou maoyi qu" 孕育中的中韓自由貿易區 (The incubation of a China-Korea free trade area). *Guoji wenti yanjiu* 國際問題研究 (Journal of International Studies), no. 1.

Liu Shaohua 劉少華. 2007. "Lun Dongmeng zai Dongya quyu hezuo zhong de lingdao nengli" 論東盟在東亞區域合作中的領導能力 (The leadership capability of ASEAN in East Asian regional cooperation). *Dangdai yatai* 當代亞太 (Contemporary Asia Pacific), no.9.

Liu Shuxia 劉淑霞. 2007. "Tang dai Zhong Yin wenhua jiaoliu ji qi lishi qishi" 唐代中印文化交流及其歷史啟示 (The historical significance of China-India exchanges in the Tang Dynasty). *Tangdu xuekan* 唐都學刊 (Tangdu Journal), no. 7.

Liu Yuan 劉遠. 2007. "Zhongguo yu dongmeng jingmao hezuo: Xianzhuang yu qianjing" 中國與東盟經貿合作：現狀與前景 (China-ASEAN economic and trade cooperation: Present and future). *Shijie jingji yu zhengzhi luntan* 世界經濟與政治論壇 (Forum of World Economy and Politics), no. 6.

Lu Guozheng 盧國正. 2007. "Huhui huying de Zhong La jingmao guanxi" 互惠互赢的中拉經貿關係 (The win-win situation of China-Latin American economic and trade relations). *Zhongguo jinrong* 中國金融 (China Finance), no. 16.

Lu Jianren 陸建人. 1999. "Dongmeng de fazhan daolu" 東盟的發展道路 (ASEAN's path of development). *Dangdai yatai* 當代亞太 (Contemporary Asia Pacific), no. 8.

Lu Jinyong 盧進勇. 2001. *Rushi yu Zhongguo liyong waizi he haiwai touzi* 入世與中國利用外資和海外投資 (WTO Accession and China's Use of Foreign Investment and China's Overseas Investment). Beijing: Foreign Economy and Trade University Press.

——, and Du Qihua 杜奇華. 2006. *Guoji jingji hezuo* 國際經濟合作 (International Economic Cooperation). Beijing: University of International Business and Economics Publishing House.

Luo Chunhua 羅春華. 2007. "IMF zongcai cheng Zhongguo zheng daidong shijie jingji zengzhang" IMF 總裁稱中國正帶動世界經濟增長 (IMF Managing Director Said China Drives World Economic Growth). *Renmin ribao* 人民日報 (People's Daily), January 22.

Makesi En'gesi xuan ji 馬克思恩格斯選集 (Anthology of Marx and Engel). 1995 . Beijing: People's Publishing House, vol.1.

Ma Zhengang 馬振崗, ed. 2007. *Jianshe hexie shijie de zhanlue huanjing yu lilun tansuo* 建設和諧世界的戰略環境與理論探索 (Exploring the Strategic Context and Theory for Building a Harmonious World). Beijing: Contemporary World Publishing.

——, ed. 2008. *Quanqiuhua beijing xia de shijie yu zhongguo* 全球化背景下的世界與中國 (The World and China against the Backdrop of Globalization). Beijing: World Affairs Publishing.

Mao Lei 毛壘. 2008. "Zhongguo congfen fahui huiyi waijiao de youshi—Quanguo renda changweihui fumishuzhang Cao Weizhou tan quanguo renda duiwai jiaowang" 中國充分發揮議會外交的優勢—全國人大常委會副秘書長曹衛洲談全國人大對外交往 (China Fully Utilizing Parliamentary Diplomacy—NPC Standing Committee Vice Secretary-General Discusses Foreign Exchanges of the National People's Congress). *Renmin ribao* 人民日報 (People's Daily), March 10.

Ministry of Commerce 中國商務部. "Zhongguo fuwu maoyi fazhan baogao" 中國服務貿易發展報告2007 (China Service Trade Development Report 2007). http://tradeinservices.mofcom.gov.cn/g/2008-06-13/48292.shtml.

Ministry of Economy, Trade and Industry 經濟產業省. Relevant years. *Tongshang baish* 通商白書 (White Paper on International Trade).

Ministry of Finance 中國財政部. 2008a. "Jiaru shimao simian Zhongguo kede gaofen shunli jinru hou guoduqi" 加入世貿四年中國可得高分順利進入後過渡期 (China Enters Post-Transition Period with High Scores after Four Years of WTO Membership), May 19, 2008. http://www.mof.gov.cn/caizhengbuzhuzhan/zhengwuxinxi/caijingshidian/xinhuanet/200805/t20080519_22332.html.

———. 2008b. "2008 nian yiyue yihao qi woguo jinchukou guanshui shuize jiang zuo jinyibu tiaozheng" 2008年1月1日起我國進出口關稅稅則將做進一步調整 (Further Revision of China's Import Tariffs from January 1, 2008), December 21. http://www.mof.gov.cn/caizhengbuzhuzhan/zhengwuxinxi/caizhengxinwen/200805/t20080519_27942.html.

Ministry of Foreign Affairs of Japan 日本外務省. Relevant years. *ODA baishu* ODA白書 (White Paper on Official Development Assistance).

Pei Changhong 裴長洪, ed. 2006. *Zhongguo duiwai jingmao lilun qianyan (4)* 中國對外經貿理論前沿（4）(The Frontier of Theory on the External Economy and Trade of China, Volume 4). Beijing: Social Sciences Academic Press.

Po Yingji 朴英姬. 2006. "Zhongguo dui Feizhou zhijie touzi de fazhan lichen yu weilai qushi" 中國對非洲直接投資的發展歷程與未來趨勢 (Past development and future trends of China's direct investment in Africa). *Haiwai touzi yu chukou xindai* 海外投資與出口信貸 (Overseas Investment and Export Credit), no. 5.

Qiu Jiafeng 邱嘉鋒. 2008. "Kuaguo gongsi fazhan de shi da qushi" 跨國公司發展的十大趨勢 (Ten most important trends in the development of multinational companies). *Jingji xue dongtai* 經濟學動態 (Economic Perspectives), no. 6.

Ren Yan 任彥. 2008. "Ying Fei guanxi zoujin yibu" 印非關係走近一步 (One Step Closer in India-Africa Relations). *Renmin ribao* 人民日報 (People's Daily), April 10.

Ren Yujun 任毓駿. 2001. "Mei Yin guanxi zai shengwen" 美印關係再升溫 (U.S.-India Relations Heats Up Again). *Renmin ribao* 人民日報 (People's Daily), May 21.

Shao Qiwei 邵琪偉. 2007. "Hua zaici tiqian lü xing luyou ye ru shi chengnuo" 華再次提前履行旅遊業入世承諾 (China Tourism Sector Again Implements WTO Accession Commitment Ahead of Schedule), January 23, 2007. http://chanye.finance.sina.com.cn/ly/20070123/310912.shtml.

Shen Danyang 沈丹陽, and Nie Pingxiang 聶平鄉. 2008."Liyong waizi: Zhengce tiaozheng yu fazhan qushi" 利用外資：政策調整與發展趨勢. (Foreign investment utilization: Policy adjustment and development trends). *Guoji jingji hezuo* 國際經濟合作 (International Economic Cooperation), no. 1.

Shu Yunguo 舒運國. 2001. "Shishi Zhong Fei jingmao guanxi de tedian" 試析中非經貿關係的特點 (Analyzing the features of Sino-Africa relations). *Shanghai shifan daxue shifan daxue xuebao* 上海師範大學學報（社會科學版）(Shanghai Normal University Journal (Social Studies)), no. 7.

——. 2007. Lun Zhong Fei maoyi guanxi 論中非經貿關係 (On China-Africa trade relations). *Shanghai shifan daxue xuebao* 上海師範大學學報 (Academic Journal of Shanghai Normal University) (Philosophy and Social Science edition), no. 2.

——. 2008. "Zhong Fei jingmao guanxi: Tiaozhan yu duice" 中非經貿關係：挑戰與對策 (Challenges and solutions in China-Africa economic and trade relations), July 14. http://ias.zjnu.cn/Academic/kyyy.asp?id=6.

Song Zhiyong 宋志勇. 2006. "Shilun Zhong Fei maoyi mocha" 試論中非貿易摩擦 (About trade frictions between China and Africa). *Xiya Feizhou* 西亞非洲 (West Africa), no. 8.

Strange, Susan. 1990. *Guojia yu shichang: Guoji zhengzhi jingji xue daolun* 國家與市場：國際政治經濟學導論 (States and Markets: Theory in International Political Economy). Beijing: World Affairs Publishing.

Su Liping 蘇麗萍. 2006. *Duiwai zhijie touzi: Lilun, shijian he Zhongguo de zhanlüe xuanz*e 對外直接投資：理論、實踐和中國的戰略選擇 (Foreign Direct Investment: Theory, Practice and China's Strategic Choice). Xiamen: Xiamen University Press.

Sun Peijun 孫培均. 1991. *Zhong Yin jingji fazhan bijiao yanjiu* 中印經濟發展比較研究 (Comparative Study of the Economic Development of China and India). Beijing: Peking University Press.

Sun Tingting 孫婷婷. 2008. "Waizi maoyi hangye Zhongguo sanshinian fazhan huimou" 外資貿易行業中國三十年發展回眸 (A Review of the 30 Year Development of Foreign Invested Trade in China). *Renmin wang* 人民網 (People's Daily Online), July 28. http://mnc.people.com.cn/GB/7570129.html.

Sun Xiliang 孫希良, and Zhang Aijun 張愛軍. 2007. "Zhongguo yu Lamei de guanxi: Yi jingji quanqiuhua wei shijiao" 中國與拉美的關係：以經濟全球化為視角 (China-Latin American relations: From the vantage point of economic globalization). *Xueshu tansuo* 學術探索 (Academic Exploration).

Tan Xiao 談蕭. 2003. *Zhongguo "zouchuqu" fazhan zhanlue* 中國"走出去"發展戰略 (Development Strategy of China "Go Global"). Beijing: China Social Sciences Publishing.

Tang Bin 唐彬, and Guo Kai 郭凱. 2008. "Zhongguo-Dongmeng ziyou maoyi qu de fazhan he weilai zhanwang" 中國－東盟自由貿易區的發展和未來展望

(The development and future prospects of the China-ASEAN free trade area). *Shangchang xiandaihua* 商場現代化 (Market Modernization), no. 1.

United Nations Committee on Trade and Development (UNCTAD) 聯合國貿易發展改革委員會. *"2007 shijie touzi baogao"* 2007 世界投資報告 (World Investment Report 2007). UNCTAD.

Viner, Jacob. 2003. *Qingxiao: Guojimaoyi zhong de yige wenti* 傾銷：國際貿易中的一個問題 (Dumping: A Problem in International Trade). Beijing: Commercial Press.

Wan Dianwu 萬典武, and Li Xihua 李禧華. 2008. "Woguo shangye tizhi gaige qude xianzhu jinzhan" 我國商業體制改革取得顯著進展 (Obvious Developments in China's Commercial System Reform). *Renmin ribao* 人民日報 (People's Daily), July 8. http://www.ce.cn/xwzx/gnsz/gdxw/200807/08/t20080708_16080336.shtml.

Wang Dexun 王德迅, and Zhang Jinjie 張金傑. 2004. *Guoji huobi jijin zuzhi* 國際貨幣基金組織 (International Monetary Fund). Beijing: Social Science Academic Press.

Wang Guo'an 王國安, and Fan Changzi 范昌子. 2006. "Zhongou maoyi hubuxing yanjiu" 中歐貿易互補性研究 (The complementarity of China-Europe trade). *Guoji maoyi wenti* 國際貿易問題 (Journal of International Trade), no. 3.

Wang Haoyong 汪浩泳, and Kong Xian 孔嫻. 2003. "Waishang zhijie touzi dui Zhongguo chanye anquan de yingxiang" 外商直接投資對中國產業安全的影響 (The impact of foreign direct investment on China's production security). *Jiye jingji* 企業經濟 (Enterprise Economy), no. 1.

Wang Jian 王建. 2000. "Zhong La jingmao guanxi xianzhuang xianjing" 中拉經貿關係現狀 (The present and future of China-Latin American economic and trade relations). *Lading Meizhou yanjiu* 拉丁美洲研究 (Journal of Latin American Studies), no. 2.

Wang Jiarui 王家瑞. 2007. "Jiji tansuo Zhongguo tese zhengdang waijiao xin geju" 積極探索中國特色政黨外交新格局 (Proactively Exploring the New Situation of Party Diplomacy with Chinese Characteristics). *Renmin ribao* 人民日報 (People's Daily), September 28.

Wang Peng 王鵬. 2005. "2004 nian Zhong La guanxi huigu" 2004 年中拉關係回顧 (Review of China-Latin American relations, 2004). *Lading meizhou yanjiu* 拉丁美洲研究 (Journal of Latin American Studies), no. 4.

Wang Sanxing 王三興. 2007. "Quanqiuhua tiaojian xia de zhongou maoyi chanpin jiegou yu maoyi bu pingheng fenxi" 全球化條件下的中歐貿易產品結構與貿易不平衡分析 (Analyzing the product structure and trade imbalance of China-Europe trade under conditions of globalization). *Guoji shangwu* 國際商務 (International Commerce), no. 2.

Wang Shaoxi 王紹熙. 1994. *Zhongguo duiwai jingji maoyi lilun he zhengce* 中國對外經濟貿易理論和政策 (Theory and Policy of China External Economic and Trade Relations). Beijing: China External Economic and Trade Publishing.

Wang Shouchun 王壽椿, ed. 1988. *Zhongguo duiwai jingji guanxi* 中國對外經濟關係 (China External Economic Relations). Beijing: External Trade Education Publishing.

——, and Xu Yu 許煜, eds. 1988. *Zhongguo duiwai jingji guanxi* 中國對外經濟關係 (China External Economic Relations). Beijing: External Trade Education Publishing.

Wang Shouzheng 王守貞. 2007. Dongya jingji yitihua 東亞經濟一體化：回顧與展望 (East Asia economic integration: Review and outlook). *Dongnanya zhongheng* 東南亞縱橫 (Around Southeast Asia), no. 4.

Wang Tingdong 王庭東. 2005. "Lun Zhongguo 'fei shichang jingji diwei' wenti de shizhi" 論中國"非市場經濟地位"問題的實質 (On the substance of the "non-market economy status" of China). *Shijie jingji yanjiu* 世界經濟研究 (World Economic Study), no. 6.

Wang Xinlu 王新祿. 1999. "Zhong La guanxi de xianzhuang he fazhan qianjing" 中拉關係的現狀和發展前景 (Current status and future development prospects of China-Latin American relations). *Lading meizhou yanjiu* 拉丁美洲研究 (Journal of Latin American Studies), no. 1.

Wang Yi 王毅. 2007. "Shizhong buyu zou heping fazhan daolu" 始終不渝走和平發展道路 (Always walking the path of peaceful development). *Qiushi* 求是 (Seeking Truth), no. 23.

Wang Yong 王勇. 2007. *Zhong Mei jingmao guanxi* 中美經貿關係 (Sino-American Economic and Trade Relations). Beijing: China Markets Publishing.

Wei Jianguo 魏建國. 2004. *"Keji xingao zhanlue shi shixian maoyi qiangguo de biyou zhi lu"* 科技興貿是實現貿易強國的必由之路 (Technology driven trade is the necessary path for the realization of a strong trading nation). October 20. China Electronic Manufacturer Expo, Suzhou. http://kjs.mofcom.gov.cn/aarticle/c/200410/20041000297970.html.

Wei Qin 魏琴. 2007. "Fazhan Zhong Fei jingmao guanxi de yiyi" 發展中非經貿關係的意義 (The significance in developing China-Africa economic and trade relations). *Jingying yu guanli* 經營與管理 (Operations and Management), no. 6.

Wu Bangguo 吳邦國. 2004. "Zengjin huxiang liaojie gongchuang meihao weilai 增進相互瞭解共創美好未來 (Increase Mutual Understanding, Build a Positive Future). *Renmin ribao* 人民日報 (People's Daily), June 4.

Wu Guoping 吳國平. 2005. "Zhongguo yu Lamei jingji hezuo de jichu he qianjing" 中國與拉美經濟合作的基礎和前景 (The foundation and prospect of economic cooperation between China and Latin America). *Zhongguo jinrong* 中國金融 (China Finance), no. 20.

Wu Hongfei 吳宏飛. 2002. "Lishi shang Zhong Yin zhijian de keji jiaoliu" 歷史上中印之間的科技交流 (Technology exchange between historical China and India). *Yunnan shehui kexue* 雲南社會科學 (Yunnan Social Science).

Wu Hongyang 吳宏陽. 1995. "Lun Zhong Yin de jingmao guanxi" 論中印的經貿關係 (China-India Economic and Trade Relations). *Zhengzhou daxue xuebao* 鄭州大學學報（哲學社會科學版）(Zhengzhou University Academic Journal (Philosophy and Social Sciences)), no. 2.

Xian Guoming 冼國明, and Wen Dongwei 文東偉. 2008. "Kuaguo gongsi zai hua zhuangkuang zongshu" 跨國公司在華狀況綜述 (Overview of multinational companies in China). *Guoji jingji hezuo* 國際經濟合作 (International Economic Cooperation), no. 1.

Xiao Haiquan 肖海泉. 1994. *Zhongguo duiwai jingji maoyi gailun* 中國對外經濟貿易概論 (Overview of External Economic Relations of China). Nanjing: Nanjing University Press.

Xiao Hong 肖虹. 2001. *Zhongmei jingmao guanxi shilun* 中美經貿關係史論 (The History of Sino-American Economic and Trade Relations). Beijing: World Affairs Publishing.

Xing Guangcheng 刑廣程. 2006. *2005 nian: Yingdui tiaozhan* 2005 年：應對挑戰 (The Year 2005: Facing the Challenge). Beijing: Social Sciences Academic Press.

——, ed. 2007. *2006 nian: Eluosi Dong'ou Zhongya huangpishu* 2006 年：俄羅斯東歐中亞黃皮書 (The Year 2006: Yellow Paper of Russia, Eastern Europe and Central Asia). Beijing: Social Science Academic Press.

Xing Houyuan 邢厚媛. 2008. "Sanshi nian fengyu jiancheng: duiwai gongcheng chengbao ye zai jiegou tiaozheng zhong zouxiang chengshu" 三十年風雨兼程：對外工程承包業在結構調整中走向成熟 (Thirty years of ups and downs: International contracting matures as industrial structure is adjusted). *Guoji jingji hezuo* 國際經濟合作 (International Economic Cooperation), no. 3.

Xu Baokang 徐寶康. 2008. "Gongchuang Zhong han guanxi xin jumian" 共創中韓關係新局面 (Jointly Creating a New Landscape in China-Korea Relations). *Renmin ribao* 人民日報 (People's Daily), August 27.

Xu Chaoqing 徐朝清, and Wu Guo 吳戈. 1998. *Lanse jiaoyi—Zai Zhong Mei miqie wanglai de beihou* 藍色交易—在中美密切往來的背後 (Blue Transaction: Behind the Close Interaction of China and the United States). Beijing: China External Economy and Trade Publishing.

Xu Fu 徐復, ed. 2006. *Zhongguo duiwai maoyi* 中國對外貿易 (External Trade of China) Beijing: Tsinghua University Press.

Xu Ningning 許寧寧. 2007. "Zhongguo yu dongmeng shiwu nian jingmao hezuo zongshu" 中國與東盟十五年經貿合作綜述 (Overview of 15 years of economic and trade cooperation between China and ASEAN). *Jinri Zhongguo luntan* 今日中國論壇 (China Today Forum), no. 2–3.

Xu Wenkai 許文凱. 2003. Guoji gongcheng chengbao 國際工程承包 (International Contracting). Beijing: University of International Business and Economics Publishing House.

Xu Yisheng 徐以升. 2008. "Lin Yifu: Ba fazhanzhong guojia xuezhe de jingyan he xikao daidao shixing" 林毅夫：把發展中國家學者的經驗和思考帶到世行 (Justin Lin Yifu: Taking the Experience and Thoughts of an Academic from a Developing Country to the World Bank). *Diyi caijing ribao* 第一財經日報 (China Business News), February 13.

Yang Liming 楊麗明. 2004. "Oumeng tuoyan Zhongguo 'rushi'neimo hou" 歐盟拖延中國"入市"幕後 (Reasons behind EU delaying the recognition of China's market economy status). *Qingnian cankao* 青年參考 (Elite Reference), no. 6.

Yang Wenwu 楊文武 and Ni Chunqin 倪香芹. 2007. "Zhong Yin jingmao hezuo xianzhuang, wenti ji qi duice" 中印經貿合作現狀、問題及其對策 (The current situation, problems and solutions in China-India economic and trade relations). *Shehui kexue* 社會科學 (Social Science), no. 9.

Yao Guimei 姚桂梅. 2004. "Zhongguo yu Feizhou de shiyou hezuo" 中國與非洲的石油合作 (China-Africa oil cooperation). *Guoji shiyou jingji* 國際石油經濟 (International Oil Economy), no. 11.

You Anshan 尤安山. 2004. "Zhongguo jingji jueqi yu dongmeng de jingmao guanxi" 中國經濟崛起及與東盟的經貿關係 (China's rising economy and its economic and trade relations with ASEAN). *Shijie jingji yanjiu* 世界經濟研究 (World Economy Study), no. 9.

Yu Peiwei 于培偉. 2006. "Zhong Fei maoyi qiantu wuliang—Zhong Fei maoyi bange duoshiji de fazhan huigu yu zhanwang" 中非貿易前途無量—中非貿易半個多世紀的發展回顧與展望 (Bright future in Sino-Africa trade: A review and projection of 50 years in Sino-Africa trade relations). *Jingji yanjiu cancao* 經濟研究參考 (Economic Research Information), 2006, no. 6.

Zhang Chengnan 張晟南. 2006. "Feinengyuan kaungchan hezuo qianjing" 非能源礦產合作前景 (Prospects for cooperation in non-energy mining resources). *Guotu ziyuan* 國土資源 (Land and Resources), no. 11.

Zhang Chunyan 張春燕. 2006. "Zhong Yin zhanlüe guanxi zhong de zhiyue yinsu yu dongle" 中印戰略關係中的制約因素與動力 (Constraining factors and motivation in China-India strategic relations). *Nanya yanjiu jikan* 南亞研究季刊 (South Asia Studies Quarterly), no. 2.

Zhang Minqiu 張敏秋. 2002. "Shishi fazhan Zhong Yin guanxi de jida zhangwai" 試析發展中印關係的幾大障礙 (An analysis of several major obstacles in China-India relations). *Guoji zhengzhi yanjiu* 國際政治研究 (Study of International Politics), no. 4.

Zhang Xinsheng 張新生. 2000."Lamei jingji fazhan qianjing yu Zhong La guanxi" 拉美經濟發展前景與中拉關係 (Latin America Economic Development and China-Latin American Relations). *Lading meizhou yanjiu* 拉丁美洲研究 (Journal of Latin American Studies), no. 2.

——. 2001. "Shiji chu de Zhongguo yu Lamei guanxi" 世紀初的中國與拉美關係 (China and Latin America relations in the beginning of a new century). *Xiandai guoji guanxi* 現代國際關係 (Modern International Relations), no. 5.

Zhang Yanhua 張豔華. 2007. "Zhong Yin jingmao guanxi xianzhuang yu qianjing" 中印經貿關係現狀與前景 (The present and future of China-India economic and trade relations). *Jingji shi* 經濟師 (China Economist), no. 7.

Zhang Youwen 張幼文 et al. 2007. *Xin kaifang guan—Duiwai kaifang lilun yu zhanlüe zai tansuo* 新開放觀—對外開放理論與戰略再探索 (New Open Door Perspective: Re-exploring the Theory and Strategy for the Economic Reforms). Beijing: People's Publishing House.

Zhang Youwen 張幼文, and Wang Renwei 黃仁偉 et al. 2007. *2007 Zhongguo guoji biwei baogao* 2007中國國際地位報告 (Report on the International Status of China, 2007). Beijing: People's Publishing House.

Zhang Yu 張昱, and Li Yuxia 李玉霞. 2006. "Zhongguo dui oumeng shangpin maoyi yanjiu—Dui shuangbian yenei maoyi shuiping de shizheng fenxi" 中國對歐盟商品貿易研究—對雙邊產業內貿易水準的實証分析 (Commodity trade between China and the European Union: Empirical evidence and analysis of the bilateral horizontal trade). *Dangdai caijing* 當代財經 (Contemporary Finance and Economics), no. 9.

Zhao Bole 趙伯樂. 2003. *Dangdai nanya guanxi* 當代南亞國際關係 (International Relations of Contemporary South Asia) Beijing: China Social Sciences Publishing.

Zhao Chunming 趙春明, and Liu Zhenlin 劉振林. 2002. "Lun Zhongguo-Dongmeng ziyou maoyi qu de qianjing he tiaozhan" 論中國—東盟自由貿易區的前景和挑戰 (On the prospects and challenges for the China-ASEAN free trade area). *Shijie jingji yu zhenzhi* 世界經濟與政治 (World Economy and Politics), no. 11.

Zheng Yu 鄭羽, ed. 2005. *Dulianti* 獨聯體 (Commonwealth of Independent States). Beijing: Social Sciences Academic Press.

Zheng Yun 鄭雲. 2006. "Zhongguo yu Oumeng maoyi zhong de bijiao youshi ji guoji fengong diwei" 中國與歐盟貿易中的比較優勢及國際分工地位 (Competitive advantage and international division of labor of the trade between China and the European Union). *Guoji shangwu* 國際商務 (International Commerce), no. 5.

Zhongguo duiwai jingji maoyi nianjian 中國對外經濟貿易年鑒 (Yearbook of Foreign Trade Statistics of China). Relevant years. Beijing: China Economy Publishing.

"Zhongguo Gongchandang dishiyi jie zhongyan weiyuanhui disan ciquanti huiyi gongbao" 中國共產黨第十一屆中央委員會第三次全體會議公報 (Report from the 3rd Plenary Session of the 11th Central Committee of the Communist Party of China). 1992. *Zhonggong zhongyang dang xuanbian* 中共中央檔選編 (Selected Documents of the Central Committee of the Communist Party of China). Beijing: Publishing House of the Central Party School of the Chinese Communist Party.

Zhongguo tongji zhaiyao 中國統計摘要 (Selected Statistics of China). 1998. Beijing: China Statistics Publishing House

"Zhongguo waimao zai jiegou tiaozheng zhong jiasu fazhan" 中國外貿在結構調整中加速發展 (The Development of China's External Trade Accelerated in Structural Adjustments). *Guoji shangbao* 國際商報 (International Business Daily), February 21, 2008.

Zhou Hong 周弘. 2004. *Gongxing yu chayi: Zhong Ou huoban guanxi pingxi* 共性與差異：中歐夥伴關係評析 (Similarities and Differences: Commentary and Analysis of China-Europe Partnership and Relations). Beijing: China Social Sciences Press.

Zhou Lin 周林. 2002. "Ru Shi—Zhongguo duiwai jingji guanxi fazhan de xin jieduan" 入世—中國對外經濟關係發展的新階段 (WTO accession: A new phase for the development of external economic and trade relations of China). *Waijiao xueyuan xuebao* 外交學院學報 (Journal of China Foreign Affairs University), no. 3.

——. 2003. "Zhongguo chanpin chukou yu meiguo zhizaoye" 中國產品出口與美國製造業 (The export of Chinese products and the American manufacturing sector). *Waijiao xueyuan xuebao* 外交學院學報 (Journal of China Foreign Affairs University), no. 4.

——. 2006. "Zhongmei jingmao mocha fenxi" 中美經貿摩擦分析 (An analysis of Sino-American friction in economy and trade). *Waijiao xueyuan xuebao* 外交學院學報 (Journal of China Foreign Affairs University), no. 3.

——. 2007. "Ru Shi 'hou guodu qi' Zhongguo duiwai jingji guanxi fazhan de tedian" 入世"後過渡期"中國對外經濟關係發展的特點 (Features of external economic relations development of China after WTO accession). In *di wu jie WTO guoji nianhui lunwen ji* 第五屆WTO國際年會論文集 (Papers Presented at the 5th WTO Annual International Conference). Beijing: Commercial Press of China.

Zhou Yingfeng 周英峰, and Wang Youling 王優玲. 2008. "Kaifangxing jingji jinru xinjieduan 開放型經濟進入新階段 (The Open Economy Enters a New Phase). *Renmin ribao* 人民日報 (People's Daily), February 23.

Zhu Caihua 竺彩華. 2008. *FDI waibuxing yu Zhongguo chanye fazhan* FDI 外部性與中國產業發展 (The External Nature of FDI and Industrial Development of China) Beijing: Economic Science Press.

Zhu Chenghu 朱成虎. 1998. *Zhong Mei guanxi de fazhan bianhua ji qi qushi* 中美關係的發展變化及其趨勢 (Changes and Trends in the Development of Sino-American Relations). Nanjing: Jiangsu People's Publishing House.

Zhu Liqun 朱立群. 2008. *Guojitixi yu Zhong Ou guanxi* 國際體系與中歐關係 (International systems and China-European Union Relations). Beijing: World Affairs Publishing.

Zhu Wenhui 朱文暉. 2004. "Quanqiuhua xia de Zhongguo yu Lamei maoyi guanxi de xin qushi" 全球化下的中國與拉美貿易關係的新趨勢 (New trends in China-Latin America relations under globalization). *Lading meizhou yanjiu* 拉丁美洲研究 (Journal of Latin American Studies), no. 3.

Non-Chinese materials:

Bergsten, Fred C., Bates Gill, Nicholas R. Lardy, and Derek Mitchell. 2006. *The Balance Sheet: What the World Needs to Know about the Emerging Superpower*. New York: Public Affairs.

Giannakopoulos, Themistoklis K. 2006. *A Concise Guide to the EU Anti-Dumping/Anti-Subsidies Procedures*. Kluwer Law International.

International Labor Organization. 2005. *Towards a fair deal for migrant workers in the global economy*. International Labor Conference, 92nd Section.

Ivanov, Igor. 2002. *New Diplomacy of Russia*. Beijing: Contemporary World Publishing.

The Korean Foundation: *Korea focus*, various issues.

Kurlantzick, Joshua. 2006. *Beijing's Safari: China's Move into Africa and Its Implications for Aid, Development and Governance*, Carnegie Endowment for International Peace, 2006.

Lai, Hong Yi. 2007. "China's oil diplomacy: Is it a global security threat?" *Third World Quarterly* 28 (3).

Linsenmann, Ingo. 2007. *Economic Government of the EU: A Balance Sheet of New Modes of Policy Coordination*. Palgrave MacMillan.

Liu, Saili. 1996. "ROK's Position and Role in the Economic Cooperation of Northeast Asia, World Economy and China." *China & World Economy* 4 (2).

Meyn, Mareike. 2006. *The Impact of EU Free Trade Agreements on Economic Development and Regional Integration*. Peter Lang Publishing.

Review of the Anti-dumping Regime applicable to Russia and China, European Commission, 2000.

Shutov, A. D. 1999. *Postsovetckoe prostranstvo* Постсоветское пространство (Post-Soviet Space), M., 1999.

Tull, Denis M. 2006. "China's engagement in Africa: Scope, significance, and consequences." *Journal of Modern African Studies* 44 (3).

Vneshniaia torgovlia Stran sodruzhestva nezavisimvikh gosudastv Внешняя торговля Стран содружества независимых государств (Foreign trade of the Commonwealth of Independent States), M., 2000.

Websites:

Asian Development Bank, http://www.adb.org/

The Central People's Government of the People's Republic of China: http://www.gov.cn/

China Association of Travel Services, http://www.cats.org.cn/

China Banking Regulatory Commission, http://www.cbrc.gov.cn/

China Business News, http://www.chinacbn.com/

China Development Gateway, http://www.chinagate.cn/

China Economic Net, http://www.ce.cn/

China Enterprise Management, http://www.ceceo.cn/

China Finance Online, http://www.jrj.com.cn/

China Insurance Regulatory Commission, http://www.circ.gov.cn/

China Investment and Finance Online, http://www.cnfol.com/

China Securities News Online, http://www.cs.com.cn/

China Securities Regulatory Commission, http://www.csrc.gov.cn/

Chinese Academy of International Trade and Economic Cooperation, Ministry of Commerce, http://caitec.mofcom.gov.cn/aarticle/s/u/as/200408/20004800261590.html/

Development Marketplace, The World Bank Group, http://www.developmentmarketplace.org.cn/

European Commission, "Anti dumping," http://ec.europa.eu/trade/issues/respectrules/anti_dumping/index_en.htm/

European Commission Delegation to China, http://www.delchn.cec.eu.int/cn/eu_and_china/EU_Agreements_China.htm/

Forum of China-Africa Cooperation, http://www.focac.org/
General Administration of Customs, http://www.customs.gov.cn/
International Labor Organization, http://www.ilo.org/global/langen/index.htm/
International Monetary Fund, http://www.imf.org/
Japan External Trade Organization, http://www.jetro.go.jp/
Korea Foundation, http://newsletter.kf.or.kr/
Ministry of Commerce, http://www.mof.gov.cn/
Ministry of Finance of Japan, http://www.mof.go.jp/
Ministry of Foreign Affairs of Japan, http://www.mofa.go.jp/
Ministry of Foreign Affairs, People's Republic of China, http://www.fmprc.gov.cn/
Mission of the People's Republic of China to the European Union, http://www.chinamission.be/chn/sbgx/RIU/default.htm/
National Bureau of Statistics of China, http://www.stats.gov.cn/
National Reform and Development Commission, http://www.sdpc.gov.cn/
State Administration of Taxation, http://www.chinatax.gov.cn/
State Intellectual Property Office, http://www.sipo.gov.cn/
Summit of the Forum of China-Africa Cooperation, http://www.focacsummit.org/
Transparency International, http://www.transparency.org/
People's Bank of China, http://www.pbc.gov.cn/
People's Daily Online, http://world.people.com.cn/
United Nations Statistics Division, http://unstats.un.org/unsd/comtrade/
The World Bank, http://web.worldbank.org/
The World Bank in China, http://www.worldbank.org.cn/
World Trade Organization, http://www.wto.org/
Xinhua, http://www.xinhuanet.com/

Index